THE *AFRICAN AFFAIRS* READER

The *African Affairs* Reader

Key Texts in Politics, Development, and International Relations

Edited by

NIC CHEESEMAN, LINDSAY WHITFIELD,
AND CARL DEATH

OXFORD
UNIVERSITY PRESS

OXFORD
UNIVERSITY PRESS

Great Clarendon Street, Oxford, OX2 6DP,
United Kingdom

Oxford University Press is a department of the University of Oxford.
It furthers the University's objective of excellence in research, scholarship,
and education by publishing worldwide. Oxford is a registered trade mark of
Oxford University Press in the UK and in certain other countries

First Edition published in 2017

Impression: 1

Published in the United States of America by Oxford University Press
198 Madison Avenue, New York, NY 10016, United States of America

British Library Cataloguing in Publication Data
Data available

Library of Congress Control Number: 2017931832

ISBN 978-0-19-879428-8 (hbk.)
ISBN 978-0-19-879429-5 (pbk.)

Printed and bound by
CPI Group (UK) Ltd, Croydon, CR0 4YY

*This book is dedicated to the memory of Stephen Ellis,
a great editor of* African Affairs

The papers included in this volume were published by two or more of the following *African Affairs* editors:

Lindsay Whitfield
Carl Death
Nic Cheeseman
Rita Abrahamsen
Sara Rich Dorman
Tim Kelsall
Stephen Ellis
David Killingray

Contents

Notes on Contributors

Deborah Bräutigam is the Bernard L. Schwartz Professor of International Political Economy at Johns Hopkins University School of Advanced International Studies, where she also directs the SAIS China Africa Research Initiative. An authority on Chinese engagement in Africa, she has also published on development strategies, governance, and foreign aid.

Catherine Boone is Professor of Comparative Politics at the London School of Economics and Political Science. She is author of *Property and Political Order in Africa: Land Rights and the Structure of Politics* (Cambridge University Press, 2014), *Political Topographies of the African State* (Cambridge University Press, 2003), and *Merchant Capital and the Roots of State Power in Senegal* (Cambridge University Press, 1993 [2006]). She is now working on questions of territory, spatial inequalities, and land rights formalization in Africa.

David Booth is a Senior Research Fellow at the Overseas Development Institute in London. He is the author, with Diana Cammack, of *Governance for Development in Africa: Solving Collective Action Problems* (Zed Books, 2013). He is currently working on institutional challenges in African export manufacturing and politically smart approaches to aid programme design.

Nic Cheeseman is Professor of Democracy at Birmingham University. He is the founding editor of the *Oxford Encyclopedia of African Politics* and the author of *Democracy in Africa: Successes, Failures and the Struggle for Political Reform* (Cambridge University Press, 2015). In addition, he is a columnist for Kenya's *Sunday Nation* newspaper, a former editor of *African Affairs*, and a writer for and advisor to Kofi Annan's Africa Progress Panel.

Frederick Cooper is Professor of History at New York University. He is the author most recently of *Citizenship Between Empire and Nation: Remaking France and French Africa, 1945–1960* (Princeton University Press, 2014), and *Africa in the World: Capitalism, Empire, Nation-State* (Harvard University Press, 2014).

Carl Death is Senior Lecturer in International Political Economy at the University of Manchester. His research focuses on environmental politics in Africa, including the international politics of sustainable development and climate change. His most recent book is *The Green State in Africa* (Yale University Press, 2016).

Stephen Ellis was a respected scholar of Africa whose research broke new ground and set new research agendas. In addition to being a widely respected editor of African Affairs for many years, he edited Africa Confidential, was the General Secretary and later Director of the African Studies Centre in Leiden, and published a number of important books. He passed away in 2015.

Frederick Golooba-Mutebi is Professor Extraordinarius at the Archie Mafeje Research Institute, University of South Africa, and Honorary Senior Research Fellow at the School of Environment and Development, University of Manchester, UK. He has published on politics and the politics of development in leading journals. He is a columnist for the regional newspaper, *The East African*, and writes articles and features for other local, regional, and international current affairs publications.

Ben Lampert is a Lecturer in International Development, based in the Development Policy and Practice Group at the Open University, UK. He is a human geographer and his research is primarily concerned with the role of migrants and diaspora communities in development.

Tom Lodge is Professor of Peace and Conflict Studies and Dean of Humanities and Social Sciences at the University of Limerick. In 2011, he published *Sharpeville: An Apartheid Massacre and its Aftermath* (Oxford University Press, 2011). At present his research is focused on a history of the South African Communist Party.

Peace Medie is a Research Fellow in the Legon Centre for International Affairs and Diplomacy at the University of Ghana and an Oxford-Princeton Global Leaders Fellow. She is studying states' implementation of gender-based violence norms in Africa and civilian self-protection. Her work has appeared in *International Studies Review* and *Politics & Gender* and she was awarded the 2012–13 *African Affairs* African Author Prize.

Giles Mohan is Professor of International Development at the Open University, UK. His recent research has examined the political economy of China as an international development actor. He has published in geography, development studies, and Africanist journals. He has also acted as consultant to Open University/BBC productions including *African School, Indian School, Reith Lectures*, and *Why Poverty?*

Tim Murithi is Extraordinary Professor of African Studies, Centre for African Studies, University of the Free State, Bloemfontein, South Africa. His research interests include the African Union peace and security architecture, peace-building, transitional justice, governance, gender, and development in Africa. He is the editor of the *Routledge Handbook for International Relations* (2014).

J. Shola Omotola is Head of the Socio-Political Unit of the Research and Training Department at the National Institute for Legislative Studies, National Assembly, Abuja, Nigeria. His primary research interests are in comparative African governance institutions, democratization and election studies, legislative studies, and oil and environmental politics in the Niger Delta. He is co-editor of *The State in Contemporary Nigeria: Issues, Perspectives and Challenges* (John Archers Publishers, 2016) and *Horror in Paradise: Framework for Understanding the Crisis of the Niger Delta* (Carolina Academic Press, 2014).

Anja Osei is a Senior Research Fellow at the University of Konstanz, Chair of International Politics and Conflict Management. She holds a PhD from the University of Leipzig. Her research focuses on parties and parliaments in Africa, democratization, and political elites.

Stefano Ponte is Professor of International Political Economy at the Department of Business and Politics, Copenhagen Business School. He has worked extensively on the political economy of commodity trade, the governance of global value chains, and on transnational environmental governance, with particular focus on Africa.

Mark Shaw is SARChI Chair in Justice and Security in the Faculty of Law at the University of Cape Town and Director of UCT's Centre for Criminology. He also directs the Geneva-based Global Initiative against Transnational Organised Crime.

Lindsay Whitfield is Associate Professor of Global Studies at the Department of Social Sciences and Business, Roskilde University, Denmark. Her current research focuses on economic transformation, industrial policy, and the competitiveness of domestic firms in non-traditional export sectors in a number of African countries. Her most recent book is *The Politics of African Industrial Policy: A Comparative Perspective* (Cambridge University Press, 2015).

Crawford Young is Professor Emeritus of Political Science at the University of Wisconsin. His chapter draws upon ideas in gestation for his 2012 capstone volume, *The Postcolonial State in Africa: Fifty Years of Independence* (University of Wisconsin Press, 2012). It also builds upon analysis in his 1994 work, *The African Colonial State in Comparative Perspective* (Yale University Press, 1994).

1

An Introduction to *African Affairs* and African Studies

Nic Cheeseman, Carl Death, and Lindsay Whitfield

THIS BOOK PROVIDES an essential guide to the big topics in African studies through the lens of *African Affairs*.[1] It uses contributions to the journal over the last 30 years as a way to review and reflect on key debates and what they tell us about the continent. To do this, we have drawn together a set of seminal articles that capture important conversations concerning how we think about the African state, the political economy of development, democracy, and African international relations, and make significant contributions to those debates theoretically and empirically. As with the journal, this volume is interdisciplinary, drawing on important insights from political science, international relations, development studies, sociology, anthropology, and beyond to provide a rounded view of the continent.

The book also explains how research on Africa has evolved over the last 30 years. As time passes, African economies, polities, and societies change, and so do the analytical tools and theoretical frames with which scholars try to make sense of them, resulting in new debates in the pages of *African Affairs*. In a series of essays that accompany each group of articles, the editors of the journal introduce these arguments and outline the current thinking on some of the most important issues of the day. Taken together, we believe that this collection provides an overview of the state of African studies and will thus serve as an excellent introductory text for those entering African studies or learning about African politics and economies for the first time. At the same time, this volume aims to share some of the key ideas and arguments that have helped to illuminate our understanding of Africa over the past 30 years as widely as possible—especially to those who lack a subscription to the journal.

---

[1] African Affairs is the No 1 ranked journal in African Studies and Area Studies according to Impact Factor. To download free articles and see if you are eligible for a discounted or free subscription, visit <http://afraf.oxfordjournals.org/> (27 August 2016).

African Affairs is not only a source of empirical studies and theoretical debates about Africa. Its history and the changing contents of its pages also have much to tell us about power relations concerning who produces knowledge about Africa, for what purpose, and from what perspectives. The politics of knowledge with relation to African studies has changed immensely since the journal's founding, but further transformation is needed to ensure that African voices are heard. Just as who writes about Africa has changed, so has how the continent is studied, leading to new discussions about what kinds of methodological tools are feasible, appropriate to understanding causal processes, and ethically acceptable. In this introduction, we discuss some of the issues related to the politics of knowledge and the study of Africa, as they are vital to any introduction to African studies, before introducing the themes and parts that follow.

THE POLITICS OF KNOWLEDGE

African Affairs, initially called the *Journal of African Studies*, was founded in 1901, when the "scramble for Africa" and the Anglo-Boer War in South Africa were coming to a close. It was an imperial instrument, as Chris Youé points out, 'for the gathering of knowledge about Africa to facilitate the colonial project that was being launched'.[2] As such, the voices heard in the journal were the business and colonial elite of Great Britain. Relaunched in 1935 as the *Journal of the Royal African Society*, the revised publication's contents reflected the colonial period, the need to understand Africa's peoples in order to rule them more effectively, and a colonial mentality of "modernizing" Africa.[3] Thus, articles consisted mainly of talks given by colonial officials at various events in Britain or the British Empire, as well as contributions by missionaries, educators, aristocrats, and some academics.

This began to change in the 1960s, and by 1970 the journal, renamed *African Affairs*, was an academic enterprise and had editorial autonomy from the Royal African Society. This change was driven by the decline of the British Empire and the emergence of African studies as a field of study in British universities. Not only did the journal become exclusively academic, but it also became a platform for "radical" discussions, where academics rejected the Eurocentric mentality of the colonial era and debated the nature and

---

[2] Christopher Youé, 'The Royal African Society, African affairs, and apartheid: The Mustoe controversy of 1970', *African Affairs*, South Africa Virtual Issue (2013), pp. 1–12, p. 3 <http://www.oxfordjournals.org/our_journals/afrafj/southafrica.html> (1 March 2016).
[3] *Ibid.*

extent of capitalist development in African countries and their position in the global economy.[4]

However, the production of knowledge about Africa remained largely in the hands of Europeans. Some of the political elite that emerged in the colonial period wrote influential political texts and even published articles in *African Affairs*, but in general there were limited African voices in the journal.[5] A number of factors explain this, but one of the most important was the lack of investment in African universities. In the colonial era there was a systematic disregard for educating Africans in the social sciences. Although the University of Fort Hare provided important opportunities for black African students from 1918 onwards in South Africa, similar developments occurred much later on the rest of the continent. In West Africa, it was not until 1948, a decade before political independence, that the University of Ghana and the University of Ibadan (Nigeria) were established. Similarly, although Makerere University in Uganda was set up as a technical institute in 1922, it was only in 1949 that it became a university college and even later, in 1963, that it evolved into the University of East Africa.[6] Moreover, it was only when the University of East Africa was divided into three independent institutions in 1970 that the University of Dar es Salaam and the University of Nairobi were created. The late development of higher education had a lasting legacy. Zambia, for example, entered independence with just 101 university graduates, and none in the social sciences.

Although some of these educational establishments enjoyed a golden era in the 1970s, many postcolonial African governments soon tired of the criticisms of university professors and students. As authoritarian rule spread across the continent, political science departments soon found themselves in conflict with the state. Along with a period of protracted economic decline, this led to a prolonged period of political interference and funding cuts in the university sector in general, and the social sciences more specifically. These barriers did not prevent African scholars such as Ali Mazrui and Mahmood Mamdani from making vital contributions to African studies,[7] but they did contribute to a situation in which most of the research on Africa is written by non-Africans. While the proportion of articles authored by women in *African Affairs* and the

---

[4] For example, there were intense exchanges about the dynamics of capital accumulation in South Africa between neo-Marxists and neoliberals.

[5] For example, speeches to the Royal African Society by Julius Nyerere, President of Tanzania, were published in *African Affairs* in 1976 and 1985.

[6] For more details, see J. F. Ade Ajayi, Lameck K. H. Goma, and G. Ampah Johnson, *The African Experience with Higher Education* (Ohio University Press, Athens, OH, 1996).

[7] See, for example, Ali A. Mazrui and Alamin M. Mazrui, *The Power of Babel: Language and Governance in the African Experience* (University of Chicago Press, Chicago, 1998); Mahmood Mamdani, *Citizen and Subject: Contemporary Africa and the Legacy of Late Colonialism* (Princeton University Press, Princeton, NJ, 1996).

Journal of Modern African Studies increased between 1993 and 2013, the proportion written by African-based authors declined.[8]

The under-representation of African voices is clearly to the detriment of African studies, which is missing out on a great deal of local knowledge, in addition to valuable alternative theoretical perspectives that often represent a better fit with how Africa is understood by Africans. Many of the academic journals based in the West recognize that they have an important role to play in reversing this trend and have responded by holding writing workshops in Africa and providing dedicated support to young African researchers.[9] It also requires journals and reviewers based in European and North American institutions to evaluate submissions on their own merits, and to avoid penalizing papers from the continent that do draw on alternative methods and literatures. However, even these innovations will only take us so far. More far-reaching change is unlikely until scholars based in Africa have the support and funding they require to be able to prioritize research. This means paying lecturers more so that they are not placed under financial pressure to take second jobs, or international consultancies, to pay the bills. It also means more time for fieldwork and writing, smaller teaching loads, bigger research budgets, and greater institutional incentives to publish in leading journals. Where these things are in place, as in the top ranks of South African universities, publication rates are significantly higher.

The good news is that more Africans are going to university than ever before, up from 200,000 in 1970 to around 10 million today.[10] The bad news is that this has placed faculty under greater pressure. Although overall education budgets have increased in many countries, Africa is the only continent in which the public expenditure per student has declined. Over the last 15 years, the amount allocated by governments per student has fallen by approximately 30 percent. As a result, the African Higher Education Summit estimated that the continent had a funding gap of approximately US\$50 billion in 2015.[11] The net effect of these trends is that more Africans are studying social science than ever before, but this is having a detrimental impact on the capacity of many of their teachers to play a leading role in research.

---

[8] Ryan Briggs and Scott Weathers, 'Gender and location in African politics scholarship: The other white man's burden?', *African Affairs* 115, 460 (2016), pp. 466–89.

[9] *African Affairs* launched its African Author prize to recognize excellent scholarship by early career African researchers that all too often does not reach audiences outside of the continent. Two of the articles that have won the prize are included in this volume (J. Shola Omotola and Peace Medie).

[10] Nic Cheeseman and Sarah-Jane Cooper Knock, 'Higher education in Africa, four key challenges', *Democracy in Africa*, 2 November 2015, <http://democracyinafrica.org/higher-education-in-africa-four-key-challenges/> (27 August 2017).

[11] African Higher Education Summit, 'Press release: Africa needs a sharp increase in spending on education', 12 March 2015, <http://www.adeanet.org/en/system/files/press_release_dakar_12-03-2015_investment_in_african_higher_education.pdf> (27 August 2016).

THE STUDY OF AFRICA

Two of the key characteristics of African studies have been the prominence of historical perspectives and in-depth country or local studies—often at the expense of broader comparisons. As a result, the vast majority of articles published in *African Affairs* in the last century were, for want of a better term, case studies. In part, the durability of this methodological approach to studying Africa owed as much to necessity as it did to the specific choices of Africanist researchers. The limited and low quality "off the shelf" data available on the continent in books and (later) online ensured that Africanists had to create their own evidence, and this required spending a considerable amount of time doing surveys, interviews, and direct observation. In turn, the relative lack of cross-national datasets and the high sunk costs that were generated by the need to undertake months—if not years—of fieldwork, meant that many Africanists became single-country experts. Together with the great variety of social structures and political systems that exist across the continent, this has also meant that social scientists of Africa have often been reluctant to generalize.

The dominance of historical and case study approaches, combined with the absence of reliable economic data and the difficulty of collecting survey data during the authoritarian decades of the 1970s and 1980s, ensured that the quantitative turn that swept through North American social sciences from the 1960s onwards had relatively little impact on Africanist political science or sociology. This is not to say that these disciplines stood still in terms of applying insights from quantitative and comparative methods. The rapid expansion of political studies in the dying days of colonial rule was sustained in the 1960s when researchers sought to apply social science approaches that had been used elsewhere, such as the Nuffield approach to election studies, to the "new states".[12] A small number of pioneering researchers, such as Joel Barkan, conducted their own original survey work and published articles in disciplinary journals such as the *American Political Science Review*. At the same time, the opportunity to publish research on the continent substantially increased with the emergence of the *Journal of Modern African Studies* in 1963 and the *African Studies Review* in 1970.[13] However, despite the growth of this literature in terms of quantity, sophistication, and diversity, outside of the field of economics it remained predominantly qualitative in approach. Consequently, as the use of quantitative methods became increasingly necessary

---

[12] So named because it originated from Nuffield College, Oxford University. Goran Hyden and Colin Leys criticized the use of this approach, which focused on identifying trends in public opinion, for missing what was significant about African elections in the one-party state. Goran Hyden and Colin Leys, 'Elections and politics in single-party systems: The case of Kenya and Tanzania', *British Journal of Political Science* 2, 4 (1972), pp. 389–420.

[13] Initially established as the *African Studies Bulletin* in 1958.

for publication in leading political science journals, the amount of research on Africa appearing in these forums started to decline.

The relatively low level of quantitative work encouraged a number of rich theoretical and methodological innovations, which both drew on and contributed to wider debates. For example, the approach taken by some qualitative scholars was shaped by various trends including the so-called "linguistic turn" in critical theory. Articles using discourse analysis, postcolonial theory, and discussion of cultural artefacts including films, novels, and music have become more prominent, alongside more traditional fieldwork, interviews, and archival research.[14] Rather than simply regarding Africa as a site of fieldwork in order to generate "data'" for theory-building which takes place elsewhere, leading critical theorists like Siba Grovogui, Achille Mbembe, Mahmood Mamdani, Francis Nyamnjoh, AbdouMaliq Simone, and Aili Mari Tripp have sought to use African experiences, imaginaries, and realities as a platform from which to retheorize world politics and advance broader debates. This can be seen as part of what Jean Comaroff and John Comaroff term 'theory from the south', in which the lived realities of cities like Lagos become more and more relevant to global trends of urbanization, inequality, and environmental degradation.[15] Insights from feminist theory and gender studies have been particularly influential in bringing to light forms of power relations that were often hidden from view, and problematizing concepts such as 'violence', 'the private sphere', and 'development'.[16] Similarly, wider theoretical debates over positivist and post-positivist epistemology, normative and empirical research questions, and ontological questions of structure and agency in a complex world, have frequently been raised and advanced in African studies.[17]

From the early 1990s onwards, both qualitative and quantitative approaches to understanding the continent began to develop in new and important ways, as the introduction of multiparty politics simultaneously triggered fresh interest in the continent's political systems and made it far easier to conduct

---

[14] See, for example, Francis B. Nyamnjoh and Jude Fokwang, 'Entertaining repression: Music and politics in postcolonial Cameroon', *African Affairs* 104, 415 (2005), pp. 251–74; Ebenezer Obadare, 'The uses of ridicule: Humour, "infrapolitics" and civil society in Nigeria', *African Affairs* 108, 431 (2009), pp. 249–61; Kristof Titeca and Theophile Costeur, 'An LRA for everyone: How different actors frame the Lord's Resistance Army', *African Affairs* 114, 454 (2015), pp. 92–114.

[15] Jean Comaroff and John L. Comaroff, *Theory from the South; Or, how Euro-America is Evolving Toward Africa* (Paradigm, Boulder, CO, 2012).

[16] Maria Eriksson Baaz and Maria Stern, 'Whores, men, and other misfits: Undoing "feminization" in the armed forces in the DRC', *African Affairs* 110, 441 (2011), pp. 563–85; Jonathan Haynes, 'Political critique in Nigerian video films', *African Affairs* 105, 421 (2005), pp. 511–33; Ogbu U. Kalu, 'Safiyya and Adamah: Punishing adultery with sharia stones in twenty-first-century Nigeria', *African Affairs* 102, 408 (2003), pp. 389–408.

[17] See, for example, Rita Abrahamsen, 'African studies and the postcolonial challenge', *African Affairs* 102, 407 (2003), pp. 189–210; and the *African Affairs* virtual issue on Research Notes <http://www.oxfordjournals.org/our_journals/afrafj/vi.html>.

research. This change, combined with the emergence of a range of datasets and the increasing focus of American and some European universities on quantitative methods, has made new kinds of comparative and quantitative analysis possible. Four kinds of data are particularly worth mentioning here. First, following the onset of multiparty politics, some African governments became increasingly willing to share economic and social data.[18] Second, the formation of the Afrobarometer in 1999 by researchers at Michigan State University, the Institute for Democracy in South Africa, and the Centre for Democratic Development in Ghana made public opinion data available for the first time for an increasing number of African states.[19] Third, a number of global datasets emerged that included information on African cases, such as the Minorities At Risk database, which collects information on the status and conflicts of politically active communal groups, and the National Elections Across Democracy and Autocracy dataset on electoral management and quality. Finally, the greater availability of research funding from universities, foundations, and international governments enabled an increasing number of researchers to collect their own data by carrying out surveys, randomized controlled trials (RCTs) and "laboratory games" in the field.

In many ways, this has been a positive development. The availability of new sources of quantitative data means that articles on Africa are now more likely to appear in disciplinary journals and shape comparative debates. However, these trends have not been uncontroversial. Many of the Africanists who cut their teeth in the 1970s and 1980s remain unconvinced about the quality of these data and about the benefits of broad generalizations. Their concerns have been strengthened by the research of Morten Jerven, which demonstrates that many of the economic statistics available on Africa are of dubious quality, raising questions about the reliability of analysis based on these data.[20] At the same time, the increasing use of surveys and RCTs, together with the fact that few African researchers have the funds to undertake similar projects in the West, has raised concerns that Africa has once again become a testing ground for foreign ideas.[21] In turn, this has further highlighted some of the tensions around the kind of global knowledge inequalities discussed earlier. In response to these debates, and others, *African Affairs* launched a new

---

[18] Some countries have signed up to Open Data projects that have made an increasing amount of material available online. However, although this has made over 150 datasets available for Kenya alone, many of these governments retain tight control of their most sensitive information, especially that relating to elections and the census.

[19] The Afrobarometer began with ten countries but now surveys over 35. See <http://www.afrobarometer.org/> (1 March 2016).

[20] Morten Jerven, 'The Relativity of Poverty and Income: How reliable are African economic statistics?' *African Affairs* 109, 434 (2010), pp. 77–96.

[21] Nic Cheeseman, 'An Introduction to African Politics', in Nic Cheeseman (ed.), *African Politics: Major Works* (Routledge, Oxford, 2016), pp. 1–27.

publication category, *Research Notes*, in early 2016. These are short essays on pressing methodological and ethical issues designed to encourage Africanists to share their experiences and to reflect on the strengths and weaknesses of new techniques.

Although the increasingly quantitative bent of the social sciences represents the biggest shift in the way in which the continent has been studied in recent times, it is important not to exaggerate the extent to which this trend has changed the complexion of African studies. In 2015, 19 out of 25 papers (80 percent) published in *African Affairs* focused on a single case, and the vast majority adopted a qualitative approach. Moreover, it is important not to lose sight of the fact that qualitative studies have also evolved considerably in recent years, becoming more ambitious and rigorous. Researchers have become increasingly confident in deploying comparative analysis and a range of different research techniques such as process tracing, political settlements frameworks, and critical juncture theory. Indeed, many of the innovative new strategies developed by quantitative and qualitative Africanists to study topics such as corruption, ethnicity, and traditional leadership have informed and shaped the practices of researchers elsewhere in the world.

As a result of these developments, the papers published in *African Affairs* today encapsulate a wide diversity of methods and theoretical perspectives for studying Africa, including a growing number of papers that draw on a mixture of different methods to illuminate a particular subject. This reflects both recent developments within African studies and the journal's belief that the continent can be profitably understood from a number of different perspectives: it is often by bringing the lessons generated through different methods into a conversation that old debates can be moved forwards.

KEY THEMES IN AFRICAN STUDIES

This book is divided into four parts, each of which presents a selection of articles from *African Affairs* on one of the research areas that has animated African studies over the past 60 years. Each part is introduced by an essay that highlights the key issues, explains the way in which research has evolved, and places the articles included here in their relevant context.

Part I deals with research on the African state. There are two reasons why this represents a productive starting point. On the one hand, how one understands the African state—that is the architecture and system of government—shapes how one understands a range of other issues on the continent. For example, whether you think that the African state is little more than a bundle of personal networks or is better understood as a particular set of political institutions will influence what you think about the prospects for building stronger states, more effective economies, and more stable democracies. On the other hand, the debate over the nature of the African state has been one of the most fierce and prolonged in African studies. For the past 60 years or so, Africanists have debated whether it makes more sense to understand African politics in terms of personal networks and community identity, à la neopatrimonialism, or inequality and class, à la Marxism, or an alternative framework entirely. They have also discussed the capacity of the state to influence developments, with some schools of thought identifying the state as central to economic and political developments and others arguing that in fact the power of the African state is illusory because it is either failed, or vacuous, or subservient to foreign powers. These debates are significant not just because it is difficult to discuss African politics without mentioning the state—however important one thinks it is—but also because at root these discussions are about a much deeper and broader question: what is the key logic and motivating force of African political and economic life?

Part II covers the political economy of economic development in Africa. It describes more than half a century of economic improvement and decline, and the equally dynamic nature of the academic debates that have sought to understand and explain this volatility. The story begins in the 1950s and 1960s, when nationalist movements on the continent began to seek not only political independence but also economic independence. The early African governments tried to deliver this by changing the structure of their economies away from "colonial trader economies" that were locked in exploitative trade relations in which they exported primary commodities to, and imported manufactured goods from, the metropole. However, efforts to industrialize in order to generate value-added economic activity at home were mixed, and came to an end when changes in the global economy in the late 1970s and early 1980s sent most African economies into crisis. In turn, the curtailment of state-led development saw the re-emergence of economic systems that were dependent on natural resource exports, and so extremely vulnerable to changes in the prices of goods such as coffee, copper, and tea on world markets.

In recent years, the limited development of African economies, combined with the example of successful industrializers outside of the continent—most notably the Asian "tiger economies"—has inspired scholars to once again ask 'can Africa industrialize?' This has led to the reopening of old debates about the need for economic transformation, and raised a number of important questions about the policies and politics that are conducive to achieving it.[22] Can African governments intervene in markets to drive industrialization, or do all interventions end in rent-seeking and corruption? Are government interventions even necessary, or will markets do the trick on their own?

---

[22] John Page, 'Can Africa Industrialise?', *Journal of African Economies* 21, AERC Supplement 2 (2012), pp. ii86–ii125.

Does foreign direct investment help foster economic transformation, or inhibit it? Is political clientelism the cause of underdevelopment, or can it be a driver of development? Are African economies at the mercy of the dominant players in global capitalism, or do they have the ability to shape their own economies? These questions have been at the heart of debates about African political economy over the past 30 years, and will remain so in the future. But while some of the questions remain the same, the answers put forward by scholars have changed, bringing fresh insights to the study of the political economy of development.

Part III looks at an alternative way to frame Africa's travails over the last 70 years, in terms of the struggle between democracy and authoritarianism. Independence represented a fight against arbitrary foreign control, and in favour of majority rule. However, in most countries nationalist movements subsequently failed to establish open and inclusive systems of government. With the exception of Botswana, Gambia, and Mauritius, the 1970s and 1980s was dominated by military takeovers, one-party states, and personal dictatorships. It was only in the early 1990s that multiparty elections started to be reintroduced, but this did not always signal an improvement in the quality of civil liberties. While competitive politics has led to the transfer of power in countries such as Benin, Ghana, and Zambia, it has also gone hand in hand with higher levels of repression in countries such as Uganda and Zimbabwe, as governments struggle to retain political control. This chequered history has given rise to a number of likely and important debates. The first of these looks at the prospects for democracy in Africa and asks a number of pertinent questions: Why has it proved to be so difficult to construct stable democratic systems in Africa? Is it actually feasible to do so? If it is, does democracy need to be "Africanized" to make it work? Can international donors help with this, or does their involvement undermine the prospect for the emergence of more home-grown solutions?

Other debates have focused more on how multiparty political systems are actually playing out on the continent. Following the experience of the last two decades, Africanists are painfully aware that simply holding elections does not equal democracy. But this raises a second set of questions: Under what conditions do elections deliver political change? Does repeatedly holding elections increase the quality of democracy over time, or intensify communal identities and increase the prospects for civil strife? Have elections led to better representation for women and historically marginalized communities? How can the electoral process be protected from manipulation? The answers are significant in terms of the Africanist literature, but they also have real policy implications for the strategies of African governments, civil society organizations, political parties, electoral commissions, international donors, and more.

Part IV situates the study of Africa within the broader context of international politics. While there have at times been tensions in the relationship between the disciplines of African studies and International Relations (IR), all students of African politics can agree that it is impossible to understand the continent without taking into account transnational and global processes of conflict and cooperation, colonialism and capitalism. Each of the articles in this part considers the interplay between global structures and processes (including the rise or fall of great powers like Britain, France, the United States, and China) and the various forms of African agency, extraversion, and resistance. While some scholars have emphasized the continent's dependence on international finance and political support, others have stressed the capacity of African leaders to manipulate the international community for their own ends, whether one is talking about the United States, the United Nations, or China. In part because of the focus on these issues, the international relations of Africa itself have often been overlooked. This is unfortunate because the development of regional organizations such as the East African Community and the Economic Community of West African States, and the political and trade networks that criss-cross the continent, will have a profound impact on its future. Indeed, the final article in the volume, perhaps appropriately, assesses the contribution of the African Union to pan-African unity, and promoting peace, security, democracy, and development in the continent and in the world. These remain continuing challenges for all students of African politics. As one of the continent's most famous sons once remarked, 'after climbing a great hill, one only finds that there are many more hills to climb'.[23]

---

[23] Nelson Mandela, *Long Walk to Freedom* (Abacus, London, 1995), p. 751.

Part I

The African State

2

An Introduction to the African State

Nic Cheeseman, Carl Death, and Lindsay Whitfield

THE AFRICAN STATE looks quite different to many of the models developed within political science and sociology, which imagine a dominant political organization capable of broadcasting its authority over a given territory.[1] By contrast, in Africa[2] the state's control over territory has often been partial and fragmentary, with large swathes of countries such as Somalia, the Democratic Republic of the Congo, and even Northern Nigeria, outside of central control. Legitimate violence is often not the sole prerogative of the state, and states struggle to prevent traditional authorities, religious groups, and well-established clandestine networks from enforcing their version of the law. Economies are divided between the formal (registered, tax-paying) and the informal, where a large portion of economic activity is located. Populations in rural areas can exist with little direct intervention from or loyalty to the nation-state, and regional, ethnic, or religious identities are in many cases stronger than national ones. With these features, how can we best characterize the African state? Scholars inspired by the work of influential sociologist Max Weber tend to follow two diagnoses: the first is that African states function as neopatrimonial regimes, and the second is that state structures in Africa are failed or failing.

The concept of neopatrimonialism has been used to describe the exercise of authority in newly independent countries that inherited formal political structures based on a Western model, but in which the "traditional" characteristics of African societies created a logic of power based on patron–client relations, in stark contrast to the rational-legal (impersonal) bureaucratic authority that was intended to underpin such institutions. Despite the fact that in reality political structures do not always conform to the rational-legal ideal type in the West, and that not all African institutions are riven with clientelism and

---

[1] Jeffrey Herbst, *States and Power in Africa: Comparative Lessons in Authority and Control* (Princeton University Press, Princeton, 2000); Charles Tilly, *Coercion, Capital and European States, AD 990–1992* (Blackwell, Oxford, 1992).

[2] We refer here to sub-Saharan Africa, the area covered by *African Affairs*.

personalized networks, the neopatrimonial model has often been taken to be an accurate representation of the way that politics works across the whole continent.[3] However, the common application of neopatrimonial frameworks has not prevented researchers from disagreeing about the implications of this form of politics. Whereas some scholars have argued that 'Africa works' because the personal networks permeating the state function effectively—at least from the position of those in power[4]—an alternative verdict has been that African states lack the capacity to perform the most basic functions and on this basis can be seen to have failed. State failure has been variously defined as 'a state's loss of control over the use of force' or an 'inability to perform development functions'; 'a political entity that lacks the institutional capacity to implement and enforce policies' or a decline in 'the capacity of the state to command loyalty', that is 'the right to rule'.[5]

Those who reach this verdict often emphasize the foreign imposition of the state in Africa, which left it poorly embedded in local societies and often in conflict with established and rival centres of power. From this perspective, it was not just the state that was in crisis in Africa, it was the very idea of the state and modern political order.[6] However, in recent years researchers have become increasingly critical of both the neopatrimonial and state failure literatures, pointing out that they tend to oversimplify and overgeneralize politics on the continent. Moreover, the weakness of state institutions and the existence of alternative political structures does not equate to the absence of order. Alternative forms of political authority exist that are historically rooted, resonate deeply within African societies, and constitute relatively stable sets of power relations—even if they bear little resemblance to Weberian rational-legal bureaucracies.

As a result, scholars have increasingly shed the theoretical baggage of the Weberian tradition and applied new frameworks of understanding. These new approaches have branched out in different theoretical directions, demonstrating that the state can be profitably studied and understood from a range of perspectives. For example, the political settlements approach disaggregates 'the state' by focusing on the relationships and competing interests among actors within the bureaucracy, ruling political coalition, and businesses, which

---

[3] With the exception of South Africa, which is usually exempted given its distinctive political history.

[4] Patrick Chabal and Jean-Pascal Daloz, *Africa Works: Disorder as Political Instrument* (James Currey, Oxford, 1999).

[5] Jean-François Bayart, *The State in Africa: The Politics of the Belly*, 2nd edition (Polity, Cambridge, 2009), pp. 74–9; Christopher Clapham, *Africa and the International System: The Politics of State Survival* (Cambridge University Press, Cambridge, 1996), p. 15; Robert H. Jackson, *Quasi-States: Sovereignty, International Relations and the Third World* (Cambridge University Press, Cambridge, 1993).

[6] Siba N. Grovogui, 'Sovereignty in Africa: Quasi-Statehood and Other Myths in International Theory', in Kevin C. Dunn and Timothy M. Shaw (eds), *Africa's Challenge to International Relations Theory* (Palgrave, Basingstoke, 2001), pp. 29–45.

are embedded within a particular distribution of power in a given society. By contrast, more anthropological takes on the 'everyday state' draw on theorists like Michel Foucault and Gilles Deleuze to show how states are the product of the crystallization and sedimentation of daily practices, interaction, and discourses, shaped by a global context of neoliberal techniques of new public management. Such analyses have led to fresh debates over the degree to which postcolonial states are being shaped in the image of the West, or are still largely particular and locally inscribed. The *African Affairs* articles included in this volume contribute to these debates and reflect on a number of pertinent issues including the usefulness of the concept of the "postcolonial state", the way in which property rights shape the nature of state authority, and the role of land politics in processes of state formation.

THE NEOPATRIMONIAL STATE AND THE INTERACTION OF FORMAL AND INFORMAL INSTITUTIONS

Max Weber outlined several ideal types of domination (or forms of ruling) that captured cultural variations in the way in which compliance with authority could be constructed and the legitimate exercise of power could be framed. Patrimonialism corresponds to a traditional type of domination: obedience is to the personal authority of the individual due to his traditional status, and he runs his kingdom similar to a household. While patrimonial power was acknowledged to exist in modern Western states, it did so alongside a strong institutionalization of power and a distinction between the public and private resources. Proponents of the neopatrimonial conception of African states argue that contrary to the European experience patrimonialism emerged as the overriding from of authority, which resulted in the personalization of power and the tendency for the ruler to treat public resources as their own property.[7] In other words, they suggest that the performance of the "modern" state formally introduced under colonial rule was compromised as a result of the interaction of political institutions such as legislatures and judiciaries with pre-existing social norms and "traditional" forms of authority.

---

[7] See the literature reviews in Gero Erdmann and Ulf Engel, 'Neopatrimonialism reconsidered: Critical review and elaboration of an elusive concept', *Commonwealth and Comparative Politics* 45, 1 (2007), pp. 95–119; Anne Pitcher, Mary Moran, and Michael Johnston, 'Rethinking Patrimonialism and Neopatrimonialism in Africa', *African Studies Review* 52, 1 (2009), pp. 125–56; Thandika Mkandawire, 'Neopatrimonialism and the Political Economy of Economic Performance in Africa: Critical Reflections', *World Politics* 67, 3 (2015), pp. 563–612.

In its initial formulation, neopatrimonialism was pitched as a simplified framework of how politics operated that should be treated as a model that would not always apply. As one of the most prominent early theorists, Jean-François Médard, wrote in 1982: 'there is more than neo-patrimonialism to Africa. This concept should be used as an ideal type: in systematically checking, for each particular political system, the reality of the model, we can measure the distortions.'[8] However, as the literature developed Médard's words of caution were often ignored. Instead, as Gero Erdmann and Ulf Engel have argued, research on the African state has at times assumed the existence of neopatrimonialism rather than testing for it, implying that the nature of politics is fundamentally the same no matter what country is being discussed.[9] This tendency became increasingly pronounced during the late 1980s and 1990s, when a number of researchers criticized the neopatrimonial framework not for overgeneralizing and simplifying the African experience, but rather on the basis that it had exaggerated the significance of political institutions and the colonial experience.

In Médard's formulation, neopatrimonialism 'began life as a framework through which to understand the impact that formal and informal structures had *on each other*'.[10] Against this, influential authors such as Patrick Chabal and Jean-Pascal Daloz suggested that the effect of colonial rule and the institutions it left behind had been overstated. In their widely read treatise *Africa works*, Chabal and Daloz argued that 'the visible institutional branches [of the state] are less significant that the subterranean roots issued from the complex world of factional struggles and local rivalries'.[11] As a result, they developed a new way of understanding African politics as an "institution-less"[12] arena in which the clue as to how politics operates can only be gleaned by looking at 'the ways in which individuals, groups, and communities seek to instrumentalise the resources which they command within this general political economy of disorder'.[13] In other words, Chabal and Daloz claim that the continent should be studied through the lens of its informal networks and relationships because African states are not really states at all.[14]

---

[8] Jean-François Médard, 'The Underdeveloped State in Tropical Africa: Political Clientelism or Neo-Patrimonialism', in Christopher Clapham (ed.), *Private Patronage and Public Power: Political Clientelism in the Modern State* (Francis Pinter Press, London, 1982), pp. 162–92, p. 51.

[9] Erdmann and Engel, 'Neopatrimonialism reconsidered'.

[10] Nic Cheeseman, 'Understanding African politics: Bringing the state back in', in Nic Cheeseman (ed.), *Institutions and Democracy in Africa: How the Rules of the Game Shape Political Developments* (Cambridge University Press, Cambridge, 2017), p. 14.

[11] Patrick Chabal and Jean-Pascal Daloz, *Africa Works: Disorder as Political Instrument* (James Currey, Oxford, 2010), p. 10.

[12] Cheeseman, 'Understanding African politics'.

[13] Chabal and Daloz, *Africa Works*, p. xix.

[14] Formal institutions refer to "bricks and mortar" organizations such as legislatures and judiciaries—the official codified rules of the game. Informal institutions refer to social norms and

Another set of scholars arrived at a similar conclusion by a different route. In *Creating political order*, Aristide Zolberg argued that political analysis of Africa had tended to exaggerate the significance of political institutions by imagining them to have a far greater geographical reach than was actually the case.[15] More specifically, Zolberg suggested that Africa featured a profound centre–periphery divide in which governments often had little presence outside of the capital city, with diminishing authority the further away one was from the seat of power. Ever since, the limited logistical capacity of the African state has been a constant preoccupation for Africanist political scientists. Most notably, Zolberg's early insights were later built on by Jeffrey Herbst, whose book *States and Power in Africa* explains how the institutional inheritance of colonial rule, absence of inter-state conflict, and ability to survive without the need to extend the tax base has discouraged African leaders from investing in strong borders and establishing control over rural areas.[16] Herbst's argument is subtle and complex, but in its most basic form suggests that African leaders have not constructed infrastructurally strong states because they did not inherit them and had few incentives to take on the high costs of state-building after independence.

The weakness of African states identified in these two literatures raises an important question: If political systems on the continent are so fragile, why have there been so few changes to state borders over the last 70 years? One of the most influential answers to this question was provided by Robert Jackson and Carl Rosberg, who conducted a survey of the African state in 1982 and concluded that it had no 'empirical' reality.[17] On this basis, they suggested that the survival of the African state could not be rooted in any domestic factors, and was rather dependent on recognition and support from the international state system. Subsequent accounts of state failure in Africa have tended to follow Jackson and Rosberg's example by downplaying the capacity of governments on the continent to establish effective and durable political systems capable of being reproduced over time.[18] This has been particularly true of a more policy-oriented set of work that has developed in response to the mixed fate of international interventions to curtail conflict on the continent.[19]

---

customs that can motivate and constrain behaviour because they are widely known and understood even though they are not codified—the unofficial rules of the game.

[15] Aristide Zolberg, *Creating Political Order: The Party-States of West Africa* (Rand McNally, Chicago, 1966), p. 6.

[16] Herbst, *States and Power*.

[17] Robert H. Jackson and Carl. G. Rosberg, 'Why Africa's Weak States Persist: The Empirical and the Juridical in Statehood', *World Politics* 35, 1 (1982), pp. 1–24.

[18] Cheeseman, 'Understanding African Politics'.

[19] Perhaps the classic example of this—and certainly the most influential—is Richard D. Kaplan, 'The Coming Anarchy', in Patrick O'Meara, Howard Mehlinger, and Matthew Krain (eds), *Globalization and the Challenges of a New Century: A Reader* (Indiana University Press, Bloomington, 2000), pp. 34–60.

The literatures on neopatrimonialism and the state failure in Africa have generated a number of valuable insights that help us to understand why the region has suffered considerable political instability in the form of military coups and civil wars, but they also suffer from a number of limitations that it is important to be aware of. Most obviously, the tendency to generalize the nature of the African state (as "patrimonial", as "weak") has directed scholarly attention away from the considerable variation that exists in the types of political system that are present on the continent. As Jean-Pierre Olivier de Sardan has put it, 'the suggestion that African countries exhibit a single type of real governance does not make good sense'.[20] Moreover, the notion that the drivers of African politics are at root the same means that these frameworks struggle to account for the difference in political outcomes between countries, or even within countries over time.[21] For example, efforts to tease out varieties of neopatrimonialism have tended to identify enclaves of rationality but maintain that the rest of the system is driven by patrimonial logic, leading Thandika Mkandawire to conclude that neopatrimonialism is 'too blunt and too formulaic an instrument for understanding the great variety of African experiences, and the contradictory interests, ideologies and motivations of social actors'.[22]

In a similar way, the emphasis of the state failure literature on the absence of strong infrastructures has at times come at the expense of a focus on the multiple forms of authority that underpin African states. As Daniel Branch and Nic Cheeseman have argued,[23] while many countries experienced conflict after independence, some also established durable governments. In Kenya, Senegal, Tanzania, and Zambia, presidents erected stable political systems that lasted for decades. The research of scholars such as Chris Allen and Henry Bienen suggests that in these cases political stability derived not from the recognition of state boundaries internationally, but from the construction of more viable political institutions reinforced by effective patronage networks.[24] Thus, Erdmann and Engel suggest that to account for variations in Africa we need to go back to Médard's initial formulation of neopatrimonialism and recognize that political authority in Africa is often most effective when it is underpinned by the fusion of both formal and informal power. In other words,

[20] Jean-Pierre Olivier de Sardan, 'Researching the Practical Norms of Real Governance in Africa' (London, African Power and Politics Discussion Paper No. 5, 2008).

[21] Richard Crook, 'Patrimonialism, Administrative Effectiveness and Economic Development in Cote d'Ivoire', *African Affairs* 88, 351 (1989), pp. 205–28.

[22] Mkandawire, 'Neopatrimonialism and the Political Economy of Economic Performance in Africa', p. 52.

[23] Daniel Branch and Nic Cheeseman, 'Democratization, Sequencing, and State Failure in Africa: Lessons from Kenya', *African Affairs* 108, 430 (2009), pp. 1–26.

[24] Chris Allen, 'Understanding African Politics', *Review of African Political Economy* 65 (1995), pp. 301–20; Henry Bienen, *Kenya: The Politics of Participation and Control* (Princeton University Press, Princeton, NJ, 1974).

if we frame the African state as being "institutionless" we risk missing out on a big part of the explanation of why some states have been more stable and effective than others.

In line with this insight, a new literature has developed that seeks to understand the African state not by comparing it to a European ideal type and finding it wanting, but by looking carefully at how it actually operates on the ground. This scholarship, which is united by a focus on the 'everyday state',[25] understands African politics through the experience of civil servants and other public officials, and in the process demonstrates that the way that the state performs is the product of the complex interaction between formal and informal ways of operating. Thus, according to Christian Lund, to understand the African state fully we need to go beyond a focus on how personal and patronage networks distort the way in which bureaucracies perform to consider also the way in which formal institutions shape the behaviour of non-state actors such as political and traditional leaders.[26] As Tom de Herdt and Jean-Pierre Olivier de Sardan have put it, it is only when we understand this 'patchwork' of formal and informal practices that we can make sense of 'the landscape of African governance' and understand why some states perform differently to others.[27] Further bodies of literature have also generated fresh insights as a result of their efforts to better understand and explain different varieties of state formation on the continent, and the sections below consider approaches influenced by political economy and political sociology, respectively.

TRAJECTORIES AMONG AFRICAN STATES AND THE DISTRIBUTION OF POWER

Recognizing the extent to which African states differ from one another and thus defy generalizations about 'the African state' or even 'African politics', Chris Allen proposed thinking in terms of a set of trajectories.[28] In the absence of strong class cleavages, all trajectories started with clientelist political systems, in which elites built political parties using patronage to bind local power-brokers to the party and local voters to the candidates. Allen argued that

---

[25] Giogio Blundo and Jean-Pierre Olivier de Sardan (with N.B. Arifari and M. Tidjani Alou), *Everyday Corruption and the State: Citizens and Public Officials in Africa* (Zed Books, London, 2006).

[26] Christian Lund, 'Twilight institutions: Public authority and local politics in Africa', *Development and Change* 37, 4 (2006), pp. 685–705.

[27] Tom de Herdt and Jean-Pierre Olivier de Sardan (eds), *Real Governance and Practical Norms in Sub-Saharan Africa: The Game of the Rules* (Routledge, Oxford, 2015), pp. 4–6.

[28] Allen, 'Understanding African Politics'.

against such a backdrop, post-independence ruling elites faced the formidable challenge of meeting the extensive factional demands for distribution of state resources, which in turn was a result of popular expectations for the government to deliver "development". More specifically, he suggested that the diversity of African trajectories could be best understand from the perspective of the varying degrees of success with which governments were able to manage demands for patronage.

The most common outcome was what Allen calls centralized-bureaucratic regimes, in which ruling elites proved able to centralize control over patronage through the creation of an executive presidency capable of supressing factional competition and the displacement of party organizations as the main distributors of clientelist resources by a bureaucracy answerable to the presidency. On this interpretation, one-party states were an attempt to regulate factional competition and conflict over the division of state resources. This strategy was sustainable until it was undermined by economic crisis in the 1980s. In a second set of countries, increasing clientelist competition was not resolved through centralized-bureaucratic regimes, and factional conflict became so intense that the military typically intervened. But rather than reducing clientelist competition, military involvement intensified it, leading to what Allen calls 'spoils politics'. The main characteristic of this trajectory was that the political faction in power denied access to resources to all other factions, which in turn led to endemic instability with continual attempts to overthrow governments and, in most cases, the total breakdown of civil order.

What Allen's model lacks is an explanation of why some leaders were able to establish stable one-party states while others were not, and thus why some countries where better able to manage patronage without the state failing apart.[29] The political settlements approach indicates that these different trajectories stem from variations in pre-colonial societies, colonial experiences, and the process of decolonization. In turn, this resulted in a large variation in the distribution of power in African countries at independence, and thus the composition of ruling coalitions and the pressures they faced. For example, power was much more dispersed in the Gold Coast as a result of pre-colonial and colonial factors, such that during the decolonization period there were a large class of educated elites and several bases of power in society that engaged in shifting alliances as they competed to take control of what would become Ghana when the British left. The same was true in Nigeria and Uganda, but it was not true in Tanzania, where there were fewer politically mobilized groups that needed to be accommodated within the state. This was significant,

---

[29] An earlier version of this argument was presented in Hazel Gray and Lindsay Whitfield, 'Reframing African Political Economy: Clientelism, Rents and Accumulation as Drivers of Capitalist Transformation' (LSE Working Paper 14–159, Development Studies Institute, London School of Economics and Political Science, London), <http://www.lse.ac.uk/depts/ID> (30 August 2016).

because it facilitated efforts to consolidate power within the ruling party and build a dominant political machine.[30] By contrast, this was not possible in Ghana and Uganda, where competing political factions failed to form inclusive and stable political settlements as a result of either historical and social cleavages or disagreements over fundamental issues such as property rights in land.

The political settlements approach systematizes these insights by classifying societies on the basis of the dominant institutions and the underlying distribution of power in a given case. A political settlement is defined as a 'combination of power and institutions that is mutually compatible and also sustainable in terms of economic and political viability'.[31] Institutions are the rules that guide social interaction, but they also determine the flow of resources to different groups and individuals in society. If institutions produce benefits that are not in line with the distribution of power, groups that lose out may be able to mobilize to overturn existing institutional structures, leading to political instability. Significantly, the political settlements approach defines the concept of power as the process through which individuals and groups are able to assert or maintain claims to ownership of property and income flows. Power can be exercised through violence (or the threat of violence), ideas, sociological and institutional hierarchies, and traditional authority as well as through access to economic resources. Thus, power exists in both formal institutions, such as within the state or within political parties, and within informal institutions such as patron–client networks, returning us to the idea that we need to take into account both formal and informal politics to understand the continent fully.

Significantly, political settlements approaches do not view particular agreements—or disputes—as being permanent. Instead, they recognize that African countries are in a long process of transformation in the sense that the formal and informal institutions that emerged out of particular historical distributions of power are constantly being renegotiated as a result of developments at both the domestic and international level. Such transformations have been a common experience across developing countries, in part because interactions with areas of the world that are already capitalist, with more advanced technologies and greater wealth, tend to challenge—and in some cases undermine—the status quo. Once capitalist transformation began in Africa, the pre-capitalist distributions of power on which traditional institutions were founded remained important but were typically not aligned to the

---

[30] Hazel Gray, *Turbulence and Order in Economic Development: The Political Settlement and Economic Transformation in Tanzania and Vietnam* (Oxford University Press, Oxford, forthcoming).

[31] Mushtaq Khan, 'Political Settlements and the Governance of Growth-Enhancing Institutions' (Research paper series on governance for growth, School of Oriental and African Studies, University of London, 2010), p. 4 <http://mercury.soas.ac.uk/users/mk17> (17 August 2016).

formal institutional structures that were imported under colonial rule. As a result, these institutions implied a formal distribution of benefits that did not always reflect the underlying distribution of power in African society. Consequently, informal distributions of resources such as clientelism and patronage became critical in redistributing resources towards groups that wielded great influence but lacked the political legitimacy to claim resources through formal state channels. As Mushtaq Khan notes, 'internal political stability in developing countries is maintained not primarily through fiscal policy, but through the largely off-budget and selective accommodation of factions organized along patron–client lines'.[32]

Political settlements theory provides important insights into the current and future direction of African politics, because it engages with the question of the conditions under which rational-legal Weberian states might emerge. More specifically, the political settlements framework emphasizes the point that such states are the product of capitalist development, and occur when the informal power of capitalists is large enough for them to align formal rights and institutions with their productive capitalist property rights and to finance the state to enforce these rights. In turn, such capitalist political settlements tend to create the conditions for the emergence of impersonal, rule-following adherence to formal institutions, although as Khan notes, this is not observed in every case. The situation is somewhat different in the clientelist political settlements of African countries, where there has been capitalist development but the profits generated by the capitalist portions of the economy are still relatively small and the distribution of power within society is much more diffuse. As a result, the informal power of domestic capitalists has not increased enough to effect a transformation of the state. On such an understanding, change from clientelist to capitalist political settlements, and thus the emergence of states with modern Weberian characteristics, requires the expansion of African capitalists in productive sectors.

FOUCAULDIAN APPROACHES TO EVERYDAY PRACTICES AND THE POSTCOLONIAL STATE

Many approaches to the state in Africa, such as the neo-Weberian and political settlements approaches discussed in the previous section, work by categorizing and classifying general types or models and using these classifications to assess actually existing states. An alternative approach

---

[32] Mushtaq Khan, 'Markets, States and Democracy: Patron–Client Networks and the Case of Democracy in Developing Countries', *Democratization* 12, 5 (2005), pp. 704–24, p. 711.

inspired by theorists like Michel Foucault, Achille Mbembe, and Jean-François Bayart has become increasingly influential in directing attention towards the everyday practices of the African state. Rather than identify an overarching logic, this approach draws attention to shifting networks, practices, subjectivities, and assemblages, through which postcolonial state formations govern and "conduct the conduct" of subject populations. This approach can be understood as postcolonial in the sense that it draws on a wider body of postcolonial theory that is concerned with analysing the specificity and particularity of non-Western societies (albeit in a context shaped by European colonialism and capitalism), rather than perspectives which seek to locate other societies and states in terms of previous European experiences of state formation.[33] Dipesh Chakrabarty has characterized this assumption in terms of the dictum 'first in Europe, then elsewhere', and postcolonial theorists have noted how from this starting point the African state always appears as a pathological deviation.[34] In a similar vein, John Hobson argues that what he terms 'Eurocentric theory' is defined by an implicit or explicit belief that Western civilization is superior and its values are universal, and that the aim of development should be to find the best ways to encourage or permit other societies to copy the European experience of processes such as state-building.[35]

Approaching the African state as an assemblage produced by everyday practices and discourses draws on critical theory and is often inspired by more sociological, anthropological, and ethnographic interpretations of the work of Michel Foucault. For Foucault, the 'state is a practice. The state is inseparable from the set of practices by which the state actually became a way of governing, a way of doing things, and a way too of relating to government.'[36] It follows that to research the state in Africa one should therefore start with the daily practices of governance and resistance through which the state is constituted: tax-collection, law enforcement, border control, military manoeuvres, and the provision of education and healthcare. Famously, Foucault located the quintessential sites of European statehood and power in the institutions of the prison, barracks, psychiatric asylum, school, and university.

---

[33] Rita Abrahamsen, 'African Studies and the Postcolonial Challenge', *African Affairs* 102, 407 (2003), pp. 189–210; Jean-François Bayart, 'Africa in the World: A History of Extraversion', *African Affairs* 99, 395 (2000), pp. 217–67.

[34] Dipesh Chakrabarty, *Provincializing Europe: Postcolonial Thought and Historical Difference* (Princeton University Press, Princeton, NJ, 2000), p. 7. See also Kevin C. Dunn, 'Madlib #32: The (blank) African State: Rethinking the Sovereign State in International Relations Theory', in Dunn and Shaw, *Africa's Challenge to International Relations Theory*, pp. 46–63.

[35] John M. Hobson, *The Eurocentric Conception of World Politics: Western International theory, 1760–2010* (Cambridge University Press, Cambridge, 2012).

[36] Michel Foucault, *Security, Territory, Population: Lectures at the Collège de France 1977–1978*, ed. M. Senellart, tr. G. Burchell (Palgrave Macmillan, Basingstoke, 2007), p. 277.

One of the earliest and most influential studies to employ this perspective on the African state is James Ferguson's study of development interventions in Lesotho, *The anti-politics machine*. He records how the operations of the international development industry can 'end up performing extremely sensitive political operations involving the entrenchment and expansion of institutional state power almost invisibly, under cover of a neutral, technical mission to which no-one can object'.[37] Much like Foucault's study of the prison in Europe, Ferguson concludes that while "development" has largely failed to eliminate poverty and raise living standards in many parts of the world, it has proved extremely successful at entrenching state power in alliance with networks of transnational elites.

Such an approach to the postcolonial state starts from the position that it should be studied as an assemblage of practices, institutions, customs, reforms, technologies, and discourses.[38] For Timothy Mitchell, drawing on historical analysis of the colonial state in Egypt, the state is 'an effect of detailed processes of spatial organisation, temporal arrangement, functional specification, and supervision and surveillance, which create the appearance of a world fundamentally divided into state and society'.[39] This appearance of an entity which claims a past, present, and future much larger than the day-to-day operations of tax-collection and law enforcement is a central historical product of European projects of state-building and colonialism. States claim legitimacy and sovereign supremacy, but the everyday practices of the state are often transformed, translated, resisted, and evaded.[40] Any understanding of contemporary states needs to appreciate how it is both 'a dispersed ensemble of institutional practices and techniques of governance', as well as 'the great enframer of our lives'.[41]

---

[37] James Ferguson, *The Anti-Politics Machine: 'Development', Depoliticization and Bureaucratic Power in Lesotho* (University of Minnesota Press, Minneapolis, 1994), p. 256.

[38] Maya Mynster Christensen, 'The Underbelly of Global Security: Sierra Leonean Ex-Militias in Iraq', *African Affairs* 115, 458 (2016), pp. 23–43; Erlend Grøner Krogstad, 'Security, Development, and Force: Revisiting Police Reform in Sierra Leone', *African Affairs* 111, 443 (2012), pp. 261–80.

[39] Timothy Mitchell, 'The Limits of the State: Beyond Statist Approaches and their Critics', *The American Political Science Review* 85, 1 (1991), p. 95. See also John L. Comaroff, 'Reflections on the Colonial State, in South Africa and Elsewhere: Factions, Fragments, Facts and Fictions', *Social Identities* 4, 3 (1998), pp. 321–61; James Ferguson and Akhil Gupta, 'Spatializing States: Towards an Ethnography of Neoliberal Governmentality', *American Ethnologist* 29, 4 (2002), pp. 981–1002; Michael J. Watts, *Silent Violence: Food, Famine, and Peasantry in Northern Nigeria* (University of Georgia Press, Athens, 2013).

[40] Wale Adebanwi, 'Glocal Naming and Shaming: Toponymic (Inter) National Relations on Lagos and New York's Streets', *African Affairs* 111, 445 (2012), pp. 640–61; James C. Scott, *Seeing Like a State: How Certain Schemes to Improve the Human condition have failed* (Yale University Press, New Haven, 1998); Susan Thomson, 'Whispering truth to power: The everyday resistance of Rwandan peasants to post-genocide reconciliation', *African Affairs* 110, 440 (2011), pp. 439–56.

[41] Thomas Blom Hansen and Finn Stepputat, 'Introduction: States of imagination', in Thomas Blom Hansen and Finn Stepputat (eds), *States of imagination: Ethnographic explorations of the postcolonial state* (Duke University Press, Durham, NC, 2001), pp. 14 and 37.

Bayart employs the metaphor of the rhizome to describe the state in Africa, meaning the root-like structure typical of potatoes or fungi, in contrast to a tree with a central trunk and spreading branches. The use of the rhizome is intended to complicate some of the more straightforward assumptions of distinct binaries between public/private, labour/capital, and national/international. Achille Mbembe makes a similar point, arguing that 'we need to go beyond the binary categories used in standard interpretations of domination, such as resistance v. passivity, autonomy v. subjection, state v. civil society, hegemony v. counter-hegemony, totalisation v. detotalisation'.[42] This means that in many specific situations it is very hard to discern where the state ends and society begins, or how to differentiate the domestic state from transnational networks. Religious brotherhoods in Senegal exist alongside and in 'illicit cohabitation' (to employ Mbembe's phrase) with the secular state.[43] Graham Harrison argues that the influence and penetration of World Bank institutions and discourses into 'governance states' like Tanzania, Uganda, and Mozambique is so pervasive that 'rather than conceptualising donor power as a strong external force on the state, it would be more useful to conceive of donors as *part of the state itself*.[44] Drawing attention to the African state as the crystallization of repeated rationalities of government draws attention to the influence of global discourses of state restructuring, such as neoliberalism, while also putting local practices of resistance and subversion at the heart of our analysis.[45] A central question raised by such an approach is the degree to which it is possible to observe successful implementation of governmental rationalities of managerialism, entrepreneurialism, competition, good governance, and technologies of freedom and responsibility in Africa. Some observers conclude that liberal modalities of rule have barely penetrated African state assemblages;[46] by contrast, others note the pervasive deployment of practices of auditing, benchmarking, and indexes of competitiveness, to manage the task of governing.[47] From this perspective, there are no 'headquarters'

---

[42] Achille Mbembe, 'Provisional notes on the postcolony', *Africa: Journal of the International African Institute* 62, 1 (1992), pp. 3–4.

[43] Paul Gifford, 'Religion and politics in contemporary Senegal', *African Affairs* 115, 461 (2016), pp. 688–709.

[44] Graham Harrison, *The World Bank and Africa: The construction of governance states* (Routledge, Abingdon, 2004), p. 87.

[45] Rita Abrahamsen, 'The power of partnerships in global governance', *Third World Quarterly* 25, 8 (2004), pp. 1453–67; Dunn, 'Madlib #32'; Clive Gabay and Carl Death (eds), *Critical perspectives on African politics: Liberal interventions, state-building and civil society* (Routledge, Abingdon, 2014).

[46] Jonathan Joseph, 'The limits of governmentality: Social theory and the international', *European Journal of International Relations* 16, 2 (2010), pp. 223–46.

[47] Rita Abrahamsen and Michael C. Williams, *Security beyond the state: Private security in international politics* (Cambridge University Press, Cambridge, 2011); Adebanwi, 'Glocal naming and shaming'; Carl Death, 'Governmentality at the limits of the international: African politics and Foucauldian theory', *Review of International Studies* 39, 3 (2013), pp. 763–87.

of authority or locus of control, rather power is everywhere and the state in Africa is brought into being through the everyday practices of a wide array of actors.[48]

PERSPECTIVES ON THE AFRICAN STATE

Many scholars have referred to the African state as "postcolonial" to distinguish it from the colonial state. However, the first article in Part I takes issue with the "postcolonial" label, arguing that the concept no longer has any explanatory power. Writing in 2004, Crawford Young posits that four decades after independence, little remains of the 'hegemonic apparatus' that the leaders of newly independent African states inherited. Affirming the empirical account of African statehood as fluid and contested, Young suggests that this represents in fact the erosion of the clear ascendancy of the colonial state, which enjoyed largely unchallenged hegemony in the realms of security, finance, and the rule of law. By the 1990s, he argues, neoliberal reforms and global changes had opened the political realm to a multiplicity of overlapping and conflicting actors. The article is one of the clearest and best accounts of the core features of the colonial 'command state', and it assesses which features were passed on at independence and continued to be present decades later. After the high point of the postcolonial or 'integral state' in the 1970s, the ebbing of Cold War support for state-building and the rise of the Washington Consensus precipitated a 'crisis of the postcolonial state' from which the continent had not recovered by the turn of the millennium.

Similar themes of state continuity and change are highlighted in the article by Stephen Ellis and Mark Shaw. Reflecting on the rise of a literature that documents the spread of the drugs trade and other forms of illicit exchange on the continent, they ask 'Does organized crime exist in Africa'? Ultimately, they conclude that the term 'organized crime' is not analytically useful, not because the continent does not feature a great deal of crime that is organized, but because the notion of organized crime implies a network of criminals seeking to elude detection from state authorities, which is not what is taking place in Africa. Instead, they suggest that what we are witnessing is a 'reformulation of politics and crime' into new sets of interconnected networks in which criminals seek out political leaders willing to facilitate their operations. This process, they argue, is better understood as a 'market for protection' in which businesspeople work with state officials to insulate their activities. Ellis and Shaw's argument is particularly important for how we understand

---

[48] Michel Foucault, *The Birth of Biopolitics: Lectures at the Collège de France, 1978–1979* (Palgrave Macmillan, Basingstoke, 2008), 77. See also Foucault, *Security, Territory, Population*, 109.

the state more generally because, like the work of Young, it suggests that globalization and political liberalization has had a profound impact on the way that the state is organized. While Ellis and Shaw are careful to point out that this process has gone much further in some states than others, and that not all African states have become criminalized, they also raise the prospect that what we are seeing amounts to a new form of governance in which 'the distinctions between licit and illicit economic activity become difficult to detect'. This is not an African problem—rather, the impact of financial globalization has given rise to new sets of transcontinental networks that transcend both geographical and state/non-state boundaries.

Catherine Boone's article shares Ellis and Shaw's interest in markets and state regulation, but in the case of Boone's analysis of property rights the focus is on land and legal forms of exchange. Boone's work is particularly significant because it demonstrates that the way in which the right to land is constituted shapes the kind of politics that emerge.[49] This argument has a broader relevance in terms of the debates discussed earlier, because it demonstrates that formal political institutions—the legal rules governing land ownership—can have a profound impact on the way in which politics is practised and the prospects for political violence. Boone demonstrates that colonial and post-colonial rulers who sought to build ruling political coalitions by bringing in chiefs and rural power-brokers did so by allowing control over land rights to remain in their hands at the local level. In most places, local institutions governing land rights revolved around concepts of 'the community', which reduced the land rights of migrants, as well as other kinds of rights that privileged indigenes. The long-term consequence of this was that it not only undermined the authority of the central state in these issues, but also called into question notions of national citizenship. In a second set of cases, postcolonial governments used the powers of the central state to challenge pre-existing land rights and institutions governing access and use of land. However, doing this successfully required considerable state authority at the local level, which is something that a number of African states have lacked. This helps to explain why land reform has stalled in many countries despite being such an important political and developmental issue.

Taken together, the three articles collected here highlight the challenges of characterizing the African state, and in particular of trying to generalize about the nature of "the African state". All three authors argue for more careful analysis that resists oversimplifications and generalizations, allowing us to identify different trajectories or paths across African countries, and to high-light sets of processes that seem to be more relevant in some countries than others.

[49] Catherine Boone, *Property and Political Order in Africa: Land Rights and the Structure of Politics* (Cambridge University Press, Cambridge, 2014).

3

The End of the Post-Colonial State in Africa?

Reflections on Changing African Political Dynamics

Crawford Young

AT THE MOMENT OF THE GRAND ENTRY OF AFRICAN STATES into the world consort of nations in 1960 (17 out of 53 achieved sovereignty that year), the primary discursive referent for the new polities was 'post-independent'. From an African nationalist perspective, widely shared in the academic community, the achievement of independence was a defining historical moment, the culmination of an epic struggle. Incorporating visions of liberation, transformation and uplift, the independent African state was a newborn polity. As 'new states', African polities appeared to shed the colonial chrysalis.

By subtle metamorphosis, over time the routine descriptor for African states became 'post-colonial'. This semantic shift was not innocent of meaning. Formal sovereignty and anti-colonial struggle gradually became less salient as defining attributes than the colonial origins of the African state; more crucially the wholesale importation of the routines, practices, and mentalities of the African colonial state into its post-colonial successor became evident.[1] Indeed, post-colonial studies became an influential current in the larger tides of 'post-modern' academic discourse by the 1980s.

Now that more than four decades have passed since the great wave of African independence, the question arises whether 'post-colonial' remains a serviceable designation. The vocabulary of analysis is more than a merely academic issue; terminology is constitutive of meanings. But beyond the semantic dimension, there is value in reflecting upon the extent to which new elements in the contemporary political equation add up to a basic alteration in the parameters of stateness. The lexical habit of post-colonial

---

[1] For an extended argument on this point, see Crawford Young, *The African Colonial State in Comparative Perspective* (Yale University Press, New Haven, CT, 1994).

usage to label the African political world persists, but in many countries little remains of the hegemonic apparatus which African rulers inherited and initially sought to reinforce and expand as an instrument of rapid development. Achille Mbembe in his remarkably prescient rendering of contemporary realities retains the title *On the Postcolony*, while his chapters portray an Africa 'out of the world' operated by 'private indirect government'.[2] The webs of conflict, violent social patterns and governmental dysfunctionalities in many parts of Africa make the state a far less dominating, agenda-setting actor than in the first post-independence decades. The *Bula Matari* (crusher of rocks) personification of the colonial state in the everyday expression of the Congolese subject in Belgian colonial times lived on in high Mobutist post-colonial times as a would-be leviathan (perhaps a lame one as Thomas Callaghy suggests), but the shrivelled, dishevelled and fragmented superstructure of Congo's governance in the Kabila age bears only a remote resemblance to its predecessors.[3] The paragon of the post-colonial Ivory Coast epitomized the arrival of a new, unsettling era, with the shattering of its stability in 1999, and its descent into civil disorder in 2002.

In this article, in delineating main trends since the terminal colonial period, I suggest closing the historical parentheses around the African post-colonial state, perhaps about 1990. The silent incorporation of many defining attributes of the colonial state in its post-independence successor for three decades validated the 'post-colonial' characterization. But by the 1980s a corrosive dynamic was visible, weakening most states, and by the 1990s eviscerating several. The state crisis became manifest by 1990 in the radically altered international environment of the collapse of the Soviet Union and irresistible pressures for liberalization. The reordering of politics which resulted had widely divergent results, poorly captured by the notion of post-coloniality.[4]

In developing this thesis, I begin by identifying the essential legacy of the colonial state. There follows a distillation of the core attributes of the post-colonial state. Its loss of ascendancy by the 1980s is examined, leading to

---

[2] Achille Mbembe, *On the Postcolony* (University of California Press, Berkeley, CA, 2001).

[3] On the 'lame leviathan' notion, see Thomas M. Callaghy, *The State-Society Struggle: Zaire in comparative perspective* (Columbia University Press, New York, 1984). For the *Bula Matari* metaphor and its origins, see Crawford Young and Thomas Turner, *The Rise and Decline of the Zairian State* (University of Wisconsin Press, Madison, WI, 1985). *Bula Matari*, one may note, lives on as the *nom de guerre* of a UNITA warlord, General Galieno da Silva e Sousa; see *Angola Peace Monitor*, Issue No. 6, Vol. VIII, on www.reliefweb.int, IRIN Nairobi, 26 February 2002. But compare Denis M. Tull, 'A reconfiguration of political order? The state of the state in North Kivu', *African Affairs* 102, 408 (2003), pp. 429–46.

[4] For an example of the continuing robust hold of 'post-coloniality' as a master concept, see Richard Werbner (ed.), *Postcolonial Subjectivities in Africa* (Zed Books, London, 2002); also, Rita Abrahamsen, 'African studies and the postcolonial challenge', *African Affairs* 102, 407 (2003), pp. 189–210. The applicability of this notion to some of the cases reviewed, such as southern Sudan, is dubious.

a conclusion that the 1990s and beyond are a sharply demarcated era in African politics. In high politics, the fundamental nature of post-colonial arrangements was challenged economically and politically, through demands—external and internal—for market liberalization and democratization. In ground-level politics, a multiplicity of contradictory processes were at work. The dramatic erosion of stateness itself in many cases—in the Weberian sense of the routine capacity to exercise ultimate authority within the territorial domain of sovereignty—opened space for a multitude of actors: informal traders, smugglers, warlords, arms traffickers, youth militia, local associations ('civil society'), women's organizations, religious groups, refugees. These elements operate with varying degrees of autonomy, interacting with state agents as well as international agencies, donor representatives, and the non-governmental sector. No single designation emerges to capture the cross-currents and contradictions of the era beyond the post-colonial state, although the broad-front marginalization of much of Africa in the world at large seems a common condition. The vision of an 'African renaissance' articulated with eloquence by Thabo Mbeki of South Africa, and the summons to a New Partnership for Africa's Development (NEPAD) echoed by Abdoulaye Wade of Senegal, Olusegun Obasanjo of Nigeria, and Abdelaziz Bouteflika of Algeria pledging an economically reformed, politically democratic, and governmentally accountable and transparent Africa, offer a normative notion of a renovated African state. A rather different empirical picture emerges in recent influential analyses by Mbembe and others.[5]

Legacy of the African colonial state

The legacy of the African colonial state defined its post-colonial successor in a number of important ways.[6] The colonial state formation in Africa had unique features, when compared with counterparts in other regions. The subjugation of Africa occurred relatively late in the age of imperialism, and with exceptional speed. In the last quarter of the nineteenth century, most of Africa was forcibly annexed to a half dozen European imperial domains. The conquest was highly competitive, and governed after the 1884–85 Berlin Conference by the doctrine of 'effective occupation'; imperial title was not secure until a

---

[5] See, for example, Mbembe, *On the Postcolony*; Jean-François Bayart, Stephen Ellis and Béatrice Hibou, *The Criminalization of the State in Africa* (James Currey, Oxford, 1999); William Reno, *Warlord Politics and African States* (Lynne Rienner, Boulder, CO, 1998), and Patrick Chabal and Jean-Pascal Daloz, *Africa Works: Disorder as political instrument* (James Currey, Oxford, 1999).

[6] This analysis is largely drawn from Young, *The African Colonial State*.

skeletal presence on the ground existed.[7] Meanwhile, metropolitan parliaments insisted on fiscal self-sufficiency for the new colonies, in a setting where in much of Africa subsistence economies prevailed. Africa had to pay for its own subjugation; in the absence of existing revenue flows to intercept, as in India, the only solution was to monetize the African subject by the imposition of head taxes (necessitating cash agriculture) and fiscal extraction in kind through forced labour. The resources extractable through such mechanisms imposed sharp limits on the size of the European colonial establishment to exercise hegemony; a low-cost intermediary cadre of African chiefs, co-opted from customary hierarchies or created, remunerated in status, subaltern power, and a share of the fiscal proceeds, was the indispensable local armature of the colonial state. The command state which resulted, even though its expatriate superstructure was modest, achieved unchallenged hegemony by World War I, and enjoyed an ascendancy sufficient to appropriate a significant fraction of the meagre incomes of its subjects, and direct large amounts of labour into economic pursuits desired by the colonial state for fiscal and other reasons (export crop cultivation, plantation labour, mining workforces). Though some authors view the colonial state as weak, relative to its vocation of low-cost domination (decentralized despotism, in the apt phrase of Mahmood Mamdani[8]), prior to World War II the scope of its authority is striking. Although brute force and violence were at its core, its overpowering image of strength and authority meant that coercive powers did not require constant application.[9]

Major changes occurred in the final years of the colonial state following World War II. By this time, 'colonial science' aiding, the superstructure of imperial rule had become well professionalized, its European cadres trained in specialized institutes. The African intermediary structures as well were better

---

[7] Simon Katzenallenbogen and others argue that the doctrine of effective occupation was not in a formal sense adopted as one of the articles of the Act of Berlin in 1885. Nonetheless, this critical notion, originally a creative reading of Roman law used by the British and French to contest Spanish and Portuguese claims to the entire Western hemisphere, was invoked by various imperial practitioners as if it had the sanction of settled international law, reaffirmed at Berlin. See Katzenallenbogen, 'It didn't happen at Berlin: politics, economics and ignorance in the setting of Africa's colonial boundaries', in Paul Nugent and A. I. Asiwaju (eds), *African Boundaries: Barriers, conduits and opportunities* (Pinter, London, 1996), pp. 21–34.

[8] Mahmood Mamdani, *Citizen and Subject: Contemporary Africa and the legacy of late colonialism* (Princeton University Press, Princeton, NJ, 1996).

[9] For the relative weakness argument, see Jeffrey Herbst, *States and Power in Africa* (Princeton University Press, Princeton, NJ, 2000). Bruce Berman gives detailed exposition to the limits of colonial authority in Kenya, and the need for its agents to carefully navigate the boundaries of their coercive capacities: *Control and Crisis in Colonial Kenya: The dialectics of domination* (James Currey, London, 1990). Frederick Cooper argues the relative weakness thesis differently, suggesting that the essence of colonial power was its 'gatekeeper' role, astride the intersection with the international realm, rather than its internal capacity. Cooper, *Africa since 1940: The past of the present* (Cambridge University Press, Cambridge, 2002).

honed instruments, with chiefly appointment now contingent on literacy and competence as well as customary qualifications. The command habits of the administration were deeply embedded in its practices and policies, finding sartorial reflection in the military-style uniforms worn by regional administrators when giving public performance on tour. The European command agents in the colonial hierarchy (Africans entered this echelon of state service only at the very end, or in the Belgian case never) enjoyed wide autonomy. The 'man on the spot' had broad latitude in the exercise of his powers, unless disorder broke out requiring central intervention. There was exceptional insulation from a civil society denied organizational scope by repressive colonial legislation, and from metropolitan instances which gave only distant monitoring, unless budget subsidies were requested or uprisings drew unwelcome attention. Field agents of the colonial state certainly faced a challenge in managing discontents arising within their domains; still, they enjoyed a wealth of legal and coercive instruments blended with the mystique of colonial power. Only when power transfer came into view after World War II did an African representative voice become legalized, political organization tolerated, and free expression accepted. In addition, the imperial centres reasserted their sovereignty in assuming control of decolonization negotiation.

The scope of the colonial state radically expanded in the postwar years. Developmentalism, which first appeared in the 1920s as state discourse, became central to the legitimation imperative of the terminal colonial state, now subject to an increasingly hostile international environment and a rising torrent of nationalist criticism.[10] The minimal social infrastructure, mostly provided by mission initiative earlier, now became an urgent target for expansion. Educational and health facilities multiplied. Dramatically swelling revenues facilitated this momentum of state expansion; Belgian Congo state expenditures increased eleven-fold from 1939 to 1950, then tripled in the final colonial decade; comparable fiscal bonanzas occurred in other countries, nurtured by the prolonged boom in primary commodity prices.[11] As well, for the first time substantial aid came from imperial rulers; the doctrine of colonial fiscal self-sufficiency was finally abandoned. The command hierarchy was now fleshed out with a proliferating array of technical services, greatly enlarging the rosters of expatriate agents of the colonial state. This remarkable influx, wrote John Hargreaves, 'produced a "second colonial occupation" in the form of a large-scale infusion of technical experts, whose activities not only increased the "intensity" of colonial government, but seemed to imply its continuance in some form until the new policies had an opportunity to

---

[10] Cooper, *Africa since 1940*, argues that developmentalism became the defining discourse of the late colonial state from 1940 onwards.

[11] Young, *The African Colonial State*, p. 213.

mature'.[12] But the new opportunities for state employment were not limited to European technicians; for the young Africans who began to emerge from secondary schools in large numbers in the 1950s (and universities in the 1960s), government service was the natural end object of education. For the youth generation, state expansion and then Africanization provided extraordinary opportunities for social ascension.

Wartime imperatives of controlling the supply of basic primary commodities, especially for the British, led to important new forms of state intervention in the economy. After the war, the mantra of developmentalism, and the new creed of economic planning, led to the institutionalization of a number of wartime emergency controls, and in particular consolidation of agricultural marketing monopolies under state management for key export crops. The premise of state control and management of the economy as a necessary responsibility in the struggle for development was solidly implanted in state reason well before the imperial flags were lowered.

A striking paradox of the terminal colonial state is that, in the large majority of countries where decolonization was managed by negotiation, internal security was maintained with strikingly small military forces, notwithstanding the rising challenge of an impatient nationalism. Uganda in the immediate pre-independence period was garrisoned only by a single battalion of the East African King's African Rifles. Giant Nigeria had an army of only 10,000 at independence; the Belgian Congo *Force Publique* had merely 20,000 troops in the 1950s, and was responsible for internal security in Ruanda-Urundi as well as the Congo. The disproportion between these figures and the 500,000 troops deployed in Algeria by France, and by Portugal in its African colonies, to combat armed liberation movements, illustrates the magnitude of potential military requirements, had the authority of the colonial state been violently contested.[13] I read these figures as reflecting the robust authority the colonial state continued to hold in its decolonization phase.

Anatomy of the post-colonial state

Some core elements of colonial state ideology passed intact to its successor. In the war against poverty, ignorance and disease to which African nationalism was committed, the state bore an historical mandate as manager of

---

[12] John D. Hargreaves, *The End of Colonial Rule in West Africa* (Macmillan, London, 1979), p. 41.
[13] The only other territories where metropolitan troop intervention was required in the decolonization era were Kenya and Cameroon. These uprisings had very limited armament, no external support or supply, and were repressed with a modest number of metropolitan troops.

transformation, at once the architect of development and its primary theologian. The racial subtext of colonial administration—that European agents by their presumed innate superiority and role as natural bearers of 'civilization' had an unquestioned right to rule—was transformed into a comparable prerogative of the youthful educated nationalist generation to exercise tutelage over an unlettered citizenry. The new governing elite, wrote Jacob Ajayi, 'staked their claims to leadership on their superior knowledge' of external models of rule and development, and 'took for granted the masses and the traditional elite's willingness to accept their leadership'.[14]

In part the silent incorporation of the colonial state legacy into the post-colonial state simply reflected natural inertial forces. The formal language of a state is law, and the legal codes assembled in a row of volumes on the office shelves of its agents were a colonial codification. Even where an alternative codified legal tradition was available, in predominantly Muslim states, a number of years passed before the ascendancy of imperial legal orders outside of personal status issues was challenged. The dossiers shaping the policy knowledge and guiding the actions of government servants were from the colonial files. The default option for any bureaucrat is to continue the policies in place, a choice naturally pursued in the everyday actions in most instances. Unless circumstances provide some sharp rupture, as in the case of countries winning independence after a protracted armed struggle, the subliminal forces tending towards a reproduction of the state are formidable.

But the outcome went well beyond mere continuity. Building upon the extant structures, policies and practices, the post-colonial rulers sought a rapid expansion in the mission and scope of the state. These expansive ambitions drew energy from some exceptional conjunctural factors influencing state-building designs. The developmental state was not merely a product of terminal colonial statecraft; the moment of African independence coincided with the zenith of confidence in state-led development. Ghana's President Kwame Nkrumah spoke for a generation in writing that 'most of our development so far has had to be carried out by the Government itself. There is no other way out.'[15] The command role for the 'political kingdom' promised a dazzling future; with independence, pledged Nkrumah, 'we'll transform the Gold Coast into a paradise in ten years...'[16] In part this certitude of state capacity derived from the attachment of much of the African intelligentsia to socialist doctrine in its various forms. European left parties had provided important support to nationalism, and were a natural source of policy ideas. Capitalism was represented by the colonial corporations and pariah

---

[14] J. F. Ade Ajayi, 'Expectations of independence', *Daedalus* 111 (1982), p. 2.

[15] Kwame Nkrumah, *I Speak of Freedom: A statement of African ideology* (Oxford University Press, London, 1962), p. 117.

[16] Tony Killick, *Development Economics in Action* (Heinemann, London, 1978), p. 34.

entrepreneurs of South Asian or Levantine antecedents widely viewed as alien exploiters. Further, in 1960 the Soviet Union and China appeared to enjoy remarkable double digit growth rates; not even Western specialists at the time cast serious doubt on these claims, and many years would pass before the world at large learned that the 'great leap forward' in China which inspired many young African intellectuals at the time created a famine which claimed an estimated 30 million lives. More broadly, a vision of a 'high modernity' achievable by state action inspired the young generation of post-colonial rulers: a rendezvous with abundance within a decade or two.[17]

Socialist orientation was not a necessary prerequisite for commitment to state-led development. The Western model for African intellectuals was the welfare state, especially its highest form in the Nordic states. Keynesian economic theory dominated Western economics at the time. Within the new sub-discipline of development economics, mainstream doctrine, in the words of Tony Killick, was 'highly interventionist'. It established powerful theoretical and practical arguments against reliance upon the market mechanism and advocated a strategy of development which placed the state at the centre of the stage.[18]

All available conceptual mappings of pathways towards rapid development pointed towards the same basic choices. Even the small number of countries such as Ivory Coast whose leaders did not recoil in horror when observers characterized their basic development orientation as 'capitalist', carved out a central role for the state in the management of the agricultural sector, and the creation of a very large array of state enterprises.[19] If the parastatal enterprise was not legitimated by socialist orientation, it found justification in the argument that, in the absence of indigenous capitalists, the state had to serve as surrogate collective capitalist.

African independence coincided as well with the apogee of the Cold War, guaranteeing that the new states would become a diplomatic battlefield. The two major blocs competed maximally for the affiliation of African states, or minimally to pre-empt alignment with the other side. The currency of this

---

[17] One may recollect the soaring ambitions for Congo-Kinshasa defined by Mobutu Sese Seko in 1970; '*Objectif 80*' promised massive new investments around the three 'poles of development' of Kinshasa, Kisangani, and Lubumbashi. With some discount for hyperbole, such visions seemed plausible to both domestic and international audiences at the time. On the allure of 'high modernity', see the engaging study by James C. Scott, *Seeing Like a State: How certain schemes to improve the human condition have failed* (Yale University Press, New Haven, CT, 1998).

[18] Killick, *Development Economics in Action*. The Killick monograph is a painstaking inquest into the interaction of currents of professional economics theory and Ghana development choices. See also Douglas Rimmer, 'Learning about economic development from Africa', *African Affairs* 102, 408 (2003), pp. 469–92.

[19] For data see Crawford Young, *Ideology and Development in Africa* (Yale University Press, New Haven, CT, 1982).

competition was aid, economic and military. Although 'non-alignment' was orthodoxy in African diplomacy, the doctrine had many shadings, and its effectiveness in insulating the continent from global rivalries was necessarily limited. However, the primacy of a global security reason for the major powers through the post-colonial decades provided insulation of a different sort: the state qualities subsequently coded by the donor community as 'governance' measured less than the alignment thermometer.[20] The logic of the Cold War gave all players a stake in the competitive engagement in 'state-building' and 'nation-building'.

Rapid state expansion in the early post-colonial years was driven by several potent factors. Anti-colonial mobilization was achieved through a number of promissory notes. The young militants who provided the muscle of nationalist movements expected opportunities for employment, which they counted upon the state to provide. The new intellectual class now emerging from the universities expected guarantees of incorporation into the upper ranks of the state bureaucracy, an assurance which usually continued until the 1980s even in countries such as Egypt and Senegal with large university cohorts. Parents hoped that pledges of rapid school expansion, even universal primary educa-tion, would materialize. Clinics, safe drinking water, roads: social infrastruc-ture promises resonated with rural and urban audiences. The colonial state was chastised for its lethargy in meeting these needs; the fruits of independ-ence would be social uplift. In the 1960s and 1970s, a very large down-payment on the pledges of a better life were made; a hefty fraction of the swelling rosters of state employees were teachers and agents of the technical and service sectors.

The doctrine of nationalism was far from satisfied by mere nominal political sovereignty. The colonial economy soon became a target as well, a movement powerfully abetted by the 1970s through the importation of dependency theory from Latin America. Not only was the dominant position of the colonial corporations an affront to sovereignty; it was also an engine of underdevelopment through siphoning of resources and the profits from their extraction to the metropolitan centres.[21] At ground level, often a greater irritant was the stranglehold which South Asian or Mediterranean mercantiles held over wholesale and retail trade. The impulse to assert national control over these sectors drew further inspiration from a brief assertive moment in Third World populism in the early 1970s, whose epitome was the movement

---

[20] See Christopher Clapham, *Africa and the International System: The politics of state survival* (Cambridge University Press, Cambridge, 1996).

[21] Particularly influential statements of this thesis are found in the abundant writings of Samir Amin, such as *Accumulation on a World Scale: A critique of the theory of underdevelopment* (Monthly Review Press, New York, 1974). Walter Rodney popularized the theory in his lucid polemic, *How Europe Underdeveloped Africa* (Bogle-L'Ouverture, London, 1972).

for a 'New International Economic Order' and whose dramatic culmination was the Arab oil boycott of 1973.

Across the continent, a two-front assault on alien economic dominance took shape: nationalization for the colonial corporations, indigenization for the pariah entrepreneurs. Countries operating from a self-consciously socialist orientation tended to be first to undertake nationalization of major colonial enterprises: Algeria, Guinea, Tanzania from the 1960s. Reginald Green, long an economic adviser to the Tanzanian government, reported that by the mid-1970s, 80 percent of the medium- and large-scale economic activity lay in the public sector, which accounted for 80 percent of total investment.[22]

Other countries soon followed; by 1979, ostensibly capitalist Nigeria had achieved 60 percent control of the petroleum sector through the Nigerian National Petroleum Corporation. In 1969, Milton Obote in Uganda pledged to impose state majority control over a large part of the colonial private sector in the name of a 'Move to the Left', only partially implemented by the time of his overthrow by Idi Amin in 1971.[23] Mobutu nationalized the mineral giant *Union Minière du Haut Katanga* in 1967; Kenneth Kaunda followed suit with the Zambian copper mines in 1969.[24] In tackling the multinational giants, African states were unable to control downstream operations or directly manage many production operations; profitable opportunities remained for foreign corporations through management contracts or operation as a minority holder. But the key point here is that the state role in managing resource extraction greatly expanded, and a large array of parastatal bodies emerged to assume these responsibilities.

From 1968 to 1973, a wave of indigenization measures swept Africa. The most spectacular was the racial cleansing of Asians conducted by Amin in Uganda in 1972, ordering their departure within 90 days. Of the 83,000 Asians resident in Uganda in 1970, 30,000 of whom held citizenship, only 10,000 remained by 1975.[25] In Ghana, Sierra Leone, Zambia, Malawi and Nigeria, governments enacted indigenization decrees designed to squeeze immigrant traders out of the commercial and light industrial sectors in favour of nationals. In Congo-Kinshasa, Mobutu in 1973 and 1974 issued sweeping 'Zairianization' and 'radicalization' decrees which in effect confiscated foreign-owned

---

[22] See Bismarck U. Mwansasu and Cranford Pratt (eds), *Towards Socialism in Tanzania* (University of Toronto Press, Toronto, 1979), pp. 19–45.

[23] James H. Mittelman, *Ideology and Politics in Uganda: From Obote to Amin* (Cornell University Press, Ithaca, NY, 1975).

[24] On the nationalization dynamics, see, *inter alia*, Thomas J. Bierstaker, *Multinationals, the State, and Control of the Nigerian Economy* (Princeton University Press, Princeton, NJ, 1987); Young and Turner, *The Rise and Decline of the Zairian State*, pp. 276–362; Kamitatu Massamba, 'Problématique et rationalité dans le processus de nationalisation du cuivre en Afrique centrale: Zaire (1967) et Zambie (1969)', (Ph.D. dissertation, Institut d'études politiques de Paris, 1976).

[25] See Michael Twaddle (ed.), *The Expulsion of a Minority: Essays on Ugandan Asians* (Athlone Press, London, 1975).

agricultural and commercial enterprises, allocating them as patrimonial rewards for henchmen and clients (and reserving some of the most lucrative for himself).[26] In other cases policies which did not ostensibly target immigrant minorities had the effect of dispossessing them. In Tanzania, for example, which had been generous at independence in offering citizenship to long-resident Asians and Europeans, the 1971 Acquisition of Buildings Act hit the Asian community hard; 97 percent of the nationalized buildings were owned by Asians, nearly half of whom had emigrated within three months of the act.[27] In some cases, as in Tanzania, mercantile minority assets entered the parastatal sector; more frequently, indigenization linked to state expansion more indirectly, through the channel of patrimonial aggrandizement. Such properties became prebendal goods available to lubricate ties of clientage to state managers.

The size of the state-owned sector also grew through the state role as surrogate capitalist. A corollary of the dependency perspective which influenced the African intelligentsia and ruling classes throughout the 1970s was import substitution industrialization. Virtually everywhere state initiative launched plants for processed foods, beverages, apparel, and other light industries, most frequently under state ownership. Though management might be contracted to foreign operators, liability for the capitalizing, debts and deficits of the enterprises rested with the state.

Rapid fulfilment of the high modernity visions of the post-colonial polity, in the logic of the times, necessitated the concentration of authority. Developmental energies, for a state, were finite, ran the thinking. The dissipation of such energies in political debate and conflict over the policy direction corroded state capacities for purposeful action. Further, open political competition opened the door for ethnic entrepreneurs to engage in divisive mobilization of communal partisans. The dual imperatives of state and nation-building beckoned centralization of power and erection of a political monopoly, for which the single party was the ordained instrument. 'At the present stage of Ghana's economic development,' wrote Nkrumah, 'the whole community must act in the national interest.'[28] Sympathetic academic observers proposed a reasoned brief at the time for the single-party system.[29] The most thoughtful African

---

[26] Young and Turner, *The Rise and Decline of the Zairian State* and sources cited therein provide full detail; see also Michael G. Schatzberg, *Politics and Class in Zaire: Bureaucracy, business and beer in Lisala* (Africana Publishing Company, New York, 1980), pp. 121–53.

[27] Aili Mari Tripp and Crawford Young, 'The accommodation of cultural diversity in Tanzania', in Daniel Chirot and Martin E. P. Seligman (eds), *Ethnopolitical Warfare: Causes, consequences, and possible solutions* (American Psychological Association, Washington, DC, 2001), pp. 269–74.

[28] Nkrumah, *I Speak of Freedom*, p. 117.

[29] For example, see Immanuel Wallerstein, *Africa: The politics of independence* (Vintage Press, New York, 1961); Ruth Schachter Morgenthau, *Political Parties in French-Speaking West Africa* (Clarendon Press, Oxford, 1964).

official argument for the single party was the report of the 1965 Tanzania Presidential Commission on the Establishment of a Democratic One Party State.[30]

Implementation of the single-party model quickly centralized authority in the ruler. Parliamentary institutions existed, but had little voice. Local representative institutions, often accused of paralyzing factionalism, were brought under central and party tutelage, or simply dissolved. Elimination of political competition and participation was hailed as a necessary device for the management of ethnicity: the departicipation strategy identified by Nelson Kasfir.[31] The single-party system dominated the African landscape until 1990. Military intervention became the sole mechanism to displace incumbents, but the putschist in power normally formed a new single party to legitimize permanent status for his rule. Thus citizen became once again merely subject, facing an exclusion from the public domain reminiscent of colonial times. One important difference: whereas the colonial state asked only obedience, the post-colonial polity demanded affection. Mere submission did not suffice; active participation in rituals of loyalty (support marches, assemblies to applaud touring dignitaries, purchase of party cards, display of the presidential portrait, participation in plebiscitary elections) was mandatory.

Successful centralization of power and monopolization of political space did not suffice to ensure the unhindered hegemony of the post-colonial state, which could never match the autonomy from society enjoyed by the imperial bureaucracy. The command state could not operate on the basis of ultimate impersonal authority and coercive force alone; indispensable were supplementary mechanisms translating state rule into personalized linkages with key intermediaries and their ramifying networks of clientele: the rhizome state of Jean-François Bayart.[32] At the summit, state power was personalized through cults devoted to the ruler. Not simply personalized but paternalized: in the moral matrix of legitimacy, argues Schatzberg, 'government stands in the same relationship to its citizens that father does to his children'.[33] Patrimonial webs of personalized circuits of distribution reciprocated with clientelist loyalty created a honeycomb of networks by which the ascendancy of the ruler was

---

[30] Substantial extracts from the report are reprinted in Lionel Cliffe (ed.), *One Party Democracy: The 1965 Tanzania general election* (East African Publishing House, Nairobi, 1967), pp. 438–65.

[31] Nelson Kasfir, *The Shrinking Political Arena: Participation and ethnicity in African politics, with a case study of Uganda* (University of California Press, Berkeley, CA, 1976).

[32] Jean-François Bayart, *The State in Africa: The politics of the belly* (Longman, New York, 1993).

[33] Michael G. Schatzberg, *Political Legitimacy in Middle Africa: Father, family, food* (Indiana University Press, Bloomington, IN, 2001), p. 1. See also Robert H. Jackson and Carl G. Rosberg, *Personal Rule in Black Africa* (University of California Press, Berkeley, CA, 1982).

maintained.[34] In turn, clienteles exerted great pressure for access to government resources, since state power was the key source of accumulation.

In all its aspects, the health of the post-colonial polity was entirely tributary to expanding revenues, both to pay for its proliferating apparatus and growing functions, and to lubricate the patrimonial channels assuring its legitimacy. In the first post-colonial decade, conditions were relatively favourable. Commodity prices were more volatile and less consistently advantageous than in the 1950s, but still high by historical standards. The aid flows from the former colonizer, which helped produce the robust growth of the 1950s, by and large continued, even increased. Major new sources of development assistance became available: Canada, the Nordic countries, Netherlands, Japan. The major Cold War powers—the United States, the Soviet Union, China—made their competitive entry onto the aid scene. Initially, assistance was often provided in grant form, but gradually became in large part loans. The developmental impact of the aid was uneven at best; econometric analysis could detect no relationship between aid levels and growth. Nonetheless, aid flows were a significant component of the resource base of many countries; in the case of a particularly favoured country, such as Tanzania, aid accounted for over 15 percent of the Gross Domestic Product (GDP) in more than a third of the years between 1970 and 1993.[35] Jannik Boesen and his collaborators in noting the scope of the crisis by the early 1980s identified as core factor policy choices 'increasingly concentrating all development activities in the state'. They added that few foresaw the coming crisis of the state:

> . . . it is striking that up to as late as 1979 there was no fundamental concern about overall economic developments in Tanzania. Few inside or outside the country seem to have realized the deeper problems behind the speed and pattern of development since the end of the 1960s, and fewer still expected the decline to follow after 1979.[36]

By the end of the 1960s, new funds were needed to finance state expansion. African external debt at this juncture was still negligible, and especially countries with promising natural resources could mortgage these assets for loans. With large eurodollar reserves and Western economies in the doldrums, major commercial banks briefly found African lending attractive in the early 1970s. Gigantic development projects, such as the multi-billion Inga-Shaba power scheme in Congo-Kinshasa, lined up for external public finance, with

[34] These arrangements are well dissected by Richard A. Joseph, *Democracy and Prebendal Politics in Nigeria: The rise and fall of the Second Republic* (Cambridge University Press, New York, 1987).

[35] Carol Lancaster, *Aid to Africa: So much to do, so little done* (University of Chicago Press, Chicago, IL, 1999), pp. 42, 59. See also Nicolas van de Walle, *African Economies and the Politics of Permanent Crisis, 1979–1999* (Cambridge University Press, Cambridge, 2001).

[36] Jannik Boesen, Kjell J. Havnevik, Juhani Kopenen, and Kie Odgaard (eds), *Tanzania: Crisis and struggle for survival* (Scandinavian Institute of African Studies, Uppsala, 1986), pp. 21, 66.

the major private contractors pushing hard for their governments to provide loan funds. Within a decade, the African external debt ballooned from very low levels to approach $300 billion.

At their high water mark in the mid-1970s, African post-colonial states appeared to enjoy a robust hegemony over their populations. Rulers seemed bent upon and close to realizing what Jean Copans, writing about Senegal, termed an 'integral state':

> The objective of the dominant groups in the state apparatus is the control, the maintenance, the augmentation of surplus extraction.... The lesson of recent years is the following: the interests of the Senegalese state have won over local private interests... this growing role of the state, rendered concrete through the remodeling and multiplication of institutions for control of the peasantry, leads to a new policy. The Senegalese state aims more and more at a direct administrative, ideological and political control over the dominated masses, be they urban or rural.[37]

This unencumbered dominance over civil society by comprehensive instruments of social control through single party and administrative encadrement, a pervasive security apparatus, and a total monopoly on print and other media gave the would-be integral state the appearance of unchallenged strength.[38] This was accompanied by an extravagant personalization of power, exemplified by the rapturous encomium to Mobutu expressed by then Interior Minister Engulu Baanga in 1975:

> In our religion, we have our own theologians. In all religions, and at all times, there are prophets. Why not today? God has sent a great prophet, our prestigious Guide Mobutu—this prophet is our liberator, our Messiah. Our church is the MPR. Its chief is Mobutu, we respect him like one respects a Pope. Our gospel is Mobutism. This is why the crucifixes must be replaced by the image of our Messiah. And party militants will want to place at its side his glorious mother, Mama Yemo, who gave birth to such a son.[39]

Crisis of the post-colonial state

By the end of the 1970s, the first clear signs that the post-colonial state was not only falling short of its ambitious designs, but facing a systematic crisis, began

[37] J. Copans, *Les marabouts et l'arachide: La confrérie mouride et les paysans du Sénégal* (Editions le Sycamore, Paris, 1980), p. 248. For a parallel argument based on close observation of Senegal at the same time, see Christian Coulon, *Le marabout et le prince: Islam et pouvoir au Sénégal* (Editions A. Pedone, Paris, 1981), p. 289.
[38] For insightful exegesis of the ubiquity of state security organs at the apogee of Mobutu, see Michael G. Schatzberg, *The Dialectics of Oppression in Zaire* (Indiana University Press, Bloomington, IN, 1988). See also Crawford Young, 'The shattered illusion of the integral state', *Journal of Modern African Studies* 35 (1997), pp. 249–63.
[39] Young and Turner, *The Rise and Decline of the Zairian State*, p. 169.

to appear. The then director of the United Nations Economic Commission for Africa (ECA), Adebayo Adedeji, asked mournfully in 1979, 'How have we come to this sorry state of affairs in the post-independence years which seemed at the beginning to have held so much promise?' A report submitted to the Organization of African Unity (OAU) summit in 1979 came to the sobering conclusion that 'Africa ... is unable to point to any significant growth rate or satisfactory index of general wellbeing.'[40] The summary judgement of Paul Nugent in the Ghana case illustrated a general pattern: 'State entrepreurship in the fields of agriculture and industry proved to be a monumental failure ...' leading to huge consumer shortages, a 50 percent fall in cocoa output, a 1981 inflation rate of 116 percent, and public revenue covering only half state expenditures.[41]

The post-colonial state became the object of withering criticism. An array of novels portrayed the state as predator, pirate, or even vampire, terms that crept into everyday vocabulary.[42] Questions began to appear about the 'empirical' reality of the state. Carl Rosberg and Robert Jackson suggested that its juridical sovereignty was sustained above all by the international system; such polities were mere 'quasi-states'.[43] Naomi Chazan illustrated this thesis in an influential 1982 monograph on Ghana:

> By the early 1980s it was apparent that Ghana had forfeited its elementary ability to maintain internal or external order and to hold sway over its population. Although its existence as a *de jure* political entity on the international scene was unquestionable, these outward manifestations did raise doubts as to its *de facto* viability.... Indeed, some kind of disengagement from the state was taking place ... an emotional, economic, social, and political detachment from the state element.[44]

Ghana was soon to demonstrate that state rehabilitation was possible in the later Rawlings years,[45] but the Chazan portrait came to fit a growing number of post-colonial states by the 1980s.

---

[40] Young, *The African Colonial State*, p. 4.

[41] Paul Nugent, *Big Men, Small Boys and Politics in Ghana: Power, ideology and the burden of history, 1988–1994* (Pinter, London, 1995), p. 26.

[42] The label 'vampire state' was given added currency by a former senior official of the Bank of Ghana, Jonathan H. Frimpong-Ansah, *The Vampire State in Africa: The political economy of decline in Ghana* (James Currey, London, 1991).

[43] Robert H. Jackson and Carl G. Rosberg, 'Why Africa's weak states persist: the empirical and the juridical in statehood', *World Politics* 35 (1982), pp. 1–24; Robert H. Jackson, *Quasi-States: Sovereignty, international relations, and the Third World* (Cambridge University Press, Cambridge, 1990).

[44] Naomi Chazan, *An Anatomy of Ghanaian Politics: Managing political recession, 1969–1982* (Westview Press, Boulder, CO, 1982), pp. 334–5.

[45] See Jeffrey Herbst, *The Politics of Reform in Ghana, 1982–1991* (Universiity of California Press, Berkeley, CA, 1993).

In its growing economic disarray, the post-colonial state encountered a suddenly more hostile international climate. A paradigm shift occurred in development economics, with the 'Washington consensus' taking shape within the international financial institutions and much of the donor community touting the supremacy of the market. Margaret Thatcher and Ronald Reagan aggressively articulated an anti-state ethos. The restoration of neo-classical economics to intellectual hegemony meant that African states seeking assistance encountered reform demands informed by what became known as 'neoliberalism'. Meanwhile, the Soviet bloc was confronting a deepening economic impasse of its own, and the 'new thinking' associated with Mikhail Gorbachev included a growing reluctance for aid commitments in Africa.

The 1980s were a decade of growing distress for much of Africa. For sub-Saharan countries, there was an average negative growth rate of 2.8 percent from 1980 to 1987.[46] Utterly beyond reach, save for the two deviant cases of Botswana and Mauritius, were the performances of the Asian 'tiger' economies. Overwhelmed by unsustainable debts, facing negative trends in many primary commodity markets, shunned by much of international capital, African states had little option but to accept, at least formally, the 'structural adjustment' programmes proposed by the international financial institutions backed by the donor community as the condition for continuing assistance. 'State crisis' began to seep into everyday characterizations of the post-colonial polity.

Other fatal shortcomings in the nature of the state became evident. The extreme centralization of decision-making, its consequent exposure to the policy whims or prebendal logic of autocrats, and the venal dynamics of multinational enterprise bidding for huge contracts carried high risks of outsized debts for unviable projects. The Inga-Shaba project in Congo-Kinshasa was a model of such misfortune, accounting for most of the original Congo debt. This scheme involved tapping the undeniably vast hydroelectric potential of the Congo River in its 300-metre drop between Kinshasa and the sea, with an 1,800-kilometer high tension direct current transmission line to the Katanga mineral complex. The project was plagued by cost overruns which quadrupled its initial estimated cost, and was completed five years behind schedule at a time when low copper prices had led to cancellation of new mine developments on which the financial viability of the project depended. Most fundamentally, the project was structured so that the key actors (Mobutu and the prime contractor) made their profit on the transaction, leaving the country and its citizenry liable for the long-term costs when revenues fell far short of

---

[46] World Bank, *Sub-Saharan Africa: From crisis to sustainable growth* (World Bank, Washington, DC, 1989), p. 221.

requirements for servicing the debt.[47] Inga-Shaba was unusual in its scale, but prototypical of a large number of development projects in its nature. Another equally striking example was the Ajaokuta integrated steel project in Nigeria, launched in 1977 with great fanfare. This scheme, which has yet to produce any steel, swallowed up several billion dollars in capital, mostly borrowed abroad.[48]

Beyond exposure to massive miscalculation, the post-colonial state found its parastatal sector a growing burden. Far from constituting an engine of growth by generating profits for new investment, most of the huge state-owned enterprise sector was in deficit. The state thus became liable for the parastatal sector debt, making it all but impossible to adequately capitalize the modest number of enterprises that were profitable. The privatization solution promoted with increasing insistence in structural adjustment programmes has proved nettlesome; many of the enterprises are beyond salvation and unattractive to buyers; sale of the more viable state companies often generates fierce controversy among a public quick to suspect windfall profits for foreign buyers or insider deals with cronies of rulers.

Yet another liability of the post-colonial state was the sheer magnitude of the corruption to which it gave rise. The costs of patrimonial management of politics by African rulers were modest at first, but steadily increased over time. Increasing diversion of state resources into prebendal circuits became a growing drain. Although personal enrichment also drove ruler behaviour, there was a constant need to divert state revenue flows or collect rents on power by demanding large commissions on development contracts.[49] The atmosphere of venality surrounding patrimonial politics led to huge sums being diverted and secreted abroad, and trickled down through the state apparatus to make even petty transactions with the state subject to side payments. Nigerian President Obasanjo told an OAU meeting in 2002 that an estimated $140 billion had been exported into secret holdings abroad by African rulers and leading politicians.[50]

---

[47] For detail on this development disaster, see Jean-Claude Willame, *Zaire—L'épopée d'Inga: Chronique d'une prédation industrielle* (Harmattan, Paris, 1986); see also Young and Turner, *The Rise and Decline of the Zairian State*, pp. 298–301.

[48] The Ajaokuta debt gave rise to a scam of colossal proportions even by Nigerian standards. The late, unlamented dictator Sani Abacha, through family intermediaries in league with two former ministers, created a shell company to buy for 20 cents on the dollar $2.5 billion of Nigerian debt to Russia incurred for Ajaokuta. The Nigerian treasury was then ordered to provide full repayment of the debt at par value to this combine. *New York Times*, 3 December 1998.

[49] Michela Wrong, an unusually tenacious journalist, sought to unravel the scale and location of the Mobutu fortune. She concluded that, by the end of his reign, much had been dissipated in the desperate effort to remain in power, and large sums were embezzled by his own clientele; Wrong, *In the Footsteps of Mr Kurtz: Living on the brink of disaster in Zaire* (Fourth Estate, London, 2000).

[50] *New York Times*, 14 June 2002.

Futile efforts to defend currencies undermined by large budget shortfalls and external trade deficits generated large currency black markets and accelerating inflation in a number of countries. The incapacity to sustain the personnel costs of the over-extended post-colonial state often led to the expedient of reducing the effective state payroll costs by letting inflation erode real public wages, and accumulating pay arrearages. State agents were demoralized, and survival imperatives put even more pressure upon them to extract rents from their administrative functions, and devote part of their working day to private pursuits. In addition, the budget reductions required by structural adjustment programmes compelled in practice cutbacks in social expenditures; in Tanzania, the primary school enrolment ratio fell from 93 percent to 66 percent from 1980 to 1996. Maintaining security forces tended to trump social expenditures. These trends substantially weakened states for which studies already showed that educational and health expenditures had less success in improving health and educational attainment than comparable outlays in Asia and Latin America.[51]

In this phase of economic decline, informalization permeated the public economy. The 'real economy' of Congo-Kinshasa, wrote Janet MacGaffey, was managed by parallel market traders, a number of whom accumulated surprising fortunes very quickly (and could lose them with equal speed).[52] Aili Tripp shows that structural adjustment in Tanzania by the time of its implementation generated strikingly little public resistance, in good part because the integral state economic superstructure had already been eviscerated by the informalization of the market.[53]

At the beginning of the 1980s, the external diagnosis of an emerging African state crisis was essentially economic. The influential 1981 Berg Report of the World Bank set the tone, with a naive faith that recovery could soon be achieved by abandonment of the statist economy in favour of market-based reforms and export-oriented growth.[54] But by the end of the decade, the exegesis of the post-colonial state condition led to more far-reaching conclusions: the malady afflicting Africa was not simply economic but more fundamentally political. African recovery required not just the miracle of the marketplace, but the blessings of democracy. The now deeply enrooted structures of patrimonial autocracy were not reformable by economic tinkering; the post-colonial state required political surgery in order to make a liberalized economy possible.

---

[51] Van de Walle, *African Economies*, p. 94.

[52] Janet MacGaffey, *The Real Economy of Zaire: The contribution of smuggling and other unofficial activities to national wealth* (University of Pennsylvania Press, Philadelphia, PA, 1991).

[53] Aili Mari Tripp, *Changing the Rules: The politics of liberalization and the urban informal economy in Tanzania* (University of California Press, Berkeley, CA, 1997).

[54] World Bank, *Accelerated Development in Sub-Saharan Africa* (World Bank, Washington, DC, 1981).

Reinventing the state

Thus circumstances demanded a virtual reinvention of the state. The magnitude of the challenge was widely underestimated at first. The kinds of political and economic arrangements which characterized the post-colonial state had become fundamentally unviable in a changing global environment. The necessity of a comprehensive reformulation of extant institutions, political and economic, was matched in scope only by the transition from Communism in Eastern Europe and the former Soviet Union. In spite of the optimism, even euphoria, at the prospect of rapid democratization and shock therapy marketization at the beginning of the 1990s, results fell far short of expectations.

A remarkable alignment of the planets propelled the Huntingtonian 'third wave' of democracy to wash over Africa.[55] Beginning with urban riots in Algerian cities in October 1988, street challenges to fossilized single-party autocracies sprang up in many countries, emboldened by the dramatic fall of the Berlin wall. At the beginning of 1990, a striking new pattern of civil society confrontation emerged, with Benin's ruler Mathieu Kérékou compelled by an empty treasury and a mobilized populace to accept a 'sovereign national conference', which proceeded to dissolve the existing order in favour of a democratic constitution.[56] Through the national conference process, in parts of francophone Africa, or other avenues elsewhere, nearly all regimes had to make at least some gestures towards political opening. In the initial phases of the democratic tide, the regime changes were numerous; depending on the mode of calculation, between a dozen and eighteen long-standing presidents were ousted or compelled to retire.[57]

An irresistible confluence of external and internal factors drove these changes. Externally, the wholly unexpected collapse of state socialism sent shock waves through the continent. Western powers, and even for a time the international financial institutions, made political as well as economic reform a condition for assistance. Internally, a potent contagion effect from the first episodes of successful confrontation of perennial autocrats operated. The utter

[55] Samuel P. Huntington, *The Third Wave: Democratization in the late twentieth century* (University of Oklahoma Press, Norman, OK, 1991).

[56] Against the odds of an economy of woefully limited resources and a history of unusual instability and ethnic conflict, the Beninese transition has proved exceptionally stable and effective. See Bruce A. Magnusson, 'The politics of democratic regime legitimation in Benin: institutions, social policy, and security' (Ph.D. dissertation, University of Wisconsin-Madison, 1996).

[57] See for a balance sheet on African democratization Crawford Young, 'The third wave of democratization in Africa: ambiguities and contradictions', in Richard Joseph (ed.), *State, Conflict, and Democracy in Africa* (Lynne Rienner Publishers, Boulder, CO, 1999), pp. 15–38. See also Michael Bratton and Nicolas van de Walle, *Democratic Experiments in Africa: Regime transitions in comparative perspective* (Cambridge University Press, Cambridge, 1997).

delegitimation of the post-colonial state as mere predator in the popular mind made stonewalling seem impossible.

But by the middle of the decade the euphoria regarding democratization had faded. The political opening was in many cases only partial. Some of the external trappings of democracy were adopted without its internal substance. In many instances, external presentability seemed to drive political reform rather than a genuine commitment to liberalization: 'virtual democracy', in the words of Richard Joseph.[58] From a different perspective, one might characterize the outcome as institutionalized semi-democracy.[59] But despite the cosmetic nature of a number of transitions, and the success of such perennial autocrats as Ben Ali of Tunisia, Paul Biya of Cameroon, or Gnassingbe Eyadéma of Togo in splintering and sometimes repressing opposition forces, some important changes did occur.

Some scope for opposition survived the autocratic restoration in most instances. State media monopolies were abandoned, and a critical press appeared. In some countries, such as Uganda and Ghana, new low-cost frequency modulation radio appeared, importing the 'talk show' format for political debate. Human rights groups, often with courageous leadership, documented abuses of power, assisted by their linkages with the international human rights community.[60] The infrastructure of a 'civil society' took shape, making improbable that an autocratic restoration could restore anything resembling the state ascendancy over the citizenry of the integral state years. Women in much of Africa used the opening to greatly enhance their role, supplying much of the leadership for the proliferating associations which define 'civil society'.[61] In a paradoxical way, political opening, while by no means erasing widespread public cynicism about state predation, created new demands states were ill equipped to meet. As Thomas Hansen and Finn Stepputat observe, enfeebled governments were challenged by the emergence of discourses of human rights linked to a reawakened imagining of the state as

---

[58] See Richard Joseph, 'War, state-making, and democracy in Africa', in Mark R. Beissinger and Crawford Young (eds) *Beyond State Crisis?: Post-Colonial Africa and Post-Soviet Eurasia in Comparative Perspective* (The Woodrow Wilson Center Press, Washington, DC, 2002), pp. 241–62.

[59] William F. Case, 'Can the "halfway house" stand? Semidemocracy and elite theory in three southeast Asian countries', *Comparative Politics* 28 (1996), pp. 437–64. Marina Ottaway, in an insightful analysis, argues that semi-democracy (or semi-authoritarianism) in much of Africa will prove a stable form of rule, not containing any internal propensity to evolve into a fuller democracy. Ottaway, *Democracy Challenged: The rise of semi-authoritarianism* (Carnegie Endowment for International Peace, Washington, DC, 2003).

[60] On the growth and impact of an international human rights community, see Margaret E. Keck and Kathryn Sikkink, *Activists Beyond Borders:Advocacy networks in international politics* (Cornell University Press, Ithaca, NY, 1996).

[61] For persuasive detail on the ability of women in Uganda to take advantage of the newly opened social space, see Aili Mari Tripp, *Women and Politics in Uganda* (University of Wisconsin Press, Madison, WI, 2000).

'representation of the *volonté générale* producing citizens as well as subjects, as a source of social order and stability, and as an agency capable of creating a definite and authorized nation-space materialized in boundaries, infrastructure, monuments and authoritative institutions'.[62]

Although the 1990s produced somewhat less disheartening economic trends than the 1980s, and some countries like Uganda, Ghana or Mozambique achieved respectable macroeconomic measures, performance overall failed to vindicate the optimistic promises made for 'neoliberal' policy prescriptions. A number of analysts, especially external commentators, pointed to the incomplete and half-hearted implementation of reforms, their subversion to entrenched patrimonial practice, and the shrinkage of state capacity.[63]

New patterns of civil conflict

Thus, although neither democratization nor economic reform came close to meeting the expectations of their initial advocates, taken together they did erase the earlier post-colonial state's claim to unencumbered hegemony. However, the partially reformed state proved to be substantially weakened, a condition which new forms of violence and disorder in the 1990s illuminated. Novel patterns of internal warfare dramatized the limitations of stateness in a number of countries, including much of the Great Lakes region. The scale and spread of civil disorder in Africa fed upon two altered international circumstances. At the global level, the end of the Cold War removed the motivation for outside powers to intervene militarily in support of friendly African regimes. Within Africa, a new-found disposition for involvement in armed conflicts in neighbouring states, in support of either incumbents or rebels, eroded the older OAU doctrine of non-intervention. The Tanzanian invasion of Uganda in 1979, as spearhead for Ugandan opponents of Amin, attracted criticism in much of Africa for the violation of sovereignty. By the time that eight African armies took part in the Congo-Kinshasa civil war in 1998, earlier OAU norms had all but vanished. Conflict thus readily flowed across borders, and instability had spillover effects in neighbouring countries: the 'bad neighbourhood' syndrome.

---

[62] Thomas Blom Hansen and Finn Stepputat (eds), *States of Imagination: Ethnographic explorations of the postcolonial state* (Duke University Press, Durham, NC, 2001), p. 2.
[63] The meticulous Van de Walle monograph, *African Economies*, exemplifies this approach. Many African intellectuals, on the other hand, excoriate structural adjustment, held responsible for a continued evisceration of basic social services and reducing the state to a servile instrument of the international financial institutions and the Western donor community.

Several critical new factors influenced the shape and nature of internal conflict.[64] The overthrow of Amin in 1979 in Uganda introduced a novel pattern of regime change, whose consequences have been insufficiently noted. The destruction of an incumbent government by insurgents coming from the periphery or neighbouring states injected a radically different security dynamic into ruler displacement. The military coups of the post-colonial state era merely altered the personnel at the summit; the security apparatus of the state remained intact. Overthrow from the periphery not only sends rulers into flight, but brings dissolution of the existing army. Former soldiers flee into the countryside or neighbouring states, often with their weapons. These can be sold, concealed for future use, or used as armament for emergent rebel militias. Such government overthrow by peripheral insurgents occurred eight times in the 1990s: Chad (1990), Liberia (1990), Ethiopia (1991), Somalia (1991), Rwanda (1994), Sierra Leone and both Congos (1997). Arms not disappearing with dissolving armies remain in unguarded armouries which can be emptied by local marauders; the fall of Amin provided such an opportunity to Karimojong cattle raiders to acquire a radically escalated level of armament, with devastating consequences for the level of violence in northeastern Uganda.[65]

The pool of weaponry entering the black market was huge; one may recollect that the Somalian and Ethiopian armies which dissolved in 1991 were among the largest and best equipped in Africa. In the wake of the collapse of state socialism, a number of bankrupt regimes in Eastern Europe and the former Soviet Union had huge weapons stocks for sale. Western arms merchants were also eager suppliers of warlords who had means of payment.

Disintegrated armies were also a source of recruits with some military training and knowledge; indeed, many former soldiers had no other marketable skill. Not only were rank and file soldiers available, but also erstwhile officers with advanced training at overseas military academies, or veterans of guerrilla warfare elsewhere. Thus organizers of insurgent forces could tap sophisticated military knowledge. A case in point were the 'Afghans', former

---

[64] For a parallel argument insisting on the novelty of factors producing internal warfare in the 1990s, though with a somewhat different list, see Jean-Claude Willame, *Banyarwanda et Banyamulenge: Violences ethniques et gestion de l'identitaire au Kivu* (Institut Africain-CEDAF, Cahiers Africains 25, Brussels, 1997).

[65] For detail on escalated violence and its social consequences in the Karamoja region, see Sandra J. Gray, 'A memory of loss: ecological politics, local history, and the evolution of Karimojong violence', *Human Organization* 59 (2000), pp. 401–18; Mustafa Mirzeler and Crawford Young, 'Pastoral politics in the northeast periphery in Uganda: AK-47 as change agent', *Journal of Modern African Studies* 38 (2000), pp. 407–30. The Kuria in northwest Tanzania, also a society in which cattle raiding is a social tradition, likewise acquired a windfall of automatic weapons in the 1979 Uganda invasion, profiting from their large numbers in the Tanzanian army. This too has contributed to a more violent and, in the Kuria case, commercialized cattle raiding; see Michael L. Fleisher, '"War is good for thieving!": The symbiosis of crime and warfare among the Kuria of Tanzania', *Africa* 72 (2002), pp. 130–49.

jihad fighters who played a significant role in the Algerian civil war of the 1990s, and in the Tuareg uprising in northern Mali early in the last decade.[66] Stephen Ellis shows the critical role of insurgent leaders trained in Libya in the dissident militia in Liberia and Sierra Leone in the 1990s.[67]

During the 1990s, important changes occurred in financing civil conflict. In Angola, the *União Nacional para la Independência Total de Angola* (UNITA) provisioned its insurgency mostly with South African and American assistance until the end of the 1980s. With these sources no longer available by 1990, Jonas Savimbi developed a revenue source in the diamond trade, worth several hundreds of millions of dollars at its peak. Charles Taylor in Liberia funded his warfare with timber, rubber intercepted from the Firestone plantations, and Sierra Leonean diamonds, also the financial life blood for the Sierra Leone Revolutionary United Front (RUF). In Congo-Kinshasa, the financial fuel for the civil war came from pillage of gold, diamonds, coffee, timber and columbite-tantalite (coltan) in the eastern reaches of the country, both by domestic insurgents and neighbouring armies. This kind of violent entrepreneurship, and the warlord politics it produced, bred militias whose primary motivation was control of valuable resources; civil populations as potential supporters were of little interest.[68] Groups such as the RUF, the Allied Democratic Forces (ADF) and Lord's Resistance Army (LRA) in Uganda, and the *Rassemblement congolais pour la démocratie* (RCD) factions had remarkably little real backing in the regions where they operated.

Another disconcerting innovation was the systematic utilization of child soldiers, especially prevalent in both Congos, Uganda, Liberia and Sierra Leone. The practice as a deliberate strategy was pioneered by the *Resistência Nacional Moçambicana* (RENAMO) in the mid-1980s, when faced with difficulties in obtaining adult recruits.[69] Adolescent boys could easily carry light automatic weapons; drugged, terrorized, promised supernatural protection, the child soldier could be a fearless warrior. Children were often recruited by abduction; other youngsters, in a social environment of hopelessness, joined voluntarily.[70]

---

[66] A Malian officer writes that the Malian government, which had crushed a Tuareg revolt with considerable brutality in the early 1960s, concluded that the inner cadre of 'Afghan' veterans made a military solution impossible in the 1990s; negotiations were the only avenue. See Lt. Col. Kalifa Keita, *Conflict and Conflict Resolution in the Sahel: The Tuareg insurgency in Mali* (occasional publication, US Army War College, Carlisle, PA, 1998).

[67] Stephen Ellis, *The Mask of Anarchy: The destruction of Liberia and the religious dimension of an African civil war* (New York University Press, New York, 1999), pp. 110–12.

[68] For the argument on the singular logic of such rulers and insurgent bosses, see Reno, *Warlord Politics*.

[69] For detail, see Margaret Hall and Tom Young, *Confronting Leviathan: Mozambique since independence* (Ohio University Press, Athens, OH, 1997).

[70] See the testimonials of former Sierra Leone child soldiers in Krijn Peters and Paul Richards, 'Youths in Sierra Leone: "Why we fight"', *Africa* 68 (1998), pp. 183–210. See also Rémy

The spread of civil conflict in Africa in the 1990s stood as metaphor for a weakened state; internal wars persisted over extended time even in the absence of popular backing for the insurgents. More than a quarter of African states experienced armed internal conflict during the decade, and another quarter faced prolonged political crises and turbulence.[71] Two large zones of inter-penetrated conflicts appeared, one stretching south-eastwards from the Horn to the two Congos and Angola, and the other extending from Senegal to Ivory Coast, but with a destabilizing impact that spread into neighbouring states, thus affecting much of the continent. The intrepid enumerator of civil conflicts, Ted Gurr, found Africa the exception to his arresting finding that internal warfare diminished in the 1990s in the world at large, contrary to popular perceptions.[72] Even in the countries where overt civil strife did not appear, the contraction of state effectiveness rendered far more visible the crucial importance of the local in shaping outcomes. Catherine Boone in a masterful new work documents the ways in which varying regional political 'topographies' in Senegal, Ivory Coast and Ghana sharply constrained central policy choices even when the post-colonial polity retained a higher order of capacity.[73] In most countries, deeply entrenched patterns of 'Big Man' politics permeated relationships from top to bottom of the institutional hierarchy and informal realm, a pattern Jan Vansina shows to be a millennial tradition in the equatorial polity.[74] 'Colonialism,' argues Paul Nugent, 'battened on to indigenous belief systems almost as much as on to chieftaincy structures, thereby reinforcing and disseminating elements of pre-existing ideologies.'[75] Patrimonial practice, already evident early in the post-colonial polity, multiplied in the face of state contraction and permeated the swelling informal domains as well as state politics.[76] Tributary to the disciplining mechanisms of the international political economy, the African state found its authority diluted by ramifying mechanisms of what Achille Mbembe calls 'private indirect government'.[77]

Bazenguissa-Ganga, 'The spread of political violence in Congo-Brazzaville', *African Affairs* **98**, 390 (1999), pp. 37–54.

[71] Catharine Newbury, 'States at war: confronting conflict in Africa', *African Studies Review* 45 (2002), pp. 1–20.

[72] Ted Robert Gurr, 'Ethnic warfare on the wane', *Foreign Affairs* 79, 3 (2000), pp. 52–64.

[73] Catherine Boone, *African Topographies* (Cambridge University Press, New York, 2003).

[74] Jan Vansina, *Paths through the Rainforests: Toward a history of political tradition in equatorial Africa* (University of Wisconsin Press, Madison, WI, 1990).

[75] Nugent, *Big Men*, p. 18.

[76] Jean-Pascal Daloz, *Elites et représentation politique: la culture de l'échange au Nigéria* (Presses Universitaires de Bordeaux, Passac, 2002).

[77] Mbembe, *On the Postcolony*, pp. 64–101.

Counter currents

Whither, then, the state which follows a discredited post-colonial regime? The wave of internal wars signalled one type of outcome, but other less negative itineraries were possible. In Uganda, under Yoweri Museveni from 1986 on, the possibilities of rehabilitation of a failed state were demonstrated in the 1990s (though coming into renewed question by 2002).[78] Ghana, after reaching a nadir in 1983, showed a comparable possibility of state restoration, carrying out two clean national elections in 1996 and 2001, the latter resulting in an opposition triumph, and bringing a comatose economy back to life, if not robust health. A comparable process of related state recovery is visible in Mozambique, though dependent on extraordinary levels of international support; since the civil war ended in 1992, over 50 percent of government expenditures through the 1990s came from external assistance, and the country benefited from over $4 billion foreign public debt cancellation.[79] Fragile peace accords in some of the most conflicted countries early in the new millennium (Angola, Sierra Leone, Congo-Kinshasa, Burundi, Sudan) held out some hope of halting the spread of civil disorder.

The value of stability and exemplary leadership is illustrated by Tanzania. Although the Nyerere vision of the populist socialist polity failed by any measure in the policy realm, the moral rectitude of the *Mwalimu* preserved his image as a charismatic leader dedicated to the common weal. Though *ujamaa* socialism did not deliver on its promises, neither did it serve as mere cynical cover for a predatory state elite.

Tunisia is another illustration of the value of stability and competent governance. Though the large democracy deficit is a source of intellectual unrest, by most performance indicators Tunisia fares well. On social infrastructure (education, health), it performs respectably. Radical reforms of the status of women initiated by Habib Bourguiba soon after independence have taken root.

Other positive instances can be cited. Botswana remains a model of democratic rectitude and developmental performance.[80] Despite their poverty and

---

[78] For an example of critical perspectives from Ugandan intellectuals, see Justus Mugaju and J. Oloka-Onyango (eds), *No-Party Democracy in Uganda: Myths and realities* (Fountain Publishers, Kampala, 2000).

[79] Carrie Manning, *The Politics of Peace in Mozambique: Post-conflict democratization, 1992–2000* (Praeger, Westport, CT, 2002).

[80] On the largely positive performance of Botswana as a developmental state, see also Abdi Ismail Samatar, *An African Miracle: State and class leadership and colonial legacy in Botswana* (Heinemann, Portsmouth, NH, 1999); J. Stephen Morrison, 'Divergence from state failure in Africa? The relative success of Botswana's cattle sector' (Ph.D. dissertation, University of Wisconsin-Madison, 1987).

limited economic prospects, Benin and Mali have persevered with political and economic liberalization.

Key African leaders sustain the campaign for renaissance. A normative vision of a rehabilitated state is traced by the promoters of NEPAD: a transparent, accountable, democratic government committed to economic reform. Such virtuous governance would be guaranteed by Africa itself, which pledges an African Union monitoring mechanism to ensure conformity with these principles. Indeed, the OAU had taken a serious step in this direction in 1998, by deciding to deny participation rights to any ruler who seized power by force. One can only admire this normative vision, and hope that the international community will provide the backing that it deserves.

The empirical state, however, is likely to fall well short of the praise-worthy standards of the African renaissance version. Here I may cite my conclusions in a recently published comparative study of state crisis in Africa and the former Soviet Union:

> Perhaps the most salient overall conclusion...is the protracted nature of the process of political and economic adaptation in course in both regions....To be sure, there has been an indisputable departure from the old order, which in its entirety remains discredited. Whatever the disillusions of the present, no mere restoration of the *ancien régime* in either region is conceivable. Such outcomes are precluded both by the impossibility of securing domestic acceptance and by the incompatibility of these prior regimes with the evolving international normative order. However, there no longer appears to be a clearly defined end point in the processes of adaptation in course. Although the tug of liberal democracy and market economy is strong, as a referential emblem of 'normality' and as a global cachet of respectability, given the enormous problems of stateness that afflict these regions there is no longer a certainty that these represent the eventual destinations. Rather, the interaction between the pressures of globalization, the contradictory processes of state-rebuilding, and activated social forces may well be producing some new equilibrium—one that is influenced by norms of constitutionalism and capitalism but falls far short of the theorized end-point.[81]

Beyond the post-colonial state?

Whatever the divergent forms taken by African states, most have long ceased to resemble the colonial state. The time elapsed since African independence now begins to approximate the time period during which African subjects

---

[81] Mark R. Beissinger and Crawford Young, 'The effective state in postcolonial Africa and post-Soviet Eurasia: hopeless chimera or possible dream?' in Beissinger and Young (eds), *Beyond State Crisis*, pp. 466–7.

experienced a consolidated colonial regime. New historical experience reshapes social memory and begins to obscure the colonial past. A rapidly diminishing number of Africans have any direct recollection of the colonial era. J. F. Ade Ajayi frequently reminded us that the colonial period itself was but a moment in the larger sweep of African history.[82] The same remark begins to apply to the post-colonial. Deeper continuities with precolonial social and political patterns, and novel experiences of coping with the realities of state decline in recent decades, combine to close a set of parentheses around the post-colonial as a defining condition. Indeed, Abdi and Ahmed Samatar situate this point at a normative level:

> Critical thinkers have certainly *written off* the African state in its *post-colonial form*.... However, ... their analytical animus is focused on the incapacity of the state in history *rather than the state per se*. In other words, African development has stalled because the state is of the wrong kind and, therefore, a re-thinking of its form seems to be of utmost necessity.[83]

Certainly, survivals of the colonial legacy are still apparent, especially in countries such as Cameroon, Kenya or Gabon with a large measure of continuity; there is no full erasure of the colonial and post-colonial experiences. However, these are progressively overwritten by new defining events, political practices and agendas. The tides of globalization wash over the continent, depositing sedimentary layers of social exposure and economic impact. The rise of significant diaspora populations from many countries produces novel forms of international linkage. As these many processes work their way into institutional forms, political patterns, and social memory, the explanatory power of the post-colonial label erodes. In short, the post-colonial moment appears to have passed.

Acknowledgment

Published in *African Affairs* 103, 410 (2004), p. 23–49. An early version of this paper served as a keynote address for a conference on 'Beyond the Post-Colonial State in Central Africa?' organized by the Centre of African Studies of the University of Copenhagen in December 2001.

[82] Cooper, *Africa since 1940*, p. 15.

[83] Abdi Ismail Samatar and Ahmed I. Samatar (eds), *The African State: Reconsiderations* (Heinemann, Portsmouth, NH, 2002).

4

Property and Constitutional Order

Land Tenure Reform and the Future
of the African State

Catherine Boone

MUCH OF THE DEBATE OVER LAND tenure reform in sub-Saharan Africa has been framed as a referendum on the market—that is, as a debate pitting those who advocate growth-promoting individualization and transferability of property rights against those who want to use land tenure policy to protect the use rights and subsistence rights of farmers. Recently, discussions have centred on how best to formalize existing land rights into systems that can be operated through a market economy, with many policy-oriented analysts becoming more concerned with market access, fairness, and regulation than with older debates about the pros and cons of markets *per se*. So far, less attention has been focused on the fact that today's land questions also lie at the core of a complex bundle of constitutional issues. Analysts tracking recent political liberalizations in Africa have not paid much attention to the constitutional aspects of land politics, and political science has largely ignored the links between questions of rural property on the one hand and deeper questions of African political development on the other.[1]

This article draws some of these connections. It argues that in many African countries, fundamentals of constitutional order and state character are at stake in land politics. In agrarian society, to reform the rules of land tenure is to redefine relationships between and within communities, and between communities and the state. This is what is being contemplated in more than twenty

---

[1] Some exceptions are Goran Hyden, *Beyond Ujamaa in Tanzania* (University of California Press, Los Angeles and Berkeley, CA, 1980); William A. Munro, *The Moral Economy of the State: Conservation, community development, and state making in Zimbabwe* (Ohio University Press, Athens OH, 1998), and the large literature on the politics of land and nationalism in Kenya (see, for example, Bruce Berman and John Lonsdale, *Unhappy Valley: Conflict in Kenya and Africa* (Ohio University Press and James Currey, Athens, OH and Oxford, 1992).

African countries that have undertaken in the last decade to overhaul existing land tenure legislation, design new national land policies, and/or rationalize and unify national land codes. In Côte d'Ivoire, Kenya, Uganda, Tanzania, Senegal, Mozambique, Zimbabwe, and South Africa, land policy and land law reform have been high-visibility public issues, shaping political mobilization, electoral dynamics, and far-reaching public debates about both democracy and development. Current debates over land tenure force fundamental questions of constitutional order to the centre of the political stage: in many African countries, these debates are taking shape as referenda on the nature of citizenship, political authority, and the future—indeed, the possibility—of the liberal nation-state.

The purpose of this article is to identify main contours of the reform debates and their high political stakes, and to show that the constitutional dimensions of land questions are visible in contemporary African politics. Part I discusses the role of land politics in processes of state formation in modern Africa, showing how land policy has worked to structure state–society relations and define the nature of state authority itself. Part II turns to the 'new wave' of land tenure reform that is sweeping the African continent. It provides an indicator of the scope of the legal innovation currently under way, and then concentrates on identifying three positions in current debates over land tenure reform. For the World Bank and other advocates of land titling and privatization, individualization and transferability of title are the goal. For neo-liberals, private property in land is still the economic and institutional gold standard, although Bank advocates of land tenure reform are now less confident about advocating land privatization across all of rural Africa than they were in earlier decades.[2] Recognition and securitization of user rights is a priority for many Africanist social scientists, including economic historians, anthropologists, geographers, and agricultural development experts. A prescription that differs from both of the preceding recommends that the state uphold historically grounded rights derived from communal membership (or 'communal rights'). This position is advanced by some African politicians and many neo-traditional leaders, and has also been put forward by urban-based leaders of village associations. In academic and policy analysis, communal rights are often conflated with user rights, but, as we shall see below, they can actually form the bases of very different land tenure regimes.

Part III examines the political stakes in these debates. The three land tenure scenarios are modelled as "ideal type" property regimes in order to accentuate the distinctive constitutional implications/underpinnings of each.[3] We show

---

[2] See, for example, K. Deininger and H. Binswanger, 'The evolution of the World Bank's land policy', *The World Bank Research Observer* 14, 2 (1999), pp. 247–76; Ambreena Manji, 'Land reform in the shadow of the state: the implementation of new land laws in sub-Saharan Africa', *Third World Quarterly* 22, 3 (2001), pp. 327–42.

[3] Use of ideal types as a heuristic acknowledges that (1) distinctions between these regime types may blur in practice, (2) much legal reform aims at supporting evolutionary processes in

that each type corresponds to a different notion of citizenship. Each also implies a different distribution of authority across instances of the hierarchically ordered state (different configurations of local, regional, and central authority), and differences in the extent of secularization and bureaucratization of political authority at the local level. This means that land law reform, either wittingly or unwittingly, involves decisions about the political structuring of society (unified or segmented, hierarchical citizenship rights; recognition of "groups" or individuals); alternative visions of state authority (nested, mediated, spatially fragmented, or unified and consolidated), and commitments about the locus of political sovereignty (individual, communal, central state).

For citizenries in African countries, land law reform can become intertwined with debates over citizenship rights, chieftaincy and its prerogatives, women's rights, and the legitimacy of existing social hierarchies. For politicians, land law reform can be an opportunity to reorder the hierarchical structuring of communal groups in relation to the state, or to cultivate new, narrower core constituencies. In many places, the stakes are very high: any move from the *status quo* can imply some kind of dispossession or exclusion.

Across much of Africa, discussions and debates about land law reform are taking place in public arenas that have been opened up by multi-partyism, electoral competition, and the invigoration of civil society. This means that in many places, outcomes of struggles over the meaning and allocation of property rights will be shaped in part by who manages to win political power at the national level.[4] The historical experience of the West, and indeed of many developing countries now attempting transitions to democracy, offers little guidance in this process: in much of Africa today, mass enfranchisement has come before, rather than after, the general consolidation of a market-based property regime. Across the African continent, struggles over land law are finding expression in, or contributing to, political conflict over national citizenship rights, upsurges in xenophobia, or anti-foreigner sentiment both inside and outside the electoral arena. And, for better or worse, land struggles

---

which the character of rights changes over time, and (3) some legal regimes create forms of tenure that combine attributes of ideal-type regimes (for example, private and communal "types" can be combined in a regime that gives private ownership rights to a corporate grouping).

[4] On debates over "the land question" in Africa today, see Sara Berry, 'Debating the land question in Africa', *Comparative Studies in Society and History* 44, 4 (2002), pp. 638–68 and Pauline Peters, 'Inequality and social conflict over land in Africa', *Journal of Agrarian Change* 4, 3 (2004), pp. 269–314. As Sara Berry explains, '[e]vidence of growing land pressure and increasing [land] conflict has prompted some observers to argue that land reform, once considered a low priority on a continent with plenty of land to go around, is now a matter of urgency' (pp. 638–9). Her essay stresses the diversity and complexity of land issues, as well as the centrality of debates over historical precedent in contemporary land disputes. In this article, I propose a schematic way of thinking about the role—past and present—of central state authority in shaping and reshaping land regimes, and identify some possible implications of land law reform for state–society relations, including citizenship rights.

are throwing up obstacles to what was beginning to look like neo-liberalism's nearly-inexorable march across the African continent.

Land and state building

The role of the state in defining property rights, especially rural property rights, has been decisive in shaping the locus and character of political authority in modern Africa, and in producing the successes and limitations of the nation-building project. These connections have been largely over-looked by those who study national-level political processes in Africa because political science, for the most part, has misunderstood African land tenure regimes. Land tenure relations have been seen as non-political ("traditional"), not involving the modern state ("archaic" or resistant to state control), and/or basically invariant across space ("communal" or its opposite, "freehold") except for the fact that European settlers expropriated land in some places but not in others.[5] Having removed property regimes from the larger political equation, most political scientists has gone on to conceptualize the connection between central states and African farming populations in terms of patronage relations (the downward flow of state resources, in the form of agricultural subsidies and social services, to favoured rural constituencies by way of neo-traditional leaders) and affective ethnic ties, which create feelings of group solidarity.[6] Governments have also manipulated and in some cases sought to monopolize the commercialization of agricultural commodities. For most political scientists, these are the instruments by which the central state managed the countryside. Far less attention has been focused on the intense politicization of land tenure relations, and on the role land regimes have played in defining state–society connections across rural Africa.

Both colonial and post-colonial rulers have defined, manipulated, codified, and adjudicated land tenure rules and relations in attempts to project the authority of the modern state into rural Africa. Colonial rulers interpreted and

---

[5] A restatement is found in Jeffrey Herbst, *States and Power in Africa* (Princeton University Press, Princeton, NJ, 2000). Contrast with the views of state intervention in land tenure relations offered in Liz Alden Wily, 'Reconstructing the African commons', *Africa Today* **48**, 1 (2001), pp. 77–99 and Patrick McAuslan, 'Improving tenure security for the poor in Africa: Framework paper for the Legal Empowerment [LEP] Workshop – Sub-Saharan Africa', Nakuru, Kenya, October 2006 (LEP Working Paper No. 1, Food and Agriculture Organization of the United Nations), pp. 7–9 <www.oxfam.org.uk/what_we_do/issues/livelihoods/landrights/index.htm> (15 July 2007).

[6] See, for example, Robert H. Bates, *Markets and States in Tropical Africa* (University of California, Berkeley and Los Angeles, CA, 1981) and Avner Grief and David Laitin, 'A theory of endogenous institutional change', *American Political Science Review* **98**, 4 (2004), pp. 633–52.

sought to enforce rural land rights in ways that would shore up the power of their rural allies, create political structures for governing rural populations, promote the partial commercialization of agriculture, fix some rural populations to the land, and promote the geographical mobility of others. After independence, the insinuation of state authority into the processes of defining, allocating, and adjudicating rural land rights remained a critical resource for central rulers. They used it to consolidate the power of the central state, promote national integration, accelerate the expansion of commercial agriculture, and demobilize rural populations who entered the political arena at the time of the nationalist struggle.

Eminent domain by right of conquest was a prerogative that the postcolonial state willingly inherited from its predecessor. As Liz Alden Wily, a property rights expert based in Kenya, writes,

> In a host of states from Eritrea to South Africa, postindependence governments chose not to recognize local lands as owned by their inhabitants, but vested the ownership of these lands variously in presidents, the state, or local government authorities. Customary owners, individually, as households or as communities, occupy and use their land as but tenants of state or state agencies, their property directly vulnerable to reallocation....[L]ocal rights amount to no more than permissive occupancy.[7]

In most African countries, the state itself became owner of all land not formally registered as private property.

Under Senegal's 1964 *Loi sur le domaine national*, for example, the state formally appropriated all powers and prerogatives to distribute land throughout the entire national territory.[8] Widely known as Senegal's 1964 'land reform law,' this measure was supposed to eradicate all traditional, customary, aristocratic, and feudal land dues, rents, and tithes. Inheritable rights to farmland would henceforth be granted by the state to whoever established 'user rights' by cultivating the land for three consecutive years, on the condition that the farmer resided in the community and farmed the parcel himself, with the aid of family members. The law had an explicit developmentalist thrust, for it was supposed to remove social barriers to bringing new land into productive use. By some accounts, the 1964 National Domain Law dealt the final blow to the old Senegambian aristocracies and placed Senegal in the vanguard of African socialism.

Ivoirian national domain law was also intensely statist. Côte d'Ivoire's *Code domanial* of 1963 ruled that all land not 'in use' or held under private title be registered in the name of the state. Although this registration never actually

---

[7] Alden Wily, 'Reconstructing the African commons,' p. 80.

[8] Land held under private proprietorship was excluded. Senegal's National Domain Law nationalized 95 percent of the national territory.

took place on a general scale, Ivoirian law never recognized customary, communal, or hereditary land rights. It also did not create legal foundations for the conversion of rural land into private property. Instead, the Ivoirian state put its weight behind the dictum that "the land belongs to whoever cultivates it".[9] Yves Person said that communities' rights were systematically ignored in all affairs, including land, calling it 'a Promethean drive to make all of Côte d'Ivoire *tabula rasa*'. The state's goal seemed to be 'to dissolve the basic communal units of rural society' and to concentrate in the state itself the only legally recognized power to dispose of land in a definitive manner.[10]

Liz Alden Wily writes that in Kenya the 1963 Constitution and Trust Land Act made '[t]he Commissioner of Lands, accountable only to the President, the agent of the [local government] councils in matters of land, [giving him] virtually a free hand to deal in trust lands [land not held under formal title], including for "government purposes" which remain undefined.'[11] For East and Southern Africa more generally, she explains that African landholdings were afforded a

> blanket protection-cum-supervision of sorts in the designation of native reserves and homelands, or later, trust lands (Kenya), customary lands (Malawi, Zambia), communal lands (Zimbabwe, Namibia), unregistered lands (Rwanda), or simply public lands (Uganda, Tanzania). [This creates a regime of] *virtual* government lands [under which] the subordination of the land rights of millions of Africans is most tangible....[12]

Under such land regimes, small farmers or peasants are not really "freehold-ers". The state was their landlord, or as Alden Wily puts it, their overlord.[13] This is true in the sense that the state held final rights to the land, and did not accord any formal, legal basis to other claims. This created a legal basis for establishing a direct relationship between the central state and the users of the land.

Prerogatives so claimed by the modern state gave post-colonial rulers an opportunity and an instrument for playing a major role in constituting rural collectivities, and in defining the locus and nature of political authority at the

---

[9] A. Ley, 'La logique foncière de l'Etat depuis la colonisation: l' expérience ivoirienne' in E. Le Bris, E. Le Roy, and F. Leimdorfer (eds), *Enjeux Fonciers en Afrique Noire* (Karthala, Paris, 1982), pp. 135–40; J. M. Gastellu, 'Droit d'usage et propriété privée' in E. Le Bris *et al.* (eds), *Enjeux Fonciers en Afrique Noire*, pp. 269–80, p. 275.

[10] Yves Person, 'Colonisation et décolonisation en Côte d'Ivoire', *Le Mois en Afrique: Revue Française d'études politiques africaines*, 188–9 (1981), pp. 15–30, p. 29.

[11] Alden Wily, 'Reconstructing the African commons,' p. 80.   [12] *Ibid.*, pp. 79–80.

[13] She writes of the 'widespread postindependence entrenchment of the state as overlord' (*ibid.*, p. 79). On Tanzania as an example, see Ernest T. Mallya, 'Civil society and the land question in Tanzania (first draft)' (Department of Political Science and Public Administration, University of Dar es Salaam, December 1999, published by Institute of Development Studies (IDS), 2000), p. 11.<www.eldis.org/static/Doc10844.htm> (1 June 2005).

local level. African governments tried to use these prerogatives in ways that were deemed to serve the interests of the centre, usually (but not always) taking into account the limited administrative and political capacity of the post-colonial state to overcome direct challenge or even passive resistance from small farmers and rural notables.[14]

We can distinguish the resulting land regimes, or processes, in terms of two basic types. Under the first type, African governments used their powers and prerogatives to uphold the land tenure regimes established under colonial rule, which confirmed the right of individuals to have access to land for houses and farming in localities where local authorities—who were sanctioned as such by the state—would recognize the individual or family as indigenous to that locality. Membership in local community, village, clan, or kin group (*appartenance à la collectivité locale*) conferred land-use rights. State action that upholds or ratifies these arrangements can be thought of as action that creates or "upholds" communal land tenure. It involves *de facto* (or *de jure*) state recognition of neo-traditional forms of local authority, and thus of state action that confirms or strengthens (or even grants) the land-management powers of non-elected, non-state, non-secular, local-level actors like chiefs, land chiefs and marabouts.[15] Given the prevailing legal order, lodging land-management powers in such actors should be understood as a kind of devolution of state authority (rather than as an abdication of state authority, or as the defeat of the state by 'African society').

To put this modern-day system of indirect rule into practice, the central state had to delimit the territorial scope of the authority of these local land authorities. So it was that 'the community' became inextricably associated with a territorially defined administrative jurisdiction.[16] The legitimacy of this arrangement had to be rooted in the ideological and legal premise that the

---

[14] The emphasis here is on the legal prerogatives formally claimed by, and conferred upon, central government authorities. Although central states did not always try to exert this authority, or succeed in translating *de jure* powers into effectively implemented policy, land laws usually left smallholders without formalized, legally recognized rights to land, with the myriad of political and economic vulnerabilities (and some of the flexibility and options) that this could imply. How national land laws were exercised was shaped by on-the-ground realities, including the specificities of state–society relations at the local level. See Catherine Boone, *Political Topographies of the African State* (Cambridge University Press, Cambridge and New York, 2003) for some West African examples.

[15] See Jesse C. Ribot, 'Decentralization, participation, and accountability in Sahelian forestry: legal instruments of political-administrative control', *Africa* **69**, 1 (1999), pp. 23–43, which explains that '[c]hiefs are not an alternative to the state but rather a particular manifestation of state intervention in the rural arena'. See also Jesse C. Ribot, *Waiting for Democracy: the politics of choice in natural resource decentralization* (World Resources Institute, Washington, DC, September 2004).

[16] On this distinction, see for example Abdoulaye Dièye, *Domanialité nationale et développement: l'exemple du Sénégal* (PhD thesis, Cheikh Anta Diop University of Dakar, April 2004), p. 100.

people deemed to be indigenous to that territorial jurisdiction were a naturally cohesive social and political collectivity. This "natural community" would be governed within its state-delimited *terroir*, or spatial jurisdiction, by the *de facto* local state.

Under a second type of land regime, governments used the powers of the modern state to challenge pre-existing rights, land-management processes, and land-allocation authorities by standing behind and enforcing the land claims of 'whoever farms the land'. As observers of the Ivoirian situation have insisted, where user rights regimes are actually enforced, they can sweep away hereditary or communal rights. This would happen in situations where the user rights rule enforces the land rights of farmers who are not recognized as members of the local community—that is, the land claims of persons such as immigrants or migrants ("strangers", or non-indigenes) who have created farms outside their home localities. Under the user rights regime, the central state commits itself to enforcing immigrant farmers' land rights if and when these claims are challenged by the 'original inhabitants of the land' or other holders of customary rights. Under a user rights regime, if it is actually enforced, no pre-existing or 'natural' political structuration of farming areas is recognized. Central authorities must become implicated in direct political management of localities and natural resource use therein. To extend our analogy with colonial theories/strategies of government, we can call this a modern-day form of direct rule.

In Africa today, there are many places that are governed under user rights land regimes that do not respect the primacy of historically established, communal land rights. The modern state has undertaken to expropriate, encroach upon, or compromise communal land rights in innumerable settings, and in a wide variety of circumstances. In Kenya, for example, the colonial state appropriated most land in the Rift Valley and gave it to European settlers; in the 1950s and 1960s the state bought out most of the landholders and reallocated most of the land to African farmers who were not indigenous to the Rift. The Tanzanian state carried out relocation and re-settlement on a massive scale. In Côte d'Ivoire, the post-colonial state actively encouraged Baoulé farmers to migrate and settle in the sparsely populated south-west, and has pressured increasingly land-hungry indigenous communities to allow these "strangers" to continue farming long after the autochtons were ready to bid them farewell. In the Ivoirian south-west, the land regime that guarantees the use rights of "whoever farms the land" violates communal rights. In parts of Burkina Faso, migrant Mossi farmers depend upon the state to protect their use rights.[17] In Senegal, the government gave away land in

---

[17] On Burkina Faso, see Sten Hagberg, 'Mobilization of rights through organizational structures [in Burkina Faso]' in Tom Young (ed.), *Readings in African Politics* (James Currey and Indiana University Press, Oxford and Bloomington, IN, 2003), pp. 127–38. Close analyses of how

Casamance region to outsiders for investments in groundnut farming, agro-industry, and tourism, sometimes in the face of overt opposition by auto-chtons who saw this as invasion of their region and expropriation of their land by 'the Senegalese'.[18]

For the purposes of generalization, it is possible to describe land regimes across much of rural sub-Saharan Africa in terms of these two types (or ideal types): the communal regime, and the user rights regime. Taking the generalization one step further, each type corresponds to a different model of rural government. The communal regime is the material basis of an indirect-rule political order, wherein neo-traditional authorities continue to exercise political clout and play an important role in resource allocation. The user rights regime, by contrast, creates a political order that looks like what the colonizers called 'direct rule': state agents play an on-going, hands-on role in local resource allocation and dispute resolution. Because land tenure regimes can vary across space within a single country (variations can be either *de facto* or *de jure*), it is possible to recognize examples of both types within the same national unit.[19] This means that the nature of the relationship between the state, the community, and the farmer can vary across space within one country. Meanwhile, in any given locality, the relationship between the state and the farmer will vary in accordance with the farming family's residency/membership status in a given locality. The indigene, the autochthon, the stranger, and the foreigner are in different positions *vis-à-vis* the state.

Across Africa, the Structural Adjustment Programmes of the 1990s aimed at eliminating the state from agricultural marketing circuits, and terminating most of the input-distribution programmes (seeds, credit, tools) that allowed ruling parties to patronize rural clienteles, cultivate electoral support in farming areas, and channel resources to rural political brokers. The land tenure connection, however, remains as salient as ever. In many countries, land politics are perhaps even more politically charged, given today's realities of shrinking urban opportunities, mounting land shortage, and growing pressure on the state to facilitate private investment in commercial agriculture. Where the central state can no longer distribute subsidized agricultural inputs or offer social services to rural populations, the terms of land access remain as the hard core of the social contract between the post-colonial state and rural populations.[20]

population mobility has shaped land rights, and the strategies employed by users to secure those rights, are presented in Richard Kuba, Carola Lentz, and Claude Nurukyor Somda (eds), *Histoire du peuplement et relations interethniques au Burkina Faso* (Editions Karthala, Paris, 2003).

[18] For the purposes of the present discussion, 'indigene' and 'autochthon' are taken as largely synonymous terms, although autochthony claims generally refer to more restricted geographical areas and social groups, and often imply an even stronger assertion of firstcomer rights.

[19] Such variations are documented in Boone, *Political Topographies*.

[20] This social contract is meaningful to anyone with family in the rural areas, or who hopes to return to the countryside to work, retire, and be buried among relatives. Land rights provide

Over 80 percent of all arable land in sub-Saharan Africa is currently held under some form of 'customary' or non-statutory tenure, but the politics of communal rights can differ profoundly from the politics of user rights, and have different implications for the possibility (and possible forms) of local and national-level democracy. Both these regimes can be juxtaposed to a regime of private property rights, which would be associated with yet another bundle of political, social, and economic processes and implications.

Three land tenure reform scenarios

Today, over 60 percent of the African workforce is engaged in the agricultural sector, and a majority of all African households rely on pastoralism or a family smallholding for at least part of their livelihood. The structural weaknesses of small-scale African farming are pervasive and well known: they include low productivity of land and labour compared to other world regions, dependence on rain-fed technologies and hand tools, low levels of investment (purchased inputs like fertilizer are not widely used, and in many regions, less so than they were in the 1980s), and high vulnerability to weather and pests.[21] Rates of growth and commercialization of agricultural output vary greatly across space, by farm size, and by crop. Overall food production *per capita* stagnated or actually declined in the 1990s, and today food insecurity is increasing in many regions. In most African countries, the rural areas are not producing an economic surplus at a rate or level sufficient to finance far-reaching investments in agriculture, much less investment in other domains of the economy.

The search for answers to these problems of sectoral and macro-economic performance, and to the problem of poverty, has driven the land tenure debate in African studies. From the mid-1980s to the mid-1990s, most analyses of Africa's agrarian crisis stressed the need to alter the institutional context of agriculture. Much mainstream economic analysis identified 'land tenure constraints'—especially insecurity of land tenure and/or obstacles in the way of using land to secure loans, and constraints on transferability of land rights—as limiting investment, productivity increases, and growth in output in African agriculture.[22] Other work showed that the erosion of community control over

access to subsistence and a social safety net that helps explain the considerable effort that urban dwellers invest in maintaining their political and social ties to home regions.

[21] See Alex Duncan and John Howell (eds), *Structural Adjustment and the African Farmer* (James Currey and Heinemann, London and Portsmouth, NH, 1992) and Jonathan Kydd, Andrew Dorward, and Jamie Morrison, 'Agricultural development and pro-poor economic growth in sub-Saharan Africa: potential and policy', *Oxford Development Studies* **32**, 1 (2004), pp. 37–57.

[22] On the debate over whether these forms of insecurity actually exist and limit investment, see Diana Hunt, 'Some outstanding issues in the debate on external promotion of land

common property resources could lead to overexploitation and resource degradation. Several particularly influential contributions to the discussion, especially John Bruce and Shem Migot-Adholla's *Searching for Land Tenure Security in Africa*, agreed that insecure rights could have a negative impact on agricultural performance, but argued that (1) existing land systems often offered a great deal of security of tenure, and were often flexible in ways that supported innovation and investment; (2) under certain conditions, land rights often evolved "endogenously" toward individualization and increased commercialization; and (3) factors other than land tenure rules were often the most important constraints on agricultural performance.[23] The policy prescription that flowed from this work was that in the land tenure domain, central governments could and should elaborate and support existing, incremental processes of institutional change. Since the mid-1990s, the land tenure discussion has focused on political relations of control over land as they affect the security of livelihoods, poverty and social vulnerability, and smallholder investment in agriculture.[24] The vulnerability of smallholders to arbitrary expropriation of their land rights is increasingly recognized as an important constraint on investment and innovation, as well as a threat to livelihood security.

The political and administrative decentralizations of the 1990s also had implications for land administration and land use policy in many African countries. One of the express purposes of the decentralizations was to alter

privatization', [ODI] *Development Policy Review* 23, 2 (2005), pp. 199–231. For other critiques of 'land tenure constraint' arguments, see Thomas Bassett, 'Introduction' in Thomas J. Bassett and Donald E. Crummey (eds), *Land in African Agrarian Systems* (University of Wisconsin Press, Madison, WI, 1993), pp. 3–15, pp. 4–5, and John W. Bruce, 'Do indigenous tenure systems constrain agricultural development?' in Bassett and Crummey (eds), *Land in African Agrarian Systems*, pp. 35–56. See also Thomas J. Bassett, *The Peasant Cotton Revolution in West Africa: Côte d'Ivoire 1880–1995* (Cambridge University Press, Cambridge, 2001).

[23] See John W. Bruce, Shem Migot-Adholla, and Joan Atherton, 'The findings and their policy implications: institutional adaptation or replacement?' in John W. Bruce and Shem Migot-Ahdolla (eds), *Searching for Land Tenure Security in Africa* (The World Bank and Kendall/Hunt Publishing Company, Washington, DC and Debuque, Iowa, 1994), pp. 251–66, especially p. 254. Following Esther Boserup, *Population and Technological Change* (University of Chicago Press, Chicago, 1981), they concluded that land rights tended to evolve in these ways under increased population pressure, changing technology, and the growing commercialization of agriculture.

[24] See for example Camilla Toulmin and Julian Quan, 'Evolving land rights, policy and tenure in Africa' (UK Department for International Development/International Institute for Environment and Development/Natural Resources Institute [DFID/IIED/NRI], London, March 2000), and United Nations Economic Commission on Africa (UNECA), 'Land tenure systems and their impacts on food security and sustainable development in Africa (UNECA report, ECA/SDD/05/09, UNECA, Addis Ababa, December 2004). The vulnerability of small farmers to arbitrary expropriation by politically connected 'big men' was a major theme of an influential volume, R. E. Downs and S. P. Reyna (eds), *Land and Society in Contemporary Africa* (University of New Hampshire and University Press of New England, Hanover, NH and London, 1988).

the locus and processes of decision making in natural resource use and management.[25] Decentralization has thus raised the question of reform of land tenure regimes precisely when rural economies are absorbing the shock of the massive policy changes of the 1990s, most notably the withdrawal of the state from rural input and output markets.[26] Farmers are also coping with falling world prices for African export commodities, and rising demographic and environmental stress.

In the last decade, many African countries have sought to reform land law to address questions of poverty, equity, restitution for past expropriations, investment and innovation in agriculture, and/or sustainability (see Table 4.1). The World Bank and other international lenders/donors have been major players in the initiation of these processes.[27] Since the 1990s, a new wave of donor-supported initiatives has aimed at land registration as part of a 'second generation' of structural adjustment reform in Africa. Although experts often discuss land reform in technocratic and economistic terms, the difficulty, sensitivity, and divisiveness of land questions reveal the deep political realities of the land issue. Tenure reform has implications for long-standing and unsettled issues having to do with citizenship, community, social inequality, and political authority. This helps to explain why domestic pressures for land law reform are coming to a head in many African countries that are transitioning to more democratic forms of rule, or that have experienced recent regime change.[28]

[25] See Richard C. Crook and James Manor, *Democracy and Decentralization in South Asia and West Africa* (Cambridge University Press, Cambridge, 1998); and Ribot, *Waiting for Democracy*.

[26] On the limited extent to which export crop markets have been liberalized in Tanzania, see Brian Cooksey, 'Marketing reform? The rise and fall of agricultural liberalization in Tanzania', *Development Policy Review* 21, 1 (2003), pp. 67–91.

[27] There has been 'tremendous expansion' in the World Bank's lending portfolio for land-related projects. 'While in FY 1990–94 only 3 stand-alone land projects were approved, the number increased to 19 ($0.7 billion commitment) and 25 ($1 billion commitment) in the 1995–99 and 2000–04 periods, respectively. This trend is expected to continue: FY04 projects and land-related projects...alone amount to $1B and, following the lead of the Bank, other donors are now addressing land issues much more vigorously in their programs as well', World Bank, Land Policy and Administration Homepage <http://Inweb18.worldbank.org/ESSD/ardext. nsf/24ByDocName/LandPolicyandAdministration (23 October 2005). For an overview of land law reform, 1990–2003, see Liz Alden Wily, *Governance and Land Relations: A review of decentralization of land administration and management in Africa* (International Institute for Environment and Development (IIED), London, June 2003).

[28] For example, as P. McAuslan writes, 'in all, the pressure to act [on land law] is, at least in part, the result of contested democratic politics and the perceived need to meet the concerns of rural voters. This is most obvious in South Africa but also applies in Namibia and Tanzania' Patrick McAuslan, 'Making law work: restructuring land relations in Africa,' *Development and Change* 29, 3 (1998), p. 527.

Table 4.1. Some land law initiatives, 1992–2006

Country	Initiative
Kenya	Draft National Land Policy released in December 2005, pending parliamentary debate at end of 2006.
Tanzania	1995 National Land Policy; Land Act and Village Land Act of 1999; Land (Amendment) Act, 2004.
Uganda	Land Act of 1998. National Land Policy formulation process under way in 2004.
Rwanda	Land Reform Law, September 2005.
Burkina Faso	*Réforme agraire foncière*, 1997.
Côte d'Ivoire	*Loi relative au domaine foncier rural*, 1998.
Senegal	*Plan d'action foncier*, 1996. Shelved. *Loi d'orientation agro-sylvo-pastorale*, 2004.
Benin	*Projet de loi portant régime foncier rural*, under way in May 2006.
Ghana	Land Policy of 1999 amended in 2002; official Land Administration Project (LAP) under way since 2003.
Liberia	Commission of Inquiry into Land Tenure established in 2006.
Cameroon	*Décret n. 2005/481 du 16 décembre 2005 modifiant...les conditions d'obtention du titre foncier.*
Namibia	1995 Agricultural (Commercial) Land Reform Act. Communal Land Reform Act, 2002.
Zimbabwe	Land Acquisition Act, 1992; Land Acquisition Amendment Act, 2000.
Malawi	Malawi National Land Policy approved by Cabinet in 2002, followed in 2004 by a proposed Malawi Land Reform Programme Implementation Strategy (2003–7).
Mozambique	1997 Land Act.
Botswana	Botswana National Land Policy Issues Report published in 2002 in preparation of a draft National Land Policy.
South Africa	Restitution of Land Rights Act 1994; Communal Property Associations Act 1996; Land Rights Bill of 1999 (shelved); Communal Land Rights Act, 2004.
Zambia	Land Act of 1995 under review in 2006.
Angola	National Land Law of 2004.

Here we contrast the three land reform strategies, or visions of land reform, that constitute the poles in the policy debate: (1) reinforce community rights; (2) promote private property rights; and (3) institutionalize user rights.

Strengthen communal or community rights

Those who advocate the strengthening of communal rights (or community rights) are generally calling for the restoration of a *status quo ante* in which members of a 'natural community' managed their own resources in ways that promoted collective interests. From this perspective, the problem with today's land tenure arrangements is that outside forces—the modern state, commercial investors, in-migrants or settlers, or the temptations that corrupt communal leaders—have compromised the effectiveness and legitimacy of long-established, local-level (indigenous) mechanisms of resource allocation and management. Exploitation or expropriation of community resources by opportunistic insiders or by outsiders has caused illegitimate trampling on the rights of indigenous communities, and the erosion of traditional mechanisms that ensured the downward accountability and effectiveness of community-level authorities.

Rural development experts and social scientists who advocated the strengthening of communal or community rights in the 1990s argued that with properly accountable local leadership, communities could manage their own resources well, and under many circumstances, could also achieve significant increases in agricultural production and productivity.[29] More recently, these advocates have begun to stress the importance of legal recognition of community land rights, and have emphasized the ways in which such changes can contribute to sustainable rural livelihoods and natural-resource management.[30] To make this kind of arrangement work, individual rights, if they are provided for, would be circumscribed and encumbered by community rights and decision making. Most of the current policy-oriented work focuses on East Africa, and contributors to this literature have generally ducked the thorny questions that have to do with (1) determining who is a member or 'citizen' of the community to be invested with officially recognized land rights, and (2) how legitimate political authority to manage such rights should/can be constituted at the local levels. The current covering law in the policy literature, as represented for example by Toulmin and Quan's influential *Evolving Land Rights, Policy and Tenure in Africa*, is that rules should be pragmatic, flexible, locally specific, and negotiated on an ongoing basis.[31]

Far less open-ended in their specification of exactly what kind of community rights should gain legal recognition, and how such rights should be enforced, are those who advocate the restoration of the historical land rights of the 'original occupants', and the authority of traditional chiefs. This position was embodied in the 1998 Ivoirian Land Law, which calls for a land registration process that would, in its first phases, overturn the prevailing land regime (state ownership of all non-registered land, by default) by restoring indigenous land rights to their 'natural' primacy over the land claims of non-indigenes. The 1998 law does so by recognizing only the land claims of indigenous Ivoirians, and by creating an initial land registration process that will be administered by local-level councils of chiefs whose decision making

---

[29] For example, Bassett in Bassett and Crummey, *Land in African Agrarian Systems*.

[30] There is debate over whether formalization of communal rights works to uphold communal rights, or whether this should be understood as the death knell for these rights. Herbst, for example (*States and Power*, pp. 186–7), describes state recognition of customary tenure as essentially disruptive. Most policy analysts, development practitioners, and land rights advocates, however, assume that state recognition of community rights will help preserve these rights, and will strengthen communities in their confrontations with outsiders and the state.

[31] Toulmin and Quan, *Evolving Land Rights*.

would be guided by their own political judgements and interests (presumed to be synonymous with those of the communities under their jurisdiction). The aspects of this land law that have proved to be politically explosive in Côte d'Ivoire are those that provide for a 'retraditionalization' or neo-traditionalization of land allocation processes in ways that elevate chiefly authority and enforce the political and economic subordination (via *de facto* expropriations of acquired land rights, or user rights) of non-indigenes.[32]

Echoes of the Ivoirian experience can be heard in the political debates surrounding the 1998 Uganda Land Act. In Uganda, Baganda petitioners, politicians, and local government councillors are seeking to reinforce and institutionalize the collective claim of the Baganda people on land in their home region. They have mounted broad opposition to the government's 1998 Uganda Land Act, which promised to securitize user rights by registering the land rights of farmers who had occupied a parcel of land for more than 12 years without paying rent. As Elliott Green explains, Baganda leaders who oppose this law want control over land administration in Buganda to be lodged in a regional land board that would act on behalf of the Baganda king, the Kabaka, in his role as land trustee. Advocates of this solution believe that such arrangements will curb the power of the central government to expropriate land in their region, and stem the tide of outsiders (western Ugandan and Rwandan 'squatters' and investors) and foreign investors who are demanding access to land in Buganda. The government of Uganda resists these demands on the grounds that creating a Buganda Regional Land Board in Mengo would 'revive historical conflicts and rivalries in respect of land.'[33] The central government also resists this strengthening of Buganda regional government and the monarchy, surely recognizing that such a change would come at the expense of the central state, and that it would compromise the principle of national citizenship.

An unresolved tension in the international land rights advocacy literature is the fact that supporting communal or community rights can often mean, in actual practice, reinforcing or legitimizing rules of access to land and other natural resources that discriminate on the basis of ethnicity, gender, age, and other ascriptive status markers. When put into practice, strategies of land tenure reform that aim at reinforcing communal rights can be patently non-democratic in the ways they cater to, and act to shore up, neo-traditional authority and institutions.[34] South Africa's attempt to write and enact a

---

[32] Jean-Pierre Chauveau, 'Question foncière et construction nationale en Côte d'Ivoire', *Politique africaine* 78 (2000), pp. 113–14.
[33] Elliott Green, 'Ethnicity and the politics of land tenure reform in Central Uganda', *Commonwealth and Comparative Politics* 44, 3 (2006), p. 383.
[34] On this, see Ribot, *Waiting for Democracy*.

Communal Land Rights Act (signed in 2004 but under legal challenge) has been bedevilled by these political contradictions.[35]

In the present analysis, we have constructed the 'communal rights' regime as an ideal type in order to extract the constitutional implications of reforms that centre on communal rights. Some of today's land rights discourse, however, suggests that collective forms of land tenure would be, or could be, founded on a secular and liberal-democratic model of community and community rights. In practice, these strategies often embody the contradictions that this article seeks to highlight.[36]

Promote capitalist farming—privatization through land registration and titling

The World Bank has been a consistent advocate of land registration and titling programmes, even if its enthusiasm has cooled somewhat since the late 1990s.[37] The idea is that formalization and individualization of control and disposition of land will transform arable land into private property, which can then be mortgaged, bought, and sold in accordance with market incentives and dictates. Once land is a full commodity, labour will soon follow. Land will be mortgaged to secure an inflow of new investment to modernize production techniques and finance intensification. Capitalist production units and production processes will gradually emerge. By this scenario, Africa will follow England down the path of capitalist transformation. Kenya's land titling programmes of the 1950s (under the Swynnerton Plan) have often been taken as a historical precedent, although evidence from central Kenya suggests that registration and titling alone are insufficient to achieve full commoditization of land.[38]

---

[35] For a brief review of the arguments and of the legal challenge, see Martin Adams and Robin Palmer (eds), 'Independent review of land issues, vol. III, 2006–2007: Eastern and Southern Africa', p. 36, <www.oxfam.org.uk/what_we_do/issues/livelihoods/landrights/index.htm> (29 July 2007).

[36] See discussion (below) of Communal Property Associations in South Africa.

[37] See World Bank, *Sub-Saharan Africa: From crisis to sustainable growth* (World Bank, Washington, DC, 1989, pp. 90, 100–4), as cited by Bassett, 'Introduction' in *Land in African Agrarian Systems*, pp. 4, 14; Deininger and Binswanger, 'The evolution of the World Bank's land policy', 1999; and commentary by Devesh Kapur, who writes that private property rights 'have acquired an almost hallowed status in the World Bank's thinking in recent years. The 1997 WDR [World Bank, *World Development Report 1997*, p. 45] does recognize that in certain settings strengthening communally-based property rights may be the better option' (Devesh Kapur, 'The state in a changing world: a critique of the 1997 *World Development Report*' (Working Paper 98–02, Harvard University, Weatherhead Center for International Affairs, Cambridge, MA, 1998), p. 6.

[38] On Kenya's experience, see Bruce and Migot-Adholla (eds), *Searching for Land Tenure Security*.

There are some supporters of individualization, titling, and transferability of land rights whose concerns are less grandiose and developmentalist. African and Africa-based investors who seek land for commercial purposes, such as for the expansion of fruit and vegetable production in peri-urban areas, or for investment in tourism projects, seek to expand and facilitate access to private land title. Meanwhile, as Aili Mari Tripp explains, women's movements across much of Africa have endorsed privatization and titling as a way of enhancing their access to land:

> Women's movements in Africa have developed a rights-based approach that challenges…[the] new consensus among policy makers around the view that sees land tenure policy as building on customary systems and giving them legal recognition. [Uganda land politics] have given rise to one of the most active women's movements challenging customary land tenure practices.[39]

Tripp describes calls for 'rights-based' land systems that 'improve women's ability to buy, own, sell, and obtain titles on land,' and would thus allow women to escape the patriarchal biases of customary land law as it is now practised in Uganda and elsewhere. In national political arenas, such attempts are 'often perceived as an attempt to disrupt gender relations, and society more generally. This explains why so much is at stake in these battles over women's rights to land….'[40]

Herbst wrote in 2000 that 'individual freehold is the avenue that many African countries are attempting to pursue', citing a 1996 University of Wisconsin-Madison Land Tenure Center report by K. Elbow *et al.*, who wrote that 'the majority of African countries are increasingly favoring individualized landholdings as economies based on the production of commodities become more developed, as populations and land pressures increase, and as international donors [like the World Bank] support widespread legal reform.'[41] It is true that land law changes in Zambia (1995), Uganda (1998), and Malawi (2002) are explicit in aiming to ease the way for full commoditization of land.[42]

From the perspective of 2006, however, it is far from clear that a general trend or legal movement toward land privatization is actually under way. Current land politics and policy reform in some countries suggests that under some conditions, we may see an opposite trend of 'retraditionalization'

---

[39] Aili Mari Tripp, 'Women's movements, customary law, and land rights in Africa: the case of Uganda', *African Studies Quarterly* 7, 4 (2004), pp. 1–19, p. 1.

[40] *Ibid.*, p. 2.

[41] Herbst, *States and Power*, p. 182, citing Kent Elbow *et al.*, *Country Profiles of Land Tenure: West Africa* (Land Tenure Center, Madison, WI, 1996).

[42] In theory, land rights registration is usually viewed as an incremental process by which legal rights are secured initially at low cost, with the option of more formal (expensive) titling further in the future.

of control over land. In the Sahelian countries of Senegal and Burkina Faso, recent decentralization programmes have reinforced the land prerogatives of established communities and of long-standing local elites.[43] Reformed land laws in Niger (1993) and Côte d'Ivoire (1998) bolster historical and communal rights that circumscribe market forces, and this is what the advocates of Baganda land claims are calling for. Arguments about the socially disruptive and disintegrative impact of land individualization have been advanced by chiefs in Zambia, who have contributed to the largely successful opposition to implementation of the 1995 Zambia Land Act, which attempted to strengthen the central government's ability to issue freehold titles to land.[44]

Secure the use rights of farmers

The World Bank has advocated a process of land titling that will gradually transfer land use and access rights away from partly or mostly self-provisioning small farmers, who have little capacity to invest in the land, and into the hands of capitalist producers. By contrast, the user rights strategy calls for land registration and titling as a means to stabilize the land access and use rights of the small farmers now cultivating the land. Whereas the privatization/commodification strategy envisions a process whereby African farming comes to look more and more like large-scale commercial farming in the West, those advocating legal recognition of small farmers' use rights envision African countrysides organized along the small-holder farming models of Taiwan and Japan. Advocates of user rights securitization argue that this land strategy would help the poor by protecting them from arbitrary dispossession, and that it could eventually foster the development of prosperous smallholder agriculture by making investment and technological change less risky for the average farmer.[45]

---

[43] See for example Mayke Kaag, *Usage foncier et usage dynamique sociale au Sénégal rural: L'histoire d'un bas fond et de ses défricheurs* (Rosenberg Publishers, Amsterdam, 2001), p. 258 *inter alia*; and Hubert Ouedraogo, 'Law and community based property rights in West Africa', *Common Property Resource Digest* 57 (2001), pp. 1, 5. Meanwhile, however, there was discussion within the World Bank of a pilot land titling programme for Senegal to take place in FY2005 (World Bank, 'Country assistance strategy: Senegal,' 23 March 2003, p. 23 <http://web.wor ldbank.org> (30 March 2006).

[44] See Joseph Mbinji, 'Getting agreement on land tenure reform: the case of Zambia', in Esther Mwangi (ed.), 'Land rights for African development: from knowledge to action' (Collective Action and Property Rights (CAPRi) policy brief, Consultative Group on International Agricultural Research, United Nations Development Project, and International Land Coalition (CGIAR/ UNDP/ILC), 2006), p. 33.

[45] Here, we have modelled 'the securitization of user rights' as one broad approach to land law reform. However, among the advocates of such a strategy, there are differences of opinion and prescription (and/or agnosticism) about whether registration and titling would or should lead to full commoditization of land rights, a gradual process of smallholder dispossession, and the

Proponents of this position are generally agnostic about the political mechanisms at the local level that would promote and sustain land tenure regimes centred on user rights. Presumably, this is at least partly due to the recognition that the full political implications of user rights strategies would vary a great deal across space. This is one reason why the user rights approach is generally considered to be the most flexible, pro-poor, and practical way forward, and also why it can be useful as a sort of generic, pro-farmer stand on the land rights question. Because the point of departure is the ratification of the on-the-ground, *status quo* land distribution, it is a strategy that could circumvent indeterminate debates over historical claims, and over what belonged to whom in the past.

The user rights position is often taken as consistent with, and as improving upon, positions that call for the strengthening of communal or community rights. This is because in many situations upholding user rights would indeed mean confirming the rights of farmers who gained access to land as members of communities claiming ancestral rights as 'original inhabitants' or first-comers. In this article (and under some conditions), however, communal rights and user rights appear as stark alternatives. The purpose here is to show that the constitutional underpinnings of the user regime are very different from the constitutional underpinnings of the communal regime. The point is important because in many African situations, 'users' are not community members: the users may be in-migrants (strangers, foreigners, newcomers, lessees, sharecroppers, workers) who have displaced, moved in alongside, or entered into a contingent farming contract with indigenous communities or community members. In these cases, the communal rights regime and the regime that gives primacy to user rights are stark alternatives: they conflict with one another.

This distinction lies at the heart of Côte d'Ivoire's 1998 land law. The Ivoirian law bars non-nationals from transforming acquired land rights into full ownership rights, and gives responsibility for certifying land claims to committees of village-level chiefs and elders who aim to affirm the land rights of those who have ancestral claims to the land. Here, user rights lose out to rights based on communal membership. Similarly, in the Buganda region of

---

concentration of land ownership. Most advocates of user rights securitization envision a very gradual (and geographically uneven) process of adaptation and change in land law and how it is implemented. In the forums of land law reform that were held in the rural areas of Senegal by Senegal's *Conseil national de concertation et de coopération des ruraux* (CNCR) in 2003, many smallholders in the groundnut basin expressed support for registration and titling if this could be done in a way that strictly limited the transferability of land rights. See CNCR, 'Réflexion des organisations paysannes sur la reforme foncière: compte rendu de l'atelier regional de Diourbel/Louga, Bambey, 2003' (unpublished manuscript, 17 pages, CNCR, Dakar, 2003), pp. 3, 6, 8–9. See also CNCR, 'Séminaire national des ruraux sur la reforme foncière: rapport introductif, réflexion des OP [organisations paysannes] sur la reforme foncière, Dakar, Hôtel Novotel, 12–15 January 2004' (unpublished manuscript 18 pages, CNCR, Dakar, 2004). Information also gathered from interviews, Dakar, 1–5 August 2005.

Uganda, Baganda nationalists are pressing to vest authority over land in Baganda land boards, with the aim of defending Bagandan land rights against government encroachment, and against the claims of non-Bagandan land purchasers and squatters. The government's resistance to these demands has given rise to 'one of the most difficult political struggles of [Museveni's] first fifteen years in government'.[46] Sandra Joireman wrote that in 1998, 'parliamentary debate over the [land act] was vigorous, inciting such great controversy over the specifics of the Land Act that the government feared civil unrest'.[47]

Both the user rights regime and the communal rights regime differ from the private property regime, which envisions the development of national land markets.

Constitutional profiles of alternative land tenure regimes

The remainder of this article considers political concomitants of each of the different land reform scenarios sketched out above, and in various ways debated in many African countries today. What do these different visions of land tenure reform imply for the relationship between the individual, the community, and the state? The contrasts are summarized in Table 4.2.

Communal rights

William Munro suggested that in Africa, the land tenure regime determines whether the state will be pegged to the individual or the community.[48] Where regimes uphold communal land tenure, the state is pegged to the community. Under such land tenure regimes, the central state defines communities as (1) territorial entities, (2) administrative jurisdictions, and (3) political collectivities that are nested within the wider polities of the modern state and the "nation" it creates. A land tenure regime that upholds communal rights recognizes these political collectivities as the natural (pre-state) constituent units of the modern nation that the post-colonial state seeks to bring into being. State recognition of these communities as natural units confers upon them the kind of sovereignty (as least in the moral sense) that the individual holds in liberal constitutional philosophy. It also constructs local political

---

[46] Green, 'Ethnicity and the politics of land tenure reform', p. 377.

[47] Sandra F. Joireman, 'Enforcing new property rights in Sub-Saharan Africa: The Ugandan Constitution and the 1998 Land Act', *Comparative Politics* **39**, 4 (2007), pp. 463–80.

[48] Munro, *The Moral Economy of the State*, p. 40.

Table 4.2. Constitutional implications of property rights (PR) regimes

	Private	Communal	User-Rights
Citizenship	Individual, national Can underpin liberal political rights.	Communal, local (nativist) Segmented, hierarchical. Groups are recognized.	Occupation/land-use over time confers citizenship and confirms access rights.
Structure of society	Individuals as the basic unit	Segmented groups, hierarchically ordered within territorial jurisdictions	Farming households (or individuals?)
Moral basis of land claim	*De jure* ownership via legal purchase	Autochthony confers entitlement.	Investment of labour (sweat equity)
Building state authority/ relations between levels of state apparatus	Central state as agent of citizen. Unified state structure; constit'l enforcement of PR	Local authorities have PR prerogatives. Political authority is mediated or nested. Indirect rule (or a federal structure?)	Unified structure with centralized or decentralized government. Citizens governed by basic law made by central state.
Bureaucratization of political authority	High	Low, but could incr. with formalization of local government. Partial secularization is possible.	High
Adjudication/ reallotment of PR	By market, with state enforcing *de jure* PR.	By local authorities with (neo)traditional pedigree.	By central state, but with constraints on arbitrary expropriation of user-rights.
Locus of political sovereignty	The individual	The "natural community"	Central state
Possibility for democratization of local authority	Possible	Restricted democracy is possible: full local franchise limited to "natural community"	Possible, if franchise is conferred by national law to those with recognized user-rights

jurisdictions whose political legitimacy pre-dates the founding of the modern African republics.

A land tenure regime that upholds communal rights (that is, land rights derived from membership in ancestral communities) thus has direct implications for political jurisdiction and authority. As Mamdani's work suggests, it consolidates local states.[49] The national state, therefore, comes to be

---

[49] Mahmood Mamdani, *Citizen and Subject* (Princeton University Press, Princeton, NJ, 1996), and M. Mamdani, 'Indirect rule and the struggle for democracy: a response to Bridget O'Laughlin', *African Affairs* **99**, 1 (2000), pp. 43–6.

constructed as a mosaic of local states or local political orders, which are governed by local-level authority figures whose legitimacy is based on their ability to see and reproduce the boundaries of the "natural community". For Mamdani, these are local despots, because their authority is at least partly derived from, and exercised through, non-democratic principles or practices. More generally, this arrangement looks very much like a modern form of indirect rule of rural populations.[50] The territorial jurisdiction of the modern state is fragmented into a multitude of local microstates, within which the relationship between the central state and individuals, households, and rural communities is mediated by local elites who have political authority and also (some) economic authority over their subjects.

Along with local states come sub-national citizenship rights, identities, and legal entitlements. If land access, and subjection to neo-traditional communal authority in land affairs, is to be governed by a person's status as indigenous or not in a given "natural" community, then indigeneity is a political classification that is an integral part of the modern African state. Extending the logic of Mamdani's arguments regarding ethnicity, membership in the local community is a legal status and a political identity—that is, as a relation to the state, rather than just a state of mind.[51] Even more, this status confers a material *entitlement* (to land access). Those not indigenous to a given locality are recognized as strangers therein. They do not have any *a priori* rights to land access.

The existence of local citizenship as an institution also has implications for representation. It implies that the right to be a local leader and to represent local populations in their transactions beyond the locality is reserved for members of the ethno-kinship group that is officially recognized as indigenous to the locality. Those of non-local or non-indigenous origins are second-class citizens, or marginal subjects of the local state. They have no moral authority or legitimate claim to represent the community.

Institutionalization of local citizenship thus competes with the project of developing truly national citizenship. It means that, in practice, no single and unique set of property rights, no uniform set of rules of access to resources, and no uniform set of citizenship rights applies to all the citizen subjects of the central state, or prevails throughout the national space. Institutionalization of a communal land tenure regime thus imposes a kind of discrimination (or system of reserved rights) based on birthplace.[52]

---

[50] See Ribot, 'Decentralization'.

[51] Mamdani, 'Indirect rule and the struggle for democracy,' p. 43.

[52] An article in *The Nation* (Nairobi), dated 1 April 2005 and entitled 'Kenyans are "free to live anywhere"' <allafrica.com> (31 March 2005), opens with 'Kenyans have the right to live anywhere in the country, the government has reaffirmed....Kenyans have a right to buy property, reside, conduct business, live and die anywhere in Kenya. Kenya belongs to all Kenyans.'

Dilemmas that communal or community-based property rights regimes pose for the modern, central state have been made very concrete in South Africa, where the secularization of land administration has already gone very far indeed, by African standards. As Ben Cousins explains, in the late 1990s the Department of Land Affairs experimented briefly with transferring land ownership rights in 'communal areas' to groups that coalesced to form legal entities (such as Communal Property Associations).[53]

> Multiple problems and conflicts emerged in the test cases: Could land be transferred to "tribes", as some groups demanded? In [that] case, how could the state ensure democratic decision-making, principles of equity, and rights of due process? In some cases, one group within the community expressed support for traditional structures but was opposed by others who preferred "democratic" structures....Another challenge was the definition of what constituted a democratic majority—where did the boundaries of the group lie, particularly in situations where smaller and larger groups were in conflict?[54]

In other countries, proposals from "civil society" for constitutional or legal reform to vest land title (Kenya) or land administration (Uganda) in communal institutions have raised similar dilemmas. In Kenya, the National Civil Society Conference on Land considered the future status of land whose legal status was derived from the colonial category of Tribal Trust Land.[55] The Conference recommended that radical title to these lands be vested in community-based institutions that would be created by and entrenched in the national constitution, thus raising many questions about how these community institutions would be defined and governed, about locating the power of eminent domain in the local rather than the national state, and about the power to classify and reclassify individuals as members of the communities in which they live. As mentioned above, Uganda's President Museveni has resisted proposals for a Buganda Regional Land Board on the grounds that this would revive 'historical land rivalries'.

[53] Ben Cousins, 'Legislating negotiability: security, equity, and class formation in Africa's land systems' in Kristine Juul and Christian Lund (eds), *Negotiating Property in Africa* (Portsmouth, NH: Heinemann, 2002), pp. 67–106. On this, see also Thembele Kepe, 'The problem of defining "community": challenges for the land reform programme in rural South Africa', *Development Southern Africa* 16, 3 (1999), pp. 435–46.

[54] Cousins, 'Legislating negotiability,' p. 89.

[55] National Civil Society Conference on Land (Kenya), 'A summary of land policy principles' (Kenya Ministry of Lands and Settlement, Nairobi, 2 April 2004) <http://www.oxfam. org.uk/what_we_do/issues/livelihoods/landrights/downloads/kenya_land_policy_principles. rtf> (27 June 2006).

Private property

The full development of land markets would break existing links between African governments, rural communities, and farmers. Control over land would be transferred from the political sphere to the market. Some people think this is a good thing: it is a *sine qua non* of the political and economic changes that would produce liberal states in Africa. One could even argue that democratization of national-level electoral processes without land tenure reform dooms much of rural Africa to the decentralized despotism that Mamdani trenchantly criticized in *Citizen and Subject*.

In settings where communal rights prevail, moves toward individualization of control and disposition of land are, by definition, changes that erode communal coherence and structure. By removing land allocation from the portfolio of local authorities, the power of these local notables is diminished. The economic autonomy of individuals *vis-à-vis* extended families, community leaders, and the community at large is greatly enhanced—this enhances the individual's political autonomy as well. The state would not recognize any political communities as primordial or natural (other than perhaps the nuclear family); rather, the existence of political communities or collectives would be the product of the voluntary, individual choices that produce "associational life".

Where the central state is now positioned as the protector of the land rights of 'strangers', moves to full privatization of land would put an end to this particular form of political dependency. The patron–client tie that now links the central state to stranger groups with highly tenuous land rights would be severed. This would be a particular expression of the more general process by which land becomes subject to market-based allocation, rather than authority-based allocation. As a 1996 Government of Senegal study of a possible move toward commercialization of land rights put it, land tenure would be transformed from 'a right granted by the state to a property right that is recognized by the state.'[56]

With fully commoditized land rights, all citizens would be free to buy and own land throughout the national space. This would provide a necessary (although not sufficient) condition for the rise of national markets as well as unified, national citizenship rights.[57] As owners of private property in land (or if not land, at least their own labour!), individuals would enjoy the economic

---

[56] Government of Senegal, 'Plan d'action Foncier (PAF) du Sénégal, Octobre 1996' (Archives Nationales du Sénégal (ANS) poIII 4° 4016).

[57] As Giddens writes, the rise of land markets 'frees labor from both proprietary *and localized* relations to the means of production' (emphasis added). A. Giddens, *Capitalism and Modern Social Theory* (Cambridge University Press, Cambridge, 1971), p. 51.

autonomy *vis-à-vis* the state that is prized in liberal political thought as the wellspring of democracy.

Meanwhile, as Karl Polanyi pointed out, the rise of well-functioning markets presupposes an enormous increase in the scope and intensity of the administrative functions of the state.[58] The state must not only supervise, enforce, and adjudicate contracts and other regulatory arrangements, but also assume many of the wider political/administrative tasks previously carried out by the local state—that is, by local-level political intermediaries or brokers—as well as some of the repressive functions previously served by local-level social controls. The implications of this are well appreciated by state agents and members of the policy community involved in land law reform in Africa. As Cotula *et al.* write, 'There are very serious implementation problems in a variety of policy areas', including lack of human and financial resources to implement land laws, and the need to create new institutions for land management.[59]

Effective privatization thus transforms the nature of the state's insertion in rural society in profound ways. It also has revolutionary implications for rural society itself. Where the process of land law reform is taking place in the context of public consultation, many of these implications are cast in stark relief. Major issues that emerge time and time again have to do with the future of customary authority and the security of existing rights, especially for the poor. These concerns are intertwined in complex ways. The private land titling called for by many women's rights groups in Uganda and elsewhere not only reins in customary authority, but also exposes those with and without land titles to the pressures and compulsions of the market. In Zambia, Malawi, and Senegal, proposed or enacted measures to accelerate privatization of land have encountered strong protest from defenders of peasants' land rights. In central Senegal, where small-scale farmers and *organisations paysannes* joined the *Conseil national de concertation et coopération des ruraux* (CNCR), the government proposed a market-promoting land law reform in 1998 that met with blanket opposition from the CNCR, whose argument was 'We will not [simply] disappear.'[60]

---

[58] Karl Polanyi, *The Great Transformation* (Beacon, Boston, MA, 1957 [1944]). Jean-Philippe Platteau makes the same point in 'The evolutionary theory of land rights as applied to sub-Saharan Africa: a critical assessment', *Development and Change* 27, 1 (1996), pp. 29–85, p. 42).

[59] Lorenzo Cotula, Camilla Toulmin, and Ced Hesse, *Land Tenure and Administration in Africa: Lessons of experience and emerging issues* (International Institute for Economic Development (IIED), London, 2004), p. 31.

[60] See Jacques Faye, 'Pour une nouvelle agriculture familiale et une nouvelle ruralité', *Le Quotidien* (Dakar), 10 May 2000, p. 8; Jean-Matthew Tamba III, 'Farmers tell government: we will not be sacrificed', *Panos* (London), 10 August 2004 <allafrica.com> (10 September 2004); and CNCR, 'Le CNCR dans le cyclone de la privatisation de la SONACOS: partenariat ou jeu de cache cache?' (Dakar, n.d.) <www.cncr.org> (7 July 2004).

Privatization's implications for the distribution of land rights cannot be understood in terms of market effects only. In most of Africa, land rights are multiple and overlapping. It is therefore true *by definition* that individualization of control over land—understood as full privatization over the use and disposition of land—dispossesses all others holding claims to a given parcel of their rights. Where communal controls prevailed in the earlier period, the losers would be members of extended families (including future generations) and communities. Where user rights are enforced against the claims of autochtons, the losers are the indigenous landlords, communal groups, and their descendants. Moves toward privatization of land are, by definition, some kind of expropriation, although the real meaning of this would vary by context. As a matter of public policy, it is conceivable that the victims of this expropriation could be compensated: user rights could be bought out. In South Africa, for example, some individuals whose claims for land restitution were honoured by the post-apartheid state received monetary recompense in place of a literal "return" of their land.[61] It is, however, difficult to imagine that in most situations, such a solution could be implemented to the extent that would actually be required to assuage redistributive conflict. The spectre of dispossession and expropriation is the most explosive dimension of the land tenure debate.

User rights

What are the constitutional implications of land regimes that aim at securitization of user rights? By what political mechanism could such land regimes be enforced?

Legal reforms that shore up user rights explicitly embrace political modes of land allocation over market allocation. The critical questions therefore have to do with the locus and nature of this political authority. A user rights regime implies a secularization of political authority, since land access would be stripped of its connection to ancestral rights, and separated from the politics of reproducing these metaphysical and spiritual connections. In much of Africa, this would produce some levelling of ascriptive political hierarchy at the local level, since the power of former land chiefs would be diminished or usurped. For many international and Africa-based land rights activists, securitization of user rights is a politically attractive option because it contains the possibility of progressive and democratic reform at the local level, does not throw African smallholders on the mercy of the market, and seems to embrace

---

[61] Cousins, 'Legislating negotiability'.

the principle of incrementalism as a strategy of land regime modernization. Yet the politics of this strategy are complicated.

To say that secular authority will be vested in formal institutions that work to securitize (rather than fully or immediately marketize) user rights leaves open the question of the locus of that authority (national/central vs local), the question of how democratic it would be, and questions about whether securitization of user rights would restrain or expand the arbitrary authority of the central state.

A user rights regime could imply that the central state would administer localities directly (via local outposts of the central state, or deconcentrated instances of the state apparatus), as is now the case in south-western Côte d'Ivoire and most of Kenya. As a constitutional matter, these arrangements are grounded in whatever claims to legitimacy and accountability the central state has mustered. Alternatively, land reforms aimed at securitizing user rights could create conditions for the building of new secular political institutions at the local level, and vesting these with some autonomy *vis-à-vis* the centre. In theory, democratic mechanisms can provide these institutions with legitimacy and make them accountable. This was the ideal guiding the Shivji Commission recommendations that helped shape debate over the 1999 Village Land Act in Tanzania.

Tanzania's law was founded on the user rights principle, and aimed at more explicit institutionalization and secularization of local land administration.[62] The main controversy surrounding this innovation centred on the distribution of prerogative between central and local government, with the assumption being that local government could be more democratic, since it is closer to the people. Shivji argued that, ultimately, the law strengthened the land powers of the central state, and therefore failed to deliver on the promise of grassroots democracy:

> The most striking feature of the two [land] bills is the enormous powers over the ownership, control, and management of village land placed in the hands of the Ministry [of Lands], and through the Ministry, the Commissioner. The Commissioner has even greater powers over reserved and general land. The role of more elective bodies, like the village assembly, as been virtually done away with.[63]

---

[62] See Mallya, 'Civil society and the land question;' and Robin Palmer, Land Policy Adviser, Oxfam GB, 'The Tanzanian Land Acts, 1999: an analysis of the analyses' (Oxfam Great Britain, March 1999) <http://www.oxfam.org.uk/what_we_do/issues/livelihoods/landrights/downloads/tananaly.rtf> (30 July 2007).

[63] Issa G. Shivji, 'Protection of peasants and pastoral rights in land: a brief review of the bills for the Land Act 1998 and the Village Land Act 1998' (paper presented to the Parliamentary Committee for Finance and Economic Affairs Workshop on the Bills for the Land Act and Village Land Act, Dodoma, Tanzania, 26–28 January 1999), cited in Manji, 'Land reform', p. 334.

Others remained more optimistic about the possibility that the Tanzania land law would expand local democratic control over land matters, since the village assemblies with land prerogatives would be elected, allow for more local participation (than a centrally driven process), and be easier for villagers to monitor and sanction.[64]

One general question that ran through the Tanzania debate is whether the line ministries of a democratically elected national government can implement laws securitizing user rights in a way that would have democratic legitimacy. The answer may be "no" for the simple reason that a decisive legal shift to a user rights regime would raise the problem of redistributive conflict in ways that, in Tanzania and most African countries, would be difficult or impossible to adjudicate in terms of existing national law or constitutional principle.

The issue is not purely hypothetical—in many parts of Africa, moves toward a regime that securitizes user rights would imply a massive redistribution of land rights. Legal reforms that securitize existing land use rights actually expropriate the rights of those who claim ancestral entitlements to, and political authority over the land (including those who are not current users or have not yet activated their land access rights).[65] Where communal rights exist, securitization of user rights can imply a revolutionary exertion of state power to transfer rights from one group of claimants ("indigenous inhabitants") to another (in-migrants, settlers, newcomers). This is how reforms centred on the securitization of user rights can polarize rural localities along indigene-stranger lines, as we have seen in Côte d'Ivoire. Similar politics define the land rights question in Kenya's Rift Valley.

The second kind of expropriation or usurpation that would come with moves to a user rights regime has already been mentioned: it is the usurpation of the right of the "natural community", as a political collectivity, to govern land. Indeed, according primacy to user rights spells the end of the community as a political collectivity that "owns" resources in common.

This discussion underscores the extent to which general success of the vision of land law reform that accords primacy to user rights, and envisions that authority over land will be vested in local democratic institutions, depends upon constitutional and legal innovation at the level of the central state. It is true that the user rights regime constrains the ability of central rulers to arbitrarily expropriate the land rights of recognized users. The difficult part is deciding whose rights to recognize, and finding the mechanism by which such decisions are made. In many parts of Africa, conflicts over land access are rife

---

[64] Manji, 'Land reform'.

[65] On the *Loi sur le domaine national* as it was applied in the Siin region of Senegal, see Dennis Galvan, *The State Must Be Our Master of Fire: how peasants craft culturally sustainable development in Senegal* (University of California Press, Berkeley and Los Angeles, CA, 2004).

at the local level. Under such conditions, one cannot expect that securitization of user rights will promote or be accompanied by a smooth transition to democratic, community-based land management. Especially in cases were the securitization of land rights is a redistributive process, it is obvious that the question of whose rights will prevail should be determined at the national level—that is, at the level of the central state. And wherever good land is scarce, relying on locally elected officials to carry out the political allocation of land could create conditions for the rise of clientelism, and enhance the vulnerability of minorities. It therefore seems that the democratic functioning of local land-allocation institutions will have to be founded upon a set of prior, national laws that define the scope of the local community (the local franchise, that is), and principles to guide the political allocation of land. These political challenges cannot be kicked down to the local level.

Conclusion

It is surprising that the vast literature on "dual transitions" in the developing world has paid little attention to the question of rural property rights. Notable exceptions include Mamdani's work on Africa (which focused more on chieftaincy and ethnicity than on land *per se*, although these are intertwined as we have argued above), the policy-driven literature on rural decentralization and resource management in Africa, work on land rights and democracy in South Africa, and recent studies of indigenous peoples' rights/movements in Central and Latin America.[66] Some of the Africa-focused work argues that communal land regimes as they are currently constituted do not support democratic decentralization. This article extends this observation by noting that the larger land tenure debates also have implications for electoralism, land politics, the possibility of democracy, and the shape that democracy in Africa might eventually assume.

In Côte d'Ivoire, Kenya, Uganda, Tanzania, Senegal, Zimbabwe, and South Africa, where land policy and land reform have been high-visibility public issues, these constitutional choices about property, citizenship, and the character and locus of political authority are being debated in the electoral arena. Electoral mobilization around land issues is thus taking place in situations where governments can exercise wide powers to redefine land rights and even reallocate land. In these situations, the redistributive stakes of electoral competition become extraordinarily high for some constituencies. The destructive

[66] See, for example, Deborah Yashar, *Contesting Citizenship in Latin America: The rise of indigenous movements and the postliberal challenge* (Cambridge University Press, Cambridge, 2005).

potential of this kind of competition has been on full display in Côte d'Ivoire in the last decade.

What are the implications of these observations for classic theories about the endogenous evolution of rural property rights in Africa and beyond? Boserup and others have argued that the privatization of rights is likely to occur from below as land values are driven up by population growth and growing land scarcity.[67] Yet the endogenous evolution scenario may be premised on the assumption that property rights are evolving within a fixed and well-specified constitutional framework—that is, the classic theories assume that the locus of authority over property rights creation, enforcement, and adjudication, is stable and not widely contested. In fact, however, there is no such agreed upon constitution in much of rural Africa; this may help explain why property rights change does not always follow the endogenous evolution path. Where demographic and environmental stress (shortage of arable land) intensifies, there is likely to be conflict in areas where these fundamental questions of local political authority and citizenship are highly contested.

In much of Africa, successful negotiation of land tenure reform and modernization must be predicated upon political choices about the kinds of property rights states will enforce, the extent of bureaucratization, secularization and democratization of state authority, and the scope and content of national citizenship. Ultimately, these are constitutional-level choices that must engage broad citizenries, and that require consensus building over basic questions of political order and community. They are logically prior to policy choices about land management, rural investment policy, or even the specifics of local government design. Open acknowledgement of these complexities brings questions of most vital interest to Africa's rural and semi-rural majorities to the centre of discussions about reform and reconstruction of the African state.

Acknowledgment

Published in *African Affairs*, 106, 425 (2007), p. 557–586. This article was presented as a paper at the 2005 annual meeting of the American Political Science Association (Wardman Park Marriott, Washington, DC, 2 September 2005), and the 2006 annual meeting of the African Studies Association, 17 November 2006 (San Francisco Westin, San Francisco, CA). It grew out of discussions held at the Social Science Research

---

[67] Esther Boserup, *The Conditions of Agricultural Growth: The economics of agrarian change under population pressure* (George Allen and Unwin, London, 1965); Platteau, 'The evolutionary theory of land rights'.

Council Regional Advisory Panel (SSRC RAP) for Africa 'Planning Meeting on Citizenship', 27 September 2003, in Amsterdam. I thank the West Africa Research Centre in Dakar for logistical support, and interviewees in Dakar in July 2004 and July–August 2005 for helpful discussions. Jesse Ribot and Sandra Joireman, along with anonymous reviewers, provided thoughtful and useful comments.

5

Does Organized Crime Exist in Africa?

Stephen Ellis and Mark Shaw

On 2 April 2013, agents of the United States' drugs enforcement administration arrested on the high seas five citizens of Guinea-Bissau whom they had entrapped in an elaborate sting operation.[1] One of the five was Admiral José Américo Bubo na Tchuto, chief of the Bissauan navy. A veteran of Guinea-Bissau's liberation war against Portugal and a leading figure in the country's armed forces, he had long been suspected by the US authorities of cocaine trafficking on a massive scale. The five suspects were taken to the US, where Bubo na Tchuto pleaded guilty in court to the charges against him. His trial is currently in progress.

Over the last decade, Guinea-Bissau has become notorious for its participation in the large-scale import of cocaine from Latin America, particularly since the publication in 2007 of a report on the subject by the United Nations Office on Drugs and Crime.[2] Following news of Bubo na Tchuto's arrest, there were reports that many of the Latin American and other international drug traffickers who had based themselves in Guinea-Bissau in previous years had taken fright and moved to the neighbouring Republic of Guinea, also known as Guinea-Conakry. There, the drug trade appears still to be flourishing, as it has done at least since the closing years of the presidency of General Lansana Conte, who died in December 2008. There is evidence from interviews with law-enforcement officers and others that leading military figures in these two neighbouring countries, Guinea and Guinea-Bissau, have conspired to trade drugs internationally for the last decade at least.[3]

---

[1] Richard Valdmanis, 'U.S. agents seize suspected Bissau drug kingpin at sea' (Reuters US edition), <http://www.reuters.com/article/2013/04/05/us-bissau-traffickers-idUSBRE93400H2020130405> (25 November 2014).

[2] United Nations Office on Drugs and Crime (UNODC), *Cocaine trafficking in West Africa: The threat to stability and development (with special reference to Guinea-Bissau)* (UNODC, Vienna, 2001).

[3] The authors have made repeated research trips to both countries.

In describing activities like these, external law-enforcement officials often refer to them as 'organized crime'. This, however, is a term rarely used by Africans themselves, with only a few exceptions, such as in South Africa where it is generally used to describe external rather than domestically rooted networks. The lack of agreement on vocabulary raises an interesting set of questions about what organized crime is recognized to be in the African context, by some observers at least, and whether the term is ever useful to describe African realities. Our approach is to study the characteristics of some of the activities in Africa that would be included in almost any definition of the term, with a view to identifying its specific features in African contexts.[4] We then proceed to analyse the features of the markets for criminal protection that have emerged in recent years in Africa and that have been the subject of study in other contexts.[5] We conclude with some remarks on how this is contributing to the continuing formation of African states.

The intertwining of crime and state politics in Africa has a genealogy that can be traced back for at least half a century. Some African countries had already developed a characteristic style of rule that the sociologist Stanislav Andreski in 1968 dubbed 'kleptocracy', in reference to the systematic use of fraud, bribery, and similar illegality as instruments of governance.[6] Andreski made clear some of the deep social and political roots of this mode of rule, which can be found in at least some African countries. However, the emergence of nationalist governments on the continent was from the outset associated not just with domestic corruption but also with a distinctive globalized form of rent seeking. In West Africa, for example, as politicians in search of funds formed alliances with foreign businessmen in search of contracts, the safeguards that prevented politicians and civil servants from doing corrupt deals with foreign contractors 'evaporated in some instances'[7] at an early date. The United Kingdom's first High Commissioner to Nigeria had 'no doubt...that foreign firms are largely to blame' in regard to corruption of this sort, just one year after independence.[8] African politicians who took bribes from foreign firms became vulnerable to blackmail, with the result that 'corruption, foreign influence, and domestic politics became hopelessly entangled'.[9]

---

[4] We are well aware of the difficulties in researching activities that are essentially clandestine, but we are able to make use of a wide range of publications on comparative crime, for example in regard to the Sicilian mafia, as well as personal interviews with actors on various points of the spectrum from law breaking to law enforcement.

[5] Federico Varese, *Mafias on the move: How organized crime conquers new territories* (Princeton University Press, Princeton, NJ, 2011).

[6] Stanislav Andreski, *The African predicament: A study in the pathology of modernisation* (Michael Joseph, London, 1968), p. 109.

[7] Henry L. Bretton, *Power and politics in Africa* (Longman, London, 1973), p. 128.

[8] National Archives of the United Kingdom, London, DO 186/10, fol. 37: Head to Clutterbuck, 5 May 1961; and fol. 56, Head to Clutterbuck, 8 November 1961.

[9] Bretton, *Power and politics in Africa*, p. 129.

As a result of these processes, economies became politicized in a new and very specific sense. Also in Nigeria, a young American businessman who took up a job in 1962 discovered that foreign companies were writing inflated invoices in respect of imported goods as a systematic means of expatriating their profits. 'Most foreign-owned companies', he recalled, 'were doing largely the same thing.'[10] A different model emerged in Africa's French-speaking countries, where the development from late colonial times of a close relationship between foreign businesses and African politicians formed part of the relationship dubbed 'Françafrique' by Côte d'Ivoire's long-serving president Félix Houphouët-Boigny–who intended this term to be understood positively. An evolving feature of Françafrique, which has transformed it into a pejorative term, has been a complex of Franco-African corruption overseen by a small and durable circle of officials whose centre of power is in the Elysée palace. A significant part of the rents generated has reportedly been channelled to French politicians and their parties.[11] What these experiences suggest is a complex interweaving of criminal networks and everyday politics that revolves around the provision of political protection for illicit activities, a development that we refer to as 'markets for protection'.

In this article, we aim to determine whether it is accurate to speak of organized crime in Africa. We investigate how the concept could be made operational and suggest how else we might describe recent patterns of organized criminal activity in Africa if it is not appropriate. We believe that the concept of markets for protection provides a useful analytical grille for studying the intersection of politics, business, and crime in Africa—one that we hope will be of use to other researchers in this area.

Understanding crime in Africa

The concept of organized crime emerged in the USA, where it originally reflected the government's interpretation of traditional patronage networks among Italian immigrants involved in crime. Since then, the phrases "organized crime" and "mafia" have gained a greater or lesser degree of acceptance in many countries, always in circumstances that differ slightly or not so slightly from one place to another.

The original mafia, rooted in Sicily, has been described as 'a shadow state, a political body that sometimes opposes, sometimes subverts, and sometimes

---

[10] Raymond Baker, *Capitalism's Achilles heel: Dirty money and how to renew the free-market system* (John Wiley and Sons, Hoboken, NJ, 2005), p. 12.

[11] There is no fully satisfactory summary of la *Françafrique*, but see Antoine Glaser and Stephen Smith, *Ces Messieurs Afrique* (Calmann-Levy, Paris, 2005).

dwells within the body of the legal government'.[12] Historically, it developed by supplying protection in situations where the enforcement of law by the state was inadequate.[13] In recent decades the spread of southern Italian crime networks to new locations has been facilitated by their ability to exploit a lack of effective law enforcement in parts of northern Italy and elsewhere in the world where new labour forces have come into existence, suggesting that a rise in organized criminal activity may be related to the emergence of new markets.[14] In Russia, organized crime groups were relatively unimportant during the heyday of Soviet government but gained political purchase during the upheavals of the 1980s as enforcers of contracts in new markets.[15] 'What was organized crime in the Soviet Union?', asks a leading Russian commentator. 'At least after Andropov's time [1984], it began to be part of the system, under the control of the KGB. The only people who the bandits were afraid of were the state security officers. And this evolved into its present-day form.'[16] In Colombia, by contrast, organized crime has developed from a strong sense of local and provincial identity in a historically weak state.[17]

If we accept that something that can reasonably be called "organized crime" exists in many places, it is nevertheless apparent that this existence takes particular forms in various countries. Similar diversity should be expected in Africa, where patterns of organized criminal activity emerge from the continent's own circumstances and history, as indeed they do everywhere. Arguably these problems emerge from continuities in Africa's history, including in the many cases where corruption is embedded, incorporating older practices of gift giving and honour.[18] It is also important to note the consequences of the structural adjustment policies of the 1980s in forming a new political and economic climate.

We therefore think it advisable not to begin by adopting one of the many definitions of organized crime offered by the relevant literature, which is

---

[12] John Dickie, *Cosa Nostra: A history of the Sicilian mafia* (Palgrave Macmillan, London, 2005), p. 291.

[13] Diego Gambetta, *The Sicilian mafia: The business of private protection* (Harvard University Press, Cambridge, MA, 1993).

[14] Varese, *Mafias on the move*.

[15] Vadim Volkov, *Violent entrepreneurs: The use of force in the making of Russian capitalism* (Cornell University Press, Ithaca, NY, 2002).

[16] Kirill Kabanov, head of the National Anti-Corruption Committee, as quoted in Charles Clover, 'A death retold', *Financial Times*, 19 February 2009, <http://www.ft.com/intl/cms/s/0/41f7ac0c-fe26-11dd-932e-000077b07658.html#axzz3Yht9Gibk> (29 April 2015).

[17] Manuel Castells, *End of millennium*, Vol. 3 of The information age: Economy, society, and culture (Blackwell, Malden, MA, 2000), pp. 202–6.

[18] Giorgio Blundo, 'La corruption et l'état en Afrique vus par les sciences sociales', in Giorgio Blundo and Jean-Pierre Olivier de Sardan (eds), *État et corruption en Afrique: une anthropologie comparative des relations entre fonctionnaires et usagers (Bénin, Niger, Sénégal)* (Karthala, Paris, 2007), pp. 39–43.

mainly based on the study of Europe and North America,[19] and then testing its relevance to Africa. While there is no globally agreed definition of organized crime, most extant definitions include reference to the scale of activities, the degree of permanence and cohesiveness of those involved, and their propensity to violence. To take one or other definition as our point of departure, we believe, will show simply that in almost any African context there is a wide variety of illicit or "grey" activities that conceivably could be described as organized crime, without gaining much explanatory power from our use of that term. We find it more productive to study relevant empirical data with a view to ascertaining what the phenomenon under scrutiny may look like in a variety of locations on the African continent, to see how it has evolved in recent decades, and to consider how it links to a wider set of global developments.

Organized criminal activity in African countries has specific features that make it possible to situate such activity on a spectrum extending from state-legitimated to purely private. Many African countries have weak law enforcement and have experienced a rapid growth of a wide variety of globalized markets in recent years. Organized criminal activity was a late starter in Africa, for example in the arrival of Russian organized crime groups in Sierra Leone in the 1980s[20] and the transformation of youth gangs in Cape Town into organized crime groups via their entry into the drugs trade and their linkages with the apartheid state.[21] In all but a handful of cases, the rise of organized crime in Africa became perceptible at a time of extensive political and economic change. These particularities make African countries rather different from many other places where the concept of organized crime is longer established.

Patterns of law breaking in Africa that reasonably may be considered as organized crime are not confined to so-called 'weak' or 'failed' states, but are readily apparent in some of the continent's middle-income states as well.[22] An example that has been the subject of recent attention is the extent of operations in Africa by the Sicilian mafia, notably in South Africa, Angola, and Kenya, generally regarded as some of the continent's most important

---

[19] Nikos Passas, 'Introduction', *Organized Crime* (Dartmouth Publishing Co., Aldershot, 1995), pp. xiii–xix. The negotiators of the one global United Nations instrument on the subject could only agree a rather loose definition of what constitutes an organized crime group.

[20] Robert I. Friedman, *Red mafiya: How the Russian mob has invaded America* (Little, Brown, and Co., New York, NY, 2000), pp. 57–8.

[21] Don Pinnock, *The brotherhoods: Street gangs and state control in Cape Town* (David Philip, Cape Town, 1984); Irvin Kinnes, *From urban street gangs to criminal empires: The changing face of gangs in the Western Cape* (Institute for Security Studies, Pretoria, Monograph No. 48, 2000).

[22] Mark Shaw, 'Transnational organized crime in Africa', in Jay Albanese and Philip Reichel (eds), *Transnational organized crime: An overview from six continents* (Sage, Los Angeles, CA, 2014), pp. 93–115.

countries.[23] For the purposes of a macro-analysis, it is legitimate to consider major criminal activities from a wide variety of African states together, or at least to compare and contrast them. Some habitual distinctions seem to lose their incisiveness in the African context, such as that between organized crime and corruption. As Etannibi Alemika has pointed out, corruption is simply the objective of the most serious organized criminal groups in Africa, not a facilitating activity as it is often held to be in the literature on organized crime elsewhere.[24] Even the terms 'illegal' or 'illicit' may present problems, as there may be no laws in place to regulate activity that outsiders consider criminal, or alternatively, the state (or actors within it) may have provided the requisite paperwork to make a specific activity legal for bureaucratic purposes. A good example is high-level oil smuggling in Nigeria, which may make use of genuine official documents procured from senior state officials who are party to a smuggling operation.

In many parts of Africa where organized criminal activity can be identified, it is associated with a set of relationships generally involving senior figures within the state or important local power brokers, as well as professional criminals. Organized criminal activity is often concerned with channelling or directing resource flows from or to African countries over a period and in an organized way for the purpose of illicit gain. Drug trading, kidnapping, embezzlement, the large-scale theft of minerals, or other plainly criminal activities exist on a sustained basis in many parts of Africa, in both "weaker" and "stronger" states. In the case of fragile states, such criminal activities seem to be most important if they concern high-value natural resources—such as in the Democratic Republic of Congo (DRC)—or occur on major trafficking routes. In cases like these, trafficking flows tend to shape politics, as in Libya since 2011.[25]

Some important elements of organized criminal activity in Africa could better be subsumed under the term 'criminal enterprise',[26] as a good deal of such activity is the work of networks of entrepreneurs who traverse the boundaries of the public and private and of the legal and illegal sectors. In the absence of a clear legal framework that is enforced consistently, enterprise crime may be considered to entail any activities that commonly would be considered illegal, and—although we realize that this is a subjective judgement

---

[23] See the investigations listed at <http://www.journalismfund.eu/MafiaInAfrica> (4 May 2015).

[24] This point is made in the opening chapter of Etannibi Alemika (ed.), *The impact of organized crime on governance in West Africa* (Friedrich Ebert Stiftung, Abuja, 2013), p. 25, and also in personal communications.

[25] Mark Shaw and Fiona Mangan, *Illicit trafficking and Libya's transition: Profits and losses* (United States Institute of Peace, Washington, DC, 2014).

[26] R. T. Naylor, 'From underworld to underground: Enterprise crime, "informal sector" business and the public policy response', *Crime, Law and Social Change* 24, 2 (1995–6), pp. 79–150.

in itself—that are contrary to what might be considered the public good. But 'enterprise crime' is not an accurate label, either.

In the end, we can find no generally accepted term that does justice to the characteristic ways in which organized criminal activity takes place in Africa, involving as it does professional criminals, local or foreign, doing business regularly with state officials and politicians and legitimate businesses, the latter very often headquartered overseas. While an erosion of the frontiers between politics, crime, and business is detectable in many parts of the world, the process has at least three specific features in African countries. First, their state bureaucracies are often weak. Second, there are strikingly different outcomes depending on whether the key alliances with organized crime are made at the level of central government (for example in Zimbabwe) or at provincial level, as in Libya since 2011. Third, the rise of organized crime in Africa occurred at a relatively late date, towards the end of the last century, at a time when financial globalization was resulting in vastly increased flows of money and resources.

The question of understanding what organized crime may mean in Africa is more than an academic exercise. Interventions by the United Nations Security Council in regard to what it calls 'organized crime in Africa' have increased significantly in the past decade,[27] going from four statements or resolutions on organized crime in Africa in 2004 to 15 in 2014.[28] These resolutions use the term 'organized crime' or 'illicit trafficking' to refer to a diverse array of activities, including drug trafficking, the illicit movement of natural resources, different forms of environmental crime, and maritime piracy. If there is one thing all these UN statements have in common it is that they concern states in conflict, or emerging from it. However, since issues of peace and security are the very reason the Security Council is examining crime in a specific country or region, it cannot therefore be assumed that armed conflict is a necessary accompaniment to organized crime. Nevertheless, it is apparent that the issue of what the United Nations itself often terms 'organized crime' in Africa is of growing interest to international policy makers, particularly when it concerns 'weak' or 'failed' states.

International concern is understandable inasmuch as each of the world's nearly 200 sovereign states is responsible for promulgating and implementing law within its own territory, and each one enjoys privileges, including the right to mint currency and to sign treaties or make other legally binding agreements

---

[27] See Ministry of Foreign Affairs of the Netherlands and Global Initiative Against Organized Crime, 'Development responses to organized crime' (Background paper for the Development Dialogue, hosted by the Ministry of Foreign Affairs of the Netherlands and the Global Initiative against Transnational Organized Crime, The Hague, 8–9 April 2014).

[28] On conflict and organized crime in Africa, an important contribution is William Reno, 'Understanding criminality in West African conflicts', in James Cockayne and Adam Lupel (eds), *Peace operations and organized crime: Enemies or allies?* (Routledge, New York, NY, 2011), pp. 68–83.

with other states. State failure, therefore, is a matter of concern to the international community in its own right—as the Security Council resolutions demonstrate. State failure is all the more concerning if it has a relationship, even a weak one, with criminal activity that promotes regional instability and funds armed conflict.[29]

For their part, the rulers of African states, whether such polities are considered strong or weak, generally understand very well the importance of being seen to uphold the rule of law, since this is essential to continuing international recognition of their sovereignty. This was well articulated by a Nigerian police chief who in 2004 stated that 'Nigeria is a distinguished member of the international community and as such we must, at all times, conform and be seen to conform with all norms, conventions and rules that are sine qua non to peaceful living and respectable human co-existence.'[30] (Ironically, the same police chief was later jailed for embezzlement.) In many cases, the theoretical primacy of the rule of law is purely formal, for political and social reality may actually be formed by patterns of illicit activity that include smuggling, the formation of militias, and so on. It is therefore essential for an understanding of crime in Africa to appreciate the distinction between the principle of the rule of law and its actual substance, as only then is it possible to identify the space between the letter of the law and the reality of political and economic life where people go about their business.[31] As the West Africa Commission on Drugs that was convened by Kofi Annan and chaired by Nigeria's former president Olusegun Obasanjo recently concluded: 'traffickers can reshape relationships between and among political and security actors, the citizenry, and the business community within and beyond borders'.[32]

If this is indeed so, it is inappropriate to use the traditional state-versus-crime distinction in situations where the state may itself be a major player in organized crime or may have been extensively infiltrated by those with a criminal purpose. Of course, standard definitions of organized crime do recognize connections between state and criminal actors, but this is usually in regard to facilitating activities, as in the case of corruption. While the term 'captured states' has now become more widely used (not least in the case of Guinea-Bissau, but also globally),[33] it is analytically blunt in so far as it implies that a state is either 'captured' or not, whereas in the

---

[29] A review of the evidence finds that 'patterns of transnational crime are imperfectly correlated with state weakness'. See Stewart Patrick, *Weak links: Fragile states, global threats and international security* (Oxford University Press, Oxford, 2011), p. 12.

[30] Interview, Inspector-General of Police Tafa Balogun, *Tell* magazine, Lagos, 6 September 2004.

[31] Jean-François Bayart, Stephen Ellis, and Béatrice Hibou, *The criminalization of the state in Africa* (James Currey, Oxford, 1999), pp. 19–22.

[32] West Africa Commission on Drugs, *Not just in transit: Drugs, the state and society in West Africa* (West Africa Commission on Drugs, 2014), p. 22.

[33] Moisés Naím, 'Mafia states: Organized crime takes office', *Foreign Affairs* 91, 3 (May–June 2012).

vast majority of cases in Africa the reality lies somewhere in-between. That is not to say that crime does not undercut state capacity, or is not changing the nature of the state itself—as we argue below—but we nonetheless find that the notion of 'criminal capture' implies a set of relationships that is too simplistic to represent what we believe to be occurring. This speaks to the conceptual challenges of drawing a linkage between the phenomena associated with organized crime in different contexts, and by so doing identifying what we mean by 'enterprise crime' and the protection economies it spawns.

An appreciation of the distinction to be made between the juridical nature of sovereignty and the frequent absence of effective law enforcement in social reality[34] makes it easier to discern an important feature of organized criminal activity in Africa, namely the requirement of criminal entrepreneurs to receive 'protection' in a variety of forms and from a variety of actors. Since the use of protection has always been a defining feature of mafia-type organizations,[35] it seems imperative to understand how mafia-style protection is acquired and applied in African contexts today if we are to analyse correctly the evolving forms of criminal enterprise that blur the boundary between politics, the state, business, and society. Any business, whether dealing in licit or illicit goods, requires protection—but in a state that has lost its monopoly of violence, this cannot be offered as a free public service by state law-enforcement agencies. The provision of protection in return for payment may easily become an interface between something that may be recognizable as 'traditional' organized crime (associated with the ability to inflict violence) and activities more easily recognizable as politics and business. The state, no matter what its strength or form, plays a key role in regulating and channelling illicit financial flows to foreign jurisdictions. In that respect, the state remains influential even in countries where the influence of criminal groups is evident and where the state itself may be weak institutionally, or have limited control over its territory.

International linkages and global changes

Activities that reasonably could be considered as enterprise crime in Africa usually have important international linkages. These range from the collusion

---

[34] Cf. Robert H. Jackson and Carl G. Rosberg, 'Sovereignty and underdevelopment: Juridical statehood in the African crisis', *Journal of Modern African Studies* 24, 1 (1986), pp. 1–31; Robert H. Jackson, *Quasi-states: Sovereignty, international relations, and the third world* (Cambridge University Press, Cambridge, 1990).

[35] Gambetta, *The Sicilian mafia*.

of major international companies in bribery and corruption[36] to the cooperation of mining companies with unofficial militias in the exploitation of minerals in the eastern DRC[37] and the role of foreign banks—sometimes major ones—in aiding illicit financial flows.[38] Given the important role of foreign companies, as well as of clearly criminal groups such as Latin American drug trafficking organizations, it is necessary to situate activities that could be considered as organized crime in Africa within a global context, especially as there appears to have been a rise in organized crime worldwide,[39] or what might be termed a blurring of distinctions between politics, organized crime, and business.[40]

The mingling of state politics, crime, and legitimate business in recent decades is not a uniquely African development, and some of the causes of enterprise crime in Africa can be attributed to global changes that have had comparable effects elsewhere.[41] In 1996, the sociologist Stanley Cohen published an article with the provocative title 'Crime and politics: Spot the difference' that was inspired partly by events in the Balkans at that time.[42] Cohen argued that new patterns of wealth seeking allied to political power were making it more difficult to apply conventional definitions of crime, and that politics and crime, rather than being two fairly distinct fields of activity, were becoming inextricably mixed. Not the least of the analytical problems such situations cause is in knowing how to think about state institutions in cases where they are themselves deeply implicated in crime, for, as Cohen wrote elsewhere, the rules of the international system require that crime and the state be officially regarded as distinct and opposed entities. 'Governments

---

[36] One example among many is the *prima facie* collusion of European arms manufacturers in South Africa's 1998 arms scandal: Paul Holden and Hennie van Vuuren, *The devil in the detail: How the arms deal changed everything* (Jonathan Ball, Cape Town, 2011).

[37] This has been documented by UN expert reports on the DRC, such as 'Letter dated 2009/11/23 from the Chairman of the Security Council Committee Established Pursuant to Resolution 1533 (2004) Concerning the Democratic Republic of the Congo…' (S/2009/603, United Nations, New York), <http://www.un.org<Docs/journal/asp/ws.asp?m=s/2009/603> (7 June 2014).

[38] See, for example, reports on Riggs Bank and Citibank by the US Senate Permanent Subcommittee on Investigations, Committee on Governmental Affairs, <http://www.levin.sen ate.gov/imo/media/doc/supporting/2004/0924psireport.pdf> (6 January 2015); United States Senate, 'Role of US correspondent banking in international money laundering' (Paper S. Hrg. 107–84, *Hearings before the Permanent Subcommittee on Investigations of the Committee of Governmental Affairs, first session*, Vol. 1 of 5, Washington, DC, 2001).

[39] Misha Glenny, *McMafia: Crime without frontiers* (Bodley Head, London, 2008).

[40] Eva Joly, *Est-ce dans ce monde-là que nous voulons vivre?* (Les Arènes, Paris, 2003), especially p. 190.

[41] See for example, H. Richard Friman and Peter Andreas (eds), *The illicit global economy and state power* (Rowman and Littlefield, London, 1999); Josiah McC. Heyman (ed.), *States and illegal practices* (Berg, Oxford, 1999).

[42] Stanley Cohen, 'Crime and politics: Spot the difference', *The British Journal of Sociology* 47, 1 (1996), pp. 1–21.

and their agencies do not commit crimes,' he noted, 'but only because the criminal law does not take cognisance of them as criminal actors.'[43]

Accordingly, it is helpful to list some of the changes in global conditions that have resulted in some fields of legitimate activity becoming associated with crime. An evident starting point is the effect of the end of the Cold War. At that time, political elites and secret services in the former Soviet bloc with no ingrained respect for law made common cause with existing crime barons in a profound reconfiguration of power.[44] The establishment of markets where none previously existed created opportunities for well-placed individuals to make huge fortunes overnight.[45] Criminal groups are generally more nimble than government regulators in exploiting new markets, but in African cases the growth of organized crime is not primarily because of deficiencies in regulation so much as in the willingness of politicians to envisage relationships with professional criminals. However, even in Western democracies, where respect for law is comparatively stronger, the relationship between politics and crime has changed. This is partly because of the burgeoning cost of political campaigning, which requires politicians to raise colossal sums of money, thereby causing them to have recourse to contributions from people or businesses engaged in illegal activity that are prepared to make large campaign contributions because they require political protection. Scandals of this sort have occurred in the United States and other democracies. A technique available to incumbent politicians especially is to make arrangements with companies that provide them with slush funds in return for political favours, as has happened in France, Germany, Italy, Spain, the United Kingdom, and some other European countries.[46]

Multinational corporations play a key role in the corruption of state officials in many countries. As the European colonial empires disappeared from the map in the mid-twentieth century, prominent national companies reorganized themselves to do business in the world then emerging. They lobbied the governments of new states with a view to creating a legal environment favourable to the requirements of the companies themselves. Multinational companies or even individual businesspeople could request a government to formulate laws in return for money or other favours, while politicians discovered that the legal principle of sovereignty itself could be used to generate cash. A spectacular example was the Seychelles, where in 1995 the National Assembly amended the constitution in order to open the way for legislation

---

[43] Quoted in David O. Friedrichs (ed.), *State crime*, Vol. 1: *Defining, delineating and explaining state crime* (Ashgate, Aldershot and Brookfield, VT, 1998), p. 51.

[44] Stephen Handelman, *Comrade criminal: Russia's new mafiya* (Yale University Press, New Haven, CT, 1995).

[45] Castells, *End of millennium*, pp. 183–90.

[46] A partial list of funding scandals in European countries can be found in Perry Anderson, 'The Italian disaster', *London Review of Books* 36, 10 (2014), pp. 3–5.

guaranteeing immunity from criminal prosecution for any foreign business operator investing a minimum of $10 million in the islands. The Economic Development Bill proposed immunity from prosecution for all investors meeting these requirements 'for all criminal proceedings whatsoever except criminal proceedings in respect of offences involving acts of violence and drug trafficking in Seychelles'.[47]

New forms of financial globalization have affected commercial and political relationships of all descriptions. Measures that have contributed to this process include market reforms undertaken by the Chinese government from 1978, the abolition of foreign exchange control in the United Kingdom in 1979, deregulation and tax cuts enacted by the first Reagan administration in the USA, the European commitment to creating a single European market, the collapse of the Soviet Union in 1991, and India's move away from protectionism in the same year. Beginning in the 1980s, leading financial powers advocated the light regulation of financial institutions, and, in this environment, banks in the world's most developed countries found methods of marketing debt that were dependent on new information technology and that were often without legal precedent, placing them in a grey zone between legal and illegal.[48]

Major companies developed systems of accounting designed to hide the extent of their debts. The cumulative impact has been to create vast quantities of debt beyond the oversight of official regulators. Lack of stringent regulation of the huge international transfers of money facilitated by financial globalization 'has enormously increased the scope and profitability of transnational organized crime', one specialist writer has noted.[49] Another has pointed out how criminal markets that were formerly 'small and isolated'[50] have become integrated into the legal economy. Legitimate business and criminal enterprise have become difficult to distinguish from each other as they meet in a legal grey zone.

This exists above all in regard to banking, as both legitimate businesses and criminal syndicates use similar techniques to move their money around the world, whether the purpose is primarily to avoid taxes or to hide the profits of criminal activity. It appears that most of the 'dirty' money moved in this way originates with multinational companies that arrange corporate locations and business transactions in such a way as to record profits in low-tax jurisdictions, although these actions may not on the face of it be illegal. According to

---

[47] *Indian Ocean Newsletter* (Paris, Indigo Publications, 18 November 1995).

[48] Frank Partnoy, *Infectious greed: How deceit and risk corrupted the financial markets* (PublicAffairs, New York, NY, 2009).

[49] David Beetham, 'Foreword', in Felia Allum and Renate Siebert (eds), *Organized crime and the challenge to democracy* (Routledge, London and New York, NY, 2003), p. x.

[50] R. T. Naylor, *Wages of crime: Black markets, illegal finance, and the underworld economy* (Cornell University Press, Ithaca, NY, and London, 2004), p. 3.

the research organization Global Financial Integrity, 'about 80 per cent of illicit outflows' in recent years have been 'channe[l] led through the deliberate misinvoicing of trade', effectively a process in which volumes of trade being transacted are falsified in official documentation.[51] Smaller amounts are deposited by crime barons or corrupt politicians hiding their loot. It is estimated that, between 2002 and 2011, developing countries lost no less than US$5.9 trillion to illicit financial flows,[52] while the figure now stands at a massive one trillion dollars per year.[53] One group of just 33 sub-Saharan countries is estimated to have lost a total of $814 billion dollars from 1970 to 2010.[54]

It is in this global context that the contours of states all over the world have been reshaped, and nowhere has this been more evident than in Africa, which underwent such extensive economic and political reforms in the last years of the twentieth century. When political tensions have contributed to armed conflict in Africa, this too has been within a global context that has changed greatly in recent decades as conventional wars have become largely obsolete, to be replaced by war among the people.[55] In the 1970s, Africa received large quantities of weapons, provided notably by the Soviet Union as it struggled for control of the Third World, which it hoped would give it the upper hand in the Cold War.[56] The first Ronald Reagan administration (1981–5) contributed to the privatization of war by instigating a global attack on governments that it considered pro-Soviet, most famously in Afghanistan and Nicaragua but also in Southern Africa, especially Angola. Senior officials in the USA coordinated an extensive semi-official network of private funding for arms deliveries to anti-Soviet groups, arranging for one US ally to help another, such as by encouraging wealthy and pious Saudi citizens to support the *mujahideen* in Afghanistan.

Arrangements of this nature brought intelligence agencies closer than ever before to major unofficial or even criminal networks in the arms trade and its associated financial circuits, at the same time putting weapons into the hands of non-official groups in a number of regions. These changes stimulated the emergence of civilian combatant groups funded by illicit trades, often sponsored by the intelligence services of allied states. As the Soviet Union

---

[51] Dev Kar and Sarah Freitas, *Illicit financial flows from developing countries: 2001–2010* (Global Financial Integrity, Washington, DC, 2012), p. j.

[52] *Ibid.*, p. 13.

[53] Raymond Baker, 'The impact of organized crime on finance, development, business and democracy', workshop on organized crime in Africa held at the Rosa Luxemburg Foundation, Johannesburg, 14 November 2014.

[54] James K. Boyce and Léonce Ndikumana, *Capital flight from sub-Saharan African countries: Updated estimates, 1970–2010* (Political Economy Research Institute, University of Massachusetts, Amherst, MA, 2012).

[55] Rupert Smith, *The utility of force: The art of war in the modern world* (Penguin, London, 2006).

[56] Christopher Andrew and Vasili Mitrokhin, *The world was going our way: The KGB and the battle for the Third World* (Basic Books, New York, NY, 2005), pp. 455–81.

disintegrated, governments in Eastern Europe and Central Asia transformed the international arms market by selling off surplus Warsaw Pact arsenals at rock-bottom prices.

As a consequence of changes such as these, there now exists a connection between the types of crime characteristic of a diversity of African states, on the one hand, and high finance and big business in rich countries, on the other hand. Both are associated with the offshore world, used by multinational businesses to avoid taxes and to make the payments necessary to secure contracts as well as by crime bosses laundering their money.[57] In fact, a successful crime boss who has grown wealthy from a criminal trade in the global South, such as in drugs, may wish to access the facilities of a developed state on a permanent basis. This is because today's biggest fortunes are made less often from the manufacture or production of physical commodities than from the promise of future profits, obtained by shaping markets in such a way as to become a magnet for investors. This is possible only in an environment where confidence in the future is sustained by durable institutions, including organs of state, banks, and insurance companies, which permit the infinite generation of credit. African criminal enterprises—at least those that really count, in terms of either political influence or scale of profits—almost always have significant global linkages, in respect both to how they conduct illegal commercial activities and how they invest their money.

Centuries ago plunder and piracy were central to the formation of capitalism in Europe.[58] In more recent times, non-violent free trade has typically been confined to the centre of the capitalist system, with violence being more common on its geographical margins. Illegal markets governed by private violence raise huge sums for legal investment, and legitimate public violence and illegitimate private violence often blend into one another.[59] With regard to Africa today, this might imply that enterprise crime represents both a new form of governance and a new style of integration into the global economy.

State criminal enterprises and organized crime

Changes associated with financial globalization put African states under intense financial pressure from the late 1970s onward, to the extent that

---

[57] Ronen Palan, 'Crime, sovereignty, and the offshore world', in H. Richard Friman (ed.), *Crime and the global political economy* (Lynne Rienner, Boulder, CO and London, 2009), pp. 35–48.

[58] Janice E. Thompson, *Mercenaries, pirates, and sovereigns: State-building and extraterritorial violence in early modern Europe* (Princeton University Press, Princeton, NJ, 1994).

[59] Wolfgang Streeck, 'How will capitalism end?', *New Left Review*, 87 (2014), pp. 35–64.

many of them turned to the International Monetary Fund (IMF) for emergency loans. The response of the IMF and the World Bank was to require far-reaching economic reforms in the form of structural adjustment programmes. The expression 'Washington consensus' was coined to designate a range of liberal reforms on which Washington-based financial institutions were broadly agreed,[60] with the support of reformers in some other parts of the world. The hallmark of the Washington consensus was a deliberate strategy of loosening the control of states over national economies, including by eliminating some of the techniques by which states, or those who governed them, had previously extracted rents from economies that were often state-run, including by manipulating currencies that were overvalued. At more or less the same moment, Africa's dozens of one-party states found themselves under enormous pressure from within and without to liberalize their constitutions in order to allow multi-party elections.

Incumbent elites, struggling to preserve their grip on power, were desperate for new sources of income to replace their lost rents, and this became a powerful stimulus for the coming-together of politicians and state officials with some highly professional criminals. In the 1980s, a number of sovereign states came to rely on criminal networks in this way, taking the form of so-called 'fusion regimes',[61] and this decade witnessed the configuration of a nexus of crime and politics in some countries that has existed ever since. Strong evidence of this process emerged from Sierra Leone, where diamonds became a vital source of political finance,[62] but perhaps the most notorious case in which professional criminals became a source of funding for politicians is that of Guinea-Bissau. The evidence suggests that key members of Bissau's tiny elite sought illicit sources of funding at a time when established licit forms of accumulation were drying up as structural adjustment began to bite, and old forms of aid transfer weakened.[63] This was during the years when 'Nino' Vieira, the former president who had gone into exile after losing the civil war of 1998–9, was preparing a comeback that saw him regain the presidency in 2005. It appears to have been in this period that he made the acquaintance

---

[60] John Williamson, 'What Washington means by policy reform', in John Williamson (ed.), *Latin American adjustment: How much has happened?* (Institute for International Economics, Washington, DC, 1990), Ch. 2; Joseph E. Stiglitz, *Globalization and its discontents* (W. W. Norton, New York, NY, 2002).

[61] William Reno, 'Illicit commerce in peripheral states', in H. Richard Friman (ed.), *Crime and the global political economy* (Lynne Rienner, Boulder, CO and London, 2009), pp. 67–84.

[62] William Reno, *Corruption and state politics in Sierra Leone* (Cambridge University Press, Cambridge, 1995). On the Russian mafiya in Sierra Leone, see Friedman, *Red mafiya*, pp. 57–8.

[63] See the chapter on Guinea-Bissau in Walter Kemp, Mark Shaw, and Arthur Boutellis, *The Elephant in the room: How can peace operations deal with organized crime?* (International Peace Institute, New York, NY, 2013), pp. 17–31.

of some of the Latin American drug traders who were to enjoy the use of the country's military facilities when Vieira duly regained the presidency.[64]

National and international decision makers were aware of some of these tendencies and in several countries in the late 1990s and early 2000s they developed policies intended to counter illicit activities. These efforts, however, were largely unsuccessful, entailing further implications for the relationship between criminal and state actors. For example, the failure to stem the cocaine trade in West Africa at a relatively early stage led to a very rapid expansion of cocaine trafficking in Africa's coastal states, which in turn had a wider impact in the Sahel. In Mali, patterns of state protection for the illicit trade in cocaine (and wider patterns of corruption) comparable to the experience of Sierra Leone and Guinea-Bissau occurred in the context of a decentralization of power in the north. A 'hollowing out' of the Malian state precipitated the coup of 2012 and a prolonged crisis that has yet to be resolved.[65] In some cases, states have effectively lost or renounced their sovereign monopoly over the use of force and their ability to enforce contracts, which has then encouraged the emergence of a market for protection and contract enforcement.

It has been suggested that criminal violence in post-colonial societies typically 'does not so much repudiate the rule of law or the licit operations of the market as appropriate their forms.... Its perpetrators create parallel modes of production and profiteering', thus creating a possibility for 'vastly lucrative returns' in the zone of ambiguity between the presence and the absence of law.[66] This description fits such cases as the warlord militias of eastern DRC and various other armed groups, which often negotiate with multinational mining companies for the sale of minerals.[67] In this region, economic activity has been accompanied by violence for decades. If a strict definition is applied, we may even describe successive governments of the DRC as being in effect organized crime groups, with little claim to define

[64] Interview, former senior official of the *Partido Africano da Independência da Guiné e Cabo Verde*, Accra, 30 October 2013. This was confirmed in interviews in Bissau. See Mark Shaw, 'Drug trafficking in Guinea-Bissau, 1998–2014: The evolution of an elite protection network', *Journal of Modern African Studies* 53, 3 (2015) (forthcoming).

[65] Morten Bøås, 'Castles in the sand: Informal networks and power brokers in the northern Mali periphery', in Mats Utas (ed.), *African conflicts and informal power: Big men and networks* (Zed Books, London, 2012), pp. 119–34. The French intervention known as Operation Serval may have had only a limited impact on trafficking. See Global Initiative Against Transnational Organized Crime, 'Illicit trafficking and instability in Mali: Past, present and future' (Global Initiative Against Transnational Organized Crime, Geneva, January 2014).

[66] John L. Comaroff and Jean Comaroff, 'Law and disorder in the postcolony: An introduction', in Jean Comaroff and John L. Comaroff (eds), *Law and disorder in the postcolony* (University of Chicago Press, Chicago, IL, 2006), p. 5.

[67] On the DRC, see Ertuğrul Apakan, 'Letter dated 2009/11/23 from the Chairman of the Security Council Committee Established Pursuant to Resolution 1533 (2004) Concerning the Democratic Republic of the Congo...' (S/2009/603, United Nations, New York), <http://daccess-dds-ny.un.org/doc/UNDOC/GEN/N09/601/43/PDF/N0960143.pdf> (4 May 2015).

legality.[68] In some cases criminalized militias connected to illicit mining might have a high degree of support in specific communities, not least because they represent the main form of economic activity.

The organization of large-scale violence is not, however, leading to the emergence of new civic forms of authority that are able to call warlords or other controllers of military power to account in ways that might parallel the emergence of accountable states in European history.[69] In Nigeria, state corruption is so extensive that some of the large-scale theft of oil appears to be the work of state officials, or is at least facilitated by them.[70] As with other cases in which the object of criminal activity is to obtain minerals, oil theft requires the collusion of foreign businesses, including oil shippers and traders and others in the oil business.[71] In Kenya, large-scale professional drug traders have infiltrated politics to the extent of forming a distinct bloc in the national parliament.[72]

It is evident that crime develops in relation to the state and society with which it coexists. Thus, South Africa, with a deeply institutionalized state, is home to crime groups that bear a fairly close resemblance to what a European or US police officer might recognize as organized crime, and indeed some such groups in South Africa are of foreign origin, although almost all have developed close relations with some elements of the state. But in South Africa, too, networked criminal activity occurs over a wide spectrum, and some aspects of the development of organized crime in this comparatively advanced economy, such as a growing overlap between the state, business, and the criminal underworld in the last decade in particular, already exist elsewhere. A country with a less robust state, such as the DRC, thus may exhibit a different form of crime, but with some characteristics common to other countries on the continent.

It seems that in some African countries local groups and networks have developed into organized crime. Conversely, foreign groups have sometimes been attracted to the continent and have settled there. These two developments are often interconnected. In both cases the cause is the rapid emergence of new, global markets that law enforcement agencies have been unwilling to police, not least because African police forces seldom have the skills to respond effectively to complex crimes, and in many cases may be prevented politically from doing so.

---

[68] Thierry Vircoulon, personal correspondence, 17 November 2014.

[69] As argued famously by Charles Tilly, 'War making and state making as organized crime', in Peter B. Evans, Dietrich Rueschmeyer, and Theda Skocpol (eds), *Bringing the state back in* (Cambridge University Press, Cambridge, 1985), pp. 169–91.

[70] Christina Katsouris and Aaron Sayne, *Nigeria's criminal crude: International options to combat the export of stolen oil* (Chatham House, London, 2013).

[71] *Ibid.*

[72] Peter Gastrow, *Termites at work: Transnational organized crime and state erosion in Kenya* (International Peace Institute, New York, NY, 2011).

The emergence of protection markets

If we are to consider such a wide range of activities as we have mentioned as constituting the same phenomenon, we need to specify the features they have in common. Perhaps their most obvious shared feature is the existence of markets for protection and, hence, of economies of protection. In this section we develop a sketch of how we might conceptualize markets for protection, which we believe provides a useful tool for analysing new formations of politics and crime. The protection economy may be considered as the set of transactions entered into for the purpose of ensuring the facilitation, sustainability and safety of a set of activities, licit or illicit, undertaken by a criminal enterprise. In almost all cases, some elements of the state are involved, and indeed in African countries, the state (no matter how weak) is often the defining element in protection markets, either as a direct participant, facilitator, or regulator. In some cases, businesses may buy the political protection of one or more senior official and also pay the police directly, in effect turning the police into a privatized service. In other cases, a criminal enterprise may hire a legally constituted private security company. In still other cases, an unofficial militia, whose roots might be in organized crime or in a militarized insurgency, provides protection. In every case there exists a market for protection whose contours can be analysed. It might even be possible to establish market prices for protection in specific locations. New entrants into African markets, particularly if they are illicit ones, usually need to buy protection at very senior levels of the state in order to ensure their ability to operate without impediment and to avoid prosecution. Or, if they are operating on a largely regional level in a situation where the reach of the central authorities is limited, they may need to secure the alliance of the pre-eminent local powerbroker. The higher up the scale of political power new entrants go, the greater the transaction costs. Single payments to key powerbrokers are easier to manage than payments to multiple local gatekeepers and facilitators, and reduce the overall chance of an effective response from the state.

It must be emphasized that the protection economy is not limited to the provision of violence or the threat thereof but also includes the 'ability to manipulate and exploit social relationships'. In other words, criminal groups or networks 'accumulate and employ social capital. Therefore, they are specialists in violence and, at the same time, experts in social relationships: it means that they are capable of constructing a system grounded on constraint and of structuring a system of relationships based on variable forms of social consensus.'[73]

---

[73] Rocco Sciarrone, 'The business of the grey area: Relationships of complicity and collusion in the economic field', in Claudio La Camera (ed.), *The grey area of the Ndrangheta* (Aracne, Rome, 2014), p. 81.

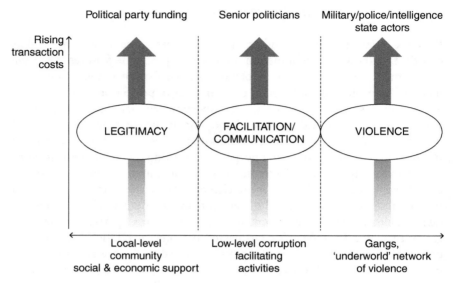

Fig. 5.1. The political economy of criminal enterprise protection.

Thus, transactions to secure the protection of illicit activities by criminal enterprises fall into three categories along a spectrum, as shown in Figure 5.1. The first set of transactions in a market for protection concerns the use or threat of violence, as recruiting people or networks with a capacity for violence is perhaps the most obvious way of ensuring protection. This is particularly so when moving illegal goods through contested territory. The actors involved range from street thugs to agents of the state such as military, police, or intelligence units. In the latter case, buying protection from state security institutions has important implications, as it leads to internal competition within the security apparatus and strengthens some parts over others.

An excellent example is provided by the role of the Zimbabwean military and intelligence service in diamond mining.[74] In some cases, when illicit accumulation becomes central to the existence of security institutions, in a state with a declining ability to raise the taxes with which to fund them, security actors become resistant to cutting themselves off from these sources. This process seems well under way in Zimbabwe, where the military increasingly relies on illicit sources of funds and is thus less responsive to calls from political leadership to withdraw from them.[75]

---

[74] Global Witness, *Financing a parallel government? The involvement of the secret police and military in Zimbabwe's diamond, cotton and property sectors* (Global Witness, London, 2012).

[75] In a recent example, senior military commanders have resisted withdrawing from a large game concession they had seized, despite a direct request from President Mugabe for them to do so. Interviews, civil society representatives, Harare, May 2014.

It has been suggested that what is emerging in such states is a bargain between political and security/military elites: incumbent politicians close their eyes to the illicit activities that the security establishment uses to fund itself, while the security establishment agrees to limit its political interventions in the shape of coups and the like.[76] While this may be a sweeping statement, the general point is that patterns of illicit accumulation by the military and the security establishment may have a more decisive long-term impact on civil–military and civil–security relations in African countries than is currently understood. The role that different African intelligence services play in respect of the nexus between government, business, and criminal relationships is in urgent need of analysis.

The second set of transactions in a market for protection is in the field of facilitation and communication. A criminal entrepreneur seeking protection may enter into a market transaction for services in this field because corrupting elements of the state in order to ensure the facilitation of illicit activities is a time-honoured way for people involved in illicit activities to secure protection. Corruption for this purpose may extend from low-level pay-offs of police constables and customs officers to the bribery of senior politicians. At the senior level, the relationship between the political leadership and criminal enterprises is often more complex than may be recognized in much of the literature concerning 'state capture'. It may not require a politician to engage directly in a criminal enterprise, but simply to provide the space for such activities to occur in return for payment. Importantly too, a transaction may involve communicating those connections to others. For example, in an important Southern African country that we prefer not to name, a particular private business venture (which could equally be labelled in relation to some of its activities as a criminal enterprise) usually invites the president to its premises once a week for drinks and entertainment.[77] The presidential motorcade arrives and things proceed. At the same time, other guests or business partners are invited, not to meet the president but to see that he is present. It is a kind of indirect transaction to ensure space or protection for the criminal enterprise.[78]

The third set of transactions that must be taken into account concerns legitimacy. Criminal entrepreneurs may seek legitimacy for their activities by measures extending from the provision of low-level social and economic support to families and communities in order to ensure an ability to operate locally, right up to political party funding. If so, an important implication is

---

[76] Thierry Vircoulon, 'International Crisis Group presentation to the Development Dialogue' (The Hague, International Crisis Group, 9 April 2014).

[77] Personal communication, investigative journalists working on the story, April 2014.

[78] Important work conducted outside of Africa is helpful to understanding these forms of communication and facilitation. See Diego Gambetta, *Codes of the underworld: How criminals communicate* (Princeton University Press, Princeton, NJ, 2011).

that an investment in investigative journalism or civil society responsiveness may increase the costs of political facilitation or communication by exposing such links to public scrutiny. In Figure 5.1, as one moves up the vertical axis, transaction costs increase, as does the level of engagement with the state. As suggested here, if a criminal group finds it necessary to intervene at the local or community level (for example, to secure local legitimacy), this may provide an incentive for local communities themselves to engage in illicit activities.

We believe that studying the market for protection constitutes a simple but effective analytical tool for four reasons. First, it can be applied to almost all activities in a diverse range of African states and includes the role of state actors. It therefore has a wide ambit, providing many points of entry for journalists or other investigators. Second, it takes into account the role of diverse internal and external actors, and seeks to understand the often complex nature of the interface between them, including the role of state and security institutions as key gatekeepers for some forms of criminal activity. Third, analytical work on the protection economy can provide price indications for protection as an essential good or commodity in its own right. Fourth, it means that if the price for protection can be raised, it may improve the prospects for changing the calculus for criminal enterprises.

Organized crime and state formation

The development of protection economies is a much more complex arrangement than the seeking of rents by political or security elites to allow illegal activities. Any cogent analysis requires taking into account the totality of any given network and the associated transactions for protection need to be analysed with due regard for the political, economic and social context in which they occur. It is arguable that some such networks could in time become stable and develop an ability to reproduce themselves, making them possible precursors of state formations of the future.[79] This brings to mind a well-known argument made by the sociologist Charles Tilly, who, describing the precursors of Europe's modern states in early modern times, famously described how war making came to require larger and more efficient armies in an age when wars were generally associated with the urge to capture treasure, booty, and territory from a rival. The necessity to organize larger, better-armed, and more effective armies in turn created a need for princes to acquire a regular income in the form of taxation, which then required a higher degree of bureaucratic efficiency than had previously existed. This created a

---

[79] Volkov, *Violent entrepreneurs.*

self-reinforcing logic that drove state development. In his own formulation, 'war made the state and the state made war'.[80]

However, the differences between twenty-first century Africa and early modern Europe are more striking than the similarities. Every major European country had a long tradition of centralized government accompanied by some degree of bureaucratic capacity even before the military developments associated with the age of gunpowder. In some countries, such as England, medieval kings had developed a quite extensive machinery of government and taxation. It is true that some African countries, such as Rwanda, also have a history of centralized government that makes a comparison with early modern Europe viable, and it is possible that in such cases the type of militarized and systematic plunder that the Rwandan government has sponsored in DRC could indeed lead over time to the formation of a stronger and more formidable Rwandan state. But in the majority of cases this seems unlikely as the logic of war and the financing of war are leading not to the development of more extensive and better organized civil services, but rather to an informalization of power whereby rulers prefer personal client systems to impersonal bureaucracies. In other words, capturing the resource flows generated or conveyed by organized crime is leading to the formation of what have memorably been called 'successful failed states'.[81]

Thus, the speculation that organized crime "buys power" in a simple transactional arrangement—with the implication that this may destroy certain states in Africa, as sometimes suggested by the United Nations[82]—is open to doubt. Whether the presence of organized crime is a stimulus to violent conflict seems to vary from case to case, according to whether the resulting flows of money and influence are retained by the head of state or the group in power (for example, in Zimbabwe) or whether they are captured by provincial warlords or militias, as in Mali and Libya.

Conclusion

How then can we answer the question posed by the title of this article? Organized crime exists in Africa, but it is increasingly taking a form that

---

[80] Charles Tilly, *The formation of national states in Western Europe* (Princeton University Press, Princeton, NJ, 1975), pp. 299–300.
[81] Ricardo Soares de Oliveira, *Oil and politics in the Gulf of Guinea* (Hurst and Co., London, 2007), pp. 20–1. The phrase 'successful failed state' seems to have been invented by Gérard Prunier and Rachel Gisselquist.
[82] United Nations Office on Drugs and Crime, 'Organized crime and its threat to security: Tackling a disturbing consequence of drug control' (Commission on Narcotic Drugs, 11–20 March 2008, Vienna; and Commission on Crime Prevention, 16–24 April 2009, Vienna), p. 4.

disqualifies the term 'organized crime', which generally does not take into account the degree to which criminal activities constitute a nexus between a fluid state and political, economic, and social actors. In our view these interactions are themselves redefining the nature of the state,[83] and the terminology of organized crime seems inappropriate to signify this, originating as this vocabulary does in a more limited Western discussion of law breaking. The notion of criminal enterprises captures more accurately (although still imperfectly) a set of interactions between key members of elites in a specific location. It implies a focus on the nexus of exchanges at the very heights of the state, society, and economy, rather than a narrower discussion around organized gangs in any African city engaged in more minor crimes like car theft or low-level fraud. The latter may be organized crime, and indeed often has some lower-level linkage to official actors, but it is not an enterprise we consider to be at the heart of the changing nature of the African state. The role of the state in a specific criminal enterprise and the degree to which resources for the public good are syphoned off into private hands or to meet private objectives are defining aspects of enterprise crime. Enterprise crime therefore often has elements of corruption, another term that does scant justice to the complex economic, political, and social transactions involved.

Understanding the meaning in African contexts of the type of large-scale, political-criminal entrepreneurship that we have evoked will increasingly drive both internal and external policy discussions, as these become directed to finding remedies. What is clear, given the complex phenomenon that we have outlined, is that law enforcement interventions alone will do little to make a difference. A discussion is emerging as to how to develop more effective political responses in this sector, the best example being the high-profile West African Commission on Drugs, but also how initiatives aimed at development can have greater impact on high-level criminality.

While there is still a long way to go on this score, understanding in detail the transaction costs of protection is a key analytical tool that can aid policy makers to understand where development interventions may take place and how they may be aligned with other interventions in a more strategic way than occurs at present. In this regard, the key function of development interventions must be to change the incentive structures that make these transactions possible. Indeed, this may be all that development interventions are able to do.

As we have tried to demonstrate, markets for protection are the nexus between business, crime, and politics. The existence of a high-level agreement

---

[83] For recent observations along lines similar to these, see Louise I. Shelley, *Dirty entanglements: Corruption, crime, and terrorism* (Cambridge University Press, New York, NY, 2014); and Francesco Strazzari, 'Captured or capturing? Narcotics and political instability along the "African route" to Europe', *European Review of Organised Crime* 1, 2 (2014), pp. 5–34.

on protection that draws in actors from all three sectors—business, crime, politics—at the apex of societies is often connected to lower-level entrepreneurs of violence, who constitute the foot soldiers of protection enforcers. Analysis of protection economies, as well as helping us trace the contours of the politics/ business/crime nexus in individual countries and regions, may also have the advantage of allowing comparison between different African cases.

Acknowledgment

Published in *African Affairs*, 114, 457 (2015), p. 505–528. This article is a fusion of two unpublished workshop papers, one on changes in the global context, by Stephen Ellis, and another on protection economies, by Mark Shaw. The authors are grateful to the Global Initiative Against Transnational Organized Crime and the Rosa Luxemburg Foundation for funding workshops on this issue in Cape Town on 27–28 March (a report is published at http://www.global initiative.net/unholy-alliances-organized-crime-in-southern-africa) and 13–14 November 2014. This work is based on research supported by the South African Research Chairs Initiative of the Department of Science and Technology and National Research Foundation of South Africa (Grant No. 47303). Any opinion, finding or conclusion, or recommendation expressed in this material is that of the authors and the NRF does not accept any liability in this regard. The authors are grateful for comments from Elrena van der Spuy, and from two anonymous reviewers and the editors of *African Affairs*.

Part II

The Political Economy of Development

Part II

The Political Economy of Development

6

An Introduction to the Political Economy of Development

Lindsay Whitfield

POLITICAL INDEPENDENCE CREATED EXPECTATIONS in Africa that it would lead to more self-sustaining economies, more economic opportunities for African entrepreneurs, and improvements in the general welfare of the population through public investments in health, education, and infrastructure. These expectations were buttressed by dominant ideas in the field of development economics after World War II that newly independent countries should pursue industrialization through national planning, in order to change the structure of their economies and achieve welfare improvements. Governments typically pursued import-substitution industrialization strategies, in which the new manufacturing firms, often set up by the state, focused on production for the domestic market to reduce reliance on foreign imports.

These attempts at state-led industrialization largely failed, but there were considerable differences across countries. Manufacturing in Africa grew by nearly 7 percent per year between 1960 and 1980, from a low base, but it was concentrated in textiles and food processing and in a small number of countries.[1] In many countries, overvalued exchange rates and producer prices set by marketing boards discouraged the production of agricultural exports, as did the rise of black markets and smuggling, and some governments' neglect of the need to improve the productivity of peasant farming.[2] This led to a decline in exports. At the same time, governments increasingly turned to foreign loans in order to finance the imported equipment and technology that the new firms and

---

[1] Frederick Cooper, *Africa Since 1940: The Past of the Present* (Cambridge, Cambridge University Press, 2002), p. 100.

[2] On Tanzania, see Deborah Fahy Bryceson, 'Peasant Commodity Production in Post-Colonial Tanzania', *African Affairs* 81, 325 (1982), pp. 547–67; On Ghana and Sierra Leone, see Jeff Haynes, Trevor Parfitt, and Stephen Riley, 'Debt in Sub-Saharan Africa: The Local Politics of Stabilisation', *African Affairs* 86, 344 (1987), pp. 343–66.

mechanized farms required. The combined effect of these trends meant that by the early 1980s most African governments were in a state of economic crisis, saddled with large trade and budget deficits as well as debt repayments that they could not meet. Facing insolvency, they turned to the International Monetary Fund (IMF). The structural adjustment programmes prescribed by the IMF and the World Bank and adopted by African governments led to deindustrialization and decades of austerity, which resulted in falling private and public investment and dependence on Western aid to shore up budget deficits.

However, in the mid-2000s the pendulum swung the other way. China's rapid industrialization drove up global commodity prices, which had fallen gradually from the 1950s and then rapidly after 1975.[3] The commodity price boom led to a decade of higher growth in many African countries, and countries began accessing international capital markets, boosted by low interest rates and a high demand for African government bonds. In a parallel development, China's rise as the second largest economy in the world meant that it offered African countries new sources of trade, foreign direct investment, and official aid. When China's export-driven industrialization push slowed in the mid-2010s, most commodity prices fell and so did the growth of several African economies: government revenue and foreign exchange earnings shrunk and the borrowing costs on international capital markets surged as investors worried about growing budget deficits and the ability of African economies to weather the growing financial storm. Thus, countries such as Ghana, Angola, and Mozambique had to seek bailouts from the IMF.

Macroeconomic problems related to exchange rates and trade deficits are central to the political economy of development in Africa, as are external shocks from changes in the global economy. While such factors affect all countries, including southern European ones, they are particularly acute for most African countries due the narrower and more shallow structure of their economies. Despite the growth turnaround in the 1990s and 2000s, there was limited structural change of African economies. Although many of the continent's economic systems are more robust now than they were in the 1980s, the extensive developments in the service sectors such as telecommunications and banking have not helped countries overcome foreign exchange constraints if they are still dependent on a small number of natural resource exports and must import manufactured goods and basic food products. Tellingly, it is typically only those countries that managed to undertake greater structural change by developing new export sectors and by increasing production for the domestic market that have been able to withstand the downturn.

This experience led to the resurgence of arguments that African countries required economic transformation in order to generate self-sustaining growth

---

[3] Masuma Farooki and Raphael Kaplinsky, *The Impact of China on Global Commodity Prices: The Global Reshaping of the Resource Sector* (Routledge, London, 2012).

and rising incomes, which in some sense echo the debates of the early post-independence period.[4] This resurgence took place against the backdrop of two decades of international and national policy agendas focused on the provision of social services, largely funded by official development assistance.[5] The focus on human development goals, while important, had the negative effect of shifting attention away from the issue of how to catalyse the economic transformation required to make such goals achievable in the absence of foreign aid. Growing recognition of this fact after 2010 led increasingly to a reorientation of donor and government priorities in which the focus on poverty reduction was replaced with one on economic transformation and industrial policy.

The return of industrial policy to national and international agendas and debates has been accompanied by discussions of what kinds of politics are necessary to support industrial policy, and whether this kind of politics can be found in African countries.[6] These discussions regarding the present opportunities for economic transformation contained within them a re-evaluation of African countries' past economic performance. The evolution in thinking regarding these contentious issues is demonstrated in this chapter through a review of the main arguments and disagreements in the literature since the 1970s. The *African Affairs* articles included in this volume demonstrate that in some ways debates have come full circle, although how these debates have played out has been very different this time around.

DEBATING THE CAUSES OF ECONOMIC DECLINE

The ultimate causes of Africa's economic decline from the mid-1970s and stagnation until the mid-1990s has been the subject of much debate, with arguments usually emphasizing either external (commodity prices, exploitative trade deals) or internal (poor governance, political instability) factors. The debates start by analysing the nature of the colonial economies that newly independent governments inherited. Most of them depended on a small basket of primary commodity exports and the importation of manufactured goods, because they had been developed to meet the economic needs of the colonial metropole. The settler economies in East and Southern Africa had large-scale capitalist agricultural production, run mostly by white farmers,

---

[4] K. Y. Amoako, 'Transforming Africa—Start Now, We Can't Wait', *African Business* 45, 377 (2011), pp. 24–7; UNCTAD, *Economic Development in Africa Report 2012: Structural Transformation and Sustainable Development in Africa* (UN, New York, 2012).

[5] Graham Harrison, 'The Africanization of poverty: A retrospective on "Make Poverty History"', *African Affairs* 109, 436 (2010), pp. 391–408.

[6] Lindsay Whitfield, Ole Therkildsen, Lars Buur, and Anne Mette Kjær, *The Politics of African Industrial Policy: A Comparative Perspective* (Cambridge University Press, Cambridge, 2015).

while in West Africa food production remained dominated by smallholder farmers and was largely inadequate to meet the needs of the increasingly urbanized population. The "commanding heights" of African economies were still controlled by Europeans, and the black African capitalist class was small and weak, partly as a result of discriminatory colonial policies and partly as a result of their inability to compete against large European companies. Import-substitution industrialization strategies were intended to reduce the vulnerabilities of these colonial economic structures. To fund such strategies, governments relied on revenue from taxes on imports and exports, as well as state monopolies on the external marketing of agricultural exports through marketing boards that had been set up during the colonial period.

The industrialization drive would have worked, argued scholars who emphasized the external causes of the economic crisis, if African countries' had not faced a continuous decline in their terms of trade (except for the blip in the early 1970s), compounded by the global oil price hikes in 1973–4 and 1979. In the face of a shortage of foreign exchange, most governments enacted import licensing and exchange controls, rather than devalue their currencies. They also tried to reduce expenses while continuing politically necessary expenditures, which required taking foreign commercial and official loans. Against this backdrop, the rise of US interest rates in 1979 as part of the US government's domestic economic strategy led to higher debt repayments[7] at the same time that the prices of African exports were falling, and further borrowing to rollover debt was not possible as international capital was sucked into the US. In turn, this rendered many African economies untenable and the output produced by locally owned farms and firms (the continent's gross national product) fell by 20 percent between 1976 and 1986.[8] One after another African governments were unable to meet their debt payments.[9] For example, Zambia experienced a drastic change in its terms of trade (which effectively measures the purchasing power of the country's exports against its imports), which dropped by 70 percent between 1974 and 1985.[10] This collapse was underpinned by the falling price of copper (which accounted for 90 percent of Zambia's exports) and rising prices of imports, which led to a fall in government revenue and greater budget deficits.[11]

---

[7] Rising nominal interest rates in the US, and then the UK and Germany, caused an increase in the cost of borrowing, especially as African countries took loans on the international capital market at *variable* interest rates. See Paul Mosley, John Toye, and Jane Harrigan, *Aid and Power*, volume 1 (Routledge, London, 1985), pp. 4–8.

[8] Cooper, *Africa Since 1940*, p. 106.

[9] They were not alone, as most developing countries were caught in the same situation, but developing countries that had diversified their exports and moved into manufactured exports recovered rather quickly, while commodity-exporting countries in Africa and Latin America were caught in a trap that they could not get out of.

[10] Kenneth Good, 'The Reproduction of Weakness in the State and Agriculture: Zambian Experience', *African Affairs* 85, 339 (1986), pp. 239–56, p. 252.

[11] Jürgen Wulf, 'Zambia Under the IMF Regime', *African Affairs* 87, 349 (1988), pp. 579–94, p. 579.

Researchers who emphasize the external causes of Africa's economic crisis argued that the fundamental problem lay in the structure of global capitalism and that reshaping African economies could only occur in the context of restructuring the international economic order. This argument was linked to the New International Economic Order initiative that was put on the agenda of the United Nations in 1974 by less-developed countries, which focused on generating higher prices for primary commodities as well as support in industrializing their economies. More specifically, it emphasized that developing country economies had been co-produced[12] through global capitalism and colonialism and that in light of global economic imbalances, it was not the sole responsibility of former colonial states to adjust to the economies of industrialized countries.

On the other side of the debate, scholars argued that bad domestic policies were the main cause of Africa's economic crisis. They pointed to the tendency of governments to manipulate their economies to protect urban consumers from economic downturn by keeping the price of food low, in the process providing disincentives for the agricultural sector to increase production, and to provide insufficient investment to fund industry and public sector activities. Furthermore, they argued that these policies were driven by the political calculations and personal benefits accruing to ruling political elites, which led them to keep in place policies that were clearly detrimental to their economies and populations.[13] This approach is exemplified in the work of Robert Bates, who argued that state interventions created rents (income), which generated rent-seeking by those who sought to capture these resources. This in turn provided government officials with power to buy political support—often from a coalition of urban-based interest groups—in exchange for rents.[14] Arguments constructed in this way typically drew on the New Political Economy approach, which assumes the state is an arena where politicians and bureaucrats are motivated by, and pursue, rational maximizing self-interest, operating under the influence of interest groups in society, and that all rents and rent-seeking behaviour diverts resources away from their most efficient use and thus have negative economic impacts.[15]

From the late 1970s onwards, an impasse ensued between arguments about the internal and external causes of African economic decline. Upon reflection, it

[12] Fredrick Cooper's article in this volume makes this argument about African economies being co-produced, and Crawford Young's article in this volume mentions the role of the New International Economic Order.

[13] For example, see Francis Teal, 'Domestic Policies, External Constraints and Economic Development in Nigeria since 1950', *African Affairs* 87, 346 (1988), pp. 69–81.

[14] Robert Bates, *Markets and States in Tropical Africa* (University of California Press, Berkeley, CA, 1981).

[15] The New Political Economy approach applied the assumptions of neoclassical economics to the study of the state. For an overview, see Mosley, Toye, and Harrigan, *Aid and Power*, pp. 13–25.

is clear that both sides of the debate contain an element of truth, but also miss some important factors. The external constraints were real and affected all developing countries, and import-substitution industrialization was driven by macroeconomic necessity. Nevertheless, African politicians inherited the accumulated funds from state marketing boards and used them to fund public investments as well as party political activities and various forms of patronage to constituencies within their ruling coalition. As a result, argued Frederick Cooper, politics became a contest among political elites to control the allocation of public revenues generated from exports and imports, not just for themselves but also for their political constituencies.[16] Increasing claims on government revenues began to outpace declining earnings from marketing boards, and the need to regulate foreign exchange in light of falling export revenue led to various state controls which were not necessarily created in order to extract political gains from rent-seeking, but often came to be used that way.[17]

This process was seen to play out more extremely in "rentier states": countries where governments are in control of massive revenues derived from exporting large volumes of oil, gas, and minerals. These countries, such as Angola, Chad, Equatorial Guinea, and Nigeria, face a particular set of challenges that are collectively referred to as the resource curse.[18] The resource curse literature emphasizes two processes that cause poor economic performance in resource-rich countries. On the economic side, these countries are not able to pursue export-led growth successfully because the sale of oil abroad leads to exchange rate appreciation, which tends to render agricultural and manufacturing export sectors uncompetitive. On the political side, governments become less accountable to their citizens because they gain most of their revenues from oil exports and so are freed from the need to levy domestic taxes. Furthermore, the presence of large resource revenues controlled by the state encourages the misuse and misallocation of resources.

While these arguments focus on political clientelism and corruption, other scholars emphasizing internal factors have pointed to an entirely different set of issues. They argue that the generally poor performance of import-substitution industrialization strategies across African countries, compared to other

---

[16] Cooper, *Africa Since 1940*.

[17] Gavin Williams, 'Why Structural Adjustment is Necessary and Why it Doesn't Work', *Review of African Political Economy* 60 (1994), pp. 214–25.

[18] Jedrzej George Frynas, 'Corporate and State Responses to Anti-Oil Protests in the Niger Delta', *African Affairs* 100, 398 (2001), pp. 27–54; Philippe Le Billon, 'Angola's Political Economy of War', *African Affairs* 100, 398 (2001), pp. 55–80; Scott Pegg, 'Can Policy Intervention Beat the Resource Curse? Evidence from the Chad-Cameroon Pipeline Project', *African Affairs* 105, 418 (2006), pp. 1–25; Jedrzej George Frynas, 'The oil boom in Equatorial Guinea', *African Affairs* 103, 413 (2004), pp. 527–46; Luke A. Patey, 'Crude Days Ahead? Oil and the Resource Curse in Sudan', *African Affairs* 109, 437 (2010), pp. 617–36; Dominik Kopiński, Andrzej Polus, and Wojciech Tycholiz, 'Resource Curse or Resource Disease? Oil in Ghana', *African Affairs* 112, 449 (2013), pp. 583–601.

developing country regions, was due to poor management within domestic firms, whether private or state-owned, and their failure to build technological capabilities.[19] This is because industrialization requires not only hard technology and the foreign exchange to pay for it, but also soft technology such as managerial and organizational capabilities that can only be learned through experience. African governments invested capital, but did not usually invest in acquiring organizational capabilities to run state-owned factories efficiently or in supporting private firms to do so.

Furthermore, African countries started at a disadvantage due to the nature of their colonial encounters. Alice Amsden shows that developing countries that were the most successful in their industrialization drives after World War II were those countries that had manufacturing experience, and African countries scored particularly low on that account.[20] John Iliffe and Paul Kennedy, among others, have shown how early capitalist developments that occurred through the interactions of farmers and merchants with the global economy were subsequently obstructed by colonial policies.[21] As a result, black African capitalists had limited technological capabilities and managerial experience at independence, and they typically did not play a significant role in key exporting sectors, which were dominated by peasant-production and state- or foreign-controlled companies. The small and weak black African capitalist class affected the kinds of strategies that post-independence ruling political elites pursued.[22] This situation led some governments to rely on foreign firms or to create state-owned firms. In others, it led governments to pursue "Africanization" policies, such as in Nigeria.[23] On average, however, government industrialization strategies did not support local private firms, and in some cases actively marginalized or repressed them, especially those who were not linked to the political elites and thus seen as a potential political threat.[24] In Tanzania and Uganda, governments also expropriated the companies of East African Asian capitalists.

---

[19] Frances Stewart, Sanjaya Lall, and Samuel Wangwe (eds), *Alternative Development Strategies in Sub-Saharan Africa* (Macmillan, London, 1992).

[20] Alice Amsden, *The Rise of the Rest: Challenges to the West from Late-Industrializing Economies* (Oxford University Press, Oxford, 2001), pp. 15–16; Alice Amsden, 'The Wild Ones: Industrial Policies in the Developing World', in Narcís Serra and Joseph Stiglitz (eds), *The Washington Consensus Reconsidered: Towards a New Global Governance* (Oxford University Press, Oxford, 2008), pp. 95–118.

[21] John Iliffe, *The Emergence of African Capitalism* (Macmillan Press, London, 1983); Paul Kennedy, *African Capitalism: The Struggle for Ascendancy* (Cambridge University Press, Cambridge, 1988).

[22] Whitfield et al., *The Politics of African Industrial Policy*.

[23] Chibuzo Ogbuagu, 'The Nigerian Indigenization Policy: Nationalism or Pragmatism?', *African Affairs* 82, 327 (1983), pp. 241–66.

[24] See the edited volumes by Bruce Berman and Colin Leys (eds), *African Capitalists in African Development* (Lynne Rienner, London, 1994);Paul Lubeck (ed.), *The African Bourgeoisie: Capitalist Development in Nigeria, Kenya, and the Ivory Coast* (Lynne Rienner, Boulder, CO, 1987).

THE IMPACTS OF STRUCTURAL ADJUSTMENT
AND GOOD GOVERNANCE

In the debate about external and internal causes of economic decline, the proponents of the New Political Economy school can be said to have exerted a greater influence over global policymakers. Their ideas fed into the IMF and World Bank structural adjustment programmes, and as a result African economies were forced to adjust to the new global economic reality.[25] Structural adjustment reforms entailed currency devaluations and the introduction of floating exchange rates in order to reduce the reliance of imports and boost exports. In addition, they required trade liberalization, the elimination of foreign exchange controls, and a reduction in budget deficits in order to reduce the supply of money circulating in the economy and thus combat the inflation that would be generated by devaluation. The main mechanisms used to reduce budget deficits were the privatization of state-owned enterprises and a reduction of the public sector payroll. It is worth nothing that these are the same adjustment conditions that the IMF recommends today, for example in Ghana's IMF bailout signed in 2015.

African governments implemented just enough of the prescribed reforms to get access to foreign exchange, concessional lending, and donor grants to pay for imports and to cushion the effects of austerity, while limiting the political costs of adjustment and arguing against the economic merits of one-size-fits-all conditionality.[26] In the 1990s, 'good governance' political conditions were added to loans from the World Bank and other donors, which emphasized that democratization and accountability reforms were necessary for the structural adjustment agenda to be successful. These conditions were inspired by the argument that state interventions make markets inefficient but are difficult to remove because they are sustained by rent-seeking and corruption, which in turn are maintained because they benefit a small group of unaccountable political elites (see Chapter 2). Political reforms, it was thought, would empower the majority to make leaders accountable.[27]

A debate ensued in African studies as to whether structural adjustment reforms were necessary. One side argued that some aspects of structural adjustment were essential, because they helped to achieve macroeconomic

---

[25] Michael Hodd, 'Africa, the IMF and the World Bank', *African Affairs* 86, 344 (1987), pp. 331–42, p. 332.

[26] Paul Mosley, 'The Politics of Economic Liberalization: USAID and the World Bank in Kenya, 1980–84', *African Affairs* 85, 338 (1986), pp. 107–19; Lindsay Whitfield (ed.), *The Politics of Aid: African Strategies for Dealing with Donors* (Oxford University Press, Oxford, 2009).

[27] Mushtaq Khan, 'Growth and Governance: History, Ideology and Methods of Proof', in Akbar Noman, Kwesi Botchwey, Howard Stein, and Joseph Stiglitz (eds), *Good Growth and Governance in Africa: Rethinking Development Strategies* (Oxford University Press, Oxford, 2012), pp. 51–79.

stability through increasing the production of traditional commodity exports and making them more competitive on world markets, and removed types of state intervention that in practice turned out to be more harmful than helpful for economic development.[28] But it was also argued that Western countries should provide African countries with additional finance to fund social services in order to reduce the negative impact of adjustment on the poorest sections of society.[29] Another critique of structural adjustment was that it was too ideologically pro-market, and prevented state interventions that would help local firms and farms to become competitive and increase productivity in the new liberalized environment. The result, as Howard Stein pointed out, was deindustrialization.[30] At the same time, Stefano Ponte and Peter Gibbon have shown that the dismantling of state marketing boards for export crops led to a decline in their quality and the takeover of marketing by multinational corporations.[31]

The debate continued into the 2000s. Steven Radelet began a discourse on Emerging African Economies by showing that 17 African countries experienced continuous growth from the mid-1990s to the end of the 2000s as a result of structural adjustment and good governance reforms.[32] But other economists such as Ernest Aryeetey and John Page pointed out that this growth was driven by increases in international commodity prices, new discoveries of natural resources, and government spending fuelled by foreign aid.[33] Economic liberalization had led to the allocation of resources to, and foreign direct investment in, sectors in which African countries already had or could quickly create competitive advantages. Thus, structural adjustment reforms provided a short-term solution to a longer term problem, and by the twenty-first century, most African countries had economies that closely resembled the ones inherited at independence.

What structural adjustment and the good governance reforms did accomplish was to reignite the process of primitive accumulation, which had stalled after the economic crisis in the 1970s. The privatization of state assets, in many cases ending state monopolies and reducing economic controls, opened up new opportunities that led to accumulation outside the state. Political elites presiding over liberalization reforms often benefited significantly from them.

---

[28] Williams, 'Why Structural Adjustment is Necessary'.

[29] Giovanni Andrea Cornia, Richard Jolly, and Francis Stewart (eds), *Adjustment with a Human Face* (Oxford University Press, Oxford, 1987), two volumes.

[30] Howard Stein (ed.), *Asian Industrialization and Africa: Studies in Policy Alternatives to Structural Adjustment* (St Martin's Press, New York, 1995).

[31] Peter Gibbon and Stefano Ponte, *Trading Down: Africa, Value Chains and the Global Economy* (Temple University Press, Berkeley, CA, 2005).

[32] Steven Radelet, *Emerging Africa: How 17 Countries are Leading the Way* (Center for Global Development, Washington, DC, 2010).

[33] See the special issue of the *Journal of African Economies* 21, African Economic Research Consortium (AERC) Supplement 2.

A new generation of domestic capitalists emerged but still firmly within the ruling coalition, as primitive accumulation occurred based on political connections that were used to access privatized assets, secure state contracts, and so on. There were also now opportunities for accumulation that were not tied solely to the state, especially in new export sectors and in sectors not highly dependent on the state. The double transition of economic and political liberalization created two simultaneous imperatives for ruling political elites (see Chapter 10). They needed more financing to build and maintain their ruling coalitions in the context of multiparty elections, even for dominant parties that won elections by a wide margin such as in Tanzania. Previous strategies of reliance on state resources were no longer sufficient due to the economic reforms, so ruling political elites sought financing from the private sector and by using their position in public office to start or expand new businesses. In a subset of African countries, the need for more political financing was met through party-owned businesses, which provided an independent base for party funding as well as economic influence.

A small group of countries have been considered outliers to Africa's general economic trend: Botswana, Mauritius, and South Africa. Botswana was seen as a star economic performer as it experienced sustained economic growth since independence, did not have external debt problems leading to structural adjustment reforms, and its state was seen to have managed its natural resources without falling into the resource curse. Therefore, some scholars claimed it to be a developmental state. Ellen Hillbom challenged this view, arguing that Botswana was similar to other African countries, sparking a debate in the pages of *African Affairs*.[34] For her part, Hillbom emphasized the fact that Botswana's economy remained dependent on natural resource exports and had not developed industry or agricultural production. In other words, rather than building a more diversified economy, the government had simply done a better job of managing the distribution of export revenues than other African countries.

South Africa is also usually seen as exceptional. This is because it was successful in using state interventions to build competitive industries in a few sectors during the apartheid era, but faces challenges in the post-apartheid period of deracializing the capitalist sector by promoting a black capitalist class and redressing racial imbalances in the labour market.[35] However,

---

[34] Ellen Hillbom, 'Botswana: A Development-Oriented Gate-Keeping State', *African Affairs* 111, 442 (2011), pp. 67–89; Ian Taylor, 'Botswana as a "Development-Oriented Gate-Keeping State": A Response', *African Affairs* 111, 444 (2012), pp. 466–67; Ellen Hillbom, 'Botswana: A Development-Oriented Gate-Keeping State—A Reply to Ian Taylor', *African Affairs* 111, 444 (2012), pp. 477–82.

[35] Nimrod Zalk, 'South African Post-Apartheid Policies Towards Industrialization: Tentative Implications for Other African Countries', in Akbar Noman, Kwesi Botchwey, Howard Stein,

despite its left-wing credentials the African National Congress (ANC) government pursued its own version of structural adjustment starting in 1996, in which trade and financial liberalization were the key pillars of the government's economic strategy. This move was highly controversial and led to a fierce and prolonged debate about the motivations for, and consequences of, the policy. In line with some of the points made in this chapter, an important recent contribution by Shaukat Ansari argues that the ANC's policy platform generated fewer benefits than other strategies such as developing a stronger industrial sector. One reason for this is that it created an overvalued exchange rate that benefited a small number of well-placed players—including a coalition of international investors, businesses in mining and financial services, and ruling political elites—by giving them access to cheap foreign credit with which to fund their activities.[36]

Mauritius, on the other hand, has achieved economic transformation, moving from sugar exports to garments to tourism and finance, as shown in Deborah Bräutigam's article included in this volume (Chapter 8). But this small Indian Ocean island with a tiny population only required one dynamic export sector at a time in order to drive up the national wage and standard of living. From this perspective, the "Mauritius miracle" seems less exceptional, but rather faced a less daunting set of economic challenges.

AFRICAN ECONOMIC TRANSFORMATION IN THE TWENTY-FIRST CENTURY

By 2010, it was clear that the structural adjustment and good governance reforms had led to disappointing results in terms of increasing employment and rising incomes. Instead, many countries had large informal economies, weak agriculture and dependence on food imports, few new export sectors, and continued vulnerability to volatile global commodity prices. They also tended to have small manufacturing sectors and featured only a handful of internationally competitive, locally owned firms. Former World Bank chief economist Joseph Stiglitz openly proclaimed that structural adjustment policy prescriptions had failed because the assumptions on which they were based did not take into account the need to support local firms and farms to build up

and Joseph Stiglitz (eds), *Good Growth and Governance in Africa: Rethinking Development Strategies* (Oxford University Press, Oxford, 2012), pp. 345–71.

[36] Shaukat Ansari, 'The Persistence of Market Orthodoxy in Post-Apartheid South Africa: The Neoliberal Incentive Structure and the Absence of the Developmental State', *African Affairs* (advance access) DOI: https://doi.org/10.1093/afraf/adw074.

their productive and organizational capabilities.[37] This is the context in which the pendulum swung again, and many mainstream economists, international financial institutions, and African governments advocated the need for economic transformation and industrial policy. The Ethiopian People's Revolutionary Democratic Front government has been one of the most outspoken on the topic.[38] In turn, these arguments reignited a discussion on what kinds of industrial policies were required to drive transformation and avoid the problems of the past, what kinds of business–state relations would support them, and what role for foreign direct investment. The three articles in Part II contribute to this discussion.

Stefano Ponte's article examines the politics of ownership in the context of liberalization and privatization reforms in Tanzania, in particular the reform of state marketing boards. Ponte's article demonstrates that the theoretical lens of the New Political Economy approach, and the neopatrimonial arguments that it draws on, does not acknowledge that state interventions can be driven by economic rationality and political objectives that are not linked to corruption and personal gain. It demonstrates this by looking at the impacts of liberalization on the coffee export sector, and investigating why the government moved to reinstate some forms of state regulation and control. Ponte explains the government's actions through the politics of ownership, in which locally owned firms operating in coffee buying, processing, and exporting activities demanded that local control be maintained over key markets and economic assets. As a consequence of liberalization, the large group of local firms previously participating in the sector could not compete very well against multinational companies. In other words, the controversy generated in Tanzania around coffee, and which can be seen in other sectors as well, was triggered by what many African countries experienced in the wake of rapid liberalization and privatization—the return to foreign domination of many economic sectors. In this way, Ponte's argument is valuable not only because it demonstrates that state interventions can be driven by economic rationales, but also because it highlights the dangers of foreign capital. More specifically, foreign direct investment can have negative effects for economic development if multinational firms dominate sectors and crowd out less-developed local firms.

---

[37] Joseph Stiglitz, 'Is There a Post-Washington Consensus Consensus?', in Narcis Serra and Joseph Stiglitz (eds), *The Washington Consensus Reconsidered: Towards a New Global Governance* (Oxford University Press, Oxford, 2008), pp. 41–56.
[38] Meles Zenawi, 'States and Markets: Neoliberal Limitations and the Case for a Developmental State', in Akbar Noman, Kwesi Botchwey, Howard Stein, and Joseph Stiglitz (eds), *Good Growth and Governance in Africa: Rethinking Development Strategies* (Oxford University Press, Oxford, 2012), pp. 140–74; Arkebe Oqubay, *Made in Africa: Industrial Policy in Ethiopia* (Oxford University Press, Oxford, 2015).

On the other hand, foreign direct investment is one of the best ways for local firms to learn how to produce in new sectors and gain new productive capabilities.[39] For this to happen, however, African governments must actively pursue strategies to incentivize technology transfer and learning between foreign and local firms. Deborah Bräutigam makes this point effectively. Her article shows that foreign capital and capitalists can be important drivers of economic transformation because transnational networks provide access to capital, credit, and export markets that indigenous entrepreneurs do not initially have. For this reason, new export sectors are usually started by diaspora capitalists or foreign direct investment, which then provide opportunities for local entrepreneurs to learn, as she shows in the case of Mauritius. Looking at Nigeria, she shows that local entrepreneurs in the motor part sector benefited from engagement with foreign business networks, but because Taiwanese firms did not make direct investments in the local economy the opportunities for Nigerian firms to learn from their Taiwanese counterparts were limited. Bräutigam's argument is important because foreign capitalists and diaspora have often been seen as a major cause of underdevelopment in the African studies literature, both in the Dependency School debates of the 1970s and also more recently. In contrast, she emphasizes that foreign capital has a positive role to play. Creating new export sectors in African countries requires that local firms be able to enter and remain competitive in global value chains, and diaspora capitalists, transnational networks, and foreign direct investment are key to doing this.

Finally, the article by David Booth and Frederick Golooba-Mutebi is representative of a group of scholars who argue, in opposition to New Political Economy and good governance approaches, that the creation and distribution of rents as well some forms of clientelism are necessary for capitalist economic transformation. This article is groundbreaking because it shifts the emphasis of explanations of Africa's economic difficulties from the absence of a Weberian rational-legal, impersonal bureaucracy to a focus on the variety of clientelist political systems that exist on the continent, and their different economic impacts. Booth and Golooba-Mutebi argue that the form of clientelism found in Rwanda is conducive to pursuing economic transformation and implementing industrial policies because it involves centralized rent creation and managing rents in a way that increases production and thus incomes in the longer term, rather than focusing on maximizing incomes in the short term through consumption or redistribution to political constituencies.

---

[39] This was one of the key critiques of dependency theory, which was influential in African studies in the 1970s and led to the debate on African capitalism. See Paul Kennedy, 'African businessmen and foreign capital: Collaboration or conflict?', *African Affairs* 76, 303 (1977), pp. 177–94; Penelope Hetherington, 'Explaining the crisis of capitalism in Kenya', *African Affairs* 92 (1993), pp. 89–103.

Their article also emphasizes the importance of rents in financing the learning costs of an initial generation of locally owned firms in acquiring technological capabilities. This can take different forms, and in the case of Rwanda the ruling political elites of the Rwandan Patriotic Front (RPF) capitalized on productive capabilities generated during the civil war to establish party-owned enterprises, which became the central tool in the RPF government's industrial policy. Other scholars have taken this work further by using political settlements theory to explain the variation in clientelist systems across African countries and their implications for the ability of some governments to centralize and manage rents and rent-seeking better than others.[40]

These articles have been selected because they bring fresh insights to old debates and make new contributions to the debate about how African states can strengthen the structure of their economies. They also raise questions about what aspects of clientelism and rent-seeking are harmful and which are necessary for economic transformation. At the same time, the articles included here demonstrate that foreign direct investment can be either a catalyst or constraint on building strong local firms, depending on the specific context. Taken together, they therefore call for a more nuanced and complex approach to the challenges of economic transformation.

---

[40] Whitfield et al., *The Politics of African Industrial Policy*; Hazel Gray, 'The Political Economy of Grand Corruption in Tanzania', *African Affairs* 114, 456 (2015), pp. 382–403; Sonia Languille, 'The Scramble for Textbooks in Tanzania', *African Affairs* 115, 458 (2015), pp. 73–96; Sylvia Croese, 'State-Led Housing Delivery as an Instrument of Developmental Patrimonialism: The Case of Post-War Angola', *African Affairs* 116, 462 (2017), pp. 80–100.

7

The Politics of Ownership

Tanzanian Coffee Policy
in the Age of Liberal Reformism

Stefano Ponte

IN THE LAST FEW YEARS THE GOVERNMENT OF TANZANIA has made a number of interventions in the country's coffee industry which seem to go against the grain of neo-liberal market reform. This article describes these changes and locates them in the wider literature on liberal reform in Tanzania and Africa. Currently, analyses of the dynamics of reform in Africa tend to fall into two (sometimes overlapping) categories: techno-economistic approaches focusing on 'appropriate interventions' and 'hurdles in the path of implementation';[1] and political science approaches focusing on 'rent-seeking', 'patron-client' and 'patrimonial' practices.[2] While political scientists rightly criticize the techno-economistic approach for its political naiveté, my aim in this article is to show that the political science literature is too reductive and too cynical. I do so by introducing the idea of the 'politics of ownership', a concept formulated in relation to empirical analysis of the reform process in the coffee sector in Tanzania.

Much of the political science literature on economic reform draws inspiration from the study of both economics and sociology. Key to its analysis is the concept of rent-seeking. In economic theory, the supplier of a good or service

---

[1] For recent examples on Tanzania, see A. Bigsten and A. Danielson, *Tanzania: Is the ugly duckling finally growing up?*. Research Report No. 120 (Nordic Africa Institute, Uppsala, 2002); and World Bank, *Tanzania at the Turn of the Century: From reforms to sustained growth and poverty reduction* (World Bank, Washington, DC, 2002).

[2] See, among many others, P. Chabal and J.-P. Daloz, *Africa Works: Disorder as a political instrument* (James Currey, Oxford and Indiana University Press, Bloomington, IN, 1999); and N. van de Walle, *African Economies and the Politics of Permanent Crisis* (Cambridge University Press, Cambridge, 2001).

earns economic rent—i.e. above-average profit—whenever demand for the good outstrips its supply. Rent-seeking analyses argue that by interfering in markets—for instance, by granting monopoly privileges in the manufacturing sector—African governments generate opportunities for earning rent. Symmetrical possibilities exist for monopsonistic buyers, for instance in the export crop market. These lucrative opportunities create incentives to bribery and corruption, as economic actors compete to win the favour of the officials and politicians at whose discretion the rent-earning opportunities are granted.[3]

The literature on rent-seeking is frequently married to analyses grounded in (neo)Weberian social theory, which use the concepts of 'patrimonialism' and 'neo-patrimonialism'.[4] In the Africanist literature, patrimonial authority is often figured as a pyramidal form of personal rule in which the ruler, chief or patron maintains the loyalty of his staff, followers or clients, by means of patronage benefits.[5] The discretionary power to permit clients the right to operate in uncompetitive markets, and thereby to earn economic rent, constitutes one lucrative source of patronage, as does the ability to delegate that discretion to lesser officials and politicians. Thus interference in markets is construed in this literature as a cynical and unprincipled strategy for granting private fortunes and maintaining personal power.

Over the past two decades Tanzania has introduced a series of economic and political reforms with the aim of enhancing competition in markets and elections.[6] However, some scholars have argued that these reforms are competing with new (or transforming existing) forms of patrimonialism, while a spate of anti-liberal policy measures taken in the late 1990s and early 2000s has prompted some observers to argue that a process of reform reversal, used for

[3] Exemplary of this approach is Robert Bates, *Markets and States in Tropical Africa* (University of California Press, Berkeley, CA, 1981), Chapters 6 and 7.

[4] Put crudely, a neo-patrimonial system is one in which a system of personal rule exists behind, or alongside, elements of bureaucratic, legal-rational rule. For a fuller discussion see U. Engel and G. Erdmann, 'Neopatrimonialism reconsidered—critical review and elaboration of an elusive concept'. Paper presented at the 45th annual meeting of the African Studies Association, Washington, DC, 4–9 December 2002.

[5] A sophisticated discussion can be found in J.-F. Médard, 'The underdeveloped state in tropical Africa: political clientelism or neo-patrimonialism?', in C. Clapham (ed.) *Private Patronage and Public Power: Political clientelism in the modern state* (Pinter, London, 1982), and celebrated neo-Weberian analyses in Richard Joseph, *Democracy and Prebendal Politics in Nigeria* (Cambridge University Press, Cambridge, 1987). More recently, Patrick Chabal and Jean-Pascal Daloz make liberal use of the concept in *Africa Works*. See also Richard Sandbrook, *The Politics of Africa's Economic Stagnation* (Cambridge University Press, Cambridge, 1985).

[6] On Tanzania, see J. Gould and J. Ojanen, *Merging in the Circle: The politics of Tanzania's poverty reduction strategy*, Policy Paper 2/2003. (Institute of Development Studies, Helsinki, 2003); T. Kelsall, 'Shop windows and smoke-filled rooms: governance and the re-politicisation of Tanzania', *Journal of Modern African Studies* 40, 4 (2002), pp. 597–619; T. Kelsall, 'Governance, democracy and recent political struggles in mainland Tanzania', *Commonwealth and Comparative Politics* 41, 2 (2003), pp. 55–82.

purposes of patronage, cronyism and rent-seeking, is taking place.[7] By analyzing the Tanzanian coffee industry, the present article seeks to show that,
while interference in markets is not free from considerations of patronage, we
need also to understand it as a form of action undertaken on grounds of
principle. The principles can be ones of economic rationality: for example,
questions of quality control in the coffee market; or ones of social identity:
the idea, for instance, that indigenous people should benefit from economic
reforms.

The article focuses on how ideals of local control of key markets and
economic assets have shaped the rules dictating who is allowed to compete
in specific industries or sectors and who is not—what I call the politics of
ownership. In the specific instance of the coffee industry, this politics is
translated into practices affecting the perceived (il)legitimacy of foreign ownership of assets (processing plants, warehouses) and of the commodity itself
before it is exported. What I aim to show is that the rent-seeking and neo-
Weberian literature provides an impoverished, one-dimensional view of the
reform process and its partial reversals. I also aim to show, through an analysis
of the politics of ownership, that Tanzanian actors' understanding of 'local'
and 'indigenous' interests and identities is discursively constructed and shifts
over time. By doing so, I add another dimension to recent studies of the
indigenization debate in Tanzania.[8]

The material presented here is based on six months of fieldwork carried out
in Tanzania in the second half of 2000. At production level, the fieldwork
entailed interviews with owners or managers of 15 large-scale estates, a sample
survey of 250 households in Hai District (Kilimanjaro), and 32 focus groups
with coffee farmers (covering ten out of eleven districts with an estimated
coffee production of at least 2,000 tons). I carried out fieldwork in the
following districts: Arumeru in Arusha Region; Moshi, Hai and Rombo in
Kilimanjaro Region; Mbozi and Mbeya in Mbeya Region; and Bukoba, Muleba
and Karagwe in Kagera Region. I am indebted to David Kapinga for fieldwork
in Mbinga District, Ruvuma Region. Interviews were also carried out with
other types of actors in the domestic marketing chain downstream from
producers. These included people handling coffee (agents, traders, co-
operatives, curing/hulling plants, exporters, local roasters, transporters) and
providers of services to the industry (finance, inputs, extension, research,
brokerage, quality control, auditing, information, logistics). Work at the

---

[7] This argument is made most directly in B. Cooksey, 'Marketing reform? The rise and fall of
agricultural liberalisation in Tanzania', *Development Policy Review* 21, 1 (2003), pp. 67–91.
Others have made a similar point in relation to a number of eastern and southern African
countries (see T. S. Jayne *et al.*, 'False promise or false premise? The experience of food and input
market reform in eastern and southern Africa', *World Development* 30, 11 (2002), pp. 1967–85).

[8] R. Aminzade, 'From race to citizenship: the indigenization debate in post-socialist Tanzania', *Studies in Comparative International Development* 38, 1 (2003), p. 45.

Tanzania Coffee Board (TCB) included interviews, data collection, and attendance at the weekly auction for five months. The overall research project also involved short-term fieldwork in Kenya (in 2000) and Ethiopia (in 2002). Four months of fieldwork were carried out in Uganda in the first half of 2002. All information included in this article comes from primary fieldwork material—unless otherwise stated.

The restructuring of coffee markets in Tanzania

In the pre-reform period in Tanzania (before 1993/94), the domestic coffee trade was under the control of co-operatives and/or marketing boards. Formally, coffee did not change hands until it was sold to private exporters at the auction in Moshi. Farmers (through the co-operatives) owned the coffee up to the export point and bore the risk of price fluctuations. However, the payment system allowed a smoothing out of price variations within the marketing year. The handling and payment systems were fairly laborious and slowed down the flow of coffee from the farmer to the importer. Overhead costs associated with these procedures were high, meaning that farmers received a lower proportion of the export price than they would have had under a more efficient system (quality considerations being equal). Payments to farmers were often delayed and resources were siphoned out of the system at various levels. However, price stabilization was ensured within one season. Most important, the system provided quality incentives to co-operative societies and (less directly) to farmers. The organization of exports was built around a mandatory auction system, in which all domestically purchased coffee had to be sold to registered private sector exporters. The monopolistic system in the domestic trade ensured that coffee remained in 'local' (mostly African Tanzanian) hands up to the auction. At the export level, smaller (mostly Asian-owned) Tanzanian export companies were able to compete with Kenya-based exporters and the subsidiaries of multinational corporations. This meant that competitive bidding characterized the auction, especially for top-quality coffees.[9]

The adoption of the 1993 Crop Boards Act marked a profound change in the regulatory framework of Tanzanian coffee marketing. In the 1994/95

---

[9] See S. Ponte, *Coffee Markets in East Africa: Local responses to global challenges or global responses to local challenges?* CDR Working Paper No. 01.5 (Centre for Development Research, Copenhagen, 2001); and S. Ponte, 'Brewing a bitter cup? Deregulation, quality and the reorganization of coffee marketing in East Africa', *Journal of Agrarian Change* 2, 2 (2002), pp. 248–72. For an analysis of the global coffee chain, see S. Ponte, 'The "latte revolution"? Regulation, markets and consumption in the global coffee chain', *World Development* 30, 7 (2002), pp. 1099–122.

season, domestic trade was opened up to private traders and processors. However, the Tanzania Coffee Board (TCB) retained numerous regulatory powers, and maintains licensing powers and the function of running the coffee auction, allowing domestic traders to buy coffee only at authorized buying posts. It does not permit farm-gate buying, although the rule is not observed in some areas of the country (see section on Kagera coffee politics). Finally, the TCB does not allow the movement of coffee from one area (southern, northern, western) to another.

Liberalization of the coffee market in Tanzania has yielded mixed results. On the one hand, farmers are paid cash on delivery and receive a higher proportion of the export price than in the pre-liberalization period.[10] On the other hand, input-credit schemes have collapsed, the volume of coffee exports has not improved,[11] and there are strong indications that coffee quality has decreased because farmers are paid one price for all coffee—irrespective of quality.[12] Most importantly for the discussion of the politics of ownership (see next section), liberalization saw the dramatic capturing of the Tanzanian coffee market by foreign companies at all levels (domestic trade, processing and export) except for farming—where 95 percent of coffee is still produced by smallholders. At the same time, foreign investors have recently come to dominate the estate production sector.[13]

At the export level, the shift in ownership can be assessed through analysis of the data in Tables 7.1 and 7.2. During the first season of liberalized marketing (1994/95), of the top five export companies three were foreign (see Table 7.1), controlling 41 percent of total exports (see Table 7.2). By 1999/00, this share had increased to 64 percent, and all top five companies were foreign. Following liberalization, foreign companies not only came to dominate exports but also the domestic coffee trade. In the mid-1990s, a number of independent local companies and co-operative unions were still operating in the domestic market. By 2000, their market power had been severely curtailed. Only a few large unions survived—Kilimanjaro Native Co-operative Union (KNCU), Kagera Co-operative Union (KCU), Karagwe District Co-operative Union (KDCU). In other coffee-growing areas, the

[10] A. Temu, 'Market liberalisation, vertical integration and price behaviour in Tanzania's coffee auction', *Development Policy Review* **19**, 2 (2001), pp. 207–24; and A. Winter-Nelson and A. Temu, 'Institutional adjustment and transaction costs: product and inputs markets in the Tanzanian coffee system', *World Development* **30**, 4 (2002), pp. 561–74.

[11] According to ICO export data, in the last eight years before liberalization (1987–94), Tanzania exported an annual average of 49,600 tons of coffee. In the eight years after liberalization (1995–2002), this average fell to 45,600 tons.

[12] Ponte, 'Brewing a bitter cup?'

[13] Out of about 25 coffee estates in the process of privatization in Kilimanjaro, I was able to trace ownership information on 19 of them. Four were still in the hands of co-operative societies and/or the government. Two had been leased to African Tanzanians, one to an Asian Tanzanian, and 12 to foreign investors.

Table 7.1. Market share and characteristics of top coffee exporters in Tanzania (1994/95 and 1999/00)

	1994/95			1999/00		
Rank	Name of company/sister company	Market share %	Company type	Name of company/sister company	Market share %	Company type
1	Tchibo Estates	23.62	foreign	Dorman (T)	15.05	foreign
2	SB/Tropex	10.09	local	Tchibo Estates	14.64	foreign
3	Mazao/City Coffee	9.95	foreign	Taylor Winch	12.84	foreign
4	Sherif Dewji	8.40	local	Olam (T)	12.59	foreign
5	Dorman (T)	7.46	foreign	Mazao/City Coffee	8.62	foreign
6	ACC/Milcafé	6.58	local	SB/Tropex	5.00	local
7	Tanzania Coffee Est.	5.57	local	Coffee Exporters	4.34	local
8	Taylor Winch	4.65	foreign	ACC/Milcafé	4.13	local
9	Unieximp (T)	3.79	foreign	Sherif Dewji	3.82	local
10	Coffee Exporters	3.52	local	Unieximp (T)	3.63	foreign

Source: Tanzania Coffee Board.

Name of company/sister company	Notes
ACC/Milcafé	partly owned by a small international trader, and partly by a Tanzanian investor; managed for an extended period of time by a European who was well integrated locally and spoke fluent Kiswahili; perceived as local company in the industry.
Coffee Exporters	partly owned by a medium-sized multi-commodity trading group and partly by Asian Kenyan investors; perceived as local.
Dorman (T)	owned by a white Kenyan; linked to a medium-sized international trader; perceived as foreign.
Mazao/City Coffee	subsidiary of a major international coffee trading company; perceived as foreign.
Olam (T)	owned by a medium-sized multi-commodity international trader; perceived as foreign.
SB/Tropex	owned by an Asian Tanzanian; perceived as local.
Sherif Dewji	owned by an Arab Tanzanian family; perceived as local.
Tanzania Coffee Est.	subsidiary of TCB; government-owned.
Taylor Winch	subsidiary of a major international coffee trading company; perceived as foreign.
Tchibo Estates	subsidiary of a large German coffee roasting company; perceived as foreign.
Unieximp (T)	subsidiary of a medium-sized multi-commodity international trader; perceived as foreign.

Source: field interviews.

Table 7.2. Market share of Tanzania coffee auction purchases by type of company (1994/95 to 1999/00)[a]

	1994/95	1995/96	1996/97	1997/98	1998/99	1999/00
Active export companies (n)	23	26	24	–	27	22
Market share of top 5 companies (%)	59.52	63.83	62.09	–	62.24	63.73
of which foreign	41.03	55.68	52.32	–	53.75	63.73
of which local	18.49	8.15	9.77	–	8.50	0.00
Market share of top 10 companies (%)	83.64	86.98	87.67	–	87.25	84.65
of which foreign	49.48	60.41	62.05	–	58.50	67.36
of which local	34.17	26.57	25.62	–	28.75	17.29
Market share of companies ranked 11th to 20th (%)	15.89	11.32	11.55	–	11.41	15.18
Market share of other companies (%)	0.46	1.71	0.78	–	1.34	0.17
Market share of total auction purchases (%)	51.04	60.41	62.05	–	59.92	67.36

Note: [a] Sister companies are counted as one company.
Source: Elaboration from TCB data.

Table 7.3. Co-operative share of domestic coffee market in Tanzania (1994/95–1999/2000)

Marketing season	Market share of co-ops
1994/95	83.2
1995/96	61.4
1996/97	32.7
1997/98	12.3
1998/99	16.5
1999/2000	26.4

Source: Tanzania Coffee Board.

co-operative unions folded.[14] Primary co-operative societies closed, re-organized themselves into smaller unions, worked as agents of private buyers, or started to sell their coffee directly at the auction. The share of the domestic coffee market of co-operative unions fell from 83 percent in 1994/95 (the first year of liberalized markets) to 26 percent in 1999/2000 (see Table 7.3). Independent local traders suffered a similar fate. As long as international prices were stable or rising (1994/95, 1996/97, 1997/98), they managed to survive. At times

---

[14] Only in Mbozi District, in the southern highlands, smaller unions—the Isansa and Iyula Co-operative Union (ISAYULA), and the Mbozi Co-operative Union (MBOCU) were able to grow from the ashes of the defunct regional union—Mbeya Co-operative Union (MBECU). The remaining three unions (in Usambara, Mwanga and Arusha), while still formally in existence, were unable to purchase substantial amounts of coffee in 2000.

of falling prices (1995/96, 1999 to the present), they suffered major losses and either disappeared or started to act as agents of major exporters. Finally, foreign companies also came to dominate the processing segment of the coffee industry (curing for mild arabica and hulling for hard arabica and robusta)—albeit to a lesser extent than in the export and domestic trade segments.

Previous to the market reforms, domestic coffee marketing in Tanzania was in the hands of co-operative societies and unions. Despite the bureaucratic and corruption-related problems with this marketing system, the industry had a strong sense of local ownership. Coffee remained in local hands from the farm level all the way to the auction floor. At the auction, local companies were able to compete with foreign companies. As already shown in this section, foreign companies have increased their market presence at the export level and have become substantially involved in domestic trade and processing of coffee as well. Although a couple of local trade processing and export companies survive, the bulk of the industry is now in the hands of foreign interests. In the next section, I show how this change has prompted a variety of responses, which I call the politics of ownership.

The politics of ownership in the Tanzanian coffee industry

The expropriation of the industry by foreign companies has created growing tensions in the coffee industry in Tanzania, especially in Moshi, where most of these companies are based and where the weekly auctions take place. Some senior TCB officers, while following the official line of support for liberalization, expressed discontent in private. This anti-liberalization stance does not necessarily represent a market-unfriendly position. These officers support competitive trade as long as local companies constitute the main actors. Their discontent is also based on a sense of powerlessness in the face of the perceived decrease in the TCB's regulatory powers (if not *de jure*, at least *de facto*). If, on the one hand, they are worried about their jobs and the institutional survival of the TCB, on the other hand they echo a more widespread sentiment of unease in relation to the foreign domination of the coffee industry. Self-serving motives overlap with identity politics.

Donors and foreign companies interpret a number of critical issues in the coffee industry through a rent-seeking/patrimonial explanatory framework. For one thing, cumbersome licensing procedures and the rule that coffee should be bought only at established buying posts are alleged to be used for soliciting bribes, especially at the local level. The same is said in relation to the proliferation of local government taxes in the coffee sector, especially in the south. Finally, continuation of the auction, even though it made little sense in the eyes of exporters in 2000, is seen as being justified in terms of providing the TCB with resources and with 'something to do'. This allows donors and foreign companies to continue arguing (without much success so far) for a complete liberalization agenda embedded in the parlance of 'proper interventions' and hurdles in their implementation.

Yet, a reading of the tensions that emerged in the coffee industry after liberalization, focusing exclusively on rent-seeking and patrimonial options, is misplaced. Discontent also rests on a widespread feeling among Tanzanians that the coffee market is at present largely controlled by foreign companies. This is most evident at the auction, where a small number of expatriates run the show—sometimes in a fairly arrogant way.[15] The dichotomy between foreign and local interests should not be overstated. In some companies, foreign and local interests co-exist and are fairly balanced. In other situations, partial foreign ownership and/or white expatriate management are still hidden under the perception of locality, because the manager may have been living in the country for a long time, be married to a local, or speaks good Kiswahili. If, in the pre-liberalization period, Asian Kenyan ownership may have been conceived as foreign, in the late 1990s it was considered more local than ownership by large multinational coffee companies.

The politics of ownership is thus distinct from the politics of nationalism as embedded in the political discourse of the 1960s and 1970s in Tanzania. It is also different from the debates around indigenization—which seeks to promote African Tanzanian interests *vis à vis* Asian or Arab Tanzanian ones. Previous to the mid-1990s, this latter politics was embedded in a division of labour along the coffee marketing chain, in which the domestic trade and processing functions were by and large in the hands of African Tanzanians and the export industry had a substantial involvement of Asian and Arab Tanzanian (or Kenyan) interests. In the post-reform period (after 1993/94), this debate, while still in existence, has been overshadowed by discussions along the 'local versus foreign' partition line, in which the perception of local goes beyond strictly nationalist and/or indigenous lines.

The post-reform politics of ownership in the coffee sector plays out in at least two forms. First, there is a sense among some TCB officers that important decisions about the industry are increasingly made outside the institution. Second, there is a pervasive sense among TCB officers, cooperative unions and farmers that foreign companies are engaging in price fixing. Whether this is

---

[15] Tensions are not limited to government circles. They also emerge clearly when talking to co-operative officers, independent coffee traders, and even some estate owners. Smallholders participating in focus group discussions were also aware that foreign companies were behind local agents, and they often conflated anti-private trader and anti-foreign sentiments.

the case or not, prices at the primary buying posts are all the same among companies. Price fixing used to be a function of the state before 1994, although price levels depended to some extent on international prices. Now, price fixing, albeit formally outlawed, is seen as being practised by foreign companies. The process of de-legitimization of the TCB is further compounded by the open flouting of the remaining regulations—such as how coffee should be graded at the primary buying level, what maximum level of humidity the coffee should have when it is traded, and the rule that coffee needs to be bought at established (and registered) buying posts. The TCB does not have enough resources to make sure that these rules are enforced.

Counter-measures against the expropriation of the coffee industry have been attempted at various levels and with different mechanisms. The most explicit perhaps is indicated by the interactions between exporters and the TCB auctioneers. About 80 percent of the coffee going through the weekly mandatory auction in 2000 was 'captive'. This means that the seller and the buyer are the same company holding licences for both domestic trade and export functions. As a result, nobody else on the auction floor attempts to 'snatch' a coffee lot. This has led to a practical situation where every participant at the auction knows which coffee is captive and which is free. Nobody bids against captive lots. Instead of witnessing competitive bidding among buyers, the auction is characterized by an extended (and public) argument between exporters and auctioneers on the appropriate price level. The TCB has a vested interest in increasing auction prices for financial reasons (it increases its resources), but also because a low price for captive coffee influences bidding for free coffee—pushing its price down. However, a resource-access explanation does not tell the whole story. The auction haggling demonstrates in the public realm (journalists attend the auction) that the TCB is on the side of the farmers. Haggling also raises the price that co-operatives and independent traders receive for their coffee at the auction, thus defending the financial viability of the local market players.

The TCB has also been encouraging primary co-operative societies that are not organized in unions to sell their coffee directly at the auction. It has facilitated the formation and registration of farmer groups that can sell their coffee directly at the auction, even though they are not licensed buyers. This is viewed as one way (albeit still marginal) of snatching domestic market share away from foreign companies and of providing farmers with a direct contact with the export market. In this way, the TCB can maintain the populist terrain and at the same time justify the existence of the auction on the grounds of providing information, transparency and a competitive buyer market for the few remaining local traders and co-operatives. Not surprisingly, foreign companies favour the elimination of the auction altogether.

Another way that the TCB has addressed the loss of local ownership in the coffee market has been through the manipulation of licensing procedures for processing plants. After a first wave of new licences awarded to private curing plants in the mid-1990s, no new licences were granted thereafter. This was done to save the curing plant owned by the co-operative union, the Tanganyika Coffee Curing Company (TCCCo) in Moshi. In 2000, the TCB was also playing the politics of ownership by threatening changes in the overall regulation of the industry. Proposals were circulated about prohibiting companies from concurrently holding both domestic trade and export licences. The idea was to re-empower local traders and take the auction back to its original competitive buying features. These proposals were actually incorporated in the 2001 Coffee Act, which was applied for the first time in the 2002/3 buying season. The Act, among other things, forbids exporters from holding a domestic trade licence. This ban could easily be circumvented by registration under a different company name. However, in practice, some of the large foreign companies that were heavily involved in farm-gate buying in 2000 have decided to quit buying at the domestic level and in 2003 operated only at the auction. This is a sign that they judged that there would be enough free coffee at the auction for their needs. As a result, it is likely that local traders have gained share in the domestic coffee market.

In this section, I have argued that the politics of ownership is trying to partially counteract the recent capturing of the coffee market by foreign interests. The most interesting local-level manifestation of this process has taken place in Kagera Region. Here, electoral politics played an important role, first in rescuing the co-operative unions from bankruptcy, then in banning private traders (most of whom worked for, or were agents of, foreign companies) from operating in the local market. Beyond short-term electoral politics, however, the 'Kagera experiment' had national-level repercussions in opening the way for the passage of the 2001 Coffee Act, and in the more general attempt to reverse ownership patterns in the domestic coffee trade in Tanzania.

Understanding coffee politics in Kagera Region[16]

Kagera Region may be considered the repository of coffee history in Tanzania. Coffee is thought to have been cultivated in Kagera since it was brought in by

[16] Some of the material presented in this section comes from interviews with private traders, processors, co-operative officers and local government officials in Bukoba, Karagwe and Muleba districts, Kagera Region. Other information comes from focus group discussions with farmers carried out in six villages, two in each of these three districts. Fieldwork in Kagera was carried out in late 2000, in the period leading up to the general elections. The identity of the sources of

the Bunyoro conquerors in the seventeenth century.[17] More certain is that coffee was present in Kagera at the beginning of German colonialism in the late nineteenth century, and that its commercial development dates roughly from the First World War.[18] The first coffee cooperative was formed in the 1920s. In 1953, previously existing co-operatives were organized under the Bukoba Co-operative Union (BCU), which survived until 1976—when co-operatives were abolished and their marketing functions were taken over by marketing boards.[19] In 1982, co-operatives were reinstated and the union resurfaced as the Kagera Co-operative Union (KCU). According to Smith, up to the late 1980s, the KCU was able to pay farmers with minimum delays.[20] Until 1990/91, the government continued to set coffee prices and to guarantee loans given to co-operatives by the banks. The burden of debt with the banks started to increase because the union had to pay government-set prices that were sometimes too high in relation to the international prices. The government then admitted its responsibilities and paid off the union's debt, giving it a clean start.

The Tanzania Co-operative Societies Act of 1991 mandated that only economically viable co-operatives would be registered, and that membership would be voluntary. The unions were given more autonomy and began setting their own prices. At that time, the Kagera District Co-operative Union (KDCU) split from the KCU, and the government stopped guaranteeing loans for the unions. As a result, the banks started to be more cautious in lending and the two unions failed to purchase all the available coffee. Substantial amounts were smuggled to Uganda. In the last five years before liberalization, the two unions were able to buy an average of 13,000 tons of coffee,[21] although in 1993/94 they managed to buy only 8,000 tons.[22]

information has been concealed to protect informants. A more detailed discussion of the history of coffee in Kagera and of the events summarized in this section can be found in S. Ponte, 'The politics of ownership: Tanzanian coffee politics in the age of liberal reformism', paper presented at the African Studies Association of the UK biennial conference, University of Birmingham, 9–11 September 2002.

[17] See J. W. F. Rowe, *The World's Coffee:A study on the economics and politics of the coffee industries of certain countries and of the international problem* (Her Majesty's Stationery Office, London, 1963), p. 126.

[18] See J. Iliffe, *A Modern History of Tanganyika* (Cambridge University Press, Cambridge, 1979) and R. Austen, *Northwest Tanzania under German and British Rule: Colonial policy and tribal politics, 1889–1939* (Yale University Press, New Haven, CT, 1968).

[19] See C. D. Smith, *Ecology, Civil Society and the Informal Economy in North West Tanzania* (Ashgate, Aldershot, 2001), p. 116; Iliffe, *A Modern History*, p. 464; P. Raikes, *Coffee Production in West Lake Region, Tanzania*, IDR Papers A.76.9 (Institute for Development Research, Copenhagen, 1976), p. 8; and B. Weiss, *Sacred Trees, Bitter Harvests: Globalizing coffee in northwest Tanzania* (Heinemann, Portsmouth, NH, 2003).

[20] Smith, *Ecology, Civil Society*, p. 125.   [21] Source: BUKOP.

[22] Source: TCB; figures given in clean-coffee equivalent.

In the 1994/95 season, the government opened the door to private sector participation in coffee trading and processing. By 1999/2000, the KCU and the KDCU were buying cumulatively only 21 percent of a total estimated crop of 15,000 tons. Most of the rest was bought by three large foreign companies. In the short period of five years the Kagera coffee trade—which had been in local hands more or less continuously since the early 1960s, and with an important involvement of local traders even in the first part of the century—had been completely revolutionized. An exception to this 'expropriation' trend applies to coffee hulling. Until 1993/94, all coffee in the region was hulled at the union-owned plant (BUKOP). In 1999/2000 BUKOP managed to process only 2,200 tons of coffee; the rest was hulled at eight other new private plants, all run by local entrepreneurs. In the case of coffee processing, private investors took over the co-operative market share, but local interests were not taken over by foreign ones.

Although competition was getting tougher in the mid-1990s, the unions managed to maintain a fairly large share of coffee purchases in the region (in the range of 60–70 percent between 1996/97 and 1998/99, then down to 21 percent in 1999/2000). In 1998/99, the unions paid a high price to farmers and then suffered from a downturn in international coffee prices. The KCU ended the season with a large debt. In 1999/2000, the union started much more cautiously and paid lower prices to farmers; it was able to repay the 1999/2000 loan plus part of the outstanding debt. Nevertheless, in March 2000, the Cooperative Rural Development Bank (CRDB) announced that the KCU had been put in receivership and that its assets were being seized. A similar process took place in relation to the KDCU in Karagwe. Both unions appealed to the government for help.

In April 2000, the government repaid the debt of both unions to the CRDB by issuing Treasury bonds. A bond account was opened and the unions were asked to pay back their debt to the Treasury by depositing TSh100 per kilogram of purchased coffee in this account. In May 2000, President Mkapa appointed a special committee to advise on how to save the co-operatives throughout the country from complete collapse. The committee was chaired by Mr Kahama, the MP for Karagwe since independence and at that time chairman of the board of directors of the TCB. Its report advised the President to stop private companies from purchasing coffee in Kagera Region, so that the KCU and KDCU could pay back their debt to the government. In mid-2000, the government released a statement explaining that private traders were banned from operating until further notice; private hulling plants were allowed to operate under contract with the unions.

Not surprisingly, industry operators and local government officials in Kagera linked this event with electoral politics. The manifesto of the ruling *Chama cha Mapinduzi* (CCM) party for the 1995 elections stated that cooperatives would be revived during the following legislature. But many unions and primary societies disappeared in the second half of the 1990s. In the 1995 presidential elections, Kagera had been among the regions in mainland Tanzania with the lowest percentage of votes for the CCM candidate, Mkapa—although CCM had won six out of seven parliamentary seats in the coffee-growing districts of Kagera. In the run-up to the 2000 parliamentary and presidential elections, local CCM cadres feared losing two constituencies. Furthermore, two opposition politicians were major players in the private sector coffee industry in Kagera at that time. By not licensing private traders, the governing party would be able to claim to have saved the co-operatives and, at the same time, would have cut off opposition figures from their electoral networks and direct contact with farmers. This was supposed to be a winning strategy, especially if widespread farmer discontent over not receiving prompt payment (or no payment at all) could be contained. A major slump in international coffee prices was not helping the party or the unions, since it entailed downward pressure on farm-gate prices.

As we have seen above, by the beginning of the 2000/2001 buying season the government had bailed out the unions. The CRDB even released new loans to them. These loans, however, were not sufficient to buy all the available coffee, particularly because of a bumper harvest. In September 2000, the unions wanted to lower the price paid to farmers, but the government (through the regional administration) told them not to do this—leading to further losses. As partial compensation, the government advised the unions to use the money they were supposed to deposit in the Treasury bond account to pay farmers for the coffee they had delivered months before.

At a rally in Bukoba town in late September 2000, President Mkapa promised not to open up the market to private buyers until the co-operative unions had repaid their debt. This strategy paid off: in the October 2000 general elections, the CCM won five of the seven seats available in Bukoba, Karagwe and Muleba Districts. Kahama, who maintained his seat in the Karagwe constituency, was appointed Minister for Co-operatives and Marketing. From his new position, he was able to maintain the ban on private coffee traders in Kagera, which continued until 2002. With the application of the new Coffee Act in 2002/3, the ban became unnecessary. The Act prohibits exporters from holding a domestic trading licence. In a sense, the Act formalized the *de facto* situation in Kagera between 2000 and 2002, with the difference that the co-operative unions now have to compete with other local traders.

It is tempting to explain the Kagera saga exclusively through clientelistic and patrimonial lenses, in the context of multi-party politics. It is reasonable to argue that the re-monopolization of domestic marketing of coffee in Kagera re-opened public channels of patrimonial appropriation and clientelistic opportunity that had been closed off by market liberalization. The latter would in part explain why the ban on private coffee traders lasted far longer than was necessary for electoral purposes. However, I would argue that the continuation of the ban into 2002 can also be ascribed to the desire to compensate for the loss of local ownership in the coffee industry. Furthermore, a patrimonial interpretation would not explain why only domestic trade (dominated by foreign companies) was re-monopolized in Kagera, while hulling—dominated by local entrepreneurs—was left to the free market. Also, in 2002 the government re-allowed domestic traders to buy coffee in competition with the unions in Kagera, thus closing the door for rent-seeking activities that had been opened by the process of remonopolization. Now that (foreign) exporters can not hold licences for the domestic trade, market competition is back. The apparent anti-liberal nature of the Kagera experience, and its patrimonial opportunities, was eventually enfolded within the politics of ownership. Its end result was the successful localization of the Kagera coffee trade.

A comparative perspective

In the previous sections, I suggested that the politics of ownership can help explain the trajectory of coffee politics and policy in post-socialist Tanzania. This politics has attempted to challenge the dominance of foreign interests throughout the coffee marketing chain. Although it is not formalized in a political or party manifesto and is only partially incorporated in regulation, the politics of ownership can be said to be broadly inspired by other coffee marketing systems in East Africa—which are seen as more successful in defending local interests *vis à vis* foreign ones.

A model cited by several TCB and co-operative officers is the Ethiopian coffee marketing system. In Ethiopia, foreign-owned companies are not allowed to register as exporters, unless they had been registered already before the advent of the Derg regime. Also, companies can not hold both domestic trade and export licences.[23] There is thus an artificial vertical segmentation of the coffee marketing chain and the auction is characterized by competitive bidding. The whole Ethiopian coffee industry is, to a large extent, run and controlled by local companies. There are no expatriates sitting at the daily auction. Obviously, some local exporters are reliant on financing from foreign importers, so their independence may be more virtual than real. But these exporters are not directly owned by foreign companies. In sum, local ownership is one of the points of pride of the Ethiopian coffee industry, not only

[23] R. Love, 'The Ethiopian coffee filière and its institutions: *cui bono?*', *Review of African Political Economy* 88 (2001), pp. 225–40; and R. Love, 'Political economy of the coffee filière in Ethiopia' (Ph.D. thesis, Institute for Politics and International Studies, University of Leeds, 2002).

among officers at the Coffee and Tea Authority in Addis Ababa, but also among exporters and domestic traders.

Another model often evoked by the perpetuators of the politics of owner-ship in Tanzania is the Kenyan coffee marketing system. In Kenya, coffee cannot be traded domestically; estates and co-operatives therefore own it all the way to the auction (as in Tanzania before liberalization). In 1999/2000, foreign companies in Kenya controlled an export market share that was much lower than the level registered in Tanzania.[24] The export market is still fairly fragmented, because the capital requirements for buying coffee at the auction are much smaller than what would be required to buy coffee in the domestic market. This allows local companies to compete fairly successfully with foreign companies on the auction floor. Because of the history of white European settlement and the large presence of white and Asian Kenyans in the contemporary estate and export sectors, the politics of indigenization operates more strongly in Kenya than in Tanzania and Ethiopia. But the politics of local versus foreign ownership plays an important role as well; 60 percent of coffee production is channelled through co-operative societies controlled by Kenyans. Industry actors are well aware that liberalization of the domestic market would mean that a large portion of this market could fall into the hands of foreign companies. At the export level, there is a sense of tension between local and foreign companies, even if local companies may be owned by white or Asian Kenyans.

In Kenya, coffee operators consider the Tanzanian trajectory of liberaliza-tion a model to be avoided, because it led to loss of local ownership and to a marked decline in coffee quality. In both Ethiopia and Kenya, donors are pushing for further reforms in the coffee marketing systems on the grounds that the current ones are corrupt and inefficient. Nevertheless, Ethiopia maintains important regulatory powers. Kenya has carried out only cosmetic reforms in the coffee sector in the 1990s. At the end of the decade, it was the most regulated coffee market in Africa. New reforms in Kenya are expected following the approval of a new Coffee Act in late 2001. It would be hard to deny that corrupt practices occur, especially in Kenya. But lack of 'complete' reform also achieved important objectives in terms of the politics of owner-ship: in both countries, the industry has remained in local hands without affecting the high reputation of Ethiopian and Kenyan coffees worldwide.[25]

Uganda provides an interesting contrast to Ethiopia and Kenya. The pro-cess of liberalization and deregulation started in 1991 and has reached the

---

[24] For details, see Ponte, *Coffee Markets in East Africa*; and Ponte, 'Brewing a bitter cup?'

[25] This is an instance where Van de Walle's argument that 'partial reform' is a deliberate neo-patrimonial device does not hold (see Van de Walle, *African Economies*). Also, partial reform is hardly a uniquely African feature; see O. Therkildsen, 'Understanding public management through neopatrimonialism: a paradigm for all African seasons?' in U. Engel and G. R. Olsen (eds), *Understanding the African Exception* (Routledge, London, forthcoming).

most advanced degree in East Africa. Full liberalization of the marketing chain has prompted the entrance of many private investors in all segments of the coffee industry. The co-operative sector has almost disappeared. Foreign companies were able to increase their export market share in Uganda, reaching almost a 50 percent share in 1998/99; then their share decreased to 44 percent in 2000/2001—a lower proportion than in Tanzania.[26] The domestic coffee market and processing segments of the marketing chain are controlled by local traders and processors. Foreign companies have attempted (and failed) to control the domestic market through vertical integration, and are now operating for the most part just as exporters based in Kampala. Price and supply dynamics may play a part in explaining this market structure. However, Kampala-based managers of foreign companies told me that it was simply impossible for them to carve out a substantial market share at the local level, because the entry barriers in trade were low and local traders had ready access to independent finance through other business activities or networks. In short, while regulation has preserved a sense of local ownership in Kenya and Ethiopia, the same—to some extent—was achieved in Uganda through lack of regulation. In Tanzania, half-baked liberalization and the absence of local financial outlets for local entrepreneurs led to the domination of foreign companies in the coffee market, and to challenges of the status quo through the politics of ownership.

Conclusion

This article has analyzed the reform of coffee markets in Tanzania, to address more widely the contradictions of a donor-driven transition towards an ideal type of market economy in Africa. The coffee case study shows that, although patrimonial politics is still at play in Tanzania, some anti-liberal practices may be better explained through the lens of the politics of ownership. This politics, in its current configuration, seeks to reempower local interests as a result of foreign domination of specific markets.

Before the mid-1990s, the monopolistic system of the domestic coffee trade in Tanzania ensured that coffee remained in local hands up to auction. At the export level, local companies were able to compete with the subsidiaries of large foreign companies. Liberalization saw foreign companies capturing the Tanzanian coffee market, both domestically and at the export level. This triggered a series of reactions attempting to re-empower local interests— such as manipulating licensing rules, encouraging direct selling of coffee at

[26] See Ponte, *Coffee Markets in East Africa*.

auction by independent co-operatives and farmer groups, auction haggling, threats of tightening regulation and, above all, the period of re-monopolization of domestic coffee marketing in Kagera. The objective of these actions was finally incorporated in the 2001 Coffee Act, as a result of which export companies (read 'foreign companies') have been banned from concurrently holding domestic trade licences. In other East African coffee markets, the politics of ownership operated successfully in a pre-emptive way. Ethiopia and Kenya maintained national control over coffee markets by limiting the extent of reforms. In Uganda, counteractive politics was not necessary, because open market competition led to a coffee market (at least in its domestic segment) controlled by a myriad of local companies.

Some of these actions may be read through patrimonial lenses. Licensing powers can be used to create prebends. The continuation of the auction and the re-empowerment of the co-operative unions opened up possibilities for private gain and the building of clientelistic networks based on access to public resources. Electoral politics did play an important role in rescuing the co-operative unions from bankruptcy and in banning private traders from operating in Kagera from 2000 to 2002. Yet the fact that private hullers (local entrepreneurs) were allowed to continue operating—and that the ban on private traders continued in Kagera for almost two years after the 2000 general election—also suggests that the empowerment of cooperative unions can be interpreted along the lines of reversing ownership patterns in the domestic coffee trade.

The politics of ownership incorporates elements of nationalism and indigenization. However, it goes beyond both concepts in the definition of legitimate local interests and in the defence of these. This indicates that, in different historical periods, perceived threats to local ownership may come from different configurations of identity markers. Thus, in the immediate post-colonial period, the politics of ownership in Tanzania was played primarily through nationalist practices (assertion of citizenship, nationalization of assets, monopolization of markets). When, later on, Asian Tanzanian interests were perceived as threatening, the politics of ownership was expressed through 'indigenization' arguments (empowering African Tanzanians). Finally, when ownership of key assets and control of markets fell into the hands of large foreign companies as a result of liberalization and privatization, localism was reasserted as a reaction to an overlap of white and foreign identities. As different groups gain access to different assets and markets, the perception of local interest shifts. The formation and political manipulation of identity markers are thus characterized by overlaps, contradictions and historical change.[27]

[27] In this article, the politics of ownership has been analyzed with a narrow focus on one industry in one country (with some elements of international comparison). The relevant identity

More broadly, I would suggest that loss of national ownership of key assets and markets undermines the legitimacy of the state and of public regulation in Africa. In the post-reform period, the politics of ownership may be read as a relatively low-key attempt by the state to regain political space, not necessarily (or not exclusively) for the (re)distribution of resources for private gain, but for the defence of perceived local interests. Although the politics of ownership operates within the limited margins of the contemporary political economy of African countries, it may be finding new room for manoeuvre within emerging post-conditionality regimes.[28]

Acknowledgment

Published in *African Affairs*, 103, 413 (2004), p. 615–633. An earlier version of this article was presented at the African Studies Association of the UK Biennial Conference, University of Birmingham, 9–11 September 2002. He is grateful to Jannik Boesen, Ronald Fennel, Graham Harrison, Tim Kelsall, Lisa Richey, Ole Therkildsen and Nicholas Wallis for their helpful comments. Support for the research project which generated the article was provided by the Danish Social Science Research Council and the Centre for Development Research, Copenhagen (now Danish Institute for International Studies).

markers that emerged in relation to this case study were race, citizenship and locality. This does not mean that other identity markers such as class, ethnicity, and religion do not apply to the politics of ownership in general. More research is needed on clarifying the changing configuration of this politics in other contexts and countries.

[28] The term comes from G. Harrison, 'Post-conditionality politics and administrative reform: reflections on the cases of Uganda and Tanzania', *Development and Change* 32, 4 (2001), pp. 657–79.

8

Close Encounters

Chinese Business Networks as Industrial Catalysts in Sub-Saharan Africa

Deborah Bräutigam

ETHNIC BUSINESS NETWORKS FACILITATE the exchange of inputs critical to global capitalism—finance, technical knowledge, and marketing information. In East and South-east Asia, Chinese business networks are increasingly acknowledged as an essential component of the area's industrial dynamism. In the now well-known 'flying geese' pattern, business networks facilitated the diffusion of manufacturing from the earliest industrializer, Japan, to the 'newly industrialized countries', Taiwan, Korea, Hong Kong, and Singapore.[1] In the manner of a flock of geese shifting leadership as they continue moving forward, these later industrializers in turn became new leaders as they spread their investment networks to Indonesia, Malaysia, Thailand, and coastal China.

Entrepreneurial networks and clusters in sub-Saharan Africa have not generally produced the kind of strong, transnational links that characterize Asia's 'flying geese' pattern of industrial diffusion. The reasons for this are complex; part of the explanation lies in differences in geography, in the different models provided by leading countries in the neighbourhood, and in the policies adopted by governments in the respective regions. Over the past two decades, however, Chinese businesses in Asia have increased their ties to entrepreneurs in sub-Saharan Africa, leading to consulting, input supply, and,

---

[1] On the 'flying geese model', see Kiyoshi Kojima, 'The "flying geese" model of Asian economic development: origin, theoretical extensions, and regional policy implications', *Journal of Asian Economics* 11, 4 (Winter 2000), pp. 375–401. For a critical perspective on the model, see Martin Hart-Landsberg and Paul Burkett, 'Contradictions of capitalist industrialization in east Asia: a critique of "flying geese" theories of development', *Economic Geography* 74, 2 (April 1998), pp. 87–110.

sometimes, joint ventures. There has been little attention to the dynamics of this growing phenomenon, the ways in which sub-Saharan business networks might connect with Chinese networks, or the potential of Chinese business networks to contribute to Africa's troubled industrial development.

This article explores two contrasting cases of Chinese business networks as they connected with local networks of entrepreneurs in sub-Saharan Africa. The first part of the article briefly contrasts the role of ethnic business networks in industrialization in East and South-east Asia (concentrating on the Chinese), and in sub-Saharan Africa. The second part presents two case studies of links between Asian business networks and networks of African entrepreneurs. In the first case, Chinese entrepreneurs in Mauritius helped persuade the government to establish an export processing zone, and then travelled to Asia, inviting co-ethnics from Taiwan, Hong Kong, and Malaysia to join them in joint ventures. These investments exposed Mauritians (both Chinese and non-Chinese) to the intricacies of global production and export processes, leading to dynamic, export-oriented manufacturing growth. In the second case, Nigerian entrepreneurs in the eastern Nigerian town of Nnewi used their connections to Chinese trading networks (mainly in Taiwan) to assist in the transition from importing auto spare parts, to producing them, creating a small industrial boom.

In both cases, local business networks forged links with networks of Asian capitalists, leading to the rapid establishment of a vigorous local manufacturing base. Both cases suggest that important, positive externalities can result from the linkages made possible when Chinese business networks connect with business networks in Africa, or with Chinese who have long made Africa their home. However, while the Mauritian case can be seen as an extra-Asian example of the global reach of Chinese business networks, and even evidence of the growing transnationalism of domestic capital in the Third World (as Mauritian investors expand their investments in nearby Madagascar), the Nnewi case suggests that domestic factors still present significant obstacles to industrial stimulation via transnational business networks. A detailed analysis of those domestic factors is beyond the scope of this article, but we shall return to them in the conclusion.

Ethnic business networks and industrialization in comparative perspective

Ethnic business networks comprise professional and social relationships among entrepreneurs sharing a particular ethnic or cultural background. These relations exist in at least three separate forms: kinship ties that link together components of extended family enterprises; social ties that form through shared social histories, for example attendance at the same school or membership in the same clubs; and professional ties based on connections formed in the course of repeated business transactions: buying, selling, or subcontracting. These three categories span the range from informal to formal, and they often overlap. The networks themselves are woven together with strands of information, shared contacts, sometimes finance (credit or investment), and a degree of trust (frequently backed up by group-based sanctions). An important element of exclusion is present in the notion of networks, epitomized by the term 'old boys' network'. Networks are part of why 'capitalism remains a social phenomenon, embedded in particular cultures and places'.[2]

Both East and South-east Asia and sub-Saharan Africa have strong ethnic business networks. Those in East and South-east Asia have been discussed extensively in the literature, with most attention being given to the Chinese business networks that knit together the export manufacturing success stories in Taiwan, Hong Kong, Singapore, and parts of South-east Asia.[3] Sub-Saharan Africa also has extensive ethnic business networks, but, with the exception of the settler areas of South Africa and Zimbabwe, the East African case of Kenya, and the island of Mauritius, these ethnic networks do not seem to have stimulated significant industrial development.

Asia has a long history of Chinese and Indian business networks that stretch across the region. Chinese merchants in East Asia and Gujarati Muslim traders in South Asia had expanded their trading circuits to include South-east Asia by the thirteenth century, and the Muslims brought their banking and letter of credit system to the region.[4] Chinese (and, to a lesser extent, Indians) became important parts of the population in several South-east Asian countries.[5] By the late nineteenth century, South-east Asia had many large Chinese family firms, already diversified into a number of activities, with networks that extended across borders. For example, the Khaw family began to accumulate wealth in the nineteenth century as tax farmers in Hong Kong and South-east Asia, moving in the early twentieth century into insurance, shipping, and tin mining and smelting in Siam (Thailand), Burma

---

[2] Darryl Crawford, 'Chinese capitalism: cultures, the southeast Asian region, and economic globalization', *Third World Quarterly* **21**, 1 (2000). p. 72.

[3] For an early example of this research, see Yuan-li Wu and Chun-hsi Wu, *Economic Development in South East Asia: The Chinese dimension* (Hoover Institute Press, Stanford, CA, 1980). Other good studies include Ruth McVey (ed.), *Southeast Asian Capitalists* (Cornell University, Southeast Asia Program, Studies on Southeast Asia, Ithaca, NY, 1992); and Peng Dajin, 'Ethnic Chinese business networks and Asia-Pacific economic integration', *Journal of Asian and African Studies* **35**, 2 (2000). Rajeswary Ampalavanar Brown's excellent study, *Capital and Entrepreneurship in South-East Asia* (St Martin's Press, London, 1994) surveys the South Asian business diaspora in South-east Asia.

[4] Brown, *Capital and Entrepreneurship*, pp. 11–13.

[5] Currently, Indonesia has between 5 and 6 million Chinese (2.5–3 percent of the population), while Malaysia has approximately 4.3 million Chinese (29.4 percent), and 1.4 million Indians (9.5 percent), Lynn Pann (ed.), *The Encyclopedia of the Chinese Overseas* (Archipelago Press for the Chinese Heritage Center, Singapore, 1998).

and the Malay States.[6] Indian firms also became true multinationals: by the 1930s, the Indian Sindhi company Chellarams had expanded into South-east Asia, the UK, the Middle East, the West Indies, and West Africa, while the Chandaria Group had subsidiaries in Kenya, Nigeria and elsewhere.[7]

Chinese businesses were particularly important in South-east Asia's industrial development and its export-oriented growth. In 1937, half of the capital invested in Thailand came from Chinese businesses, and the Chinese controlled almost a third of the capital in Malaya-Singapore, and 10 percent in Indonesia.[8] Yet the region's significant export-oriented trajectory was in large part a function of Japanese investment after World War II. Japanese firms in South-east Asia relied on Chinese businessmen who 'provided important distribution networks which were vital for the Japanese because they were newcomers'.[9] Over time, the trading firms that originally helped pass on the imported Japanese goods became manufacturers themselves, helped enormously by the example and knowledge they had gained through close association with Japanese producers.[10] This was the well-known 'flying geese' pattern; in only one example: in the mid-1960s, Japanese companies owned most of the textile industry in Thailand, but by the1980s, most were owned by Thai (Chinese) firms.[11]

Networks were the primary means by which Asia's Chinese and Indian business groups accessed finance, ideas, and overseas markets, as numerous case studies have documented.[12] In the Philippines and Thailand, Doner found that Chinese informal credit networks and trading company links were critical for companies trying to make the transition into export-oriented manufacturing in the auto industry.[13] Korean networks provided similar benefits as they expanded. Rhee described how Korean firms linked new

---

[6] Brown, *Capital and Entrepreneurship*, p. 87.

[7] Brown, *Capital and Entrepreneurship*.

[8] Jamie Mackie, 'Changing patterns of Chinese big business in southeast Asia', in McVey, *Southeast Asian Capitalists*, p. 164.

[9] James Jesudason, *Ethnicity and the Economy: The state, Chinese business and multinationals in Malaysia* (Oxford University Press, Singapore, 1990), pp. 58, 153.

[10] For a discussion of the Japanese links to Chinese business in the industrialization of South-east Asia, see, in addition to Jesudason, *Ethnicity and the Economy*, Akira Suehiro, 'Capitalist development in postwar Thailand: Commercial bankers, industrial elite, and agribusiness groups', in McVey, *Southeast Asian Capitalists*, and Anuwar Ali and Wong Poh Kam, 'Direct foreign investment in the Malaysian industrial sector', in K. S. Jomo (ed.), *Industrializing Malaysia: Policy, performance, prospects* (Routledge, London, 1993), pp. 77–117.

[11] Kunio Yoshihara, *The Rise of Ersatz Capitalism in South East Asia* (Oxford University Press, Oxford, 1988), p. 19.

[12] For a small sample, see Gary Hamilton, *Asian Business Networks* (Walter de Gruyter, New York, 1996); Murray Weidenbaum and Samuel Hughes, *The Bamboo Network: How expatriate Chinese entrepreneurs are creating a new economic superpower in Asia* (The Free Press, New York, 1996).

[13] Richard Doner, 'Politics and the growth of local capital in SEA: Auto industries in the Philippines and Thailand', in McVey, *Southeast Asian Capitalists*, pp. 212–13.

Bangladeshi export industries to distribution systems in Europe and the United States.[14]

At an early date, the Asian diaspora's capital and networks reached across to sub-Saharan Africa. Some sources date the origin of trade links between South Asia and Africa to the first century AD.[15] Gujarati traders followed the dhow routes from Muscat to Mombasa and Zanzibar as early as the thirteenth century, bringing Indian textiles and buying ivory and gold, and later settling along the coast. The eunuch admiral Zheng He sailed fleets of enormous Chinese junks, each carrying up to a thousand men, to the east coast of Africa between 1405 and 1433. After three officially sponsored voyages, the second Ming emperor forbade further expeditions, and these early contacts failed to establish any direct trade links between Chinese and Africans.

By the twentieth century there were significant communities of Asians in some parts of Africa. In some states such as Kenya, Uganda, and South Africa, clusters of South Asian settlers began to make the transition into industrial production.[16] Syrian/Lebanese businesses (mainly in West Africa) also made some initial industrial investments, although there is comparatively little research on their contribution. Chinese immigration was significant only in South Africa, Madagascar, and Mauritius, and in all three countries Chinese entered into manufacturing.[17] Most Asian business communities retained ties with their Asian homeland, often through business networks.

Many of sub-Saharan Africa's indigenous entrepreneurs also belong to well-established business networks. The trading networks of the Hausa and Igbo are legendary, as are the 'Mercedes mamas', market women of West Africa, who ply the region's trading circuits with their goods in large bundles. However, research on indigenous business networks in sub-Saharan Africa suggests that they are less likely than European or Asian networks (in Africa) to provide the kind of credit, information, and examples that can launch an

[14] Yung Whee Rhee, 'The catalyst model of development: Lessons from Bangladesh's success with garment exports', *World Development* 18, 2 (February 1990), pp. 333–46.

[15] In a personal communication, Dorothy McCormick (Institute of Development Studies, Nairobi, Kenya, 17 October 2001) noted that the *Periplus of the Erythraean Sea*, written in the first century AD, describes direct trade between East Africa and India, with East Africa trading gold, ivory, and slaves for Indian cloth and beads. This may also have been part of the ancient Arab-mediated 'dhow trade'. See also Shawkat Toorawa, 'Imagined territories: The pre-Dutch history of the Indian Ocean', in S. J. T. Evers and V. Y. Hookoomsing (eds), *Globalisation and the South-West Indian Ocean* (University of Mauritius/International Institution for Asian Studies, Réduit, Mauritius/Leiden, 2000), pp. 31–9.

[16] For an excellent study of South Asian industrialists in Kenya, see David Himbara, *Kenyan Capitalists, the State and Development* (Lynne Rienner Publishers, Boulder, CO, 1994). See also Keith Hart and Vishnu Padayachee, 'Indian business in South Africa after apartheid: New and old trajectories', *Comparative Studies in Society and History* 42, 4 (October 2000), pp. 683–712.

[17] In Mauritius the Chinese population reached 25–30,000, or nearly 3 percent, in Madagascar 18,000 (including children of mixed parentage), and in South Africa 20–25,000. Chinese immigration was not significant in any other African country. Pann, *Encyclopedia* (*passim*).

entrepreneur into manufacturing.[18] Much of sub-Saharan African business remains in the informal sector, and this would explain some of the limits of indigenous networks. Researchers also suggest that indigenous African business networks are segregated by ethnicity as well as socio-economic status, and that African businesses seem less likely to be linked to other groups outside the region that could provide important models, ideas, and resources. McCormick's work in Kenya's garment sector demonstrates that networks of Asian (generally, Indian) and African entrepreneurs in Kenya seldom overlap. In her study, mass producers of garments for export (with global linkages) were 100 percent Asian, while custom tailors (limited to the domestic market) were 95 percent African.[19] McCormick argues that access to entrepreneurial networks helps explain why Asian manufacturers in Kenya produce more efficiently than others, and why they have more potential for growth.

Networks among indigenous Africans may be less able to provide access to capital and credit. In Nigeria's northern plastics industry, Zakaria found that up to 60 and 70 percent, respectively, of Lebanese and Chinese factory owners got their initial capital from their extended families and networks.

By contrast, 71 percent of indigenous Hausa entrepreneurs funded their investments through personal savings.[20] Fafchamps found that, in Kenya and Zimbabwe, only European and Asian networks offered their members significant, preferential access to supplier credit, primarily because nonindigenous groups had access to information about the reliability of others in their network, but not those outside.[21]

Little research has been done on Chinese business networks in an African context. An exception, Gillian Hart's case study of Taiwanese networks in a KwaZulu-Natal, South Africa cluster of garment manufacturing, provides a rare look at the start of an investment sequence that might have represented the early stage of the flying geese model.[22] Hart's research focused primarily

---

[18] See, for example, Kinuthia Macharia, *Social and Political Dynamics of the Informal Economy in African Cities* (University Press of America, Lanham, MD, 1997). Dorothy McCormick discusses the informality of African business in Kenya in her paper 'Enterprise clusters in Africa: On the way to industrialisation?' Discussion Paper (Institute of Development Studies, University of Sussex, Brighton, 1998). For a study that includes both formal and informal businesses, see Abigail Barr, 'Enterprise performance and the functional diversity of social capital'. Working Paper 98/01 (Centre for the Study of African Economies, Oxford University, 1998).
[19] Dorothy McCormick, 'Industrial district or garment ghetto? Nairobi's mini-manu-facturers', in Meine Pieter van Dijk and Roberta Rabellotti (eds), *Enterprise Clusters and Networks in Developing Countries* (Frank Cass, London, 1997), p. 117.
[20] Yakuba Zakaria, *Entrepreneurial Ethics and Trust: Cultural foundations and networks in the Nigerian plastic industry* (Ashgate, Brookfield, 1999), pp. 25–6.
[21] Marcel Fafchamps, 'Ethnicity and credit in African manufacturing', *Journal of Development Economics* 61, 1 (February 2000), pp. 205–35; Marcel Fafchamps, 'Trade credit in Zimbabwean manufacturing', *World Development* 25, 5 (May 1997), pp. 795–815.
[22] Gillian Hart, 'The agrarian question? Agro-industrial linkages through Asian lenses', *Journal of Peasant Studies* 23, 2–3 (January–April 1996), and Gillian Hart, *Global Connections:*

on a comparison between the mode of production in Taiwan and that used by the Taiwanese industrialists in South Africa, but her study provides insights that are useful for understanding how this network worked as an extension of those operating in Asia, and how the connections were first made between Africa and the Asian firms. Hart found that the initiative rested first with local government officials in KwaZulu-Natal, assisted by their own contacts with a Hong Kong industrialist who had relocated nearby. Around 1984, with the help of this Hong Kong industrialist, municipal bureaucrats from the town of Newcastle travelled to Taiwan and Hong Kong to hold seminars publicizing the attractions of their region for Chinese investors.[23] Eventually, some 59 Taiwanese firms invested in Newcastle and other approved regions, mainly producing knitwear for the South African market. Some tried to export, but met with difficulty because frequent strikes by a mobilized labour force made it hard to meet order deadlines. Hart demonstrated how the original investors were joined by small, new firms established by their own former technicians (most of them also from Taiwan) who began to subcontract to their former firms. Some of the older firms supplied credit to the new firms.[24] In one case, a former technician who subcontracted to his former firm was a black South African. This entrepreneur, who was 'unlicensed and operates out of an old grain storage facility',[25] may represent the first glimpses of what might eventually be a 'flying geese' model, or he may represent a dead end; it is difficult to tell from the case.

Three fundamental differences between East and South-east Asia and sub-Saharan Africa may account for the fact that business networks in Asia facilitated the 'flying geese pattern' of industrialization there,while business networks in sub-Saharan Africa apparently have not done so: maritime geography, the 'neighbourhood' effect, and the policies followed by post-independence governments towards Chinese and Indian businesses. First, the historic ease of maritime travel in South-east Asia, and along the extended coast of China and southern India, meant that these areas were incorporated into extensive, dense, cross-regional trading networks as long ago as the Roman Empire. These maritime networks were extended to some parts of the coast of East Africa—Zanzibar, Kilwa, and other towns—but maritime trade was completely absent from the rest of sub-Saharan Africa until the fifteenth century. The simple fact of easy and regular transport in Asia allowed significant trading ties to build up; later, coastal East Africa was linked to networks that were already strong in South Asia.

The rise and fall of a Taiwanese production network on the South African periphery. Working Paper No. 6. (University of California, Institute of International Studies, Berkeley, CA, 1996). See also J. Pickles and J. Wood, 'Taiwanese investment in South Africa', *African Affairs* **88** (1989), pp. 507–28.

[23] Hart, *Global Connections*, p. 14.   [24] *Ibid.*, p. 19.   [25] *Ibid.*, p. 28.

Thus, maritime geography helped coastal Asia, and coastal areas of sub-Saharan Africa (but, importantly, not the rest of the continent), to become host to extended business groups that could potentially have served as a 'flying geese' conduit allowing manufacturing to spread from its earlier home to more outlying areas. This happened in East and South-east Asia. Yet two other factors were also different. In Asia, Japanese entrepreneurs came first, making contacts with the Korean, Chinese and Indian firms in the area, and eventually passing technology and leadership on to these firms. Sub-Saharan Africa had no similar neighbourhood leader who could act as an 'export catalyst' or be the first leading goose in the flying geese model. South Africa could have played this role, but instead of facilitating investment in neighbouring countries, as Japan had done, the government in South Africa chose to insulate itself in an effort to preserve its apartheid system.[26]

This brings us to the third factor: government policy. Even in those areas where Asian capital was already providing significant economic stimulus, some governments reacted by trying to crush a group they saw as a political threat. Uganda's Idi Amin expelled some 80,000 Asians, including many who had started manufacturing firms. Tanzania nationalized many Asian businesses. Asian entrepreneurs encountered perhaps the least oppression in Kenya, where the Kenyatta government (like the post-colonial government of Malaysia) chose an affirmative action approach to provide advantages to indigenous business. As a consequence, Asians owned 55 percent or more of the medium and large manufacturing firms in Kenya in 1998.[27] Finally, as many studies have pointed out, the policies of post-colonial governments in most parts of sub-Saharan Africa made industrialization difficult for private capital.[28] In part this was due to the political threat posed by business as a rival source of power. At the same time, some leaders believed that their domestic capitalists were too weak to lead the industrialization effort, and put resources into building up state-owned manufacturing as an alternative strategy. In contrast, a business-friendly policy environment in many Asian countries is

---

[26] For discussions of the experience of Indian business in South Africa, see Vishnu Padayachee and Robert Morrel, 'Indian merchants and *dukawallahs* in the Natal economy, c1875–1914', *Journal of Southern African Studies* 17, 1 (March 1991), pp. 71–102; Hart and Padayachee, 'Indian business in South Africa', p. 683.

[27] A. Bigsten, P. Collier, S. Dercon, M. Fafchamps, B. Gauthier, J.W. Gunning, A. Isaksson, A. Oduro, R. Oostendorp, C. Patillo, M. Soderbom, F. Teal and A. Zeufack, 'Contract Flexibility and Conflict Resolution: Evidence from African manufacturing', (Department of Economics, Stanford University) (mimeo), cited in Marcel Fafchamps, 'Business networks in sub-Saharan Africa', in Masahiko Aoki and Yujiro Hayami (eds), *Communities and Markets in Economic Development* (Oxford University Press, New York, 2001), p. 196.

[28] There are extensive analyses of the problematic policy environment in sub-Saharan Africa. See, in particular, Howard Stein (ed.), *Asian Industrialization and Africa: Studies in policy alternatives to structural adjustment* (St Martin's Press, New York, 1995), which provides useful comparisons.

widely agreed to be one of the fundamental components of the 'East Asian miracle', even if dispute still exists over what those policies were, and which were critical.[29]

In Africa, the dynamic business networks that brought East Asian capital and dynamism to South-east Asia and coastal China and that have received so much attention in Asia's 'flying geese model' are notable mainly for their absence. This has started to change, in small degrees. Taiwanese and Hong Kong firms began in the 1970s and 1980s to establish closer business ties in sub-Saharan Africa, leading in some cases to investment. Their reach has been quite uneven, with a small number of countries (mainly in southern Africa) receiving the bulk of interest.[30] Yet as the research reported below illustrates, the origins of some of sub-Saharan Africa's manufacturing success stories can be traced to direct links formed between Asian and African networks. Do Chinese networks operating in Africa represent an extension of the 'flying geese' model whereby a more developed trading partner begins by producing goods at home and exporting, then moves into direct production in a less-developed foreign country, providing a stimulus for investment by example, and by joint ventures, and finally moves on, bought out by local entrepreneurs, who then take over the lead? What are the possibilities for businesses in Africa to form linkages with transnational Chinese networks that enable them to reap some of the synergies of this particular model of capitalism?

Exploring these questions thoroughly would require the examination of multiple cases of Chinese networks operating in Africa. Very little research of this nature exists; Hart's study of Taiwanese investment in South Africa is an exception. My own preliminary investigation of these issues draws on fieldwork from two additional cases of Chinese networks in Africa.[31] One, the island nation of Mauritius, demonstrates the ease with which Chinese capitalists with deep roots on the island were able to reach back to East Asia and join their own local knowledge and resources with those provided by transnational Chinese networks. The second case, the decades-long relationship between Igbo trading networks in Nigeria's eastern city of Nnewi and Chinese production and distribution firms scattered across East and South-east Asia,

[29] See World Bank, *The East Asian Miracle* (World Bank, Washington, DC, 1993); Deborah A. Bräutigam, 'What can Africa learn from Taiwan? Political economy, industrial policy, and adjustment', *Journal of Modern Africa Studies* 32, 1 (1994) as well as Stein, *Asian Industrialization and Africa*, for a sample of these debates.

[30] United Nations Conference on Trade and Development (UNCTAD) Annual Report for 1997: *Transnational Corporations,Market Structure and Competition Policy* (United Nations, New York and Geneva, 1997) gives a table listing recent Asian investment in Africa.

[31] My fieldwork on these cases took place in multiple visits to Nigeria and Mauritius in the period 1991–9. In the case of Nnewi, all manufacturers of auto spare parts were interviewed. In Mauritius, interviews took place with officials of the Chinese business associations and with several influential Chinese businessmen.

demonstrates the potential, but also the limits, of a strategy of linking indigenous African networks to Chinese networks in Asia. Both the Nigerian and Mauritian cases also highlight the importance of the state in providing an environment where capitalist networks can flourish.

Chinese business networks and capitalism in Mauritius

Chinese business networks are responsible for some of the information, ideas, and capital that helped launch the small Indian Ocean nation of Mauritius as an important centre for export-oriented industry. Yet the fact that these moves required the 1970 'trigger' of legislation establishing an export processing zone (Africa's first) and were boosted in 1983 by the fears of Hong Kong industrialists as Great Britain negotiated the return of Hong Kong to China, provides an important corrective to the idea that Chinese networks might simply spread from one area to another, given the adequate density of a Chinese population.

The presence of Chinese business in Mauritius has deep roots, although not nearly as deep as those in South-east Asia. Chinese were among the earlier settlers in Mauritius, a country that was uninhabited when it was first discovered and settled by Europeans. Fujian and Cantonese merchants in partnership with French traders brought the island into the direct China trade soon after 1750.[32] Two Chinese men began planting tea on the island in 1770.[33] An early traveller reported seeing Chinese men smoking pipes in Port-Louis's tea shops and cafés in 1801, and a small but distinct Chinatown had been established by 1817.[34] By the mid-1880s, the Chinese in Mauritius numbered several thousand.[35] At that time, the Port-Louis market in Mauritius was said to be 'dominated' by Chinese traders, and one visitor reported, 'in every out-of-the-way nook and corner of the island' you found 'a Chinaman's shop'.[36] Mauritius also became an important transit point for overseas Chinese moving on to settle on the African continent and in Madagascar.

---

[32] Huguette Ly-Tio-Fane Pineo, 'Mauritius', in Pann, *Encyclopedia*, p. 351.

[33] Prof. Sir Edouard Lim Fat, 'The contribution of the Chinese in the industrialization of Mauritius', talk given at the First World Chinese Conference held in Mauritius, 23–26 April 1992.

[34] Burton Benedict, *Mauritius: Problems of a plural society* (Frederick Praeger Publishers, New York, 1965), p. 20.

[35] Mauritius was also an important destination for immigrant Indians, including Gujarati Muslim merchants, as discussed above, but this narrative will focus on the Chinese.

[36] Philip Snow, *The Star Raft: China's encounter with Africa* (Weidenfeld & Nicolson, New York, 1988), p. 55.

The Chinese in Mauritius were well organized and maintained ties with their homeland through return visits to their ancestral place of origin, often to find spouses. The colonial government banned Chinese from buying land unless they severed their ties with China, and the Chinese, who were reluctant to do so, did not become plantation owners, as did some of the wealthier Indians on the island.[37] By the early twentieth century, there were some 25 to 30 separate Chinese clans in Mauritius, mainly Hakka, but also Cantonese.[38] In 1908, Chinese businesses organized a Chinese Chamber of Commerce, only two years after the founding of a Chinese chamber in Singapore. Some of the region's earliest factories were established by Chinese: tobacco processing (1874) and alcohol distillation (1897).[39] By 1925, Chinese manufacturers were producing boots and shoes, rum, and aloe bags for shipping sugar. Seven out of eight cigarette factories were owned by Chinese families, including the clans of Ng Cheng Hin, Venpin, Lueng Pew and Ah-Fat.[40] While many Chinese lived in the rural towns of the island, each clan established a business and social centre in Port Louis, the capital. There they would find Chinese food and accommodation, and the opportunity to make business contacts, or perhaps share the cost of a truck to transport their goods to the rural areas. At the turn of the century, some 80 percent of the Chinese in Mauritius were traders, but as their level of education rose, other opportunities presented themselves, and by 1944 only 33 percent remained as merchants.[41]

Ethnic networks continued to connect Sino-Mauritians to the Chinese diaspora in Asia, even when they moved into other professions. The case of Sir Edouard Lim Fat demonstrates how helpful this was for the industrial transition in Mauritius. In 1970, Mauritius became one of the earliest developing countries to establish a duty-free export processing zone (EPZ). An institutional invention of the Irish, EPZs were rapidly adopted in the 1960s by countries in East and South-east Asia, where their tax-free incentives helped launch the region's export-led growth. An engineering professor at the University of Mauritius and also a businessman, Dr Lim Fat was one of the early visionaries pushing for the establishment of an EPZ. The idea for the zone came to him during frequent visits to Asia in the 1960s.[42] The Lim Fat family was originally from China's Canton area, and Dr Lim Fat's in-laws had fled to

[37] Kevin Shillington, *Jugnauth: Prime minister of Mauritius* (Macmillan Education, Basingstoke, 1991).

[38] Interview, Prof. Donald Ah Chuen, President of the Chinese Chamber of Commerce, Port Louis, 21 April 1999.

[39] Lim Fat, 'Contribution of the Chinese'.

[40] Chinese Chamber of Commerce, 'The Chinese Chamber of Commerce: a few historical notes', 90th Anniversary Special Souvenir Magazine (December 1998); Pineo, 'Mauritius,' p. 354.

[41] Huguette Ly-Tio-Fane Pineo, *Chinese Diaspora in the Western Indian Ocean* (Éditions de L'Océan Indien and Chinese Catholic Mission, Port Louis, Mauritius, 1985), pp. 80–1.

[42] Interview, Professor Sir Edouard Lim Fat, Port Louis, 19 April 1999; see also Dick Chan, 'Mauritius wants to be Hong Kong', *South China Morning Post* (Hong Kong), 23 January 1995.

Taiwan after 1949. (Other parts of their family emigrated to Singapore and Hong Kong.) In this case, it was the diaspora connections and social networks that provided the idea of an export processing zone, but it would be the business networks that would bring capital from Hong Kong and Taiwan, for investment in export-oriented manufacturing.[43]

Dr Lim Fat travelled to Puerto Rico to compare its EPZ with those he had seen in Asia. His research was reported in a paper delivered in November 1969 at the World Sugar Congress held in Mauritius, and later circulated widely in the government. The paper directly stimulated the December 1970 Export Processing Zones Act No. 551. Shortly after the act was passed, Sino-Mauritians such as Dr Lim Fat travelled to Asia, 'taking advantage of [their] numerous personal contacts in these Far Eastern lands' to promote the EPZ 'with ceaseless missionary zeal'.[44] The Lim Fat family established one of the first three EPZ factories, with a partner he first met in Hong Kong.[45]

Sir Jean Ah Chuen was another early investor in the EPZ.[46] Sir Jean was the first Sino-Mauritian to be nominated to the Legislative Council in Port Louis (in 1948). Active both in politics and in business, Sir Jean also had extensive connections in Asia. His sister was married to a Hong Kong businessman, Joseph Lee, originally from Shanghai, who served as the honorary consul for Mauritius in Hong Kong. Through Lee's contacts with Shanghai manufacturers who had settled in Hong Kong after the Communist victory in 1949, the Ah Chuen family bought second-hand machinery from a Hong Kong firm and established a wig factory in the EPZ. Although this venture failed after 18 months, their second venture was more successful. An effort to produce cotton t-shirts, and later on woollen knitwear, this investment (in which the Ah Chuen family was a minority shareholder) also boasted a Shanghai–Hong Kong connection through the firm Textile Industries.

The success of Sino-Mauritian business networks showed in the percentage of Hong Kong equity capital invested in the EPZ: more than 90 percent in the early years.[47] Taiwan and Malaysia also sent investors, and a few Singapore firms set up operations. Between 1971 and 1975, EPZ exports grew by 31 percent per annum. By 1982 there were more than 115 EPZ firms, and

---

[43] Investors from Europe and (less so) the United States also invested in the Zone at first; later, most of the capital came from Mauritians themselves.

[44] L. M. Lim, 'Hong Kong and the free zone', *L'Express* (Port Louis, Mauritius), 11 July 1997. See also Michael Young, 'Mauritian development strategy: Hong Kong is the model', *The Financial Times*, 5 May 1971.

[45] Ironically, his partner was German, although he met him through Chinese network connections. Interview, Port Louis, 19 April 1999.

[46] Interview with Professor Donald Ah Chuen, Port Louis, 21 April 1999.

[47] An anonymous reviewer of this article noted that many of the Asian industrialists brought in used machinery from Asia, but valued it at the price of new equipment; thus the value of this Asian investment may have been inflated.

59 percent of the capital invested in the EPZ came from Hong Kong Chinese.[48] In 1983, as the British and Chinese governments held talks about the future of Hong Kong, the Mauritian Prime Minister (who was quite aware of the fears of the Hong Kong Chinese and determined to take advantage of the situation) made an official trip to China, stopping over in Hong Kong to give two seminars on the attractions of Mauritius as an investment site. Following this up with other government contacts, the Mauritian government established itself as the partner of the Mauritian Chinese in their networks, working with them to foster Asian investment in the island.[49] The appeal of the Chinese overseas network in making Mauritius a destination for Hong Kong capital was clear, as a Sino-Mauritian remarked: 'The Hong Kong investor who comes here does not feel so much like a stranger as he would in Africa. He sees Chinese faces, he eats Chinese food, his wife has someone to talk to.'[50]

Early in the life of the EPZ, joint ventures between East Asian and local investors were common, although this was not a requirement for foreign investment. Joint ventures appealed both to Franco-Mauritians who had amassed capital in the sugar industry, and Sino-Mauritians who had become wealthy through trade and local manufacturing. Because Mauritians had the desire to learn the business, while the Asian firms needed the risk-sharing and the local knowledge and contacts, the joint ventures were genuine, not 'paper' partnerships like so many joint ventures between Indians and Africans in Kenya, for example. The importance of the initial links with Chinese businesses clearly made the EPZ concept a success from the outset, by bringing capital from Chinese in Asia to Mauritius. But these links were also important for transferring information that would reduce the risks and costs to Mauritians of embarking on export-oriented industry. A Sino-Mauritian analyst pointed this out in a 1997 newspaper article:

> Most of [the local investors] were ex-partners or employees of EPZ firms who over the years had acquired the necessary experience and know-how from the Hong Kong industrialists in such vital areas as international marketing, the latest technology and large-scale industrial production and management, and felt confident enough to start their own EPZ enterprises.[51]

This was the 'flying geese model' in action. In time, many local Mauritians invested in the EPZ. Two of the earliest firms were established by Sino-Mauritians with overseas partners: Suzy Toys (Lim Fat), and Textile Industries

---

[48] Roland Lamusse, *The Breakthrough in Export-processing Industrialization in Mauritius*. (African-American Issues Center Discussion Paper No. 13, Boston, MA, no date, c.1985).

[49] This is discussed in Shillington, *Jugnauth*, pp. 142–4.

[50] Comment by Philippe Chan Kin, former chairman of the Mauritius Export Processing Zone Association, in Blaine Harden, 'Mauritius breaks out of Africa's poverty: free export zone works wonders for tiny island', *Los Angeles Times*, 21 November 1988.

[51] Lim, 'Hong Kong and the free zone'.

Ltd, now part of the Esquel Group (Ah Chuen).[52] Other firms were established by the Lai Fat Fur and Lam Po Tang groups. Franco-Mauritians and Muslim Indian Mauritians also invested, including the Espitalier Noël family and the Currimjee group. By the late 1980s, more than half of the equity in the EPZ was local, and Mauritius had become the third largest exporter of 'Woolmark' knitwear in the world. Support industries producing boxes, thread, buttons, and packaging materials for export firms had also grown, and most of these firms were owned by local Chinese. At present, Mauritian owners account for about 60 percent of the capital invested in export manufacturing in Mauritius.[53]

The Chinese networks in Mauritius also continue to facilitate a role that Mauritius first began to play in the eighteenth century: they serve as a gateway for overseas Chinese entrepreneurs interested in investing both in Mauritius and elsewhere in Africa. Some of the promotion of Mauritius took place during large clan reunions, which have brought overseas Chinese from across the diaspora to gather in Mauritius. One such meeting of the Chung family brought some 200 overseas Chinese relatives to Mauritius, including some who were in business in Malaysia. The clan members made plans to conduct a joint mission to South Africa and Namibia to explore business opportunities there. The first World Conference of Overseas Chinese, held in Mauritius in 1992, performed a similar role.[54]

Chinese entrepreneurs in Mauritius have also formed new networks with other Chinese outside their direct kin groups. The US Africa Growth and Opportunity Act, passed in late 2000, offered duty-free entry to garments and other industrial goods produced in sub-Saharan Africa. This has reawakened interest in Africa as a production location among Asian investors who have run up against quotas in exports from Asia to the United States. In anticipation of the passage of the Act, the Federation of Textile Manufacturers and Merchants of Malaysia (largely a Chinese organization) asked the Chinese Chamber of Commerce (CCC, one of two Chinese business associations on the island) to help facilitate a 1998 visit to Mauritius and Southern Africa to explore investment possibilities in the region. Another network was expanded when Chinese business leaders from the Chinese Business Chamber (CBC) in Mauritius met the head of the Associated Chambers of Commerce and Industry of Malaysia (ACCIM—whose members are largely Chinese) at a conference organized in Mauritius by the UN Conference on Trade and Development. The two groups arranged to take CBC members from Mauritius

---

[52] *Ibid.*, p. 3.

[53] 'L'apport hongkongais dans la ZF', *L'Express*, 1 July 1997.

[54] It is not known whether any of these meetings have actually led directly or indirectly to new investment or joint ventures in continental Africa. This would be an interesting subject for further research.

to meet the ACCIM in Malaysia in 1999. The CBC promoted investment opportunities in the EPZ and the offshore financial sector, and showed a documentary put together by the Mauritius Freeport Authority, an organization headed by Dr Lim Fat. They also urged the Malaysians to consider Mauritius as a convenient gateway to the markets of the Southern Africa Development Community and the Common Market for Eastern and Southern Africa. The CBC proposed that members from the two organizations study the possibility of joint ventures in Namibia, Botswana, Mozambique, and Madagascar.[55]

In recent years, the Chinese in Mauritius have been actively exploring business opportunities in Southern Africa, where they may run into a growing number of Taiwanese and Hong Kong businesses that are investing in Lesotho, Madagascar, and South Africa. At least twenty Chinese firms have established factories in Lesotho, producing clothing for the European and American markets. Again, much of this investment came through business networks. A Hong Kong executive explained that he was 'originally from Taiwan and his friends in the business there told him about the opportunities [in Lesotho]'.[56] These examples paint a picture of Chinese business networks operating to expand Chinese investment in sub-Saharan Africa, something that by itself can help the process of industrial transformation in the region. But Chinese business networks have also facilitated industrial investments by indigenous Africans, who themselves used their own networks to connect to the information and resource channels available in ethnic Chinese networks. The case of Nnewi, below, illustrates this.

Nnewi: the 'Taiwan of Africa'

At one point in Chinua Achebe's Nigerian novel *Anthills of the Savannah*, the main character disguises himself as an itinerant peddler of motor spare parts, describing his business thus: 'Na small motor part him I de sell. Original and Taiwan'.[57] Until the 1980s, motor spare parts sold in Nigeria generally came either from the 'original' manufacturer (Peugeot, Mercedes, etc.) or were counterfeit copies made in Taiwan. However, early in that decade, a number of factories sprang up in the eastern region of Nigeria, particularly in the town

---

[55] Léon Baya, 'Mission en Malaisie: la Chinese Business Chamber confiante des possibilités de "joint-ventures"', *Le Mauricien* (Port Louis), 13 February 1999.

[56] Angela Mackay, 'Africa woos far eastern fashion factories', *Sunday Business*, 23 September 2001.

[57] 'Original' refers to parts made by Peugeot, Mercedes, Toyota, and other manufacturers; 'Taiwan' denotes the copies produced in Taiwan, and marketed in Nigeria.

of Nnewi, producing a wide variety of spare parts for automobiles, trucks, and motorcycles. By the mid-1990s, there were more than 30 fairly modern factories, using imported technology and employing more than 2,700 workers. Some of these factories were exporting to neighbouring countries in West Africa, to the Middle East, and even to Europe. The manufacturing boom attracted attention both in and outside Nigeria.[58]

Trade and institutional innovation have a lively history in the Nnewi region, in part due to the area's early incorporation into international trading circuits. The settlement of the region by the Igbo people in the sixteenth century established nearby Onitsha, on the banks of the Niger River, as a major internal trading port. In the late nineteenth century, Nnewi elites joined the many Nigerians who were producing, collecting, and transporting palm oil for the export market.[59] As transport businesses based in Nnewi grew, other traders began to supply them with spare parts. Nnewi's large Nkwo market for used and new motor spare parts grew into the largest in the region. With time, Nnewi indigenes spread their transport and spare parts outlets from the Nkwo market to other parts of Nigeria (such as the famous Idumota spare parts market in Lagos), and eventually to other cities in West Africa. The Nnewi spare parts trading networks were organized by family, and each family tended to specialize in a particular group of parts, or a particular brand.[60]

Nnewi's first factory, an aluminium foundry, was set up during the Biafran war in the late 1960s. Nnewi and other sites in eastern Nigeria became known for their innovative and desperate attempts to craft military equipment after the blockade imposed by the central government cut off their access to armaments. This resourceful spirit may have lingered after the end of the war, but it was contacts between Nnewi traders and their Taiwanese counterparts that proved the major catalyst to industrialization.

Spare parts for the Nnewi market network were imported at first primarily from Europe, but by the 1960s Asian distributors began to frequent the Nkwo market, offering to produce copies of the European 'original' brand name parts. The first Asian firms were Japanese, but they were rapidly supplanted by traders from Taiwan, who became the source of the 'Taiwan' spare parts that figured in Achebe's novel. Over time, Nnewi motor parts traders arranged to

---

[58] See, for example, 'Managing Nigeria's own Taiwan', *Tell* (Lagos, Nigeria), 4 May 1992; Obi Nwekanma, 'Industrial revolution in the east', *The Sunday Magazine* (Lagos, Nigeria), 6 March 1994.

[59] For excellent descriptions of the Nnewi transport networks in Nigeria, pre-manufacturing, see Stella B. Silverstein, 'Sociocultural organization and locational strategies of transportation entrepreneurs: An ethnoeconomic history of the Nnewi Igbo of Nigeria', (unpublished Ph.D. dissertation, Boston University, Boston, MA, 1983); and Stella Silverstein, 'Igbo kinship and modern entrepreneurial organization: The transport and spare parts business', *Studies in Third World Societies* **28** (1984).

[60] Silverstein, 'Sociocultural organization and locational strategies'.

have their own brand name products made in Taiwan.[61] During the 1970s, many Nigerian traders travelled to Asia to meet their suppliers, and were thus exposed to the dynamism of the Asian newly industrialized countries, as well as the many small and medium-sized firms still operating in Japan. The contrast with Dr Lim Fat's travels to Taiwan from Mauritius is instructive, however. Dr Lim Fat noted the success of export processing zones in Asia, and eventually helped persuade the government in Mauritius to pass legislation establishing such an institution in Mauritius. He and other Sino-Mauritians travelled to Asia in part to persuade Chinese co-ethnics to invest in Mauritius. Many did, reassured in part by the extended family and professional connections made through the Chinese diaspora. The Nnewi traders, on the other hand, used their contacts with the Chinese in Nigeria to locate distributors and producers in Asia, with whom they could trade, and later from whom they could purchase machinery and technical assistance. Without those contacts, the transition to manufacturing might not have happened, but in contrast to Mauritius, there have been no joint ventures of Chinese and Nigerians and no Chinese investment in Nnewi.

The contacts between the Nnewi trading networks and the Chinese networks primarily enabled the diffusion of information and example. As the CEO of Edison Auto Industries, a manufacturer of brake linings and brake fluid, commented, 'For eight years I imported these things [from Asia] and saw how simple they were to make.' He moved into manufacturing after studying machinery and processes in use by his supplier firms in Asia. Connections with Chinese networks like these were particularly important for the Nnewi traders who were learning how to manufacture. Many entrepreneurs had imported parts through Chinese trading companies,which themselves distributed parts made by a number of small firms in Taiwan and elsewhere. All of the Nnewi spare parts firms that established factories in the 1980s and 1990s also continued their distribution networks in Nigeria, simply adding their new brands to existing lines that they continued to import from Taiwan and elsewhere in Asia.[62]

The networks of contacts established during years of trade eased the Nnewi entrepreneurs' task of gathering information about production. One manufacturer who had imported many lines of spare parts made in Taiwan solicited bids for machinery from a number of Taiwanese companies with whom he had grown familiar. In other cases, Nnewi entrepreneurs asked for

---

[61] For an extensive discussion of the Nnewi industrialization experience, see Deborah Bräutigam, 'Substituting for the state: Institutions and industrial development in eastern Nigeria', *World Development* 25, 7 (July 1997), pp. 1063–80. For a comparison between the Nnewi cluster and two Lagos clusters, see Banyi Oyelaran-Oyeyinka, *Networks and Linkages in African Manufacturing Clusters: A Nigerian case study* (United Nations University Institute for New Technologies (INTEC) Discussion Paper No. 2001–5, Maastricht, September 2001).

[62] Bräutigam, 'Substituting for the state'.

recommendations from their Taiwanese networks for technical advisers to install the factories and train local people. Some companies, such as a producer of moulded plastic components, sent groups of workers to Asia (in their case, Shenzhen, China) for on-the-job training in Chinese factories. Others used their contacts with trading companies to identify Chinese manufacturers who were ready to sell used equipment, such as the oil filter manufacturer who purchased the entire plant of his Singapore supplier.

Business relationships with Chinese networks in Asia were strengthened, but these overlapping networks did not lead to extensions of credit, something that is common in the internal operation of ethnic business networks. For example, a businesswoman in Taiwan commented that many years of working together with a Nigerian trader, now a manufacturer, built up a certain kind of trust: 'We started business long ago, so we are very close. We trust each other already. We feel more confident.'[63] The Taiwanese trading company helped the Nigerians to locate machinery when they decided to go into business, and continued to supply them with spare parts made in Taiwan for their trading business. However, when it came down to payment, the Taiwanese firm still refused to ship the goods until the money had been wired from Nigeria. Trust and confidence had limits.

The Nnewi case demonstrates that it is possible for business networks in Asia to form productive linkages with business networks in Africa, transferring ideas and technology and facilitating the development of dynamic manufacturing sectors. Not long after their initial links with the outer edge of the widespread wave of Asian business networks, Nnewi indigenes forged strong bonds with their Asian counterparts, taking Nigerian networks to Asia, and multiplying information, resources, and marketing links. In an interesting way, the relationship in the 1960s and 1970s between the network of Nnewi spare parts traders and the Taiwanese manufacturers does resemble the early 'flying geese' relationship between Japanese manufacturers and Chinese business networks in South-east Asia described above. Nnewi indigenes were able to learn quite a lot about industrialization from their contacts with Chinese businesses in Taiwan and elsewhere. But in the absence of Chinese investment in the region, there were limits to the transfer of knowledge and the building of the kind of multiple strands (family ties, social and cultural celebrations, exchanges of credit, etc.) that characterize business networks among people from the same cultural group. Because of this, the Nnewi trader-industrialists lacked the extra advantage of the kind of learning opportunities possible for Mauritians, who had many joint ventures with, and professional opportunities to work in, overseas Chinese firms set up in the Mauritian EPZ.

---

[63] Interview, Taipei, Taiwan, 25 July 1996.

Although these two cases have focused almost entirely on the societal side of the development of transnational capitalist networks in Mauritius and Nigeria, the networks of Asian, Mauritian, and Nigerian traders and investors operate within different policy environments.[64] We can only explore these briefly, but they are critical for the successful operation of the 'flying geese' model. Without supportive investment policies, transnational relationships will generally be limited to trade, and when investment is shunned, the transfer of technology and learning is made much more difficult. Mauritius has implemented policies very similar to those in place in East and South-east Asia's most dynamic countries.[65] A well-working export processing zone is one aspect of this policy framework, but EPZs do not work in a vacuum. Economic policies also mattered. Both Mauritius and the East/South-east Asian successes have been called 'open economies', but in fact although they all have a high proportion of trade and are thus 'open' economies, they have not generally been 'open' in the sense of being 'free markets'. Exchange-rate and other, more interventionist policies strongly encouraged exports, yet at the same time many aspects of production for the domestic market were protected. Trade and capital account liberalization has taken place (somewhat) in most Asian countries (and in Mauritius), but it has been for the most part quite gradual, and does not characterize the early years when export-oriented industry was first established. In contrast, Nigeria and other sub-Saharan countries have repeatedly failed to establish an environment that would allow either domestic industry or export-oriented firms to grow and thrive.[66] Finally, local governance and social relations also matter. As Hart has pointed out, the outcome of Taiwanese network investments in South Africa was in part dependent on militant local labour relations and municipal politics that were quite different from conditions in Taiwan.[67] This highlights another important aspect of the extension of business networks, and one deserving of further research.

Conclusion

Trading networks are the connective tissue of the global economy in developing countries, but because of their ability to accumulate profits and information,

[64] I appreciate Dorothy McCormick's reminder that the policy aspects of business networks are of key importance, pers. comm. 17 October, 2001.

[65] See Bräutigam, 'What can Africa learn from Taiwan?'.

[66] There are excellent discussions of the policy environment in all the regions mentioned in this article. For Mauritius, see Rajen Dabee and David Greenaway (eds), *The Mauritian Economy: A reader* (Palgrave, New York, 2000). On Nigeria, see Howard Stein, Olu Ajakaiye, and Peter Lewis (eds), *Deregulation and the Banking Crisis in Nigeria: A comparative study* (Palgrave, New York, 2002).

[67] Hart, *Global Connections*, pp. 12–16.

traders who move into production also play a key role in industrialization. Ethnic business networks, particularly Chinese, are an increasingly recognized feature of the dynamic capitalism present in East and South-east Asia. Through the 'flying geese' model, these networks transmit information and resources efficiently, while their members serve as models and tutors for co-ethnics aspiring towards export-oriented industrialization. Sub-Saharan Africa had far fewer networks of Asian traders, even in Mauritius, South Africa, Kenya and other countries where Asian entrepreneurs flourished (relatively). Although indigenous entrepreneurs in other parts of sub-Saharan Africa have long had cross-border trade networks, and many traders sell products made in Asia, few seem to have forged the kind of strong links with Asian networks seen in Nnewi and Mauritius—links that enabled entrepreneurs to learn how to industrialize with greater ease. This is beginning to change. Over the past two decades, Chinese transnational networks have made increasingly visible forays into sub-Saharan Africa, forging links with African capitalists and stimulating industrial transitions in areas such as eastern Nigeria, and Mauritius, that had shown little industrial development before.

The case of Mauritius demonstates that Asian networks in a remote Indian Ocean island can have a powerful impact on a country's economic development, when the networks' resources and information are combined with supportive economic policies. Even though the early 'geese' have long since left Mauritius, the joint ventures they formed with local entrepreneurs persist and have expanded under Mauritian sole ownership. Export manufacturing in Mauritius remains excessively specialized in garments, but many Mauritian entrepreneurs have managed to upgrade their product continually, and to seek out new markets overseas, something they learned from the Hong Kong manufacturers who first came to the island in the 1970s.[68]

The Nnewi case shows that indigenous African networks can take advantage of specific kinds of global trade links to form very helpful connections with networks in other parts of the world. Although these links were vital for producing an industrial transition in Nnewi, these networks are unlikely to produce the kind of export dynamism of Mauritius, mainly because the policy environment has not been conducive to exports. Sub-Saharan Africa's capitalists were left disadvantaged both by their geography and by their governments. Post-independence policy regimes did little to foster indigenous industrialization, and post-1990 structural adjustment policies do not seem to be leading to industrial transformation either. States in the region are weak, and infrastructure poor. Business networks cannot substitute for a weak state, but, as institutions, they can make markets work better by providing information, lowering risks, and easing the transaction costs that accompany transitions from trade to industry, and from production for the local market

---

[68] For a critical but well-informed view of the Mauritian model, see Percy S. Mistry, 'Commentary: Mauritius – quo vadis?', *African Affairs* **98**, 393 (1999), pp. 551–69.

to production for export. As Asian and African business networks expand their global reach, these contacts and their associated benefits are likely to increase. In a supportive policy environment these business networks can be important catalysts for local industrialization in sub-Saharan Africa, as they were in South-east Asia.

Acknowledgment

Published in *African Affairs* 102, 408 (2003), p. 447–467. She acknowledges with thanks resident fellowships from the Woodrow Wilson International Center for Scholars, Washington, DC and the Christian Michelsen Institute in Bergen, Norway. Fieldwork in Mauritius and Nigeria was made possible through a Fulbright Senior Research Fellowship, and by grants from the Aga Khan Foundation, administered through the World Bank's Regional Program on Enterprise Development (RPED) and USAID under Co-operative Agreement No. DHR-0015-A-00–0031–00, respectively. Thanks are also due for helpful comments from David Hirschmann, Dorothy McCormick, Shawkat M. Toorawa, several anonymous reviewers, and participants at the International Conference on Social Capitals at Michigan State University and a public lecture organized by the Chinese Business Chamber in Réduit, Mauritius.

9

Developmental Patrimonialism?
The Case of Rwanda

David Booth and Frederick Golooba-Mutebi

DIFFERENT AFRICAN COUNTRIES ATTRACT DIFFERENT kinds of research. Especially since the 1994 genocide, Rwanda has attracted a large volume of research relative to its size, with special attention to a particular set of topics. Subjects particularly well covered include justice and reconciliation,[1] rural poverty and land,[2] power and ethnicity,[3] the management of knowledge,[4] political space,[5]

---

[1] For example, Phil Clark and Zachary D. Kaufman (eds), *After Genocide: Transitional justice, post-conflict reconstruction and reconciliation in Rwanda and beyond* (Hurst, London, 2008); Scott Straus and Lars Waldorf (eds), *Remaking Rwanda: State building and human rights after mass violence* (University of Wisconsin Press, Madison, WI, 2011), Part III.

[2] An Ansoms, 'Striving for growth, bypassing the poor: a critical review of Rwanda's rural sector policies', *Journal of Modern African Studies* 46, 1 (2008), pp. 1–32; An Ansoms, 'Re-engineering rural society: the visions and ambitions of the Rwandan elite', *African Affairs* 108, 431 (2009), pp. 289–309; Straus and Waldorf, *Remaking Rwanda*, Part IV; An Ansoms and Stefaan Marysse (eds.), *Natural Resources and Local Livelihoods in the Great Lakes Region of Africa: A political economy perspective* (Palgrave Macmillan, Basingstoke, 2011).

[3] Bert Ingelaere, 'Peasants, power and ethnicity: a bottom-up perspective on Rwanda's political transition', *African Affairs* 109, 435 (2010), pp. 273–92; Marie-Eve Desrosiers and Susan Thompson, 'Rhetorical legacies of leadership: projections of "benevolent leadership" in pre- and post-genocide Rwanda', *Journal of Modern African Studies* 49, 3 (2011), pp. 429–53.

[4] Johan Pottier, *Re-Imagining Rwanda: Conflict, survival and disinformation in the late twentieth century* (Cambridge University Press, Cambridge, 2002); Filip Reyntjens, 'Constructing the truth, dealing with dissent, domesticating the world: governance in post-genocide Rwanda', *African Affairs* 110, 438 (2011); Bert Ingelaere, 'Do we understand life after genocide? Center and periphery in the construction of knowledge in postgenocide Rwanda', *African Studies Review* 53, 1 (2010), pp. 41–59; Straus and Waldorf, *Remaking*, Part V.

[5] Danielle Beswick, 'Managing dissent in a post-genocide environment: the challenge of political space in Rwanda', *Development and Change* 41, 2 (2010), pp. 225–51; Paul Gready, '"You're either with us or against us": civil society and policy making in post-genocide Rwanda', *African Affairs* 109, 437 (2010), pp. 637–57; Andrea Purdeková, '"Even if I am not here, there are so many eyes": surveillance and state reach in Rwanda', *Journal of Modern African Studies* 49, 3 (2011), pp. 475–97; Straus and Waldorf, Remaking, Part I.

and Rwanda's role in the Congo wars.[6] This pattern of interest, understandable given the circumstances, has nonetheless resulted in gaps in research coverage, including some topics that usually figure prominently in country bibliographies: the macro-economy, state–business relations, public administration, public services, and political parties.

For related reasons, Rwanda is often also treated as sui generis. It has only occasionally figured in multi-country academic studies focused on generic issues of socio-economic or political development. The focus tends to be more normative than theoretical, with much emphasis on governmental shortcomings in relation to standards of social equity, liberal democracy, or human rights. Lately, one concept from the mainstream of political and social science—'high modernism'—has become prominent in analyses of country policies. This concept is well adapted to supporting a critical view but is not especially helpful in thinking about what distinguishes the Rwandan regime from relevant comparators.[7]

This article addresses one of the more significant substantive gaps in the Rwanda literature, and does so in the context of a cross-national comparative study with theory-building ambitions. The focus is on a well-known but under-documented aspect of the Rwandan Patriotic Front (RPF) as a ruling party: its approach to political involvement in the private sector of the economy. Central to this is the relationship between the RPF and the private-sector operations of the holding company formerly known as Tri-Star Investments and now trading as Crystal Ventures Ltd (CVL), in which the RPF owns 100 per cent of the equity.

Our analytical framework derives from research led by Tim Kelsall in the Business and Politics stream of the Africa Power and Politics Programme (APPP).[8] It draws on a systematic comparison of business–politics linkages across a large set of countries and regimes of South-East Asia and sub-Saharan Africa. The working hypothesis is that while business–politics interactions have neo-patrimonial qualities under most regimes—that is, there is a blending of impersonal/bureaucratic and personal/clientelistic features—it is important to distinguish between more and less developmental forms of neo-patrimonialism.

---

[6] Gérard Prunier, *From Genocide to Continental War: The 'Congolese' conflict and the crisis of contemporary Africa* (Hurst, London, 2009); Filip Reyntjens, *The Great African War: Congo and regional geopolitics, 1996–2006* (Cambridge University Press, Cambridge, 2009).

[7] The term, used by James C. Scott in connection with the excesses of state *dirigisme* in the Soviet Union, Tanzania, and elsewhere, is popular with several contributors to Straus and Waldorf, *Remaking*. However, Scott is unusual among those who work on the role of the state in development in his lack of concern about how, in many countries, development challenges have been overcome with the help of effective state agencies. See James C. Scott, *Seeing Like a State: How certain schemes to improve the human condition have failed* (Yale University Press, New Haven, CT, 1998).

[8] <http://www.institutions-africa.org> (19 April 2012).

The article is structured as follows. First we set out the elements of a typological theory which distinguishes what we call 'developmental patrimonialism' from the modal type of business–politics interaction in sub-Saharan Africa. We then situate Rwanda's historical trajectory as a country in relation to the modal pattern. The next two sections advance an argument about how present-day Rwanda seems to differ from the modal pattern and to approach the developmental patrimonial type, referring particularly to the relationship between the RPF and Tri-Star/CVL. We then expand the discussion to include the roles of the army's Horizon group of companies and a public–private consortium, the Rwanda Investment Group (RIG). The article concludes that, with some qualifications, the concept of developmental patrimonialism captures and helps to illuminate some distinctive features of Rwanda's current political economy.

Developmental patrimonialism in Africa

In the APPP framework, a country is said to display developmental patrimonialism when the ruling elite acquires an interest in, and a capability for, managing economic rents in a centralized way with a view to enhancing their own and others' incomes in the long run rather than maximizing them in the short run. We hypothesize that developmental patrimonialism represents a more likely scenario for achieving economic transformation[9] and social development than the one suggested by orthodox advocates of 'good governance'.[10]

We also draw on the arguments of Mushtaq Khan about the necessary role of central management of rents and other 'primitive accumulation' in the early stages of capitalist development.[11] Khan's political economy is certainly

[9] That is, structural change resulting from widespread productivity gains and not just accelerated growth, following, among others, K. Y. Amoako, 'Transforming Africa—start now, we can't wait', *African Business* **45**, 377 (2011), pp. 24–7; and UN Economic Commission for Africa/African Union, *Economic Report on Africa 2011: Governing development in Africa—the role of the state in economic transformation* (UNECA, Addis Ababa, 2011).

[10] Tim Kelsall, 'Rethinking the relationship between neo-patrimonialism and economic development in Africa', *IDS Bulletin* **42**, 2 (2011), pp. 76–87; Tim Kelsall and David Booth, with Diana Cammack and Frederick Golooba-Mutebi, 'Developmental patrimonialism? Questioning the orthodoxy on political governance and economic progress in Africa' (Working Paper 9, Africa Power and Politics Programme, London, 2010); Diana Cammack and Tim Kelsall, 'Developmental patrimonialism? The case of Malawi' (Working Paper 12, Africa Power and Politics Programme, London, 2010).

[11] Mushtaq H. Khan and Jomo K. Sundaram (eds), *Rents, Rent-Seeking and Economic Development: Theory and evidence from Asia* (Cambridge University Press, Cambridge, 2000); Mushtaq H. Khan, 'Governance and growth: history, ideology, and methods of proof' in Akbar Norman, Kwesi Botchwey, Howard Stein, and Joseph E. Stiglitz (eds.), *Good Growth and Governance in Africa* (Oxford University Press, Oxford, 2012).

heterodox, but increasingly he is in good company in this respect.[12] If he is right, the elimination of rents—and the superseding of patrimonialism—is neither feasible nor desirable until capitalist economies are far more established than at present in most of sub-Saharan Africa. The generation and sharing out of major rents is not only the key to social order and political stability, as argued by Douglass North and his colleagues;[13] it is also an essential means of financing the learning costs involved in the acquisition of technological capabilities by an initial generation of domestically owned firms.[14]

Considerable interest therefore attaches to the question of whether and under what conditions long-horizon rent centralization becomes both attractive and feasible for a country's politically dominant groups and individuals—its political elite. Feasibility, it is assumed, centres upon the ability of leaders to impose the necessary disciplines, first within the political elite itself and then within key elements of the techno-bureaucracy. An important question is what kinds of leaders acquire this sort of ability and under what circumstances?

Most of the instances of developmental patrimonialism identified in a survey of regime types in seven resource-poor tropical African countries were historical examples.[15] They belonged to the immediate post-independence era in countries like Côte d'Ivoire (1960–75), Kenya (1965–75), and Malawi (1964–78). The mechanisms used by these regimes to centralize rent management were varied, but they usually entailed a concentration of power around the person of the President or other 'big man'. There was systematic clientelism and informal use of state resources, and hence a blurring of the distinction between public (state) wealth and the private wealth of the rulers, corresponding to the standard definition of neo-patrimonialism.[16] However, as in comparable regimes in Asia (such as Indonesia and Malaysia), rents were deployed in ways that assisted national development; they did not just serve to enrich the big man and his cronies.

---

[12] See the literature on transformation cited above as well as Justin Lin and Célestin Monga, 'Growth identification and facilitation: the role of the state in the dynamics of structural change', *Development Policy Review* 29, 3 (2011) and Lindsay Whitfield, 'How countries become rich and reduce poverty: a review of heterodox explanations of economic development' (Working Paper 2011: 13, Danish Institute of International Studies, Copenhagen, 2011).

[13] Douglass C. North, John J. Wallis, and Barry R. Weingast, *Violence and Social Orders: A conceptual framework for interpreting recorded human history* (Cambridge University Press, Cambridge, 2009).

[14] Khan and Sundaram, *Rents*, Chapter 1.   [15] Kelsall, 'Rethinking'.

[16] Michael Bratton and Nicolas van de Walle, *Democratic Experiments in Africa: Regime transitions in comparative perspective* (Cambridge University Press, Cambridge, 1997), pp. 61–96. The prefix 'neo' indicates a system which combines patrimonial and legal-rational or modern bureaucratic features. In discussing the more developmental subtype, we drop the prefix solely for economy of expression.

The question obviously arises whether regimes such as those of present-day Ethiopia and Rwanda are also to be considered examples of the type. For Rwanda, the answer to this question is not completely straightforward, as blurring of the boundaries between public wealth and the *personal* wealth of members of the ruling group is not a notable feature of the model. However, developmental patrimonialism covers a cluster of subtypes in which the personalistic element in the centralization of rents is a variable. On this understanding, we argue that there are reasons for including today's Rwanda in the category.[17]

The article is based on research carried out in Rwanda between 2007 and 2011. Fieldwork included 82 semi-structured confidential interviews or other personal communications, several repeat interviews, site visits to CVL companies, and direct observation of key events, including the November 2010 CVL group management meeting. We benefited from exceptionally good access to nearly all the key players in the recent history of the RPF's business operations, an advantage that researchers in this kind of field have not often enjoyed. We also interviewed disinterested but well-positioned observers, and some with reasons to be resentful about RPF business operations or related government decisions.[18] This put us in a position to triangulate information from different and potentially conflicting formal and informal sources, and make judgements on the balance of evidence. In this way, we were able to investigate and validate or invalidate many of the claims—from the serious to the completely scurrilous—which circulate as Kigali gossip or on the internet.

Our analysis is focused on two questions. First, what features of the RPF-led regime correspond to the model of developmental patrimonialism, and with what qualifications; and second what does the Rwandan experience tell us about the general relevance of the model for understanding the options facing sub-Saharan Africa today?

We are aware that any attempt to categorize the regime in Kigali is going to be controversial. Interpretations of almost every aspect of Rwanda and its history are exceptionally polarized. Even scholarly and analytical writings tend to be pigeonholed by their critics as either apologias for or attacks upon Paul Kagame and the RPF. Compounding the problem, Rwandan public policy has been characterized by unnecessary secrecy and its inevitable counterpart, unrestrained rumour-spreading. One of the effects of this is a remarkably low level of knowledge and understanding about some of the topics that

---

[17] For comparable work on Ethiopia, see Sarah Vaughan and Mesfin Gebremichael, 'Rethinking business and politics in Ethiopia: the role of EFFORT, the Endowment Fund for the Rehabilitation of Tigray' (Research Report 02, Africa Power and Politics Programme, London, 2011).
[18] Interviewees included government and RPF officials (22); directors and managers of CVL, Horizon Group, RIG, and parastatal companies (18); other business leaders and staff (26); NGO heads, consultants, and journalists (19); and donor agency advisers (6).

concern us, even at quite senior levels in government and in the resident international community.

We do not expect to avoid being caught up in controversy. However, we should stress that the theory of developmental patrimonialism is not primarily an evaluative exercise but an effort to disentangle the empirical dynamics at the heart of different types of African regimes, past and present. All of the regimes that appear to us to exemplify the more developmental form of neo-patrimonialism pose ethically difficult questions about trade-offs between liberal freedoms and human rights, on the one hand, and development outcomes (and thus other human rights) on the other. These issues merit discussion but we firmly believe that such discussions are only fruitful when they are grounded in a good understanding not just of all the relevant facts but also of systems and linkages.

Rwanda and the African modal pattern

As a developing country, Rwanda suffers from a number of quite severe disadvantages in addition to its violent political history. Landlocked, under-endowed with natural resources other than land and climate, and with an exceptionally unfavourable person–land ratio, it continues to be extremely poor in income and human-development terms. The formal sector of the economy is tiny. As a destination for private investment, it is geographically ill-placed and lacks compelling attractions. Nonetheless, the country's economic growth in recent years has been impressive, averaging over 8 percent per year in real terms since 2005.[19] While this is growth from a low base, it compares favourably with what is being achieved by its better-endowed and more favourably located East African neighbours. In terms of poverty reduction and human development, a huge amount remains to be done, but the latest survey data show income poverty falling from 57 to 45 percent between 2005/6 and 2010/11, and substantial progress on maternal and child mortality rates.[20]

Some see Rwanda's recent progress as a good example of the gains from applying internationally recognized best practices in economic management and governance reform. There is something to this. Rwanda under Kagame is in some respects a star pupil of the Washington Consensus. The RPF-led

[19] National Institute of Statistics of Rwanda, 'Gross domestic product and its structure by activity' (NISR, Kigali, March 2011), Table 2A.

[20] Yusuf Murangwa, 'EDPRS2, EICV3 and DHS4 joint launch: key statistics highlights' (National Institute of Statistics of Rwanda, Kigali, 7 February 2012); Republic of Rwanda, *Rwanda Demographic and Health Survey 2010: Final report* (NISR/Ministry of Health/ICF International, Kigali, December 2011. See <http://www.minecofin.gov.rw/node/441> (14 February 2012).

government has been strongly committed to the private sector as the engine of development. It has recently adopted a good deal of orthodox best-practice thinking in its approach to investment promotion. That is, it has defined its role as facilitating and enabling private investment, with official bodies concentrating on the provision of pure public goods, including policy guidelines, information, standards, and regulation. Rwanda was rewarded for its strenuous efforts to meet the criteria of the World Bank's Doing Business survey when, in 2010, it was categorized as second-top global improver (after Kazakhstan), reaching a global ranking of 58th out of 183 countries and a regional ranking of 4th in sub-Saharan Africa.[21] However, to emphasize these aspects of the situation would be to miss what is most distinctive, interesting, and widely relevant about the Rwandan experience. It would capture only one of the features that distinguish the Rwandan case from what may be called the African modal pattern.

In our understanding, the modal pattern in sub-Saharan Africa today is one in which 'rent seeking' is widespread and uncontrolled, and associated with both political and administrative corruption. The pattern may be seen as having five interrelated elements.[22]

First, rent extraction is a major source of personal enrichment for the political class as a whole as well as for private business. Second, the political leadership is either unwilling or unable to deny access to rent-taking opportunities by its major supporters, because it is largely by distributing such opportunities that it remains in power. Third, policy making is driven in part by the exigency of creating rents for allocation to supporters and for replenishing the campaign funds of the party in power. Fourth, corruption reaches down to the lowest levels of the public service, partly because clientelism has become systemic and partly because the political class lacks the moral authority to maintain a clean administration. Some public servants perform their duties with dedication for idiosyncratic reasons but the dominant pattern has become the exploitation of public office for private gain. As a consequence, finally, appointments and promotions within the civil service have lost their connection to considerations of merit and effectiveness.

We would maintain that, historically, Rwanda has displayed all the elements that, other things being equal, tend to reproduce the African modal pattern. If, as we are going to argue, Rwanda today is somewhat exceptional it would therefore be a mistake to treat this as an historical inevitability. Two sorts of evidence underpin this proposition.

---

[21] World Bank and IFC, *Doing Business 2011: Making a difference for entrepreneurs* (World Bank and International Finance Corporation, Washington, DC, 2010).
[22] See Kelsall, 'Rethinking'; and for a country illustration, Brian Cooksey and Tim Kelsall, 'The political economy of the investment climate in Tanzania' (Research Report 01, Africa Power and Politics Programme, London, 2011).

First, the pre-1994 regimes in Rwanda were characterized by all or most of the features of the African modal pattern. Rwanda's long history as a state means that, in Pierre Englebert's terms, there is a high degree of 'state legitimacy',[23] which contributed to aspects of governmental effectiveness then as it does today. The introduction of multi-partyism came only at the end of the 1973–94 Habyarimana regime and helped to destabilize it. Before that there was a one-party state under which clientelistic rent seeking was generalized, competitive, and disorganized. Businesses needed 'godfathers' within the administration or the military, and through this mechanism the small business sector financed politics.[24] The Akazu, the apex of the clientelist system, was a powerful network close to but not effectively controlled by the President.[25]

Second, there have been repeated indications since 1994 that many actors in the RPF-led political system, not to speak of opposition elements abroad, would have found it both easy and desirable to resume the practices established under the former regime. Kagame's rather austere sense of public duty and strait-laced line on corruption are not to everyone's taste. Some, at least, of the early defections from the RPF government may be best explained in these terms. Of course, the question why former allies of Kagame eventually fell out with him and went into opposition or exile is controversial. The murkiness surrounding what was the eventual fate of some of these people, Hutu moderates and RPF originals alike,[26] does not help in reaching a clear position on the matter. No doubt, each case was specific, and in most of them more than one issue was at stake. Nonetheless, a plausible suggestion about some of the prominent early defectors is that they were eager for a more 'flexible' approach, permitting greater scope for using public funds to buy the political support of key players, 'the working methods of the old regime'.[27]

Even some of the more recent high-level defections are attributed by some observers to an underlying discontent with the rigours of leadership discipline

---

[23] Pierre Englebert, *State Legitimacy and Development in Africa* (Lynne Rienner, Boulder, CO, 2000).

[24] Interviews with elderly and middle-aged Rwandan businessmen, Kigali, 11 March 2009 and 8 November 2010.

[25] Uvin, *Aiding Violence*; Gérard Prunier, *The Rwanda Crisis: History of a genocide* (Fountain Publishers, Kampala, 1999); Frederick Golooba-Mutebi, 'Collapse, war and reconstruction in Rwanda: an analytical narrative on state-making' (Working Paper 2, Crisis States Research Centre, London, 2008).

[26] See especially Prunier, *Continental War*, chapters 1–2, and Joseph Sebarenzi, *God Sleeps in Rwanda: A personal journey of transformation* (Oneworld Publications, Oxford, 2009).

[27] The source of this suggestion is no doubt Kagame himself, but that does not necessarily mean it is wrong or just self-serving. It is discussed in Stephen Kinzer, *A Thousand Hills: Rwanda's rebirth and the man who dreamed it* (Wiley, Oboken, NJ, 2008), Chapter 13, and also in Rosen, 'Rising', where the direct source is the Ugandan journalist and publisher Andrew Mwenda. These are sympathetic but not uncritical commentators on Kagame's Rwanda.

under Kagame. The arrangements described below, in which politically generated opportunities for profit are comprehensively institutionalized and centralized, are seen as a little too austere. The arrests and court judgements that follow even minor infractions seem to many to be unduly severe, even if it is also true that offences are often pardoned and reputations restored quite swiftly.[28] All of this tends to confirm that Rwanda could well have gone, and could still go, the way of the African modal pattern.

From the moment when Kagame secured his leadership of the RPF and the government in 2000, the system in Rwanda has distanced itself from the African modal pattern on each of the five points listed above. We argue that the key to this is a set of arrangements for managing economic rents in a centralized way and deploying them with a view to the long term. This has several dimensions, involving the relationships between private businesses and the government on the one hand, and the army and the ruling RPF on the other. In the next two sections of the article, we focus on the most directly political of these relationships: the RPF's own business operations.

Management of economic rents: the Tri-Star dimension

A key element in the centralization of rent management is the role in the economy of the private holding company Tri-Star Investments/CVL, which is fully owned by the RPF.[29] Tri-Star grew out of the Production Unit maintained by the rebel army during the war of 1990–4. Its initial funding came from political contributions to the war effort by supporters, as part of a wider effort to attract people with business experience and capital from the Rwandan diaspora.[30] Within a few years of the RPF's accession to power, companies owned wholly or mainly by Tri-Star were in metals trading, road construction,

---

[28] Interviews, male senior government adviser, and middle-aged businessman, Kigali, 12 December 2009 and 23 February 2010.

[29] Until recently, the firm's website rather confusingly named three individuals as 'shareholders': John Mirenge, James Gateera, and Faustin Mbundu. However, the legal position is that these three are RPF members with significant business experience who act as trustees on behalf of the party. Currently, the website states that CVL 'is wholly owned by Rwandan business people who pooled resources together to meet challenges of economic recovery and take advantage of growth opportunities in a virgin environment'. See <http://crystalventuresltd.com/index.php> (24 March 2011; 25 February 2012). Both these formulas reflect the sensitivity surrounding the idea of a governing political party being a substantial private entrepreneur, not the real situation. Interviews, male senior journalist; male CVL executive; male government minister; and male senior government figure: Kigali, 20 February and 8 November 2010, 17 February and 22 April 2011.

[30] Interviews, male senior security official; male senior journalist; male former CVL executive; and male CVL executive: Kigali, 11 March 2009 and 20 February, 9 March, and 8 November 2010.

housing estates, building materials, fruit processing, mobile telephony, and printing, as well as furniture imports and security services.

In each of these fields, the Tri-Star subsidiary was initially the largest domestic firm, if not the largest investor in what was an extremely limited and depleted private sector.[31] Today, CVL has a 50 percent stake or more in 11 companies operating in Rwanda.[32] Most of these are the leading national company in their sector. With one exception, the competition they face comes primarily from either regional (usually Kenyan) or international (including notably Chinese) firms. In addition to this core portfolio, CVL has a minority stake in several joint ventures in Rwanda.[33] Outside the country, it owns a chain of coffee shops in the USA and UK,[34] and an air charter company registered in South Africa.[35]

The scale of the operation is substantial in relation to the national economy. In 2009, the group's turnover, referring to majority shareholdings only, was about US$35 million. In this restricted sense profits were around US$7 million after the payment of US$0.8 million in taxes. With the contributions from minority shareholdings, including in the Rwanda branch of the mobile phone company MTN, turnover was US$167 million, post-tax profits US$47 million, and taxes paid US$24 million. While the majority-owned CVL firms represented well under 1 percent of Rwanda's US$5.3 billion GDP, the whole group represented over 3 percent, a significant proportion given the limited size of the formal sector as a whole.[36] The taxes paid by the larger group were

[31] *Ibid.* Interview, middle-aged businessman, Kigali, 23 February 2010.

[32] Inyange Industries (water, dairy, and fruit processing), Intersec Security (private security services), Bourbon Coffee (coffee shops), Mutara Enterprises (furniture imports), Graphic Print Solutions (print and design), Media Systems Group (media services), NPD-COTRACO (roads and civil works), Real Contractors (housing estates), CVL Developers (real estate), Ruliba Clays and East African Granite Industries (building materials). The last two firms are controlled through a 50/50 joint venture with the Rwanda Social Security Board called Building Materials Industries Ltd. <http://crystalventuresltd.com/index.php> (25 February 2012) and personal communication from CVL chief executive officer, John Bosco Birungi, 20 February 2012. See also *The Independent, Rwanda: Remembering the liberation struggle* (*The Independent* Publications, Kigali, 2012), pp. 64–95.

[33] These are MTN Rwanda (mobile phones), 20 percent; Mount Meru-Soyco (cooking oil processing—a plant to be commissioned in July 2013), 20 percent; Rwanda Investment Group (see discussion below), 10 percent; and Ultimate Concepts (Kigali Convention Centre project), 20 percent. Some additional joint ventures have been registered recently, including CARCO (between Petroland Turkey and the CVL subsidiary NPD-COTRACO for commercial concrete production), NPD holding 50 percent (CEO John Bosco Birungi, 20 February 2012).

[34] Bourbon Coffee now has outlets in Washington, DC, Cambridge, MA, and London (*Independent, Rwanda*, pp. 84–7).

[35] *Independent, Rwanda*, pp. 84–7; <http://kigalipost.wordpress.com/2010/05/28/s-africa-based-luxury-jets-owned-by-rpf-nshuti/> (26 February 2011).

[36] Extract from CVL 2009 accounts provided by CEO John Bosco Birungi, 20 November 2010. The same source gave the group's employment as over 5,000, of which 3,500 are classified as permanent.

equivalent to around 9 percent of all direct taxes paid in the fiscal year 2009/10.[37]

As discussed later, the management systems of Tri-Star/CVL have changed and improved over time, but there have been two constants: RPF ownership and a private-sector legal status. The holding company has been governed throughout by a board of directors nominated by the RPF leadership and managed by an executive chair or chief executive officer. Profits from the operations of the subsidiaries have been taxed and then either reinvested or returned as dividends to the RPF.[38] The central relationship is between two formal organizations with their own corporate identities and rules.

We would argue that this arrangement is accurately described as a system for centralizing economic rents. We leave for later the question of what forms of 'rent' are included in Tri-Star/CVL earnings and the significance of this for the development of the Rwandan economy. In this section, we assume the element of rent is significant and focus on how the rent-centralization mechanism helps to shape the wider political economy, setting the Rwandan situation apart from all the five features that define the African modal pattern.

In the modal pattern, rent extraction is a major source of personal enrichment for the political class as a whole. In the current Rwandan pattern, this is not the case: Tri-Star/CVL profits accrue to the RPF corporately.

At the beginning, Tri-Star companies were concerned exclusively with responding to the acute material shortages that characterized the immediate post-war situation, using RPF financial reserves to import goods and even pay civil servants' salaries.[39] In this phase, the party was 'sponsoring the government';[40] financial returns were hardly an issue. As the Rwandan economy recovered from its deep post-genocide depression, however, the Tri-Star/CVL firms became profitable. Benefits then flowed back to the RPF in the form of dividends, at which point they became subject to the decisions of the RPF's national executive committee.[41] What the party did with these funds has not been researched by us and is probably not researchable. However, the important point is that there is no evidence of direct profit taking by individual politicians or military leaders.

For example, the most controversial form of rent extraction in which the new Rwandan elite was involved for a period, namely wartime minerals

---

[37] Calculated from NISR, 'Gross domestic product' and Rwanda Revenue Authority, 'Annual activity report for 2009/10' (Kigali, 2010).

[38] Interview, male CVL director, Kigali, 11 November 2010. The accounts are 'heavily audited'. Interview, male senior journalist, Kigali, 20 February 2010.

[39] Interview, male former CVL executive, Kigali, 9 March 2010.

[40] Interview, male government minister, Kigali, 17 February 2010.

[41] *Ibid.* Interviews, male senior security official; male senior journalist; and middle-aged businessman: Kigali, 11 March 2009, 20 February and 8 March 2010.

trading out of Congo, was in part in the hands of a Tri-Star subsidiary, Rwanda Metals. The holding company records indicate that Rwanda Metals did contribute to the corporate balance sheet of Tri-Star, although profits were not large, especially by comparison with the MTN investments discussed below.[42] Because of the international outcry about exploitation of Congolese natural resources, Rwanda Metals was sold off to a Botswana-based firm soon after the effective end of the war in 2002. We do not have any data with which to assess whether Congo minerals trading made any individuals rich in Rwanda. However, if it did, Tri-Star was not the channel through which it happened.

In the African modal pattern, the political leadership maintains itself in power by distributing rent opportunities to its major supporters. At least since 2000, this has not been the pattern in Rwanda. In the terms used by Bruce Bueno de Mesquita and his co-authors, the political system of the country has a moderately large 'selectorate' (enfranchised citizens) and a smaller winning coalition (the subset of selectors whose support is decisive to the retention of power by the incumbents).[43] More crudely, it is not at present the votes of the general population that keep the incumbents in power. Under these conditions, the theory—which applies equally to regimes that are formally democratic or authoritarian—predicts a leadership preference for providing private goods selectively to members of the coalition, as the cheapest and most reliable means of political survival.[44] Contrary to the theory, the RPF and its allies are gambling on the 'expensive' option of building support on a broad base by demonstrating an ability to provide more and better public goods.[45]

In Rwanda since 2000, policy has been driven rather exclusively by the view that economic and social development—underpinned by adequate provision of essential public goods by the state—is the only feasible route to overcoming the ethnic divisions and violent conflicts of the past. This is formally articulated in a document called 'Rwanda Vision 2020'. Moreover, contrary to what happens with equivalent documents in most countries of the region, this is a

---

[42] Interviews, male former CVL executive, and male CVL executive, Kigali, 9 March and 8 November 2010.

[43] Bruce Bueno de Mesquita, Alastair Smith, Randolph M. Siverson, and James D. Morrow, *The Logic of Political Survival* (MIT Press, Cambridge, MA, 2003).

[44] Bueno de Mesquita, *Logic*, Chapter 3.

[45] One key element in the RPF's power base, the armed forces, is no doubt well provided for corporately, as the theory would predict. However, even at the height of the interventions in Congo, individual military officers were under strong pressure not to acquire material benefits personally, in sharp contrast to the case of Uganda. This is based on interviews with senior DRC field commanders from both countries conducted by Frederick Golooba-Mutebi during the mid-2000s and reported in part in 'The Uganda People's Defence Forces in the context of its predecessor armies: continuity and change' (Draft paper, Makerere Institute of Social Research, Kampala, 2010).

real point of reference for ministers and civil servants.[46] The assumption underlying the vision is that, if economic and social progress occurs fast enough, a new generation will emerge who are capable of fully assuming their national identity as Rwandans rather than privileging what divided them in the past. Many critics of the regime see this as naïve and argue that reconciliation needs to be attended to in a more direct fashion.[47] But in so doing they also confirm that this is indeed the vision that drives policy.

In the African modal pattern, policy making is driven away from a public-goods focus by the need to create rents to allocate to supporters and more generally to finance politics. One of the things that enable the Rwandan regime to deviate from this pattern is the role played by Tri-Star/CVL. The RPF's running costs and campaign funding needs are met in the first instance by party member contributions, but these are able to be supplemented by distributed profits from the holding company. This has the side-effect of removing the pressure on the ruling party to raise political funds by methods that involve fraud, kickbacks, or other corruption.[48]

Readers who approach Rwandan reality from the angle of democratic ideals may well find it unfair that an already dominant political party can finance its activities in this way.[49] However, in the analytical and comparative perspective we adopt, the contrast with the way incumbents normally exploit their position to sustain themselves in power is the more significant feature.

In the modal pattern, corruption has become systemic. In contrast, according to most surveys corruption is quite uncommon in Rwanda's public service at any level, and corruption with impunity is largely absent.[50] 'The least corrupt country I have worked in' was the characterization offered by one experienced 'Africa hand' now in business in Kigali.[51] The explanations are to be found at two levels. First, alleged corruption at high levels has been vigorously suppressed at regular intervals and this has shaped expectations most of the way down the chain of the public administration. Second, the

---

[46] This finding is based in part on direct observation by Frederick Golooba-Mutebi of several Annual National Dialogue sessions and the testimony provided to him by participants in ministerial retreats.

[47] Straus and Waldorf, *Remaking*, pp. 3–21; Filip Reyntjens, 'Rwanda, ten years on: from genocide to dictatorship', *African Affairs* **103**, 411 (2004), pp. 177–210.

[48] Interviews, male government minister; male senior journalist; and male CVL subsidiary manager: Kigali, 17 February, 20 February, and 23 February 2010.

[49] Parties which get at least 5 percent of the popular vote are entitled to modest government funding as members of the Forum of Political Parties. President Kagame is said to be opposed to more substantial state funding for parties on the grounds that it would stimulate the formation of 'fake' parties. Interview, male senior journalist, Kigali, 20 February 2010.

[50] The East African Bribery Index for 2010 found incidents in Rwanda to be 'negligible'—78 bribery experiences out of 4,350 interactions.<http://www.transparency.org/news_room/latest_news/press_releases_nc/2010/2010_07_22_ti_kenya_eabi> November 2011); also Transparency Rwanda ASBL, 'Rwanda Bribery Index 2010' (Kigali, 2010).

[51] Interview, male senior international businessman, Kigali, 12 March 2009.

RPF/Tri-Star link has made high-level political corruption unnecessary, which has given Kagame and his immediate circle the necessary moral authority to enforce a zero tolerance policy.

Finally, the combination of factors noted above has enabled the civil service to follow a pattern that differs from the one observed in recent years in most other countries of the region. It was necessary and possible after 1994 to reconstruct the Rwandan civil administration from scratch. Former civil servants were rehired, but ministries received a good deal of fresh staffing, much of it drawn from returnees from the diaspora and, increasingly, recent products of the National University or universities in Uganda and other countries. The resulting civil service is exceptionally youthful and there has been much learning on the job. In this context, recruitment and promotion decisions are able to be based to a large extent on merit and effectiveness. In addition, administrators are motivated and disciplined by an unusually effect- ive form of performance-based contracting linked to the neo-traditional practice called *imihigo*.[52]

In at least five ways, then, Rwanda deviates from the African modal pattern. Our contention has been that this is partly explained by the way rent man- agement is effectively centralized though the RPF/Tri-Star link. To complete this part of the argument, consider what evidence would compel us to reject our claim about centralization of rent management in Rwanda. It would have to be rejected, obviously, if we were to find one instance or more of personal rent capture by a leading or middle-ranking politician which was not effect- ively sanctioned. For example, if a minister or other prominent public figure were to go unpunished after undertaking a large-scale scam at the expense of the state, we could not maintain the hypothesis that rent management was centralized.

For Kenya, Uganda, or Tanzania, it would be possible to cite many such instances.[53] We would maintain that there are no such cases in Rwanda. In Kigali, new appointees to permanent secretary or parastatal management positions are teased with the question 'Have you got your pink [i.e. convict's] uniform ready?'[54] Numerous examples may be cited where the mere suspicion of financial wrongdoing has been sufficient to prompt immediate and effective sanctions, legal and otherwise. Among the prominent individuals affected are several who were not known to be in any other respect in dispute with the leadership and, in that sense, candidates for victimization.[55]

---

[52] Theoretically inspired by an oathing ceremony performed by warriors at the royal court during the pre-colonial kingdom, the institution gets its force from the unusual level of backing, monitoring, and enforcement applied to it from the President's office downwards.

[53] See, for example, Cooksey and Kelsall, 'Tanzania'.

[54] Interview, male former senior journalist, Kigali, 13 December 2007.

[55] Important friends of the RPF in the business community who have fallen foul of the regime's stringency on financial legalities include Rwanda's top tycoon, Tribert Rujugiro, who

The 'Rwanda Briefing' document which has circulated widely on the Internet under the names of four prominent exiles makes the argument that Kagame sets very high standards of integrity for those who serve under him, but does not live by the same rules.[56] The document alleges that the President is 'responsible for financial impropriety and theft of public resources on a grand scale'. However, the route by which it reaches this conclusion does not inspire confidence. It rests partly on non-credible claims about how Tri-Star/CVL is managed[57] and partly on concerns about Tri-Star/CVL's relationship with the rest of the private sector that are widely shared, as discussed next, but have nothing to do with Kagame's personal wealth.

Tri-Star as example of long-horizon rent deployment

It appears, then, that one of the features distinguishing the Rwandan business–politics regime is an effective centralization of control of rents. Can we also distinguish the post-2000 Rwanda pattern from the equally centralized but short-termist kleptocracy that characterized a number of ill-reputed post-colonial African regimes? To what extent does it differ, for example, from the pattern in Zimbabwe, where it is also the case that the ruling party, ZANU-PF, owns significant private businesses?[58]

This is not a question of whether the intentions of the leadership are more benevolent or otherwise praiseworthy. The issue may be restricted to whether rent management is directed towards the short-term enrichment of members of the political class and its allies, or alternatively towards

---

was removed from the National Executive Committee of the RPF when the UK and South African authorities questioned his tax status; and Alfred Kalisa, who was Tri-Star's senior operator in the banking sector until he was jailed for a period over the issuing of unsecured loans. Interviews, male senior journalist, and middle-aged Rwandan businessman, Kigali, 20 February and 23 February 2010.

[56] Kayumba Nyamwasa, Patrick Karegeya, Theogene Rudasingwa, and Gerald Gahima, 'Rwanda briefing', August 2010, <http://www.scribd.com/doc/52751143/Rwanda-Briefing-by-former-RPF-RDF-members-in-Exile> (26 February 2012), p. 28.

[57] 'The assets of the RPF are, for all practical purposes, the personal wealth of President Kagame. The RPF does not have any committee or body that oversees all of its assets...President Kagame never reports to any of the organs of the RPF on the financial affairs of the RPF's business enterprises' (Nyamwasa, 'Briefing', p. 26). General Nyamwasa, one of the four people named as authors of the document, served for four years as an RPF nominee on the Tri-Star/CVL board of directors and in that capacity was a co-signatory to its accounts (Interview, male senior government figure, Kigali, 22 April 2011). He is therefore presumably aware that, as far as Tri-Star/CVL accountability is concerned, these comments are misleading.

[58] On which, see Martin Dawson and Tim Kelsall, 'Anti-developmental patrimonialism in Zimbabwe', *Journal of Contemporary African Studies* 30, 1 (2012), pp. 49–66.

'growing the pie' of the national economy, maximizing opportunities for long-term accumulation.

We believe the evidence places the RPF-led regime clearly in the second category. To some extent, this puts us at odds with a widely held view in Kigali, which emphasizes the various ways Tri-Star/CVL companies have benefited from government decisions and take advantage of their dominant position to beat down competitors. This view has been influential among the country's international donors,[59] and it is sometimes claimed that prospective foreign investors have been put off from coming to Rwanda by the knowledge that their potential rivals in the domestic market are part of a conglomerate owned by the ruling party.[60] The government itself has become sensitive to the suggestion that the role played by the party-owned enterprises is anti-competitive and thus a hindrance to the emergence of a healthy private-sector-led economy. However, we think this concern is in several respects exaggerated.

No doubt, the allegations about restrictions on competition have something in them. The members of the conglomerate certainly gain from decisions to buy goods and services from each other.[61] Tri-Star's financial power (a combination of its own resources and its financial credibility as a borrower from national banks) does give it a major advantage over would-be competitors from the domestic private sector, and this is no doubt resented.[62] At various stages, the subsidiaries have been in a position to earn monopoly profits, as the CVL website itself concedes.[63] Unsuccessful private business people in Kigali do sometimes explain their troubles by saying that they have been unwilling to bid for contracts against Tri-Star affiliates because they

---

[59] Some in government see this as primarily a donor concern. Interview, female senior civil servant, Kigali, 14 December 2007.

[60] A study of 18 cases of 'disinvestment' by foreign or local firms was recently commissioned by the semi-official Private Sector Federation of Rwanda with a view to improving investor aftercare. The report included a quotation from the US State Department's Rwanda Investment Climate Statement 2010 to the effect that 'Some private sector firms assert that companies in which the government owns shares or have close ties to the government have been beneficiary of preferential treatment with regard to access to credit and in tax compliance enforcement.' However, none of the disinvestment decisions documented by the study involved concerns of this type (PSF/FSP, 'Disinvestment and investor aftercare in Rwanda: assessment report', Kigali, July 2011, p. 10).

[61] For example, the Bourbon Coffee chain is the biggest user of the milk sachets produced by Inyange Industries; Intersec is the sole provider of security guards to the building sites of NPD-COTRACO and Real Contractors, and GPS provides printing services to several 'sister companies'. Interviews, male CVL subsidiary manager; second male CVL subsidiary manager; male middle-aged businessman; and third CVL subsidiary manager: Kigali, 23 February, 10 March, and 8 and 11 November 2010.

[62] Interviews, male senior government adviser, and male CVL subsidiary manager, Kigali, 12 December 2007 and 23 February 2010.

[63] <http://crystalventuresltd.com/index.php> (21 February 2012).

cannot believe that the playing field will be level.[64] These are all relevant considerations.

On the other hand, the Tri-Star/CVL firms do not seem to have either the overweening market power—after foreign competitors are factored in—or the ability to mobilize political leverage that is often attributed to them. Now that business is booming across East Africa, most of the CVL subsidiaries are facing quite intense competition from regionally or internationally owned firms; if they are able to grow, it is because markets are expanding.[65] Their managers naturally reject suggestions that government purchasing offices or the Rwanda Revenue Authority do them any favours. Specific examples and testimony from other sources add credibility to these claims.[66]

What distinguishes the conventional view from ours, however, is not so much a different view of the facts, but a different interpretative framework. The conventional approach takes a textbook view of competition, one that assumes the existence of a fully fledged capitalist economy. Following Khan, we believe that the challenge which applies to Rwanda's situation, even today after a decade or more of economic recovery, is not that of defending a mature private-enterprise sector against monopoly power, but that of getting capitalism started. It is a misreading of economic history to treat these challenges as the same.

For foreign firms, there are many more significant disincentives to investment in Rwanda than the possibility of unfair competition from the biggest of the local firms. They include the implications of small domestic market size for any investments in import substitution; the barriers to export production created by the country's landlocked status; land, power, and transport issues; and the comparatively limited opportunities for quick wins in natural-resource extraction, particularly in comparison with Uganda and Tanzania.[67]

[64] Interviews, male senior security official; male elderly Rwandan businessman; male former civil servant; and male private consultant: Kigali, 11 March and 12 March 2009; 19 February and 9 March 2010.

[65] Interviews, male mid-range civil servant; middle-aged businessman; male mid-range civil servant; and second middle-aged businessman: Kigali, 10 and 11 March 2010, and 8 November and 8 November 2010.

[66] For example, in 2010 furniture importer Mutara Enterprises had recently lost two large contracts (with the parastatal Electrogaz and the Ministry of the East African Community) to Zadok Furniture Systems of Kenya (interview, male CVL subsidiary manager, 16 November 2010). GPS reckons to win 70 percent and lose 30 percent of tenders despite its ultra-modern equipment. Interview, male CVL subsidiary manager, Kigali, 11 November 2010. Other examples were provided in interviews with male senior civil servant; male CVL subsidiary manager; male regional businessman; and male CVL executive: Kigali, 14 December 2007; 23 February, 12 March, and 8 November 2010. Among the 26 non-government, non-Tri-Star private business people we interviewed, a prevalent view was that the UK-trained Rwanda Revenue Authority is so harsh and inflexible that it would be unlikely to make concessions to anybody, and least of all to firms in the 'large taxpayer' category.

[67] Interviews, male senior regional journalist; male former CVL executive; and male current CVL executive: Kigali, 18 February, 9 March, and 8 November 2010.

Crucially, they also involve the risks associated with investing in an immature business environment, in which professional skills and support services are in short supply. The risks are especially large in sectors characterized by major backward and forward linkages and externalities, such as commercial horticulture.[68] As for domestic investors, many have only emerged as significant players thanks to the initial learning undertaken, and the example provided, by the politically driven operations of the Tri-Star/CVL companies.[69] As different interviewees put it, Tri-Star/CVL has been an 'ice breaker' for other firms in Rwanda's formal economy; it has shown the way, 'preaching by example'. As a result, there has been more 'crowding in' than 'crowding out' of other local firms.[70]

Our contention is that Tri-Star/CVL is playing a critical role in getting capitalism started in Rwanda. It did so initially with investments that met urgent social or political needs and subsequently earned the monopoly profits that would have accrued to any first-comer. In several cases, it is reasonable to treat the profits made as a return on risk taking and investments in learning that eventually helped to crowd in other domestic players.

The early ventures included providing housing for returnees and private security services for official buildings and installations. Investments in basic import substitution followed, such as bottled water and basic dairy products. Subsequent investments were in furniture imports, mobile telephony, road construction, housing estates, building materials, fruit processing, and printing. In most of these fields—most strikingly in the cellphone example detailed further on—the Tri-Star subsidiary was at first a pioneer in activities where there was little interest from the domestic or (more relevantly, perhaps) the diaspora private sector. For some years, the majority of firms were not highly or even moderately profitable and were supported by the RPF primarily for their social benefits. Although they operated like private companies, they were run by party cadres, some of them with little or no business experience, and were probably not very efficient. The introduction of the accounting and reporting systems that would allow us to judge efficiency only came later.[71]

The management of the Tri-Star/CVL group seems to have gone through three distinct phases. In the earliest phase, management styles within the

---

[68] PSF/FSP, 'Disinvestments'; Interviews, male middle-aged businessman; second male middle-aged businessman; and female government minister: Kigali, 8 March, 11 March, and 10 November 2010.

[69] The demonstration effects are sometimes bolstered with direct technical assistance, as in the advice provided by Inyange Industries to its main juice-bottling competitor Uribitso Enterprises, and by Bourbon Coffee to novice coffee-shop chains (interviews, male CVL subsidiary managers, Kigali, 10 and 11 March 2010).

[70] Interviews, male government minister; male senior security official; and male former CVL executive: Kigali, 17 February 2010, 11 March 2011, and 9 March 2010.

[71] Interviews, male CVL executive, and male CVL director, Kigali, 8 November and 11 November 2010.

group resembled those of the parastatal sector, but over two subsequent periods of reform (roughly 2005–8 and 2008 to the present) the companies have come to be managed more in accord with the norms of private corporate business.[72] Today, according to the CVL CEO, the model is that of 'early-stage venture capitalism'. The orientation is towards creating firms that are attractive partners for international direct investors, not just large players in domestic terms. The company's board—now consisting largely of RPF members with banking or financial-management backgrounds—is determined to raise efficiency and management reporting to the necessary standards.[73]

A continuous feature of Tri-Star/CVL operations throughout the three periods is that they have been to a greater or lesser extent risky, and in several cases involved heavy initial learning costs.[74] Thus, what emerges as most significant is the willingness of Tri-Star/CVL to use its financial clout to fund investments with high expected social benefits and/or positive economic externalities, including those associated with venture capitalism.

This interpretation applies clearly to the most important early Tri-Star investment, in MTN Rwanda. Tri-Star largely funded the initial establishment of the MTN cellphone network in Rwanda at a time when MTN and other global operators found the country's potential subscriber base uninteresting and the government of Rwanda was in no position to take the lead financially. The results of this venture were spectacularly successful, leading the MTN parent company to expand its equity share. Not long after setting up in Rwanda (July 1998), it went on to establish a network in Uganda (October 1998), with Tri-Star as one of the shareholders. Initially, Tri-Star held approximately 65 percent of the equity in the Rwandan operation and MTN South Africa 26 percent, with the government of Rwanda contributing the balance through the then parastatal Rwandatel. In the following years, Tri-Star progressively transferred holdings to the South African parent company, reducing its share to 40 percent by 2007. That year, MTN International assumed majority control (55 percent) when Tri-Star sold it a 15 percent stake, anticipating the entry into the market of two new providers—Tigo and

---

[72] Up to 2008 the company was headed by Efraim Turahirwa. In 2008 John Mirenge took over as executive chairman. In 2010 the role was divided: Professor Massaneh Nshuti became a non-executive chairman of CVL, with John Bosco Birungi as CEO. Turahirwa had been finance director of MTN and head of the Commercial Bank of Rwanda. Mirenge was recruited from Electrogaz and went on to manage the national airline. Nshuti is a former Minister of Commerce and Minister of Finance, while Birungi was hired from a US-based financial consultancy.

[73] CVL monthly managers' meeting, Kigali, 11 November 2010; Interviews, male former CVL executive; male CVL executive; middle-aged businessman; male CVL director; and male CVL subsidiary manager: Kigali, 9 March, 8 November, 8 November, 11 November, and 15 November 2010.

[74] Had the company's priority been to make large profits in a low-risk business, it would have gone into fuel importing and would have retained its early interest in banking after the financial sector started to prosper. Interview, male former CVL executive, Kigali, 9 March 2010.

the now privatized Rwandatel. Tri-Star realized 5–10 times its original invest-ments as a result of these sales.[75] In October 2011, the remaining 10 percent government stake and a further 15 percent Tri-Star (now CVL) holding in MTN Rwanda was sold to the parent company, leaving CVL with a 20 percent stake.[76]

In other words, Tri-Star helped to generate a demonstration effect and a learning experience in which one of the beneficiaries was an international firm. It thereby ensured not only that Rwanda entered the world of mobile telephony earlier than it would otherwise have done, but also that the network that was established was at least partly owned by domestic capital. There have been spill-over benefits for the wider information and communication tech-nology field, with new IT firms being established by Rwandan entrepreneurs who cut their teeth negotiating with MTN on behalf of the government.[77]

In other sectors, too, the emphasis has been on using financial clout to enable local players to undertake the risks and learning associated with getting established in competition with international suppliers. This is particularly applicable to building and road construction, where some international firms, including increasingly Chinese companies, have not only experience but a financial capacity that allows them to be free of risk-averse Africa-based banks.[78] As experience in Uganda confirms, it is hard for local firms to achieve operational competitiveness with international and particularly Chinese firms in these sectors unless there is some mechanism for financing start-up costs and learning-by-doing.[79]

In all of these operations, there is awareness that competitiveness does not depend only on having a supportive and patient financial backer. Tri-Star firms have had extremely open recruitment policies for managers, engineers, and other technical specialists. In a number of cases, diaspora professionals have been head-hunted but increasingly the firms recruit by means of open advertising within the East African region and beyond. They can and do hire globally to meet needs in some technical areas.[80] A willingness to hire

---

[75] Interviews, male former CVL executive; middle-aged information technology business-man; and male CVL executive: Kigali, 12 March 2009, 12 March 2009, and 8 November 2010; <http://www.engineeringnews.co.za/article/mtn-lifts-stake-in-rwanda-operations-to-55-2007-11-22> (26 February 2011).

[76] <http://bikyamasr.com/47832/mtn-boosts-rwanda-shares/> (21 February 2012).

[77] Today, the MTN operation is invariably one of the top two taxpayers in Rwanda. It employs 690 directly, only two of whom are expatriates. Indirect employment, including dealerships and security guards, is estimated at over 5,000. Interview, middle-aged businessman, Kigali, 12 March 2009.

[78] Interview, male CVL subsidiary manager, Kigali, 11 March 2010.

[79] David Booth and Frederick Golooba-Mutebi, 'Aiding economic growth in Africa: the political economy of roads reform in Uganda' (Working Paper 307, Overseas Development Institute, London, 2009).

[80] Interviews, male CVL subsidiary manager; second male CVL subsidiary manager; male CVL executive; middle-aged businessman; and third CVL subsidiary manager: Kigali, 23 February, 10 March, 8 November, 8 November, and 11 November 2010.

internationally for the sake of creating competitive national firms has been noted as a distinguishing feature of regimes that we have elsewhere characterized as 'developmental patrimonialisms'.[81] This would appear to be one of the features that distinguish the policies of such regimes from those of the African modal pattern, in which 'jobs for the boys' and jobs for locals take precedence over a given firm's efficiency and competitiveness.

Horizon and RIG

What the Tri-Star/CVL experience illustrates is that, in very underdeveloped capitalist economies, an incipient private sector may benefit from being led from the front and not just facilitated with the provision of a business-friendly environment. Other dimensions of the business–politics relationship that has emerged in Rwanda are also consistent with that principle. They complete the picture on central management and long-horizon deployment of economic rents.

To begin with, the privatization process was more actively supervised than has typically been the case within the African modal pattern. At the outset (1997–2004) the policy was what one interviewee called 'all-out privatization' and followed the main principles of the Washington Consensus quite closely. But subsequently a number of recently privatized firms, including Rwandatel, were taken over and then privatized for a second time when the first buyers proved incapable of providing the promised injections of capital and know-how. More recently, Rwandatel went into receivership after Libya's Lap-Green failed to meet some of the conditions of its purchase, and is to be sold for a third time. Policy makers today are more tough-minded about the likely benefits of privatization and there is stronger interest in the option of bringing private-sector discipline into remaining and newly created state-owned companies.[82]

The government has adopted a relatively activist stance in at least two other areas. First, it encouraged the army to create an investment arm with which to undertake socio-economic projects and create productive enterprises. The result was another holding company run on private-sector lines, Horizon Group. Second, it brokered the creation of a private investment consortium that brought together a group of the richest domestic and diaspora entrepreneurs. The consortium is known as the Rwanda Investment Group (RIG).

---

[81] Kelsall, 'Rethinking'; also Diana Cammack and Tim Kelsall, 'Neo-patrimonialism, institutions and economic growth: the case of Malawi, 1964–2009', *IDS Bulletin* 42, 2 (2011), pp. 88–96.
[82] Interview, former CVL executive, 9 March 2010.

Horizon Group's first venture was a construction company established with an initial gift of equipment from the government and a team of military engineers seconded from the army. It undertook a series of projects for the government, including building irrigation dykes and constructing coffee-washing stations, 'to avoid the Chinese doing everything'.[83] At an early stage, it established a cassava-growing operation and a dairy (Laiterie Nyabisindu). Subsequently, it moved into comprehensive urban site development, first on land bought from the Housing Bank in Kigali and later in collaboration with CSS-Zigama, the military's micro-finance initiative.

Horizon is now also in pyrethrum processing,[84] as the owner of the Sopyrwa plant in Musanze, in the former Ruhengeri Province, which is linked to 24 large producer cooperatives in the area. Sopyrwa, created as a parastatal in the early 1970s but recently privatized, was close to bankruptcy following the global credit crunch. Horizon was approached with a view to a takeover by the former owners, a group of private entrepreneurs, in view of the company's track record in agri-business undertakings.[85]

The operations of Horizon subsidiaries are increasingly diverse. Thus, Horizon Logistics is moving into logistical support to Rwandan peace-keeping forces in a number of locations, taking over from international firms. On the other hand, Galaxy Management Systems has recently been established to assist the Kigali City Council with street naming and house numbering, considered a precondition for efficient taxation.

Horizon Group is run as a private firm. Its board does not include serving military officers, although its CEO was seconded from the army following a previous posting with the military bank. However, as with Tri-Star, its social and political purposes are important, and according to the CEO profitability is no more than a co-equal objective.[86] The group's interest in rural construction arose from the perceived need to restore export agriculture to something approaching its previous condition. Urban housing was signalled as a vital matter when competition between returnees and displaced people for access to the limited housing stock became acute in the later 1990s. The intervention in pyrethrum was necessary to avert the collapse of a privatized parastatal, which would have harmed employment and smallholder incomes in the still politic-ally fragile north-west. Like Tri-Star, Horizon has a robustly internationalist approach to filling skills gaps in its firms, with business efficiency and the meeting of strategic social objectives taking precedence over commitments to local hiring and capacity development.[87]

---

[83] Interview, male Horizon Group executive, Kigali, 15 November 2010.
[84] Pyrethrum flowers are the raw material for an organic pesticide.
[85] Interviews, male Horizon Group executive, Kigali, 15 November 2010; male Horizon subsidiary manager, Musanze, 18 November 2010.
[86] Interview, male Horizon Group executive, Kigali, 15 November 2010.
[87] *Ibid.*

The Rwanda Investment Group SA (RIG) is also a holding company but of a different character, a public–private partnership. It was created in May 2006, at the instigation of President Kagame and in response to the difficulty of raising funds for large projects in the absence of a local capital market. Currently, it has 41 shareholders, including 31 individuals, four medium-sized companies, and six institutional investors including the Rwanda Development Bank, major insurers, and Crystal Ventures Ltd. The initial start-up capital totalled US$25 million. In effect, RIG brings together 'nearly all' of the richest and best-known businesspeople of Rwanda and the diaspora, along with the major public financial institutions.[88] At present it operates with a fairly restrictive minimum subscription of US$3.6 million, but the intention is to seek international partners and in due course float shares publicly.[89]

RIG's mandate is to raise capital for investments of particular national interest without relying on international capital markets or the local branches of foreign banks. Social objectives are less prominent than in the cases of CVL and Horizon, but the group's mission is described as a form of 'economic patriotism'.[90] A local public–private partnership appeared necessary to the founding members of the consortium at the time when the country's largest cement factory CIMERWA, a Chinese–Rwanda government joint venture under the Habyarimana regime, was being privatized and needed a substantial capital injection. As a result, RIG acquired a 90 percent stake in CIMERWA, with the government of Rwanda holding the balance.[91]

RIG subsequently invested heavily in peat mining and methane gas extraction from Lake Kivu (both potential solutions to Rwanda's acute electric power shortage). It is in a public–private partnership with the government for the establishment of the Kigali Industrial Park and several other schemes.[92] These are all initiatives that funding sources with no 'patriotic mandate', or willingness to underwrite risks, might well have considered unsuitable.[93]

A developmental neo-patrimonialism?

It seems, therefore, that the business–politics relationship in Rwanda rests upon a centralized management of rents and their utilization in a long-horizon perspective. In different ways, the RPF's holding in Tri-Star/CVL,

[88] Interview, male government minister, Kigali, 12 December 2007.
[89] <http://www.rig.co.rw/content/view/40/96/> (26 February 2011); Interview, male RIG executive, Kigali, 9 March 2010.
[90] Interview, male RIG executive, Kigali, 9 March 2010.
[91] Rwanda Investment Group SA, '2008 annual report' (RIG, Kigali, June 2009).
[92] <http://www.rig.co.rw/content/view/40/96/> (26 February 2011).
[93] Interview, male RIG executive, Kigali, 9 March 2010.

the army's involvement in the Horizon Group, and the creation of RIG all exemplify and contribute to this pattern. In other words, the Rwanda case complies with the main features of the developmental patrimonialism model. It agrees, moreover, with Khan's thesis about the constructive role that utilization of rents can play in incipiently capitalist economies.

Rwanda's developmental patrimonialism differs from the model provided by earlier regimes of this type, such as Houphouët-Boigny's Côte d'Ivoire or Banda's Malawi. The allegations of the 'Rwanda Briefing' notwithstanding,[94] the distinctive features of the regime do not seem to include a blurring of the distinction between the resources of the state and the private income or wealth of the ruler or ruling group. Generally, the boundaries between government operations and the private-sector operations of the RPF and the army are clear and quite formalized. We have argued, moreover, that one of the effects of the Tri-Star/CVL arrangement has been to enable the political elite to enforce an unusually strong anti-corruption line. For this and other reasons, the country scores well on conventional business-climate criteria.

The implication would seem to be that Rwanda since 2000 has displayed some distinctive features compared with other exemplars of developmental patrimonialism. Nonetheless, the concept of developmental patrimonialism centred on long-horizon rent management helps to illuminate what is most distinctive and important about politics–business interactions in Rwanda. Other resource-poor, landlocked African states surely have something to learn from the politically inspired economic activism represented by Rwanda's Tri-Star/CVL, Horizon, and RIG.

Acknowledgment

Published in *African Affairs*, 111, 444 (2012), p. 379–403. The research for this article was completed under the APPP, a consortium research programme funded by the Research and Evidence Division of the UK's Department for International Development (DfID) and by Irish Aid for the benefit of developing countries. The views expressed are those of the authors and not necessarily those of DfID, the UK government or Irish Aid. The authors are grateful to Tim Kelsall, the editors and three anonymous referees for comments on previous drafts, but they remain fully responsible for the contents.

---

[94] Nyamwasa, 'Briefing'.

Part III

Elections, Democracy, and Representation

10

An Introduction to Elections, Democracy, and Representation

Nic Cheeseman

IN THE EARLY 1990s, the reintroduction of multiparty politics across Africa transformed the continent's political landscape. From the release of Nelson Mandela in South Africa in 1990 to the first electoral defeats of authoritarian regimes in Benin and Zambia just a year later, the decade brought seismic changes that reverberated throughout the political, social, and economic sphere. Almost all African states now hold elections of one form or another,[1] and states such as Benin and Ghana secured impressive democratic gains. However, despite this the decade did not prove to be the "second liberation" that opposition activists had hoped for. In many countries, entrenched authoritarian leaders found ways to subvert democracy, manipulating elections in order to keep themselves in power. Old dogs, it turned out, could learn new tricks. In the process, ruling parties played on and exacerbated many of the most problematic features of the politics of the 1980s: corruption, weak institutions, and inter-ethnic tensions.

The reintroduction of multipartyism was therefore both a blessing and a curse. Over the last two decades, this duality has inspired a number of productive debates. In one of the most high profile, Staffan I. Lindberg[2] has argued that the repeated holding of elections has an independent causal effect on the quality of democracy, leading to better-quality civil liberties over time—even if the quality of the elections is poor. Against this, a number of other researchers have sounded a more cautious note, highlighting the potential for elections to trigger fresh social conflict that can reverse the democratization process. A second debate has focused on whether the reintroduction of multiparty competition has actually improved the performance of

---

[1] Eritrea and Swaziland being the exceptions.
[2] Staffan I. Lindberg, *Democracy and Elections in Africa* (Johns Hopkins Press, Baltimore, MD, 2006).

governments, whether this is measured in the amount invested in education or the presence of women in parliament.[3] In a third important debate, scholars inspired by the work of the late Claude Ake have addressed the thorny question of whether democracy needs to be "Africanized" in order to work effectively on the continent.[4]

Understanding whether democracy in Africa is consolidating or is generating new and dangerous challenges for political stability requires a degree of intellectual flexibility because in reality the impact of political liberalization has been promising in some respects and problematic in others. In other words, democratization has generated complex and often contradictory processes within the same continent, and often within the same country. This makes it particularly difficult to determine exactly how these developments will play out: in places such as Kenya and Nigeria elections appear to be contributing to both the emergence of stronger democratic norms *and* greater social tensions at one and the same time. As recent publications in *African Affairs* demonstrate, both trends have powerful roots, and it is not yet clear whether one will subsume the other or they will continue to coexist side by side for some years to come.

DEMOCRATIZATION AND AFTER

As Samuel Decalo argued in an important early article, the process of democratization in Africa was largely unheralded.[5] Most researchers writing in the 1980s shared Samuel Huntington's assumption that 'by reason of their poverty or the violence of their politics', African states were 'unlikely to move in a democratic direction'.[6] However, once the process had begun it quickly became clear that the collapse of authoritarian regimes had deep roots. By the 1980s, the legitimacy of most African leaders had been undermined by economic decline and generational change. The young men and women coming of political age towards the end of the decade had no memory of the anti-colonial struggle and were more concerned about the lack of jobs than the ruling party's nationalist credentials. However, the prohibition of opposition

---

[3] Gretchen Bauer and Jennie E. Burnet, 'Gender Quotas, Democracy, and Women's Representation in Africa', *Women's Studies International Forum* 41 (2013), pp. 103–12.

[4] Claude Ake, 'The Unique Case of African Democracy', *International Affairs* 69, 2 (1993), pp. 239–44, pp. 242–3.

[5] Samuel Decalo, 'The Process, Prospects and Constraints of Democratization in Africa', *African Affairs* 91, 362 (1992), pp. 7–35.

[6] As quoted in Decalo, 'The Process, Prospects and Constraints of Democratization', p. 7.

parties,[7] politicization of the security forces, and access to international flows of financial support, meant that most governments retained just enough control to be able to co-opt or repress those calling for regime change.

The political playing field began to shift markedly from the early 1980s onwards as a result of a number of new developments. The collapse of the Soviet Union reduced the funding available for left-leaning African states from the mid-1980s onwards, and temporarily freed Western powers to focus on promoting democracy, rather than security, abroad. Although Western support for political liberalization was never as forthright or as effective as some have suggested, where European and North American governments did not have strong financial or geostrategic reasons to side with incumbent regimes they used their economic clout to push countries towards multipartyism. At the same time, the sight of once-dominant one-party states collapsing in Europe, combined with the decision of the white minority government in South Africa to unban the African National Congress (ANC) in 1990, represented a vital shot in the arm for pro-democracy activists across the continent.

When political liberalization occurred, it often inspired the expansion of civil society and encouraged the media to pursue more critical political coverage. In turn, as Ayo Olukotun wrote in 2002, the opening up of the press played a role in 'nudging governments towards respect for human rights'.[8] Where weak ruling parties met with a unified and powerful opposition, the effect was the rapid transformation of the political system. As a result, in Benin and Zambia early elections led to comprehensive victories for the new opposition parties, suggesting that elections could be the vehicle for significant political change. Although multiparty politics in these countries did little to reduce corruption, it did create the opportunity for power to be rotated between different communities, while increasing the pressure on governments to introduce popular reforms such as free primary education. For example, Nic Cheeseman and Marja Hinfelaar found that in the Zambian election of 2008 the main parties 'were not ideologically vacuous.... Instead,... they debated the appropriate role of foreign investors in economic policy and the standard of living owed to urban workers, while carefully assimilating their rivals' most popular policy proposals'.[9]

However, this positive picture was not repeated across much of the continent. Instead, the early humbling of authoritarian regimes in Benin and Zambia alerted executives elsewhere to the precarious position that they were in. Subsequent polls were less free and fair, and far less likely to result in a transfer

---

[7] With the exception of Botswana, Mauritius, and the Gambia (until 1994), which remained multiparty from independence onwards.

[8] Ayo Olukotun, 'Authoritarian State, Crisis of Democratization and the Underground Media in Nigeria', *African Affairs* 101, 404 (2002), pp. 317–42, p. 340.

[9] Nic Cheeseman and Marja Hinfelaar, 'Parties, Platforms, and Political Mobilization: The Zambian Presidential Election of 2008', *African Affairs* 109, 434 (2010), pp. 51–76.

of power. Overall, African presidents won 88 percent of the elections that they contested between 1990 and 2010.[10] As a result, researchers searched for a new vocabulary to describe states that had all of the trappings of democracy but were not actually democratic. Borrowing from the literature on Latin America, Africanists began to speak of "quasi-democracies" and "electoral-authoritarian" states. The ability of presidents to resist the pressure for change depended on the political and economic resources at their disposal, and the strength of the constraints under which they operated. According to Caryn Peiffer and Pierre Englebert, the more vulnerable countries were to international pressure, the more likely it was that they would be forced to open up political space.[11] Relatedly, it also became clear that the presence of valuable natural resources played an important role in shaping the prospects for political reform.[12] With the possible exception of Nigeria—and, most recently, Ghana—no African petro-state has come close to being a democracy in the last 20 years. According to Patrick Molutsi and John Holm, a third important factor is the disposition of civil society, which can have a significant positive impact when it is united.[13] Putting these three points together, we can say that it was more feasible to sustain authoritarian rule when the government enjoyed a strategic importance for foreign donors, faced a divided opposition and weak civil society, and was endowed with easy-to-export natural resources firmly under its control.

Significantly, African leaders understood that it was possible to engineer such advantages where they did not exist. Water could not be turned into oil, of course, but opposition unity and relations with the international community were malleable. The potential to encourage the fragmentation of rival parties is well illustrated by Daniel Branch and Nic Cheeseman's work on Kenya, where President Daniel arap Moi quickly realized that divide-and-rule politics could be deployed to ensure that an ethnically diverse opposition would not unite.[14] In one famous incident, Moi's government capitalized on ethnic tensions within the Forum for Restoration of Democracy (FORD), by rushing to register two versions of the party—FORD-Asili and FORD-Kenya—each led by a figure from a different ethnic group, one Luo, the other Kikuyu. In the subsequent election, the combined vote of the two FORD parties was greater

---

[10] Nic Cheeseman, 'African Elections as Vehicles for Change', *Journal of Democracy* 21, 4 (2010), pp. 139–53.

[11] Caryn Peiffer and Pierre Englebert, 'Extraversion, Vulnerability to Donors, and Political Liberalization in Africa', *African Affairs* 111, 444 (2012), pp. 355–78.

[12] Michael L. Ross, 'Does Oil Hinder Democracy?', *World Politics* 53, 3 (2001), pp. 325–61.

[13] Patrick Molutsi and John D. Holm, 'Developing Democracy when Civil Society is Weak: The Case of Botswana', *African Affairs* 89, 356 (1990), pp. 323–40.

[14] Daniel Branch and Nic Cheeseman, 'Democratization, Sequencing, and State Failure in Africa: Lessons from Kenya', *African Affairs* 108, 430 (2009), pp. 1–26.

than that of Moi's, but because they split the opposition vote he was able to retain power.[15]

African leaders have also proved able to manipulate the international community for their own ends. No one better exemplifies the ability of presidents to exercise agency in the context of apparently tight international constraints than the Ugandan President Yoweri Museveni. As Jonathan Fisher's research demonstrates, 'Museveni's decision to intervene in Somalia is the most recent example of his regime's multipronged "image management" strategy in which the President has involved Uganda in numerous foreign and domestic activities to ensure that donors perceive his government in a particular way.' In so doing, Museveni 'has been able largely to avoid censure in areas of traditional donor concern such as governance', sustaining a "no-party" system until 2005 and a heavily controlled multiparty system thereafter.[16] The reintroduction of multiparty politics thus inspired a variety of different trends and responses, some of which made governments increasingly responsive to their people, while others enabled recalcitrant leaders to reassert their hegemony.

THE POWER OF ELECTIONS

One of the most high-profile debates of the last ten years has concerned whether elections improve the quality of democracy in Africa or represent a threat to political stability. Staffan I. Lindberg argues that on average the repeated holding of elections increases the quality of civil liberties for a number of reasons including that elections train voters in "democratic arts" and so inculcate democratic norms and values.[17] He also makes the important point that election campaigns often serve to focus the minds of opposition parties, civil society groups, and international donors on levelling the political playing field. Over time, incremental gains in the quality of elections, combined with the gradual consolidation of democratic norms, can help to improve the quality of democracy—even when the elections are not free and fair. Thus, according to Lindberg, the more elections that are held, the better the quality of democracy is likely to be.

Ever since Lindberg's major work, *Democracy and elections in Africa*, was published in 2006, other researchers have challenged these findings. Although

---

[15] Kenya then employed a first-past-the-post electoral system for the presidency, in which there was only one round of voting and whoever secured the most votes was elected.

[16] Jonathan Fisher, 'Managing Donor Perceptions: Contextualizing Uganda's 2007 Intervention in Somalia', *African Affairs* 111, 444 (2012), pp. 404–23.

[17] Lindberg, *Democracy and Elections in Africa*.

most scholars have accepted the idea that good-quality elections can have democratizing effects, many have questioned the idea that the same is true of poor-quality elections. To see why, let us return to the case of Kenya under President Moi. As Branch and Cheeseman have argued, the introduction of elections encouraged Moi's government to adopt an increasingly short-termist approach, playing divide-and-rule politics and sponsoring ethnic clashes in order to contain the opposition.[18] Although such strategies enabled Moi to retain power in the 1990s, the political violence and ethnic tensions that they unleashed had a deleterious effect on national identity. Most significantly, the social cleavages and militias that were strengthened under Moi's rule laid the foundations for the outbreak of post-election violence following the disputed election in 2007, which led to the death of over 1,000 people and the displacement of hundreds of thousands more.[19]

In more recent work with Carolien van Ham, Lindberg has taken this point on board.[20] Using a new dataset that includes all elections up to 2015, they find that the positive impact of elections only kicks in above a minimum threshold of democracy. When elections are held in overwhelmingly authoritarian contexts, they do not have democratizing effects. This added nuance is valuable, and demonstrates the complex and uneven impact of multiparty politics—something that becomes even more apparent when one considers that in a number of countries elections have had democratizing effects in some areas and autocratizing effects in others at the same time. The potential for these two trends to coexist within the same political system is demonstrated by Jeffrey Conroy-Krutz's analysis of the influence of election campaigns on the political knowledge of Ugandan voters. Despite Museveni's ability to manipulate elections to legitimate his dominant-party state,[21] Conroy-Krutz finds that election campaigns have increased public 'knowledge on topics such as office holders, candidates, and political institutions'. Significantly, this appears to have an empowering effect on poorer communities, because the campaign 'seems to have diminished, although not eliminated, pre-existing knowledge gaps between advantaged and disadvantaged populations'.[22] Thus, in Uganda, as in so many of Africa's electoral-authoritarian political systems, the public has been simultaneously empowered and disempowered.

[18] Branch and Cheeseman, 'Democratization, Sequencing and State Failure'.

[19] Sarah Jenkins, 'Ethnicity, Violence, and the Immigrant-Guest Metaphor in Kenya', *African Affairs* 111, 445 (2012), pp. 576–96.

[20] Carolien van Ham and Staffan I. Lindberg, 'Elections: Reassessing the Power of Elections in Multiparty Africa', in Nic Cheeseman (ed.), *Institutions and Democracy in Africa* (Cambridge University Press, Cambridge, forthcoming).

[21] Roger Tangri and Andrew Mwenda, 'Corruption and Cronyism in Uganda's Privatization in the 1990s', *African Affairs* 100, 398 (2001), pp. 117–33.

[22] Jeffrey Conroy-Krutz, 'Electoral Campaigns as Learning Opportunities: Lessons from Uganda', *African Affairs* 115, 460 (2016), pp. 516–40.

The impact of elections

A second important debate has concerned whether or not political competition delivers better government. In theory, this is one of the most important democratic dividends. The ability to kick out poorly performing leaders should give incumbent governments an added incentive to provide public services, while election campaigns should empower the public to demand that governments enact the policies they most want and need. There is some indication that these hypothesized benefits can be realized in the African context, at least in the continent's more open political systems. According to Robin Harding and David Stasavage, democracies have higher rates of school attendance than non-democracies, in large part because they are more likely to abolish school fees in response to political pressure.[23] This finding chimes with the work of Takaaki Masaki and Nicolas van de Walle, who use economic data from 1982 to 2012 to show that on average democracies perform better than their authoritarian counterparts when it comes to economic growth, and that the longer a country is democratic the greater the benefits are likely to be.[24]

However, when it comes to democracy in Africa things are rarely straightforward. Although there is evidence that in general democracies perform better in some areas, there are a number of examples of authoritarian regimes that have outperformed their more democratic neighbours when it comes to both economic growth and development. Ethiopia and Rwanda, for example, enjoyed some of the highest growth rates in Africa in the 2000s, and have performed well when it comes to poverty reduction. It is easy to see why multiparty politics might not be good for economic policy. The need to mobilize votes can encourage leaders to make unrealistic promises and to use public services to reward supporters instead of pursuing the public good. According to Michael Bratton, vote buying is a characteristic dimension of African election campaigns, while one in five Nigerians has been personally exposed to an electoral bribe.[25] In turn, the diversion of resources away from productive investments towards forms of clientelist exchange can facilitate corruption and mismanagement.[26] As a result, some scholars have argued that less competitive political systems may be able to achieve better development results, an idea that appears to be borne out by the rapid growth of

[23] Robin Harding and David Stasavage, 'What Democracy Does (and Doesn't Do) for Basic Services: School Fees, School Inputs, and African Elections', *The Journal of Politics* 76, 01 (2014), pp. 229–45.
[24] Masaki and van de Walle, 'The Impact of Democracy on Economic Growth in Africa'.
[25] Michael Bratton, 'Vote Buying and Violence in Nigerian Election Campaigns', *Electoral Studies* 27, 4 (2008), pp. 621–32.
[26] Leonardo Rafael Arriola, *Multi-ethnic Coalitions in Africa* (Cambridge University Press, Cambridge, 2012).

authoritarian China. The logic underpinning this idea is that leaders who enjoy a political monopoly are better placed to resist the demands of their supporters for patronage and hence to rule in the national interest. Greater central control can also empower the executive to force through unpopular but necessary reforms, and to constrain the level of corruption. For example, David Booth and Frederick Golooba-Mutebi ascribe some of Rwanda's recent economic success to the considerable authority that President Paul Kagame enjoys over the political and economic landscape.[27] However, while this may be true of a small number of cases, such systems of government suffer from a number of limitations, not least that they are wide open to abuse if they succumb to weak and venal leadership.[28]

What can we conclude from this debate? The mixed evidence available suggests that there is no easy relationship between multipartyism and economic development. Democracies can preside over economic catastrophes and authoritarian systems can deliver long periods of growth. To some extent, then, whether a country is democratic or authoritarian matters less to its economic performance than what kind of democracy, or what kind of authoritarian system, is in operation. This issue is discussed further in Part II.

The impact of democracy has also been inconsistent in other areas, such as the representation of historically marginalized groups. This is well illustrated by the case of female political representation. As Gretchen Bauer and Jennie Burnet argue, there is no relationship between democracy and the number of women in government in Africa. Some of the continent's most democratic states, such as Botswana, have remarkably low numbers of women in parliament, while one of the continent's most authoritarian states, Rwanda, is leading the way—not just in Africa, but in the world.[29] Moreover, even where historically marginalized groups have made it into government, this does not mean that they necessarily have the capacity to change policy—in some cases, more equal representation is little more than "window dressing" designed to improve the legitimacy of the regime. The limited transformation of the position of many minorities is therefore an important reminder that there is much more to democracy than elections. As Burnet wrote in *African Affairs* in 2008, 'the emphasis on elections in lieu of other aspects of democratic governance may reduce rather than increase the capacity of interest groups to shape policy'.[30]

---

[27] Chapter 9, this volume.   [28] Cheeseman, *Democracy in Africa*, chapter 5.
[29] Bauer and Burnet, 'Gender quotas'.
[30] Jennie Burnet, 'Gender balance and the meanings of women in governance in post-genocide Rwanda', *African Affairs* 107, 428 (2008), pp. 361–86, p. 386.

AFRICANIZING DEMOCRACY

A third important debate has focused on whether democracy needs to be "Africanized" to work on the continent. Arguments in favour of this proposition have taken a variety of forms. Writing in 1996, Carlos Lopes claimed that 'the African model of political democracy has to be rooted in the tradition of an inclusive society in which a series of inequality exist'.[31] In doing so, he was echoing the famous argument of Julius Nyerere, the former president of Tanzania, who stated that making decisions through setting up rival political parties was alien to the communities in which he grew up. Instead, Nyerere suggested that forming government policy through inclusive discussions and arriving at a consensus was more "African".[32]

Claude Ake, the influential Nigerian scholar who dedicated much of his career to the study of African democracy, had a different reason for arguing that liberal democracy in the Western image might not work on the continent. Ake suggested that 'Liberal democracy which pretends to universalism is historically specific...Contemporary Africa remains a far cry from this'.[33] More specifically, Ake pointed out that liberal democracy is premised on the idea that citizens think and act (and vote) as rational individuals motivated by their own self-interest. By contrast, he argued that 'Africa is still a communal society' in which countries are 'federations of ethnic groups or nationalities' and people participate not to advance their own self-interests but because they feel part of a wider ethnic/religious/regional community.[34] Another way to put this point is that the impact of capitalist development in Europe generated strong class identities that served to transform economic self-interest into stable party systems. The relative absence of this kind of economic transformation in Africa means that the political parties that have emerged tend to mobilize along ethnic lines because this was the most effective social identity available to them.

On this basis, Ake questioned whether political parties were appropriate vehicles to represent the will of the people in a context in which the group is often more important than the individual. As a result, he proposed a different form of democracy that would be politically inclusive and ensure the representation of key ethnic and religious groups through a combination of power sharing and decentralization. This kind of creative constitutional engineering is actually very rare in Africa, but something akin to the system advocated by

---

[31] Carlos Lopes, 'The Africanisation of Democracy', *African Journal of Political Science* 1, 2 (1996), pp. 139–53, p. 139.

[32] Julius Nyerere, 'The African and Democracy', in Julius K. Nyerere, *Freedom and Unity* (Oxford University Press, Dar es Salaam, 1966).

[33] Ake, 'The Unique Case of African Democracy'.   [34] *Ibid.*, p. 243.

Ake has been developed in the Republic of Somaliland, the self-declared state that operates as an autonomous region within Somalia.[35] The Somaliland case is instructive because it is not officially recognized as an independent state by the international community and so has not received the same kind of international democracy assistance as other countries. Partly as a result, its home-grown political resurgence has given rise to a form of democracy that is distinctive, marrying an American-style structure of checks and balances to a system of group representation in which seats in both houses of the legislature are allocated to clans on a proportional basis. The resulting set of political arrangements appear to have been relatively stable precisely because they evolved out of a process of domestic negotiations that drew on pre-existing and socially embedded practices of conflict management and resolution.

Although the political system in Somaliland remains fragile and has a number of limitations,[36] its successes—such as holding the most transparent elections ever to take place in the Horn of Africa in 2005—have led to calls for democracy to be "Africanized" in other countries. However, while it makes good sense to adapt democracy to local realities in order to strengthen its roots, it is also important not to fetishize tradition. All too often appeals to "African values" have 'been used to justify the extension of authoritarian control rather than to consolidate democracy'.[37] This was true in Tanzania, where Nyerere used the argument that political competition was "unAfrican" to legitimize the introduction of a restrictive one-party state. Similarly, while high public support for traditional leaders to play a greater role in decision-making at the local level[38] makes it tempting to think that integrating them further into the political system would strengthen democracy, it is important to consider the potential costs of such a move. In many countries, the power of chiefs to resolve family disputes has resulted in women being disinherited, and when they have played a significant political role this has often served to unfairly advantage the ruling party.[39] Thus, in the words of Claude Ake, 'Democracy has to be recreated in the context of the given realities and in political arrangements which fit the cultural context, but without sacrificing its values and inherent principles'.[40]

---

[35] Mark Bradbury, *Becoming Somaliland* (Indiana University Press, Indiana, 2008).

[36] Most notably that women comprise a tiny proportion of municipal councillors and MPs.

[37] Cheeseman, *Democracy in Africa*, p. 229.

[38] Carolyn Logan, 'The roots of Resilience: Exploring Popular Support for African Traditional Authorities', *African Affairs* 112, 448 (2013), pp. 353–76.

[39] *Ibid.*, p. 230.   [40] Ake, 'The Unique Case of African Democracy', p. 244.

MAKING DEMOCRACY WORK

What do these divergent trends mean for the state of democracy on the continent? By 2015, a number of countries were rated as "free" by Freedom House, including Benin, Botswana, Ghana, Namibia, Senegal, and South Africa.[41] However, on average the period from 2010 to 2015 witnessed a deterioration of respect for civil liberties, and only 36 percent of African states have ever experienced a transfer of power. Given the mixed picture so far, what are the prospects for democratic consolidation on the continent? The three articles included in Part III illuminate this question in very different ways, highlighting the significance of political institutions, neopatrimonialism, and elite relations.

J. Shola Omatola's sharp critique of elections in Nigeria highlights the ability of petro-state governments to maintain themselves in power by generating weak and pliant democratic institutions. Writing in 2010, when Nigeria was still a dominant-party state and had yet to experience a transfer of power, Shola Omatola argues that elections in the 2000s 'were characterized by ineffective administration at all stages and levels (before, during and after), resulting in damagingly discredited outcomes'. This is an important contribution, because it highlights the capacity for presidents to exert undue influence over democratic institutions, making it impossible to establish a level playing field. It also explains how poor electoral procedures can undermine confidence in the democratic process. In many ways, Omatola's analysis was remarkably prescient. Despite the many barriers to democratic consolidation in Nigeria, he argued that progress could be made if the Independent National Electoral Commission (INEC) was allowed to develop into a more independent and professional body. He also noted that the 'recent trend towards challenging electoral fraud in the courts' signalled a strengthening of the rule of law, giving reasons for optimism. Omatola proved to be right. Following the appointment of the widely respected Attahiru Muhammadu Jega as chairman, the quality and assertiveness of INEC progressed significantly, leading to a much-improved electoral environment in 2011. Another period of institutional strengthening between 2011 and the 2015 elections further enhanced INEC's profile. As a result, when a stronger and more unified opposition emerged under the leadership of former President Muhammadu Buhari, and secured more votes than the incumbent, President Goodluck Jonathan, INEC had the self-confidence and the authority to announce the country's first democratic transfer of power.[42]

---

[41] Freedom House, 'Freedom in the World', 2016, <https://www.freedomhouse.org/> (1 March 2016).

[42] Olly Owen and Zainab Usman, 'Briefing: Why Goodluck Jonathan Lost the Nigerian Presidential Election of 2015', *African Affairs* 114, 456 (2015), pp. 455–71.

Another article included here documents a country in which the quality and capacity of institutions was moving in the other direction. Putting pen to paper in 2014, Tom Lodge reflects on the potential for clientelism and corruption to undermine democratic checks and balances and thus facilitate both economic and political decay. In the wake of Jacob Zuma's ascension to the presidency in South Africa, and the marked increase in mismanagement and graft—reflected in a score of just 44 out of 100 on Transparency International's Corruption Perception Index—he sets out to explain the transformation of the ANC from a well-regulated party into an organization whose internal dynamics are heavily shaped by personal interests. Lodge does so by demonstrating that there have always been neopatrimonial elements within the ANC, but that these had previously been held in check by the need for discipline in the liberation struggle. Once power had been achieved, it became harder to hold these tendencies in check, especially given the party's 'historical ties to criminal networks and pressures arising from the transition to majority rule and contemporary electoral politics'. In this way, Lodge demonstrates the potential for multipartyism to exacerbate clientelism and authoritarian tendencies within ruling parties—even when they enjoy a dominant electoral position. His article also makes a further important contribution, namely that it implicitly addresses the notion of South African exceptionalism. The belief that South African politics are distinctive is built on the idea that because the country initially escaped neopatrimonial politics and features a stronger infrastructure than its neighbours, it cannot be expected to perform in the same way. By tracing the development of these tendencies within the ANC, and the increasing fragility of the state, Lodge explodes this myth and demonstrates that South Africa is not immune to the challenges facing the rest of the continent.

Part III is completed by an article that turns our attention to the important question of what makes democracy endure. According to Anja Osei, one of the main variables that shapes whether a country successfully managed to consolidate democracy is the cohesiveness of political elites. Using a social network approach, Osei argues that 'liberal democracy is impossible without a consensually united elite'. Based on 253 interviews with Ghanaian legislators, her article demonstrates that democratic consolidation in Ghana is underpinned by the fact that members of parliament (MPs) form strong networks that bridge ethnic and party divides. Partly as a result, MPs from different parties trust each other more than one might think. Osei recognizes that elite cohesion is not a silver bullet, noting that 'elite consensus does not mean the absence of political conflicts' or that more extreme political views are not expressed. However she persuasively concludes that political elites enjoy sufficient trust to be able to handle the conflicts that do arise in a non-violent way. Osei's analysis makes an important contribution to our understanding of the success and failure of Africa's democratic experiments because it highlights a factor that is so often missing—and hence overlooked—in the continent's more authoritarian states. Indeed, the Ghanaian experience stands in stark contrast to many other African countries such as Burundi, the Democratic Republic of the Congo, and South Sudan, where ethnic tensions and histories of conflict have served to undermine elite consensus.

Taken together, recent publications in *African Affairs* demonstrate that any complete analysis of democracy in Africa must take into account both structure, in terms of the capacity and autonomy of political institutions and a country's economic foundations, and agency, in terms of the attitudes and relations of the political elite and the actions of individual leaders. It is only when both were conducive to democratic consolidation that the reintroduction of elections led to more open, fair, and responsive politics.

11

Elections and Democratic Transition in Nigeria under the Fourth Republic

J. Shola Omotola

As NIGERIA CELEBRATES ITS FIFTIETH ANNIVERSARY, it is an apt time to consider its democratic development. From a minimalist perspective, elections are the first and most basic indicator of democracy. In Nigeria, however, elections have been one of the main problems of the democratization process. The country's struggles for sustainable democracy, good governance, and development have been so daunting that all previous attempts at democratic transition have been futile. The collapse of the First (1960–6) and Second (1979–83) republics, and the abortion of the Third Republic through the criminal annulment of the 12 June 1993 presidential election, are clear indicators of the failure of previous attempts at democratization. After prolonged military rule spanning close to two decades (1983–99), characterized by the wanton violation and repression of the political, economic, and social rights of the people, the re-democratization process begun in 1999 elicited renewed expectations for the consolidation of democracy in the country.[1]

At the heart of these expectations lies the pertinent issue of elections. Elections are meaningfully democratic if they are free, fair, participatory, competitive, and legitimate. This is possible

> when they are administered by a neutral authority; when the electoral adminis-
> tration is sufficiently competent and resourceful to take specific precautions
> against fraud; when the police, military and courts treat competing candidates
> and parties impartially; when contenders all have access to the public media;
> when electoral districts and rules do not grossly handicap the opposition; ... when
> the secret of the ballot is protected; when virtually all adults can vote; when
> procedures for organizing and counting the votes are widely known; and when

---

[1] Eghosa E. Osaghae, 'Democratization in sub-Saharan Africa: Faltering prospects, new hopes', *Journal of Contemporary African Studies* 17, 1 (1999), pp. 4–25.

there are transparent and impartial procedures for resolving election complaints and disputes.[2]

This article examines the place of elections, particularly their administration, in the democratic transition process in Nigeria since 1999 in order to ascertain the extent to which elections have helped to strengthen or retard democratic consolidation. The article focuses primarily on electoral governance by the electoral management body (EMB), in this case the Independent National Electoral Commission (INEC), with partial reference to other core institutional actors in the democratization process. How these institutions are organized, managed, funded, and motivated is crucially important. Are they rooted in society, and are they independent, accountable, and democratic? What are their attitudes to democracy and the rule of law? The article engages these questions and argues that the democratic qualities of Nigerian elections under the Fourth Republic (1999–2007) have been shallow because of ineffective governance. This is a result of the weak institutionalization of core institutions in the governance of the electoral processes, particularly INEC and the political parties. Notable weaknesses include lack of independence and professionalism, political interference, undemocratic attitudes, and lack of respect for the rule of law. The form and character of the Nigerian state, giving rise especially to political instability and severe underdevelopment, are other sources of the deepening crisis of electoral governance in Nigeria. However, the recent trend towards challenging electoral fraud in the courts gives some hope that elections may still contribute towards the consolidation of Nigeria's democracy.

Elections in democratic theory

The comparative literature on democratization, particularly during Africa's 'third wave', emphasizes the significance of elections.[3] Elections have been seen as central to competitive politics. Ideally, they guarantee political participation and competition, which in turn are pivotal to democratic transition and consolidation. Elections are also central to the institutionalization of orderly succession in a democratic setting, creating a legal-administrative framework for handling inter-elite rivalries. They also provide a modicum of popular backing for new rulers.[4] Implicit in these assumptions is that elections are

---

[2] Larry Diamond, *The Spirit of Democracy: The struggle to build free societies throughout the world* (Times Books, New York, NY, 2008), p. 25.

[3] Staffan Lindberg, *Democracy and Elections in Africa* (Johns Hopkins University Press, Baltimore, OH, 2006); Staffan Lindberg (ed.), *Democratization by Elections: A new mode of transition?* (Johns Hopkins University Press, Baltimore, OH, 2009).

[4] Arnold Hughes, and Roy May, 'The politics of succession in black Africa', *Third World Quarterly* **10**, 1 (1988), p. 20.

important for the institutionalization of popular participation, competition, and legitimacy, three core foundations of democracy.[5] Michael Bratton observes that 'the consolidation of democracy involves the widespread acceptance of rules to guarantee political participation and political competition. Elections—which empower ordinary citizens to choose among contestants for top political offices—clearly promote rules.'[6]

It is, however, important to note that elections are not in themselves a guarantee for sustainable democratic transition and consolidation. Elections can also be used to disguise authoritarian rule, what Andreas Schedler called 'electoral authoritarianism'.[7] Under such circumstances, elections are only held as a transitional ritual where the people have little or no choice, as has been the case in many African countries.[8] This compromises the democratization process by preventing elections from playing their crucial role.[9] It is, perhaps, with this in mind that Michael Bratton writes that while 'elections do not, in and of themselves, constitute a consolidated democracy', they 'remain fundamental, not only for installing democratic governments, but as a requisite for broader democratic consolidation'.[10] The relationship between elections and democratic transition, in other words, is not a given, but is contingent upon a number of forces, chief among which is the administration of the election. Thus:

> The regularity, openness and acceptability of elections signal whether basic constitutional, behavioral, and attitudinal foundations are being laid for sustainable democratic rule... while you can have elections without democracy, you cannot have democracy without elections. If nothing else, the convening of scheduled multi-party elections serves the minimal function of marking democracy's survival.[11]

Staffan Lindberg adds weight to this thinking, especially in the African context, when he speaks about the 'surprising significance' of African elections.[12] Lindberg observes that 'the positive effects of holding repetitive

---

[5] Staffan Lindberg, 'The democratic qualities of multiparty elections: participation, competition and legitimacy in Africa', *Commonwealth and Comparative Politics* 42, 1 (2004) pp. 61–105.

[6] Michael Bratton, 'Second elections in Africa', *Journal of Democracy* 9, 3 (1998), p. 51.

[7] Andreas Schedler (ed.), *Electoral Authoritarianism: The dynamics of unfree competition* (Lynne Rienner, Boulder, CO, 2006), pp. 1–26; Andreas Schedler, 'Elections without democracy: the menu of manipulation', *Journal of Democracy* 13, 2 (2002), p. 46.

[8] Said Adejumobi, 'Elections in Africa: a fading shadow of democracy?', *International Political Science Review* 21, 1 (2000), pp. 59–73; Tukumbi Lumumba-Kasongo (ed.) *Liberal Democracy and its Critics in Africa: Political dysfunction and the struggle for social progress* (Codesria, Dakar, 2005).

[9] Andreas Schedler, 'The nested game of democratization by elections', *International Political Science Review* 23, 1 (2002), pp. 103–22.

[10] Bratton, 'Second elections', p. 52.   [11] *Ibid.*

[12] Staffan Lindberg, 'The surprising significance of African elections', *Journal of Democracy* 16, 1 (2006) pp. 139–51.

elections are perhaps not restricted to free and fair elections, at least not in the early stages of democratization'.[13] He argues, for instance, that electoral problems such as 'inflated voters registries, political violence during the campaign and polling day, outright fraudulent voting and collation of votes, intimidation of voters and political opponents ... may stimulate activism in society even more than free elections'.[14]

Lindberg's argument, however, underestimates the overall costs of poorly governed elections, including their impact on legitimacy. It is the contention of this article that the form and character of elections, either as a reinforcement of democratic consolidation or as regression, are largely contingent upon a series of factors. The most basic of these relates to the EMB and other institutional-political frameworks that surround it—including political parties, mass media, and the judiciary—the interaction among them, and their degree of institutionalization.[15] These institutions are important for effective electoral administration because 'the indeterminacy of elections'—the possibility of elections leading to alternation of power—'is to a large extent a function of an impartial administration of elections'.[16]

Election institutions and electoral processes

The importance of electoral governance, defined as 'the wider set of activities that creates and maintains the broad institutional framework in which voting and electoral competition take place',[17] to democratic transition and consolidation cannot be overemphasized. Electoral governance is a comprehensive and multi-tasked activity, involving the three levels of rule making, rule application, and rule adjudication. Rule making involves designing the basic rules of the electoral game; rule application deals with implementing these rules to specifications to organize the electoral game; and rule adjudication entails resolving disputes arising from the game. On the whole, electoral

---

[13] Staffan Lindberg, 'Introduction: Democratization by elections: a new mode of transition?', in Lindberg, *Democratization by Elections*, p. 6.

[14] *Ibid.*, p. 6.

[15] Robert A Pastor, 'The role of electoral administration in democratic transitions: implications for policy and research', *Democratization* 6, 4 (Winter 1999), pp. 1–27; Jorgen Elklit and Andrew Reynolds, 'The impact of election administration on the legitimacy of emerging democracies: a new comparative politics research agenda', *Commonwealth and Comparative Politics* 40, 2 (2002), pp. 81–118.

[16] Adele L. Jinadu, 'Matters arising: African elections and the problem of electoral administration', *African Journal of Political Science* 2, 1 (1997), p. 1.

[17] Shaheen Mozaffar and Andreas Schedler, 'The comparative study of electoral governance—Introduction', *International Political Science Review* 23, 1 (2002), p. 7.

governance involves 'the interaction of constitutional, legal, and institutional rules and organizational practices that determine the basic rules for election procedures and electoral competition; organize campaigns, voter registration, and election day tallies; and resolve disputes and certify results'.[18] In these processes, 'the interplay of power structures and processes is central to electoral outcomes'.[19] As such, EMBs are part of 'a set of institutions and rules that together determine the probity of electoral processes, and in emerging democracies, where administrative processes are weak and distrust across political actors is high, their role at the center of electoral processes tends to be more visible'.[20] Thus whether electoral governance will contribute to democratic consolidation or regression will depend on the independence and professionalism of electoral institutions, particularly the EMB, because 'institutional structures that promote a "level playing field" at each stage of the electoral process will enhance the extent to which voters perceive their elections to be fair'.[21]

In their comparative study of Latin America to test the significance of electoral governance in the consolidation of democracy, Hartlyn, McCoy, and Mustillo established 'an important positive role for professional, independent electoral commissions on electoral outcomes', showing that 'formal-legal independence matters when the rules of the game are likely to be respected'. Moreover, 'low-quality elections are found disproportionately where incumbents seek reelection and where victory margins are extremely wide rather than narrow'.[22] This is not to say, however, that effective electoral governance alone guarantees good elections: obviously a number of forces, including all the social, economic, and political variables, intervene to play prominent roles in influencing the process, integrity, and outcome of elections. Nevertheless, good elections are not possible without effective electoral governance.[23]

It is perhaps for this reason that the new focus of research in electoral studies and democratization is gradually shifting towards electoral administration.[24] These studies demonstrate that EMBs, as the primary institutional

---

[18] Jonathan Hartlyn, Jennifer McCoy, and Thomas M. Mustillo, 'Electoral governance matters: explaining the quality of elections in contemporary Latin America', *Comparative Political Studies* 41, 1 (2008), p. 75.

[19] Adigun Agbaje and Said Adejumobi, 'Do votes count? The travail of electoral politics in Nigeria', *Africa Development* 31, 3 (2006), pp. 25–44.

[20] *Ibid.*, p. 76.

[21] Sarah Birch, 'Electoral institutions and popular confidence in electoral processes: a cross-national analysis', *Electoral Studies* 27, 1 (2008), pp. 305–20.

[22] Hartlyn *et al.*, 'Electoral governance matters', p. 73.

[23] Mozaffar and Schedler, 'The comparative study of electoral governance', p. 6.

[24] Mozaffar, 'Patterns of electoral governance'; Mozaffar and Schedler, 'The comparative study of electoral governance'; Jorgen Elklit and Palle Svensson. 'What makes elections free and fair?', *Journal of Democracy* 8, 3 (1997), pp. 34–45; Jorgen Elklit, 'Electoral institutional

mechanism, are vital to overall quality, defined as 'the extent to which political actors see the entire electoral process as legitimate and binding'.[25]

Winners and losers can accept electoral processes and results as binding provided elections are effectively administered, but effective administration is only possible if the EMB has autonomy, measured basically in terms of its structure, composition, funding and capability.[26] This is why one of the hallmarks of a mature democracy is professional, independent, non-partisan election administration. However, other relevant institutions like political parties, mass media, the security agencies, and civil society groups (CSOs) are also required to play their own roles effectively, including the provision of logistical support, which is vital to the operation of the electoral body. The oversight functions of the legislature and judiciary are also crucial.

In Nigeria, the primary responsibility of electoral administration rests with an EMB that has undergone several changes in nomenclature under different regimes, but not as much change in its structure. To be sure, between 1959 and 1999 the EMB was renamed six times. Before the civil war it was the Electoral Commission of Nigeria (ECN, 1959–63); then the Federal Electoral Commission (FEC, 1963–6). In the latter part of the 1970s it was the Federal Electoral Commission (FEDECO, 1976–9). During the Babangida regime (1986–93), it was renamed the National Electoral Commission (NEC). General Sani Abacha (1993–8) replaced the NEC with the National Electoral Commission of Nigeria (NECON), while General Abdusallami Abukakar, Abacha's successor (1998–9), rechristened it the Independent National Electoral Commission (INEC).[27] It has also been reconstituted endlessly; in 1958, twice in 1963, 1964, 1977, 1981, 1987, 1989, 1993, 1994, 1998, 2000, and 2004.[28] Despite (or perhaps because of) these changes, the EMB has not been able to administer elections effectively, and its 'autonomy and capacity' over the years have been suspect.[29]

Three major indicators of lack of autonomy are identifiable. The first is its composition, which is the prerogative of the President. Since 1999, INEC has been composed of a chairman, twelve national commissioners, and 37 resident electoral commissioners, one each for the 36 states of the federation and the

---

change and democratization: you can lead a horse to the water, but you cannot make it drink', *Democratization* 6, 4 (1999), pp. 28–51; Elklit and Reynolds, 'The impact of election administration'; Pastor, 'The role of electoral administration'.

[25] Elklit and Reynolds, 'The impact of election administration', pp. 86–7.

[26] International IDEA, *Electoral Management Design: The International IDEA Handbook* (International IDEA, Stockholm, 2006).

[27] Agbaje and Adejumobi, 'Do votes count?', p. 31.

[28] See Browne Onuoha, 'The electoral machine: the bureaucracy and the electoral process in the making of Nigeria's Fourth Republic' in Lai Olurode and Remi Anifowose (eds.), *Issues in Nigeria's 1999 General Elections* (John West and Rebonik Publications, Lagos, 2004), p. 39.

[29] Agbaje and Adejumobi, 'Do votes count?', p. 31.

Federal Capital Territory, all of whom are appointed by the federal government. This makes INEC easily susceptible to manipulation by the President and the federal authorities. The oversight role expected of the legislature in the screening of presidential nominees for INEC positions is rendered impotent by the fact that the President's party, the People's Democratic Party (PDP), has a legislative majority sufficient to secure its wishes in Parliament.

The second indicator relates to the insecure tenure of the INEC chairman and commissioners. Job security generally increases the stakes officials have in the electoral process: if they mess up the process, they may lose their positions. Unlike in Ghana, where the chair of the Electoral Commission and the two deputies have security of tenure (they enjoy the same terms and conditions of service as Justices of the Court of Appeal and cannot be removed arbitrarily until retirement at age 70),[30] Nigerian electoral officers statutorily occupy office for five years, renewable for another term. They can, however, be removed by the President on flimsy grounds. This was the fate of two successive electoral commission chairmen under Babangida, namely Professors Eme Awa and Humphrey Nwosu, who were removed from office in 1989 and 1993 respectively in questionable circumstances. The former was removed for his uncompromising stance in the management of the Electoral Commission, and the latter following the military government's decision to annul the 12 June 1993 presidential elections contrary to the position of the Commission.[31]

The third issue relates to the funding of the electoral body. Ordinarily, an independent EMB would require a consolidated account, where a specified proportion of federal revenue is allocated and under the direct control of INEC. In this way, the EMB can enjoy independent funding, thereby limiting the financial control the executive can exert. In Nigeria, however, this is not yet the case. Under the current regime, INEC does not have an independent budget or sources of funding, but instead depends almost entirely on the presidency. This significant financial control contributes to the inability of INEC to make adequate, timely planning and preparations for successful elections.

INEC's capability has been severely constrained in other ways. Two primary indicators are the appointment of people without sufficient professional and intellectual competence to lead the body. For instance, Professor Maurice Iwu, the recently removed national chairman, had no professional experience in electoral management and a health sciences background. The second is INEC's reliance on the use of *ad hoc* staff, who are usually hastily briefed for

---

[30] B. Agyeman-Duah, 'Elections and electoral politics in Ghana's Fourth Republic', *Critical Perspectives* **18** (July 2005), p. 3; and J. Shola Omotola, 'Ghana defies the odds again: the 2008 elections and the consolidation of democracy, *Politeia* **29**, 1 (2008), pp. 42–64.

[31] Humphrey Nwosu, *Laying the Foundation for Nigeria's Democracy: My account of June 12, 1993 presidential election and its annulment* (Macmillan, Lagos, 2008).

a day about their duties. After every flawed election, the tendency has been for INEC to lay the blame on the doorstep of its temporary staff, rather than accept responsibility at the leadership level.[32]

Worse still, INEC reflects the centrist proclivities of the federal democracy. The most visible evidence of this over-centralization of power is that INEC has responsibility for the administration of all federal and state elections. As well as presidential and National Assembly contests, it supervises gubernatorial and House of Assembly elections across 36 states. The only responsibility assigned to the State Independent Electoral Commission (SIEC) is the administration of local government elections.

The electoral processes since 1999

The problems of democratic transition in Nigeria, as in several other African countries, are deep-rooted and well-known.[33] Elections represent a core component of these problems. Already in the colonial era, Nigeria proved unable to organize credible elections acceptable to all democratic players, particularly the opposition parties. But under the fledgling Fourth Republic, Nigeria has for the first time in its post-independence experience been able to hold three consecutive elections at regular intervals (1999, 2003, and 2007). This section analyses the administration of these elections, underscoring their effects on the democratization process.

The Founding Election of 1999

The first election under the current democratization process in Nigeria took place in 1999. Founding elections in Africa, usually the first in a democratic transition process, have been found to exhibit certain features that tend to inhibit the democratization process. These features include the landslide victory, rejection of results by losers, and poor administration of elections.[34] The 1999 Nigerian elections shared all these negative features.

---

[32] Maurice Iwu, *The April 2007 Elections in Nigeria: What went right?* (Department of Political Science, University of Ibadan, 2008).

[33] Samuel Decalo, 'The process, prospects and constraints of democratization in Africa', *African Affairs* **92**, 362 (1992), pp. 7–35; Tunji Olagunju, Adele L. Jinadu, and Samuel Oyovbare, *Transition to Democracy in Nigeria, 1985–1993* (Safari and Spectrum Books, Ibadan, 1993); J. Shola Omotola, 'From importer to exporter: the changing role of Nigeria in promoting democratic values in Africa' in Joelien Pretorius (ed.), *African Politics: Beyond the third wave of democratisation* (Juta Academic Press, Cape Town, 2008), pp. 32–54.

[34] Bratton, 'Second elections', p. 55.

Over the course of three months (December 1998–February 1999), Nigeria had four rounds of elections. These were the local government council elections of 5 December 1998, state House of Assembly and gubernatorial elections of 9 January 1999, National Assembly elections of 20 February 1999, and the presidential election of 27 February 1999. These elections were contested by the three registered political parties: the PDP; the All People's Party (APP)—later All Nigerian People's Party (ANPP); and the Alliance for Democracy (AD). Although these parties claimed to be national in outlook, each maintained dominance in specific geographical-ethnic domains. At the end of the presidential election, Chief Olusegun Obasanjo of the PDP was declared the winner and the duly elected President of Nigeria. He won with a total of 18,738,154 votes (62.78 percent) over Olu Falae, who ran for the APP/AD alliance, with 11,110,287 (37.22 percent).[35] The PDP extended its dominance to all other elections at the national, state, and local levels, and in executive and legislative elections.

The election results were challenged. There were pockets of protest regarding the credibility of the elections, the most notable being the litigation filed by the defeated candidate, who challenged the results of the election. The elections were not credible, as attested by reports of local and international observers including the Transition Monitoring Group (TMG), the Carter Center, National Democratic Institute (NDI), International Republican Institute (IRI), and the EU. All reported widespread irregularities, including a 'miraculous' 100 percent turnout of voters in Rivers State during the presidential election.[36] Yet, the attendant protests were moderate as major stakeholders in the elections—including political parties, candidates, and civil society—decided to sheath their swords, possibly appeased by the renewed promise of democracy.[37] Because the election was meant essentially to disengage the military from politics, not much attention was paid to its credibility.

Nevertheless, allegations of electoral corruption, with the active connivance of INEC and probably the transitional military regime, challenged the administration of the election and raise basic questions regarding INEC's independence, impartiality, and accountability. INEC allegedly rigged the 1999 elections

---

[35] Solomon O. Akinboye, 'Nigeria's 1999 multi-party elections: an overview of electoral conduct and results' in Olurode and Anifowose (eds.), *Issues in Nigeria's 1999 General Elections*, pp. 146–7.

[36] The Carter Center, for example, reported widespread ballot box stuffing, inflated voter turnout, altered results, voter disenfranchisement, and inconsistent application of INEC's procedures across the country. See Carter Center, 'Postelection statement on Nigeria elections, March 1 1999'. The report was issued in response to the 27 February presidential election of 1999. See <http://www.cartercenter.org/news/documents/doc891.html>.

[37] Darren Kew, '"Democrazy, dem go craze, o": monitoring the 1999 Nigerian elections', *Issue: A Journal of Opinion* 27, 1 (1999), pp. 29–33.

in favour of Obasanjo in demonstration of military solidarity,[38] but, more importantly, the elections were rigged in order to avoid a coalition government and the pitfalls of the First Republic, when no party had enough seats to form the government. As a source puts it, 'the reason for the major rigging was to ensure that the party had an absolute majority in order to avoid the coalition and subsequent weak take-off of a new government, which was part of the crises of the transition governments of 1959 and 1979'.[39]

The susceptibility of INEC to political manipulation was due to its lack of institutional and financial autonomy. All its principal officers, including its chairman, national electoral commissioners, and resident electoral commissioners, were, as constitutionally mandated, the political appointees of the President.[40] Consequently, INEC had to rely on the executive arm, particularly the presidency, for its actions and inactions. The loyalty and accountability of INEC, therefore, was first and foremost to the executive to whom it had to go cap in hand begging for audience and funding.

On the whole, the 1999 general elections reflected some conventional wisdom about Nigerian elections. One was the influence of forces of identity, particularly ethnicity and religion, though the emergence of the two presidential candidates from the same geographical axis—the south-west—moderated their impact. Yet, the parties were each dominant along ethno-regional and religious divides. There was also the gender dimension: women were extremely marginalized, accounting for less than 3 percent of elective offices at all levels, meaning that they have 'yet to "penetrate" the core circle of politics, where the "real" things happen'.[41] Moreover, there was an unprecedented monetization of politics as "moneybags" hijacked the electoral process and engaged seriously in vote buying.[42] The situation was allowed to deteriorate to this degree because of INEC's inability to enforce political finance regulations. Nevertheless, the military eventually handed over power to President Obasanjo on 29 May 1999, marking Nigeria's return to civil rule.

---

[38] Kew aptly demonstrated the various forms of rigging perpetuated by INEC staff during the 1999 elections. He noted that, in one instance, 'the presiding officer and the two party agents—one from the APP—were busy thumb-printing as many PDP votes as they could stuff into the ballot box....' *Ibid.*, p. 31.

[39] Browne Onuoha, 'A comparative analysis of general elections in Nigeria' in Remi Anifowose and Tunde Babawale (eds.), *2003 Elections and Democratic Consolidation in Nigeria* (Friedrich Ebert Stiftung, Lagos, 2003), p. 54.

[40] Section 154 of the 1999 constitution of Nigeria provides for the composition of federal agencies, including INEC, and vests the power of appointment in the President.

[41] J. Shola Omotola, 'What is this gender talk all about after all? Gender power and politics in contemporary Nigeria', *African Study Monographs* 28, 1 (April 2007), p. 42.

[42] Emmanuel O. Ojo, 'Vote buying in Nigeria' in Victor A. O. Adetula (ed.), *Money, Politics and Corruption in Nigeria* (International Foundation for Electoral Systems (IFES), Abuja, 2006), pp. 105–23; Alade W. Fawole, 'Voting without choosing: interrogating the crisis of electoral democracy in Nigeria' in Lumumba-Kasongo (ed.), *Liberal Democracy and its Critics in Africa*, p. 160.

The 2003 Second Election

Second elections have been regarded as a crucial step towards democratic consolidation. The democratization process is seen to be on course, especially when elections come at regular intervals. Consequently, more attention is usually paid to the preparation, conduct, and credibility of a second election, at all levels. The road to the 2003 elections was full of potholes, which 'were either left unfilled or filled haphazardly before the elections were held'.[43] The registration of more political parties (increased from three to thirty) and a review of the voters' register were alarm signals amid palpable fears and tension across the country—everyone knew that the stakes were higher than in 1999. A lot of manipulation and manoeuvring went into the build-up, and the hand of the state (in other words, the presidency) was clear. Most notably, President Obasanjo changed the order of the elections through the 2001 Electoral Bill. Whereas in 1999 elections proceeded from the lower to the higher levels—local, state, national assembly and presidential—the 2001 Bill specified that the presidential election would come first. This was interpreted by the opposition as a calculated step by the PDP to facilitate a bandwagon effect in subsequent elections should Obasanjo's PDP win the first elections. The governors in particular saw the reordering as an attempt to storm their state-based strongholds. The crisis generated considerable controversy, even among people in the highest echelons of power. Then President Obasanjo, Senate President Pius Anyim, and Speaker Ghali Umar Na'Abba all traded accusations and counter-accusations over the distortions. The ensuing struggle over the legal framework of the election thus gave the impression that the playing field might not be level. In sum: 'The politics behind this was that both the President and the National Assembly wanted to secure their re-election before the turn of the governors; because the state governors have become very powerful and if elected first might use their local political machines to thwart the political ambitions of the National Assembly members and the President for re-election.'[44]

It was therefore not surprising that the 2003 elections generated massive interest domestically and internationally. Despite some protests about INEC's level of preparation, all the thirty political parties participated at one level of the elections or the other. A number of domestic and international observers also participated. The administration of the elections was generally poor. INEC's organizational weakness and lack of autonomy from political forces all hampered its effectiveness. For instance, the review of voters exercise it

---

[43] J. Shola Omotola, 'The 2003 Nigerian second elections: some comments', *Political Science Review* 3, 1 and 2 (2004), p. 130.
[44] Agbaje and Adejumobi, 'Do votes count?', p. 33.

conducted was fraught with irregularities, particularly non-registration of eligible voters and withholding and sale of voters' cards.[45]

The actual conduct of the elections left more to be desired. Some of the basic problems included the unnecessary militarization of the elections through the massive deployment of security forces. Admittedly, as mentioned above, there was tension across the country prior to the elections—particularly in states such as Kwara, Anambra, and Borno, where the battle lines had been drawn between acclaimed godfathers and their estranged sons (incumbent governors). That was not enough to justify the militarization of voting, which not only undermined voter turnout but also provided cover for the INEC to rig the elections in favour of the ruling party.[46]

The electoral results show that the PDP emerged as the winner at all levels with very wide margins. For example, this time President Obasanjo won the presidency with a total of 24,109,157 (61.80 percent) of total votes cast, while General Mohammed Buhari, the ANPP candidate, emerged runner-up with 12,495,326 (32.3 percent). This shows the firm grip of the retired military officers on Nigerian politics. The PDP also had a landslide victory in the National Assembly elections, winning 75 of the 109 senatorial seats, leaving the ANPP and AD with 28 and 6 seats respectively. The PDP's massive victory was due largely to the power of incumbency, which enabled it to have substantial and unhindered access to state machineries, including the treasury, mass media, INEC, and the security forces. As the party in power, it also enjoyed good patronage from wealthy individuals and corporate bodies in terms of financial donations in exchange for the protection of their business interests.

The most troubling dimension of the electoral trend, however, was the almost total eclipse of the AD in its traditional stronghold, the south-west. Historically, this region has been renowned for its oppositional politics. But in 2003 it was caught napping, as the PDP won the gubernatorial seats in five of the six states, as well as majorities in the state Houses of Assembly and National Assembly elections in the zone. Again this was due to the PDP's power of incumbency, but also to the attempt by the House of Representatives to impeach Obasanjo in August 2002, shortly before the elections. This attempt was interpreted by the south-west as a northern ethnic agenda to recapture power at all costs. Moreover, Obasanjo had accorded the south-west some reasonably high levels of patronage between 1999 and 2003. This was despite his rejection at the poll by the region in the 1999 presidential election. The belated electoral alliance between the PDP and AD—where the latter fielded no presidential candidate of its own, but directed its supporters to vote

---

[45] Omotola, 'The 2003 Nigerian second election', p. 131.
[46] Kunle Ajayi, 'The security forces, electoral conducts and the 2003 general elections', *Journal of Social Sciences* **13**, 1 (2006), pp. 57–66.

for Obasanjo—also contributed to the problem.[47] It was a practical demonstration of the south-western agenda to frustrate the perceived northern anti-Obasanjo agenda. No doubt all these factors contributed—but, more importantly, INEC as an agent of the presidency continued its tradition of manipulating and rigging the elections in favour of the ruling party.

The result was the sharp decline and decay of opposition politics, not only in the south-west, but across the country. The defeat of the AD in the south-west almost entirely denied the party its base, turning it into a weakling in terms of providing a credible oppositional platform to the PDP. Thus the PDP became 'the only party in town', making and unmaking public policies solely at its own discretion. This dominance was so emphatic that the PDP started behaving like a mini-army under a garrison commander, driving the country towards a one-party state.[48] The high-handedness of the PDP was partly a reflection of its dictatorial leadership and centrist organizational structure, where dissenting voices are seldom allowed a hearing.

The problem may not really be PDP's landslide *per se*, as much as the way it acquired it. If the PDP had attained such a pedigree by open, transparent and credible means, concern about the outcome would probably have been less acute. But that was not the case. The 2003 elections, according to reports of local and international observers, were fraught with contradictions, including vote buying, ballot stuffing, rigging, and violence.[49] These shortcomings were largely a result of inadequate preparation by INEC, resulting in logistical problems and inefficient officials. Pre-election activities, such as voters' registration and education, were rushed through. In particular, the display of the voters' register for verification was not carried out effectively, as a result of which voters' registration exercises created room for electoral fraud.

This situation could not have been avoided, since INEC was neither legally nor practically insulated from politics. The 2002 Electoral Law that governed the elections stipulates that those to be appointed as electoral commissioners must be qualified to be members of the House of Representatives. This can be interpreted to mean 'that those appointed as members of the electoral commission should be party members, as membership is a major criterion to be

---

[47] Omotola, 'The 2003 Nigerian second election', pp. 132–3; David O. Alabi, '2003 elections and the South West' in Hassan A. Saliu (ed.) *Nigeria under Democratic Rule, 1999–2003*, Vol. 1 (University Press Plc., Ibadan, 2004), pp. 111–35.

[48] Fatai A. Aremu and J. Shola Omotola, 'Violence as threats to democracy in Nigeria under the Fourth Republic, 1999–2005', *African and Asian Studies* 6, 1–2 (2007), pp. 53–78; Epele Alafuro, 'The 2003 elections and the rise of the one party state in Nigeria' in Godwin Onu and Abubarkar Momoh (eds.), *Elections and Democratic Consolidation in Nigeria* (NPSA, Lagos, 2005), pp. 121–40.

[49] J. Shola Omotola, 'The limits of election monitoring: Nigeria's 2003 general election', *Representation* 42, 2 (2006), pp. 157–67; Transition Monitoring Group, *Do the Votes Count? Final Report of the 2003 General Elections by the Transition Monitoring Group* (TMG, Lagos, 2003).

elected into the House of Representatives. Nigeria does not allow independent candidacy in elections.'[50] This, in itself, engenders declining public confidence in INEC and partly explains why the election results were vigorously contested to the extent that the coalition of opposition parties unanimously announced their rejection of the results. Again, this raises the question of the independence and impartiality of INEC, and of its ability to create a level playing field for all electoral players.

The 2007 General Elections

The 2007 general elections were the third in the series that maps Nigeria's democratization since 1999. It was another opportunity for change and power turnover in the country, given the seeming popular disenchantment with the ruling PDP.[51] These expectations, judging by the overall quality and outcomes of the elections, were effectively squandered.

Prior to the elections, the political atmosphere was again very tense. Among other mind-boggling incidents, President Olusegun Obasanjo condescendingly declared that, for him and the PDP, the 2007 election was 'a do or die affair'.[52] INEC too, rather than focusing on adequate preparations for the elections, was widely engaged in unnecessary distractions, most notably litigation against opposition candidates in its attempts to screen and disqualify candidates. Its insistence on preventing Alhaji Atiku Abubakar—then Vice-President and presidential candidate of a leading opposition party, the Action Congress (AC)—from contesting, although the electoral law made it clear that INEC does not have such powers, snowballed the tension. Despite INEC's jaunty expressions about its state of preparedness and ability to conduct free, fair, and credible elections, events before and during the elections proved otherwise. The political atmosphere was permeated with jaundiced views of INEC's capability, independence and impartiality.

Despite these reservations, Nigerians enthusiastically went to the polls for the gubernatorial and state Houses of Assembly elections on 14 April, and the presidential and National Assembly elections on 21 April. In the results of the elections, INEC awarded the PDP an unimaginable landslide victory at all levels—unimaginable because the last eight years of PDP leadership had not improved the living conditions of average Nigerians in any fundamental sense. Unemployment, inflation, poverty, insecurity, and violence were on the rise.

---

[50] Said Adejomobi, 'When votes do not count: the 2007 general elections in Nigeria', *News from Nordic African Institute*, 2, (May 2007), pp. 14–15.

[51] Mike Unger, 'Panel analyses upcoming Nigerian elections', *American Weekly: American University's News Paper*, 13 February 2007, p. 1.

[52] See Adejumobi, 'When votes do not count', pp. 14–15.

The much-orchestrated reform agenda was predicated on neo-liberal ideolo-gies of the free market, where the rich profit at the expense of the poor.[53] Under such circumstances, a massive victory for the ruling party is likely to be questioned.

The manner by which the PDP garnered the votes was puzzling. Across the country, there was unprecedented rigging, ballot stuffing, falsification of results, intimidation of voters, and direct assault on the people. In some extreme instances, voting did not take place.[54] This was most prominent in the south-east, south-south and south-western geo-political zones of the country, where opposition parties were believed to be most formidable. In Enugu State, for example, Ken Nnamani, then Senate president, like many others, could not vote in the presidential election because voting materials were not made available. There were instances where INEC decided to dis-qualify candidates on the eve of the elections, contrary to court orders. This was the case with opposition gubernatorial candidates in Kogi, Adamawa and Anambra states, where opposition candidates (ANPP and AC) were excluded. Substitutions of candidates who won party primaries was another major issue in the 2007 election, the most celebrated case involving the gubernatorial candidate in Rivers State. Indeed, local and international observers were unanimous in their outright condemnation of the elections.[55]

That massive irregularities marred the elections is supported by some verifiable indices. First, the results of the elections were bitterly disputed and protested in an unprecedented manner, though largely non-violently. From the conduct of the elections alone, 1,250 election petitions arose. The presi-dential election had eight, the gubernatorial 105, the Senate 150, the House of Representatives 331, and the state Houses of Assembly 656.[56] With a few exceptions, especially the gubernatorial elections in Osun and Ekiti states, most of these cases have been decided in the final appellate court. For example, the two leading opposition candidates in the presidential election pursued their cases to the Supreme Court, where the case was decided in favour of President Yar'Adua of the PDP. However, results were annulled in several states and at different levels, including the gubernatorial elections in Kogi, Edo, Kebbi, Sokoto, Adamawa, Ekiti and Ondo states. In most of these cases, a re-run was mandated, which the PDP won. In Ondo and Edo states, however,

<hr>

[53] See Daniel Omoweh and Dirk van den Boom, *Blocked Democracy in Africa: Experiment with democratization in Nigeria, 1999–2003* (Konrad Adenauer Foundation, Abuja, 2005), pp. 41–59.

[54] For a comprehensive review of the reports of local and international observers, see Paul F. Adebayo and Shola J. Omotola, 'Public perception of the 2007 Nigeria's general elections', *Journal of African Elections* 6, 2 (2007), pp. 201–16.

[55] *Ibid.*

[56] E. Remi Aiyede, 'Electoral laws and the 2007 elections in Nigeria', *Journal of African Elections* 6, 2 (2007), p. 50.

declaratory judgments were given, leading to the restoration of the electoral victory of the Labour Party and AC in the respective states. The substituted candidate in Rivers State was also rein-stated by the Supreme Court.[57]

The 1,250 election tribunal and court cases recorded are just the tip of the iceberg. This is so when elections are considered to be a combination of preelection, election and post-election events. In an astonishing revelation, *The Herald*, a national daily, reveals that the 2007 elections recorded an alarming 6,180 cases throughout the electoral process.[58] This may be correct given the high level of political gangsterism and the political culture of impunity that characterized the political scene. The most relevant example relates to the manipulation of party primaries to pave the way for anointed candidates of the godfathers, especially within the ruling PDP.[59] Where this failed, the party hierarchy, at the instance of the presidency, resorted to elimination by substituting the names of the preferred candidates for those who actually won the primaries. A typical case was in Imo State, where Senator Ifeanyi Ararume won the primaries but another candidate's name was put on the ballot nonetheless. Ararume challenged this and won in the Supreme Court, but the victory proved costly: the PDP in the state decided to expel him for anti-party activity, for it is an abomination to challenge an internal PDP decision in court. Whatever happens must be treated as a 'family affair'. The PDP also decided not to field a candidate for the governorship election in the state, and since the electoral laws do not recognize independent candidacy, Ararume was tactically pushed out of the race.[60]

Be that as it may, the resort to the courts to seek electoral justice signals the gradual acceptance of the rule of law as the most viable option for those seeking redress. Gradually, Nigerians are beginning to regain their confidence in the judiciary. This is partly a result of certain landmark judgements delivered by the judiciary in recent times, especially as the race to the 2007 elections intensified. One notable example was the Supreme Court judgements that stopped INEC from disqualifying Atiku barely a few days before the election. These are signs of political institutionalization, where political actors exploit legal avenues, as opposed to unconventional channels, to seek redress. If sustained, it is a sign of democratic deepening. That is not to say that all protests about the elections were peaceful. In some south-western states, particularly Osun, Oyo, Ekiti and Ondo, there were violent protests against

---

[57] J. Shola Omotola, '"Garrison" democracy in Nigeria: the 2007 general elections and the prospects of democratic consolidation', *Commonwealth and Comparative Politics* 47, 2 (2009), pp. 195–221.

[58] See Kayode Lawal, '2007 elections: courts receive 6,180 cases', *The Herald* (Ilorin, 12 May 2008), pp. 1 and 23.

[59] J. Shola Omotola, 'Godfathers and the 2007 Nigeria's general elections', *Journal of African Elections* 6, 2 (2007), pp. 147–8.

[60] *Ibid.*

the massive rigging and overturning of the people's will. Killing, arson, looting, and other forms of violence were pervasive in these states, leading to deplorable security situations. These shortcomings cast ominous shadows on the elections and the prospects of democratic consolidation.

Nevertheless, the 2007 elections are reputable for at least four important reasons. First, that the election took place at the expected interval is reassuring. It was the first time in the history of the country that a democratically elected civilian government completed two terms of eight years, conducted elections, and successfully handed over to another elected government. As remarkable as this seems, it should not be interpreted to mean that any sort of elections would do in the third election test—indeed the declining quality of Nigerian elections is increasingly being considered as a source of democratic deconsolidation.[61] Second, the resort to the courts to seek electoral justice is a clear deviation from the use of self-help strategies to settle electoral scores in the past. This shows that the political class is gaining increasing confidence in the judiciary as an important democratic institution. Third, the new government's publicly avowed commitment to the rule of law, keeping faith in the courts, and executing all courts, judgements on the elections, even when against the PDP, point toward the gradual emergence of democratic political culture. This was unthinkable under ex-President Obasanjo, who unilaterally selected which courts, decision to execute. Finally, the maladministration of the election has intensified civil activism for electoral reform and pressured the government to grant some limited concessions, including the ongoing electoral reform process. These developments are important for building a democratic political culture rooted in the rule of law. Though these gains do not constitute consolidated democracy, they may help reclaim public confidence in the democratization process.

Conclusion: elections and the prospects of democratic consolidation

The foregoing analysis suggests that the prospect of consolidating democracy in Nigeria through elections remains a tall order, though not impossible to deliver. Consolidating democracy through elections depends largely on the institutional foundations of the electoral processes, particularly the EMB—in this case, the INEC. A professional, capable, and independent INEC, free from partisan influence and government control, would provide better prospects of effective electoral administration. Only such an electoral body could conduct

---

[61] See IFES, *A Nigerian Perspective on the 2007 Presidential and Parliamentary Elections Results from Pre- and post-Election Surveys* (International Foundation for Electoral Systems, Abuja, 2007).

credible elections, whose outcomes will be acceptable to the majority of people, including opposition parties. From the preceding analysis, it is clear that this is not yet the case in Nigeria. In its present form and character, INEC enjoys limited legitimacy and respect among Nigerians.

There are many reasons for this. Not only is INEC grossly deficient in autonomy and professionalism, but it is also inefficient. The presidency wields overbearing influence on INEC, making it impossible for it to exercise independence and provide a level playing field to all political actors. More importantly, INEC is saddled with the task of governing the entire electoral cycle—pre-election, election, and post-election at federal and state levels. These tasks are obviously 'beyond the scope of a single body. The logistics of conducting countrywide elections mean that INEC is overwhelmed during voting and counting.'[62] The electoral laws, which can be manipulated to secure the services of politicians within the electoral body, is another dimension of the problem. Thus, INEC has been hamstrung in the effective governance of elections.

The high level of instability in the country since independence in 1960 has also contributed to the weak institutionalization of INEC. Due to frequent change of governments, it has been subjected to repeated renaming and restructuring.[63] The main considerations in these exercises have been political, rather than relating to the search for institutional autonomy and administrative efficiency.[64] The high level of instability has not allowed for the evolution and development of electoral governance culture, routinized in design and implementation. Instability has also had an impact on the cultivation of democratic political culture and citizenship, which is today responsible for the predominance of politicians who are not democrats in the true sense of the term. The dearth of democrats has also contributed to the suffocation and shrinking of the political space in which democratic institutions can operate, including INEC and political parties.

There is an urgent need to make adequate efforts to reform electoral institutions. INEC represents the most important of all the institutional foundations of elections in Nigeria. It ought to be independent, impartial, and courageous in discharging its responsibilities. The starting point would be to detach it completely from the presidency and make it an entirely autonomous body. The appointment of its political head and commissioners should be insulated from politics, while its funding should be charged to the consolidated account. Like any other federal parastatal, INEC should receive its statutory allocation in the annual budget, thus reducing its financial dependence on the presidency. Yet, for institutional reform to work well, it must be pursued along with attitudinal and behavioural reform. From historical insight, the institutional foundations of elections in Nigeria fail not because

[62] Aiyede, 'Electoral laws' p. 53.   [63] Onuoha, 'The electoral machine', p. 39.
[64] Agbaje and Adejumobi, 'Do votes count?', p. 30.

they are inherently corruptible or incapable of doing the right thing, but because main political actors design them to fail so that they can advance their self-interests. What is therefore important is a continuous process of social mobilization and political re-engineering that emphasizes value reorientation at all levels. While the political class should be the major targets, the campaign should be comprehensive and holistic, leaving out no one, at all levels of socio-political organization. In this Herculean task, the civil society and mass media are crucial. Their roles should be popular sensitization, education, conscientization, and mobilization against the anti-democratic dispositions of some political actors at all levels.

Despite all the daunting difficulties, there are reasons for optimism. Civil society organizations, pro-democracy forces and opposition parties are fighting relentlessly for a comprehensive reform of the electoral process. The Electoral Reform Network (ERN) and the Centre for Democracy and Development are leading examples; both submitted memoranda to the Uwais Electoral Reform Committee and are still following up this initiative in the National Assembly. The recent rise of the Save Nigeria Group (SNG)—a coalition of several civil society organizations, along with pro-democracy and human rights activists, to champion the cause of sustainable electoral reform and good governance—has added weight to the pressure for reform. The reforms being championed are targeted mainly at securing the institutional autonomy, administrative efficiency, and professionalism of INEC. Recent changes in the leadership of INEC, including the removal of the controversial and discredited Maurice Iwu and his replacement with Professor Attahiru Jega—a leading political scientist who is also a labour and democracy activist—are some of the gains of the ongoing reform process. Moreover, the judiciary is becoming increasingly courageous and assertive in the delivery of electoral justice. These advances, in addition to international support such as election monitoring, are essential for the institutionalization of effective electoral administration for democratic consolidation. The emerging scenarios suggest that, despite its troubled electoral history, Nigeria's fiftieth independence anniversary offers hope of an alternative future built on institutional engineering and reinforced by behavioural and attitudinal change. It is perhaps not a mere coincidence that Nigeria's first democratic decade coincides with this anniversary. It may be an indicator of better things to come.

Acknowledgment

Published in *African Affairs*, 109, 437 (2010), p. 535–553. I thank this journal's anonymous reviewers for their provocative and useful comments. I also thank Rita Abrahamsen for her ceaseless probing, which served to bring the article to its current state. I am, however, solely responsible for the views expressed.

12

Elites and Democracy in Ghana

A Social Network Approach

Anja Osei

THE QUESTION OF WHY SOME COUNTRIES become more democratic than others has been a constant issue in political science. Two main explanatory approaches can be distinguished: structural and actor-centric. Structural explanations consider wealth, urbanization, industrialization, and education as factors that are positively related to the emergence of stable democracies.[1] Actor-centric conceptions, in contrast, reject the idea that democracy rests on a set of economic and social preconditions,[2] instead emphasizing processes of elite bargaining and strategic interaction.[3] Initially, the third wave of democratization seemed to support the actor-centric idea that democracy can thrive in all kinds of settings.[4] This was especially evident in Africa, where some of the poorest countries—hitherto referred to as 'unlikely democratizers'[5]—introduced multi-party systems. Michael Bratton and Nicolas van de Walle's analysis of African transitions as processes of strategic interaction between popular protests and elite responses lends further support to the strategic approach.[6]

---

[1] Seymour Martin Lipset, 'Some social requisites of democracy: Economic development and political legitimacy', *American Political Science Review*, 53 (1959), pp. 69–105.

[2] Dankwart A. Rustow, 'Transitions to democracy: Toward a dynamic model', *Comparative Politics* 2 (1970), pp. 337–63.

[3] Guillermo A. O'Donnell and Philippe C. Schmitter, *Transitions from authoritarian rule* (Johns Hopkins University Press, Baltimore, MD, 1986).

[4] Sheri Berman, 'Lessons from Europe', *Journal of Democracy* 18 (2007), pp. 28–41.

[5] Larry Diamond, 'The rule of law versus the big man', *Journal of Democracy* 19 (2008), pp. 138–49.

[6] Michael Bratton and Nicolas van de Walle, 'Popular protest and political reform in Africa', *Comparative Politics* 24 (1992), pp. 419–42; Michael Bratton and Nicolas van de Walle, 'Neopatrimonial regimes and political transitions in Africa', *World Politics*, 46 (1994), pp. 453–89.

However, from the mid-1990s onwards, it became clear that not all cases of transition would end up as consolidated democracies. A number of successful democracies exist alongside surviving autocracies and hybrid regimes that are neither fully democratic nor autocratic. A 'new crop of preconditionists' began to refine and extend a set of arguments through which to explain the relationship between socio-economic development and democracy.[7] Various other structural variables were investigated, such as the colonial background of countries, their ethnic and religious composition, political culture, institutions, and the existence of a democratic neighbourhood. Overall, structural factors have proven to have significant explanatory power, but there remains a group of countries whose democratic achievements or non-achievements are not well predicted from structural prerequisites.[8] In these 'deviant cases', actor-centric explanations may contribute in important ways to our understanding of political transitions.[9] Interestingly, Africa hosts an unusually high number of deviant cases. In his worldwide study of the determinants of democratization, Jan Teorell finds ten such cases, six of which are in Africa.[10] Similarly, three of the five deviant cases described by Renske Dorenspleet and Petr Kopecký are African countries, as are seven of the twelve deviant cases Michael Seeberg cites.[11]

Thus there is good reason to take a fresh look at actor-centric explanations and specifically the role of elites, which in this article will refer to political elites, with a focus on MPs. Actor-centric and structural approaches are not mutually exclusive, since structures and human actions are dialectically linked and presuppose each other.[12] However, while structural variables can be tested relatively easily in quantitative studies, the relationship between elites and democracy is much harder to grasp. The aim of the article is twofold. First, it shows the relevance of elite theory to the study of democratization in Africa. Taking the premise that no democracy is possible without a consensually united elite as a starting point, this article presents a first empirical test of the Higley/Burton theory in an African case: Ghana. Second, it demonstrates that a Social Network Analysis (SNA) can be applied fruitfully to the empirical study of elite structures on the continent.

---

[7] Berman, 'Lessons from Europe', p. 31.

[8] Renske Doorenspleet and Petr Kopecký, 'Against the odds: Deviant cases of democratization', *Democratization* 15 (2008), pp. 697–713.

[9] Doorenspleet and Kopecký, 'Against the odds', p. 710; see also Jan Teorell, *Determinants of democratization: Explaining regime change in the world, 1972–2006* (Cambridge University Press, Cambridge, 2010).

[10] Teorell, *Determinants of democratization*.

[11] Doorenspleet and Kopecký, 'Against the odds'; Michael Seeberg, 'Mapping deviant democracy', *Democratization* 21 (2014), pp. 634–54.

[12] Anthony Giddens, *Central problems in social theory: Action, structure and contradiction in social analysis* (Palgrave Macmillan, London, 1979).

Ghana represents a suitable case for this article because it is clearly a country that has achieved a high quality of democracy in the absence of many of the structural conditions that are said to promote democratic consolidation. Notwithstanding the controversy over how democracy should be measured, few would dispute that Ghana belongs in this category. According to Freedom House, Ghana's quality of democracy has increased continuously over recent decades, and the country is rated as 'free'.[13] At the same time, Ghana was not blessed with a particularly promising starting point: the country is ethnically diverse; has a history of military coups and political instability; and at the start of the multiparty period recorded a low GDP and high unemployment. It is therefore intuitively plausible that an actor-centric approach may be better placed to explain Ghana's democratic consolidation. In this sense, Ghana represents what Harry Eckstein calls a 'crucial case'.[14] Crucial cases are those that 'must closely fit a theory if one is to have confidence in the theory's validity, or, conversely, must not fit'.[15] Ghana is a 'must fit' case: if the proposition that a liberal democracy is impossible without a consensually united elite is valid, then Ghana must reveal precisely the elite structure that the theory predicts.

The article is organized as follows. First, a theoretical section on united and disunited elites introduces the analytical framework and discusses how elite theory can be linked to democratization studies. Based on this foundation, the article argues that democracy requires a profound transformation of elite behaviour towards greater unity. Using SNA, this proposition is tested in the case of Ghana. Empirical evidence comes from a unique data set that maps the interaction patterns between MPs elected in 2012. It is found that the network is densely connected, and that there are frequent contacts between MPs of different party affiliation and ethnic origin. These findings provide strong evidence for the Higley/Burton thesis that elite unity promotes democratic consolidation. The concluding section of the article puts the research results into comparative perspective and highlights the causal path of elite transformation in Ghana. Special attention is paid to two important factors: the role of the two-party system in the process of transformation, and the interaction between ethnicity and party loyalties as a stabilizing factor for elite unity.

---

[13] For their evaluation of Ghana, and the methodology that they employ, see <www.freedomhouse.org> (15 July 2015).

[14] Eckstein, *Regarding politics*, p. 65.

[15] *Ibid.*; see also John Gerring, 'Is there a (viable) crucial-case method?', *Comparative Political Studies* 40 (2007), pp. 231–53.

United and disunited elites

Scholars studying the relationship between regime types and elite structures agree that elite integration fosters stability.[16] Elite integration has two important dimensions: structural integration, which involves the relative inclusiveness of communication networks among elite persons and groups; and values consensus, which involves a general consensus on the rules of the game.[17] On the basis of these dimensions, John Higley and Michael Burton develop a typology of elite structures and corresponding regime types.[18] According to their view, liberal democracy is only possible with a consensually united elite, which is characterized by 'dense and interlocked networks of communication and influence'.[19] Important elites must have access to central decision making, but they must also share basic values and norms of political behaviour, and recognize bargaining as an acceptable mode of operation.[20] The consensus on values does not necessarily refer to specific issues, but rather to the rules of the game—in other words, elites must agree to disagree.[21] Disunited elites, by contrast, are divided by cultural, ethnic, or political cleavages and deeply mistrust each other.[22] Furthermore, they lack a sufficient amount of structural integration because their communication networks do not cross factional boundaries.[23] Regimes with disunited elites tend to be unstable because competing elite factions perceive the existing regime as the vehicle of a dominant elite faction that needs to be toppled by violent means.[24] Any regime change towards democracy will therefore remain temporary unless it is preceded or accompanied by a transformation of elite structures and behaviour.[25]

Elite transformations are, however, relatively rare events.[26] They can take two forms: a sudden settlement of disputes, or a slow convergence toward shared norms of political behaviour. Settlements are most likely to take place after conflicts in which all parties suffered losses, or under the threat of an

[16] Robert D. Putnam, *The comparative study of political elites* (Prentice-Hall, Englewood Cliffs, NJ, 1976).

[17] John Higley and Michael Burton, *Elite foundations of liberal democracy* (Rowman and Littlefield, Lanham, MD, 2006).

[18] *Ibid.*   [19] *Ibid.*   [20] *Ibid.*, p. 11.

[21] Fredrik Engelstad, 'Democratic elitism: Conflict and consensus', in Heinrich Best and John Higley (eds), *Democratic elitism: New theoretical and comparative perspectives* (Brill, Leiden and Boston, MA, 2010), pp. 61–78.

[22] Putnam, *The comparative study of political elites*, p. 119.

[23] Michael Burton, Richard Gunther, and John Higley, 'Introduction', in John Higley and Richard Gunther (eds), *Elites and democratic consolidation in Latin America and southern Europe* (Cambridge University Press, Cambridge, 1992), pp. 1–37.

[24] *Ibid.*, p. 10.

[25] John Higley and Michael Burton, 'The elite variable in democratic transitions and breakdowns', *American Sociological Review* 54 (1989), pp. 17–32.

[26] Higley and Burton, *Elite foundations of liberal democracy*, p. 3.

outbreak of violence. Such initial compromises are no guarantee for the thriving of democracy, but they provide the basis for a subsequent broadening of the scope of elite unity. Settlements can only be successful if they are perceived as legitimate by wide sections of the population. Daniel Levine shows that strong parties were central to this process in the case of Venezuela, because they 'provided elites with sufficient leverage to impose settlements on rank and file members'.[27] Another important aspect is the building of new institutions and procedures for handling conflict.[28] Moreover, many authors emphasize the role of personal interactions, which reduce the probability of intra-elite conflict and help to build mutual trust.[29]

Elections are an important step in the process of elite transformation. Michael Burton *et al.* describe this as follows: first, some of the opposing elite factions realize that they can win elections repeatedly by forming broad electoral coalitions.[30] A series of defeats then convinces hostile or dissident elite factions of the necessity 'to beat the...dominant coalition at its own electoral game'.[31] As a result, they abandon anti-system stances, acknowledge the rules of the game, and become trustworthy competitors.[32] The process of elite transformation is usually completed by the electoral victory of previously dissident elites.[33] The key idea here is that consensually united elites are a precondition for democracy because they are able to manage conflicts by non-violent and institutional means. Their dense and interlocked webs of communication give elites mutual security even after missteps and during political crises.[34]

Empirical research on elite structures and behaviour has greatly benefited from the SNA approach, which allows researchers to map social structures and examine relationships between actors.[35] The method can be applied fruitfully to the Higley/Burton theory, because the authors make clear statements about the relationship between elite structures and regimes. As stated above, consensually united elites are connected by dense and interlocked networks; in other words, their networks have a high degree of cohesion. Cohesive elite networks are important for democracies because they allow information and

---

[27] Daniel H. Levine, 'Venezuela since 1958: The consolidation of democratic politics', in Juan Linz and Alfred C. Stepan (eds), *The breakdown of democratic regimes: Latin America* (Johns Hopkins University Press, Baltimore, MD, and London, 1978), pp. 82–109.

[28] *Ibid.*, p. 102.

[29] Anthony Giddens, *The class structure of the advanced societies* (Hutchinson, London, 1973). See also Putnam, *The comparative study of political elites*, pp. 112 ff.

[30] Burton, Gunther, and Higley, 'Introduction', p. 24.

[31] *Ibid.*   [32] *Ibid.*   [33] *Ibid.*

[34] Higley and Burton, *Elite foundations of liberal democracy*, p. 12.

[35] Ursula Hoffmann-Lange, 'Methods of elite research', in Russell J. Dalton and Hans-Dieter Klingemann (eds), *The Oxford handbook of political behaviour* (Oxford University Press, Oxford, 2007); David Knoke, 'Networks of elite structure and decision making', *Sociological Methods and Research* 22 (1993), pp. 23–45.

other resources to flow fast and reach a great number of people. It is further assumed that important elites have access to each other and to central decision making.[36] If this requirement is to be fulfilled, the structure of the network must be such that no single actor or faction is able to control the flow of resources, which in turn makes possible the 'politics as bargaining' that Higley and Burton emphasize. A decentralized elite network is therefore a prerequisite for democracy. In authoritarian regimes, by contrast, a star-like network would be expected, in which the most central actor—usually the leader— controls the flow of information and all other resources.

Using SNA, empirical evidence of consensually united elites has been found in Western democracies such as Australia, West Germany, and the US.[37] In all three countries, a densely connected network structure exists.[38] The few studies of disunited elites have revealed an absence of personal contacts between the main factions,[39] and studies on authoritarian regimes found network structures that are strongly centralized around the leadership.[40]

Can these ideas be applied to African countries? In Higley and Burton's book, African cases are mentioned but not elaborated on at length. The theory has attracted little attention in African Studies, where elite politics have been discussed mainly in connection with the phenomenon of neopatrimonialism. In neo-patrimonial states, a system of formal rules coexists with a clientelist system of personal relations.[41] This literature offers interesting parallels to the Higley/Burton theory because it addresses a similar problem: the relationship between elite unity/disunity, on the one hand, and political stability/regime type on the other. However, there is still not much clarity about the relationship between neo-patrimonialism and political regimes. In a recent paper, Leonardo Arriola points to the paradoxical fact that the same arguments have been used to explain both the stability and the breakdown of African regimes.[42] Many authors, including Jean-François Bayart[43] and Donald Rothchild and Michael Foley,[44] have described patronage as a mechanism of elite

---

[36] John Higley, Ursula Hoffmann-Lange, Charles Kadushin, and Gwen Moore, 'Elite integration in stable democracies: A reconsideration', *European Sociological Review* 7 (1991), pp. 35–53.

[37] Gwen Moore, 'The structure of a national elite network', *American Sociological Review* 44 (1979), pp. 673–92; Higley *et al.*, 'Elite integration in stable democracies'.

[38] *Ibid.*

[39] Higley and Burton, 'The elite variable in democratic transitions', p. 19.

[40] Higley and Burton, *Elite foundations of liberal democracy*, p. 10.

[41] Gero Erdmann and Ulf Engel, 'Neopatrimonialism reconsidered: Critical review and elaboration of an elusive concept', *Commonwealth and Comparative Politics* 45 (2007), pp. 95–119.

[42] Leonardo R. Arriola, 'Patronage and political stability in Africa', *Comparative Political Studies* 42 (2009), pp. 1339–62.

[43] Jean-François Bayart, *The state in Africa* (Polity, Cambridge, 2009).

[44] Donald Rothchild and Michael W. Foley, 'African states and the politics of inclusive coalitions', in Donald S. Rothchild and Naomi H. Chazan (eds), *The precarious balance: State and society in Africa* (Westview Press, Boulder, CO, 1988).

integration. In this view, patronage networks contribute to political stability by merging competing elite segments—the 'big men' of various ethnic, religious, or regional communities—into a relatively cohesive ruling coalition. At the same time, however, patronage can be a source of instability because elites fracture over access to it.[45] Elite conflicts often spill over into widespread violence, especially when competing elites instrumentalize ethnic, religious, or other potentially divisive identities to garner support.

Whether or not patronage can serve as a mechanism of elite integration depends to a large degree on the availability of resources. Thus, when the economic crisis of the 1980s deprived leaders of their patronage capacity, the breakdown and disintegration of elite accommodation systems resulted in violent conflict in a number of countries.[46] In other countries, it forced leaders to open up the political space and give way to multi-party politics. In a third group of countries, the incumbent regimes were able to survive even the third wave of democratization; this group includes both resource-abundant countries like Gabon and relatively poor ones such as Togo. Arriola is therefore correct to criticize the literature on neo-patrimonialism for having 'failed to specify the conditions under which patronage enhances...stability'.[47] The same argument can be made for the relationship between democracy and neo-patrimonialism: are they irreconcilable, as some authors claim,[48] or do they in fact coexist, as others believe?[49] Has the transition to multi-party elections only led to intensified competition among a relatively narrow circle of elites,[50] or have there been more substantial changes in elite behaviour?

This article proposes to move away from the 'elusive concept'[51] of neopatrimonialism and to look at elite unity or disunity more specifically. This perspective allows a better understanding of how political competition is structured in Africa, and how these elite structures are linked to democracy. Second, it links Africanist scholarship to political sociology and opens up a dialogue between area-specific and more universalist approaches. Interestingly, a number of scholars working on Africa have advanced arguments that are

---

[45] Bratton and van de Walle, 'Neopatrimonial regimes and political transitions in Africa'.

[46] William Reno, *Warlord politics and African states* (Lynne Rienner, Boulder, CO, 1998).

[47] Arriola, 'Patronage and political stability', p. 1340.

[48] Mamoudou Gazibo, 'Can neopatrimonialism dissolve into democracy?', in Daniel C. Bach (ed.), *Neopatrimonialism in Africa and beyond* (Routledge, London, 2012), pp. 79–89; Nicholas van de Walle, 'The path from neopatrimonialism: Democracy and clientelism in Africa today', in *ibid.*, pp. 111–23.

[49] Linda J. Beck, *Brokering democracy in Africa: The rise of clientelist democracy in Senegal* (Palgrave Macmillan, New York, NY, 2008). Anne Pitcher, Mary Moran and Michael Johnston, 'Rethinking patrimonialism and neopatrimonialism in Africa', *African Studies Review* 52 (2009), pp. 125–56.

[50] Patrick Chabal, 'Power in Africa reconsidered', in Ulf Engel and Gorm Rye Olsen (eds), *The African exception* (Ashgate, Aldershot, 2005), pp. 17–34.

[51] Erdmann and Engel, 'Neopatrimonialism reconsidered'.

akin to the Higley/Burton thesis discussed here. Especially in the cases of Ghana and South Africa there is some evidence that democracy has succeeded because of an underlying elite consensus.[52] Elite disunity, by contrast, is often seen as an obstacle to stable democracy.[53] While such works are important and insightful, we need more and better data to test these claims empirically. The next section will therefore introduce SNA as a promising research tool that can be deployed to achieve this aim.

Using social network analysis to test the Higley/Burton thesis in Ghana

A systematic investigation of elite unity and disunity can further our understanding of the variation between regime types on the African continent and elsewhere. On the methodological front, there is much to be gained from SNA. Although elite sociology has successfully employed it to study elite structures empirically, Africanists have used its terminology in a more metaphorical way to describe the network-like dyadic structure of clientelism.[54] SNA does not resolve the many conceptual and empirical problems inherent in the study of clientelism, but it can make the relationships between actors visible.

The ability to test theories is generally seen as the primary strength of quantitative, cross-country research.[55] As many researchers have shown, however, it is possible to test theories using single-case studies.[56] For this

[52] Lindsay Whitfield, '"Change for a better Ghana": Party competition, institutionalization and alternation in Ghana's 2008 elections', *African Affairs* 108 (2009), pp. 621–41; Alexander K. D. Frempong, 'Political conflict and elite consensus in the liberal state', in Kwame Boafo-Arthur (ed.), *Ghana: One decade of the liberal state* (Zed Books, London, 2007), pp. 128–64; Johanna Odonkor Svanikier, 'Political elite circulation: Implications for leadership diversity and democratic regime stability in Ghana', *Comparative Sociology* 6 (2007), pp. 114–35.

[53] See, for example, Nic Cheeseman, 'The internal dynamics of power sharing in Africa', *Democratization*, 18, 2 (2011), pp. 336–65.

[54] Examples include Michael Bratton and Nicholas van de Walle, *Democratic experiments in Africa: Regime transitions in comparative perspective* (Cambridge University Press, Cambridge, 1997); Patrick Chabal and Jean-Pascal Daloz, *Africa works: Disorder as political instrument* (James Currey, Oxford, 1999), and Gero Erdmann and Ulf Engel, 'Neopatrimonialism reconsidered'. In their work, all these authors make frequent use of the term 'clientelistic networks' as a metaphor to describe relationships between actors.

[55] John W. Creswell, *Research design: Qualitative, quantitative, and mixed methods approaches* (SAGE, Los Angeles, CA, 2014).

[56] Alexander L. George and Andrew Bennett, *Case studies and theory development in the social sciences* (MIT Press, Cambridge, MA, 2005); Arend Lijphart, 'Comparative politics and the comparative method', *The American Political Science Review* 65 (1971), pp. 682–93; Harry Eckstein, *Regarding politics: Essays on political theory, stability, and change* (University of California Press, Berkeley, CA, 1992).

method to work, two conditions must be fulfilled: the theory must be developed into a testable form,[57] and the case to be investigated must be carefully selected. The next section will first develop a test for the theory of interest, outlining how SNA works, and thereafter describe the process of data collection in Ghana.

With regard to the first point, the theory developed by Higley and Burton readily lends itself to deductive hypothesis testing because it makes certain clear statements about the relationship between elite structures and regimes. The hypotheses that are derived can be tested by means of SNA methods. There is no room here to provide a detailed introduction to network analysis; consequently, only a few core concepts directly related to the analysis are highlighted. To begin with, networks are composed of nodes and ties. In social networks, the nodes are the actors, and the ties are the relationships between them. There are three levels of analysis: the node level, the dyad, and the complete network.[58] Actors (nodes) have specific characteristics, such as gender and age. These characteristics often influence the formation of a dyad; in friendship networks, for example, women may have more relationships with other women, and men with other men. The network itself consists of chains of interconnected dyads. The ties in a network can be directed, meaning that one node is a sender of something that flows through a network (such as information or resources) while another node acts as a receiver. Moreover, ties can be valued. The value of a tie describes the intensity of a relationship—for example whether actors interact very often, often, or only sometimes. A number of software packages are available for the empirical analysis of social networks. For this article, all calculations were performed using UCINET.[59] In addition, Visone[60] was used for the visualization of the networks shown in Figures 12.1 to 12.4.

As previously noted, the theory of Higley and Burton has two dimensions: structural integration and value consensus. Structurally, consensually united elites are connected by cohesive and decentralized networks that integrate all important elites. In terms of behaviour, they share a basic understanding of the rules of the game. One simple but insightful concept of cohesion is network density. Density is calculated by dividing the number of ties present in a network by the number of theoretically possible ties. The density measure

---

[57] George and Bennett, *Case studies and theory development*, p. 116.

[58] Stephen P. Borgatti, Martin G. Everett, and Jeffrey C. Johnson, *Analyzing social networks* (SAGE, Los Angeles, CA, 2013), p. 2.

[59] Stephen P. Borgatti, Martin G. Everett, and L. C. Freeman, *Ucinet for Windows: Software for Social Network Analysis* (Analytic Technologies, Harvard University Press, Cambridge, MA, 2002).

[60] Ulrik Brandes and Dorothea Wagner, 'Visone: Analysis and visualization of social networks', in Michael Jünger and Petra Mutzel (eds), *Graph drawing software* (Springer, Heidelberg and Berlin, 2004), pp. 321–40.

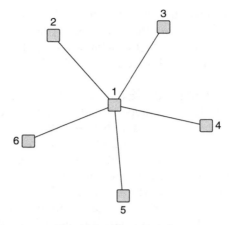

Fig. 12.1. Star network.

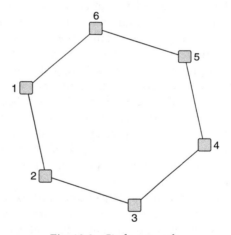

Fig. 12.2. Circle network.

takes on values between 0 (when no ties exist at all) and 1 (for a complete network in which every actor is connected to every other actor). It must be noted that density is sensitive to the overall network size: in a friendship network of five people, it is reasonable to assume that everyone will be connected to everyone else, but for a huge network like that of national elites, this is hardly possible. It follows that the larger the network grows, the sparser it will become.

While densities are best compared over networks of the same size, there are other useful measures of cohesion that are less influenced by variation in sample size—for example, fragmentation, which denotes the number of pairs that cannot reach each other. This measure takes on the value 0 when all nodes

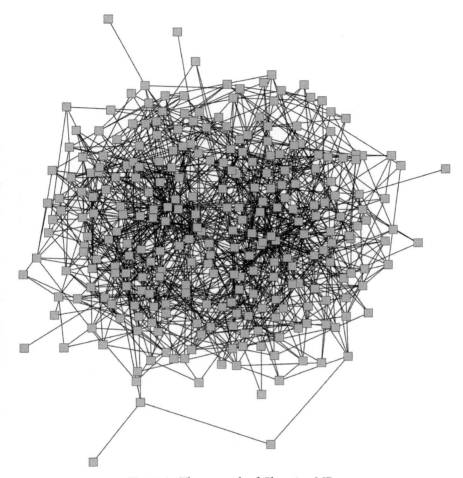

Fig. 12.3. The network of Ghanaian MPs.

are reachable and 1 when all nodes are isolates. In disconnected networks, it is also possible to examine the number of components. The component ratio is understood as the number of components divided by the number of nodes; this measure achieves its maximum of 1 when all nodes are isolates and its minimum of 0 when there is only one component.[61] In broadest terms, the bigger the main component, the greater the overall cohesion in the network.[62] There are many other concepts used to quantify the structure of a network, but the methods described above are sufficient to provide an idea of the inter-connectivity of elites. Thus the first hypothesis is: elites in Ghana form a cohesive and dense network.

[61] Borgatti *et al.*, *Analyzing social networks*, p. 151. [62] *Ibid.*, p. 151.

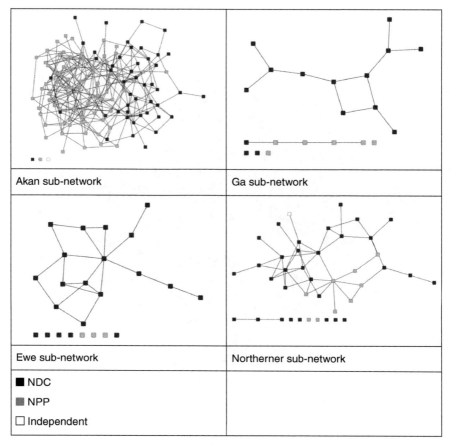

Fig. 12.4. Ethnicity and party: interaction effects.

The next concept of importance for this study is centralization. Centralization, understood as a property of the whole network, can be measured in various ways, but all measures take on the same values for two extreme scenarios: The star network (Figure 12.1) has the highest centralization score of 100 percent; whereas the circle (Figure 12.2) has the lowest score of 0 percent.

Closely related is the concept of centrality, which describes the position of individual nodes in a network. For the present article, the rather simplistic idea of degree centrality is applied. Degree centrality denotes the number of connections that a given node has. A further distinction can be made between 'out-degree', the number of ties that a node sends out to others, and 'in-degree', the number of ties that a node receives. Because there is no absolute measure or cut-off point, all we can say for the moment is that elite networks are more likely to promote democracy if they more closely resemble the circle rather than the star. This idea can be formulated as the second hypothesis: elite networks in Ghana are decentralized.

In addition, the formation of ties in a network can be related to certain attributes. One of the most familiar concepts is that of homophily, which is based on the idea that 'similarity breeds connection'.[63] Many social network studies have found contacts among similar people to be more frequent than contacts among dissimilar people.[64] Homophily is important to the study of elite interactions in two different ways. First, the theory suggests that democratic consolidation requires both a consensus on general rules and interactions among all elites—that is, there must be interactions between people of differing party affiliations and ethnic origins. Second, elite fragmentation and conflict in Africa is often discussed in relation to identity issues. The literature also argues that ethnic identities play a role in party formation and competition.[65] For a democratic country, we would therefore assume that elites engage in inter-party relations and in inter-ethnic relations. Homophily can be assessed using the E-I Index, which measures the ratio between external (E) and internal (I) ties. The normalized E-I Index takes on values between −1 and +1, where −1 indicates total homophily, and where all existing ties are formed among members of the same group. An E-I Index of +1, in contrast, denotes complete heterophily, meaning that all ties are formed between members of different groups.

Finally, the Higley/Burton framework presupposes mutual trust and shared political values. However, measuring the extent to which elites do in fact share a political value system is rather difficult. This article is therefore restricted to using inter-party trust as an indicator for a consensually united elite. The fourth hypothesis is: Ghanaian elites trust one another.

Operationalizing these hypotheses requires certain decisions to be made as to what counts as the "elite" and how data on this group can be collated. There are many different conceptions and definitions of the term 'elite'. For the sake of clarity, this article uses the definition proposed by Higley and Burton. They define elites as 'persons who are able, by virtue of their strategic positions in powerful organizations and movements, to affect political outcomes regularly and substantially'.[66] In principle, this very broad definition can include business, government, and military leaders, but also top position holders in parties, professional associations, and other interest groups. As a social stratum, the 'elite' has no clear boundaries, and the inclusion or exclusion of individuals in empirical studies is subject to the research question as well as to practical

---

[63] Miller McPherson *et al.*, 'Birds of a feather: Homophily in social networks', *Annual Review of Sociology* 27 (2001), pp. 415–44.

[64] *Ibid.*, p. 416.

[65] See Sebastian Elischer, *Political parties in Africa: Ethnicity and party formation* (Cambridge University Press, New York, NY, 2013).

[66] Higley and Burton, *Elite foundations of liberal democracy*, p. 7.

considerations (for example, constraints on time or the financial resources available). In addition, the term 'elite' has remained particularly elusive in the Africanist literature; it is therefore largely unclear how elites can be differentiated from other social groups. As a consequence, the definition of the sample of people to be included in the survey posed a great challenge for this study. Because the main focus of interest is the political system, MPs in Ghana were chosen as the target group. This selection follows the logic of the positional method, which identifies elites according to the formal positions they hold. This method may have disadvantages if one is seeking to include informal power relationships, but it has the tremendous advantage of generating a network with clear boundaries. Moreover, legislatures number among the most crucial institutions in democratizing countries.[67]

Data collection took place in close collaboration with the Centre for Democratic Governance, Ghana between June and August 2013. The Centre's excellent contacts in Ghana's Parliament proved an invaluable asset. A number of steps were taken to ensure the collaboration of the MPs. First of all, the parliamentary leadership was officially informed about the objectives of the project. In addition, a letter was sent to each MP stating that all data would be used for scientific purposes only and that no sensitive information connected to individual names would be published. Ten interviewers were then recruited for the fieldwork; four of them were employees of the Research Department of Parliament, which kindly supported our efforts.

MPs were interviewed using a standardized questionnaire. Two types of data were collected: attribute data (biographical data, career patterns, and values) and relational data. For the collection of the relational data, a name generator was used: 'Looking back over the last six months, who are the people in the Parliament of Ghana with whom you have discussed important political decisions? Please give me their names.' A similar question was first used in the General Social Survey and has since been a standard tool for obtaining network information.[68] Scholars have debated to what extent variations in the wording of name generators might yield different networks. However, on the basis of experiments, Stefanie Bailey and Peter Marsden have argued that networks do not vary substantially across various name generators.[69]

---

[67] See Michael Steven Fish, 'Stronger legislatures, stronger democracies', *Journal of Democracy* 17 (2006), pp. 5–20; Joel D. Barkan (ed.), *Legislative power in emerging African democracies* (Lynne Rienner, Boulder, CO, 2009).

[68] Ronald S. Burt, 'Network items and the General Social Survey', *Social Networks* 6 (1984), pp. 293–339.

[69] Stefanie Bailey and Peter V. Marsden, 'Interpretation and interview context: Examining the General Social Survey name generator using cognitive methods', *Social Networks* 21 (1999), pp. 287–309; Bruce C. Straits, 'Ego's important discussants or significant people: An experiment in varying the wording of personal network name generators', *Social Networks* 22 (2000), pp. 123–40.

Another issue is whether there are specific cultural dimensions that should be taken into consideration when relational data are collected. This question is particularly difficult to evaluate because there has been almost no experience with name generators in standardized surveys in Africa. The reaction of some MPs at least hints at an understanding of 'discussing political decisions' as a form of rather intense social contact, in many cases even amounting to friendship. This is further confirmed by the fact that the question on the intensity of contact shows very little variance: a large majority of MPs indicated that they interacted 'very often' with all the people they nominated (the other possible answers on a five-point scale were 'often', 'sometimes', 'a few times', and 'not at all'). Due to this consistency, these tie values are not included in the analyses in this article.

The questionnaire also included a measure of inter-party trust. MPs were asked to state how much they trusted the New Patriotic Party, National Democratic Congress, People's National Convention, and Convention People's Party on a five-point scale ranging from 'very much' to 'not at all'. For this article, an index of inter-party trust was constructed using the mean values of all four variables.

Elite unity and disunity in Ghana since independence

For the majority of the nation's history, Ghanaian elites were deeply divided. From a simplistic and generalized perspective, two broad camps can be identified. On one side, there is the Busia-Danquah tradition, which has always been associated with the wealthy professional and business elites in the south of the country, most of whom belong to the Akan ethnic group. In opposition to this group, there is a leftist tradition that has always favoured an anti-elite political orientation. This tradition began with the CPP (Convention People's Party) and Kwame Nkrumah, who was hailed for his opposition to urban elites and his sympathy for mass politics. More recently, the leftist orientation has been represented by the social-democratic National Democratic Congress (NDC).[70] Whereas the Busia-Danquah tradition has major strongholds in the Ashanti and Eastern regions, their opponents have generally found more support in less-developed areas, such as the three regions in northern Ghana and the Volta Region.[71] It is note-worthy that Ghana

---

[70] Kwesi Jonah, 'Political parties and the transition to multi-party politics in Ghana', in Kwame A. Ninsin (ed.), *Ghana: Transition to democracy* (CODESRIA, Dakar, 1998), pp. 83–107.

[71] For more on party politics and recent elections see Kevin S. Fridy, 'The elephant, umbrella, and quarrelling cocks: Disaggregating partisanship in Ghana's Fourth Republic', *African Affairs* 106, 423 (2001), pp. 281–305. See also Whitfield, '"Change for a Better Ghana"'.

currently has one of the few two-party systems in Africa. Compared to other countries on the continent, political parties have strong roots in the society and enjoy the support of great numbers of core voters.[72]

Between 1957 and 1981, power alternated between military and civilian governments. In every republic, however, party formation reproduced the polarization between the two political traditions. In 1981, the Provisional National Defence Council military government under the leadership of the charismatic Jerry John Rawlings proclaimed a revolution in defence of the common man. At first Rawlings tried to establish himself as an alternative to the two older political traditions. However, he shared a strong anti-elite and leftist rhetoric with the Nkrumahists, and his government also absorbed some of the old CPP networks and cadres to build its own power base.[73]

The first steps towards a greater elite unity were taken in the 1990s. In the face of growing reform pressure from donors and domestic groups alike, Rawlings recognized that his regime would not be able to withstand the demands for political liberalization. At first, the reform process was slow and did not involve substantial consultation with the opposition. After a constitutional referendum, the first elections were held in late 1992. The main contestants were the liberal-democratic New Patriotic Party (NPP), a party representing the Busia-Danquah tradition, and the National Democratic Congress (NDC), an organization created by Rawlings as a platform for his presidential ambitions.[74] There were also some smaller Nkrumahist parties, which did not make any serious electoral impact. In the end, Rawlings was able to win the presidential elections with a clear majority. In response, the opposition boycotted the parliamentary elections, and the NPP issued a statement that claimed a 'stolen verdict'.[75] The atmosphere following the 1992 elections was heated, increasing the pressure on the government and the opposition to agree on basic political rules. Under the threat of political chaos, a breakthrough was finally achieved by the Inter-Party Advisory

---

[72] See Staffan I. Lindberg and Minion K. C. Morrison, 'Exploring voter alignments in Africa: Core and swing voters in Ghana', *The Journal of Modern African Studies* 43, 4 (2005), pp. 565–86.

[73] Paul Nugent, 'Banknotes and symbolic capital', in Matthias Basedau, Gero Erdmann, and Andreas Mehler (eds), *Votes, money and violence: Political parties and elections in sub-Saharan Africa* (Nordiska Afrikainstitutet, Uppsala, 2007), pp. 252–75; Nicolas Amponsah, 'Political traditions and electoral politics in Kintampo North and South, Sissala West and Wa Central', in Kwame Boafo-Arthur (ed.), *Voting for democracy in Ghana: The 2004 elections in perspective* (Freedom Publications, Accra, 2006), pp. 287–307.

[74] Paul Nugent, 'Living in the past: Urban, rural and ethnic themes in the 1992 and 1996 elections in Ghana', *The Journal of Modern African Studies* 37, 2 (1999), pp. 287–319; Jonah, 'Political parties and the transition to multi-party politics in Ghana'.

[75] For more on the election, see Richard Jeffries and Clare Thomas, 'The Ghanaian elections of 1992', *African Affairs* 92, 368 (1993), pp. 331–66.

Committee (IPAC),[76] which brokered a consensus on key issues in the electoral process. The 1996 elections were again won by Rawlings, but this time the result was accepted by all opposition parties. Besides the IPAC, the Ghana Political Parties Programme, organized by the Institute of Economic Affairs, an Accra-based NGO, proved to be another facilitator of inter-party dialogue. Party leaders continue to hold monthly meetings to discuss important national issues.[77]

It can be argued that the Ghanaian experience fits well into the pattern of elite settlements, which are most likely to take place under the threat of an outbreak of violence.[78] According to Higley and Burton, the process of elite unity must be completed by the victory of formerly dissident elites.[79] In Ghana, this was the case when the opposition NPP won the December 2000 election. Each of the subsequent elections was closely contested between the NPP and the NDC, with smaller parties being increasingly sidelined. In 2008, power passed back to the NDC in another democratic election. The power transfers in 2000 and 2008 have made Ghana one of the most democratic countries in Africa. Elites seem to have reached a common understanding on electoral procedures and the norms of political competition. This is a major achievement.

However, in 2012, Ghana faced a serious test of its democratic maturity when then-Acting President Atta-Mills unexpectedly died shortly before the election.[80] The election went ahead as planned and was again won by the NDC and its presidential candidate, John Mahama. Although the process was declared free and fair by domestic and international observers, the defeated NPP claimed electoral fraud and filed a lawsuit to challenge the result. In August 2013, the Ghanaian Supreme Court finally dismissed the claims of voter fraud and declared that Mahama had been elected legitimately.

From the perspective of elite theory, this development can be interpreted in two different ways. On the one hand, the dispute over the electoral result can be viewed as a worrying sign with potentially negative consequences for democracy in the country. Ghana's growing oil industry has raised the stakes in electoral races, and the already fierce competition between the parties has become more intense. In the dispute over the 2012 results, there were strong

[76] The IPAC is a loose, non-statutory, and voluntary body that comprises the EC and all political parties. See Kwesi Jonah, 'Inter-party dialogue in Ghana' (Institute of Economic Affairs, Accra, 2005).

[77] Interview, Ransford Gyampo, Researcher at the Institute of Economic Affairs (IEA), Accra, Ghana, 24 June 2013.

[78] Michael Burton *et al.* 'Introduction', p. 15.   [79] *Ibid.*

[80] Some domestic and international media sources expressed concern over the stability of Ghana's democracy after Atta-Mills's sudden death. There were fears of civil unrest but also of increased political infighting in the NDC. See, for example, *The Guardian*, 'Will Ghana's success story continue after John Atta Mills?', 25 July 2012, <http://www.theguardian.com/global-development/2012/jul/25/ghana-success-john-atta-mills> (26 May 2015).

rhetorical confrontations in the media; however, there were no calls for violence and no riots. For this reason, the electoral petition can also be seen as a positive sign that Ghanaian elites have learned to play by the rules of the game. Instead of taking their case to the streets, the NPP sought a solution by constitutional means. The fact that the opposition finally accepted the ruling of the court without any violent protest demonstrates that a consensus on the rules of the game has indeed been achieved. Although a great deal of hostility is displayed in the media, MPs from both parties seem to intermingle quite freely in Parliament. As one MP explained, 'We disagree on politics, but we eat together.'[81] Another MP admitted that the deep antagonism between the NPP and the NDC was a delusion on the part of the voters, because 'in Parliament we are one'.[82] Interactions take place not only informally in parliamentary corridors, but also in institutions such as IPAC, which still plays an important role in national politics. The next section takes the analysis to another level to demonstrate how this consensus is reflected in the elite network structure.

Composition and Density of Ghana's Elite Network

The Sixth Parliament of Ghana consists of 275 MPs. Of these, 148 belong to the NDC, 123 to the NPP, and one to the People's National Convention (PNC). In addition, there are three independent MPs. Nearly all MPs (253, or 92 percent) took part in the survey. On average, each MP named five people with whom he or she discussed political issues at least from time to time. For this article, it is assumed that a tie between two MPs exists if at least one individual reported talking to the other. As a result, most of the non-respondents are included in the network. All calculations were performed on a symmetrized matrix, with the exception of the in-degree measure (see below). There were only three MPs (one NDC, one NPP, and one independent) who did not take part in the survey and who were not nominated by any other person. These people were excluded from the network. One additional person, the Speaker of Parliament, had to be included owing to the number of nominations.[83] Altogether, this yields a network of 273 nodes, as shown in Table 12.1. The full network is displayed in Figure 12.3.

---

[81] Interview, MP, Dunkwa, Central Region, Ghana, 10 October 2012.
[82] Interview, MP, Accra, Ghana, 28 September 2012.
[83] In Ghana, the Speaker of Parliament is elected from among the MPs of the majority party. Because the Speaker is not allowed to serve simultaneously as an MP, his or her seat in Parliament is declared vacant and is filled through a by-election.

Table 12.1. Number of respondents

Party	Number of MPs in the 6th Parliament	Number of survey respondents	Number of people represented in the network
NDC	148	139	148
NPP	123	111	122
PNC	1	1	1
Independent	3	2	2
Total	275	253	273

Table 12.2. Measures of network cohesion

Components	Component ratio	Density	Fragmentation
1	0	0.029	0

It is evident that the parliamentarians are highly connected to one another. The network consists of one big component, and there are no isolated nodes and no visually detectable fragmentations. Therefore, both the component ratio and the fragmentation measure take on the value 0. The density of the complete network is 0.029. In other words, roughly 3 percent of theoretically possible connections are realized. These measures of network cohesion are summarized in Table 12.2.

The existence of one big component (component ratio = 0, fragmentation = 0) is a strong indicator of network cohesion. In principle, each actor can reach any other actor either by direct or indirect connections. The average geodesic distance (the shortest possible path from one actor to another) is three, meaning that most actors can be reached over three nodes. The largest distance (diameter) is six. While these results quite clearly indicate the cohesiveness of the network, the density score needs some discussion. As noted before, density is sensitive to the size of the network and there is no absolute measure on whether a network is dense or not. The findings, however, compare well to other elite network studies. In their study on the US, Australia, and West Germany, Higley *et al.* find density scores ranging from 0.026 to 0.038 for networks of 227 to 418 nodes.[84] They take this as an evidence for their assumption that comprehensive elite integration has occurred in these countries.[85] Tetiana Kostiuchenko finds densities between 0.018 and 0.044 percent for various sub-groups of an elite network in Ukraine.[86] Against the background of these comparable studies the first hypothesis—that elites form a cohesive and dense network—can be confirmed.

---

[84] Higley *et al.*, 'Elite integration in stable democracies', p. 41.   [85] *Ibid.*, p. 36.
[86] Tetiana Kostiuchenko, 'Elite continuity in Ukraine: When networks matter(?)', *Historical Social Research* 37, 2 (2012), pp. 14–25.

Overall centralization in the network is 12.982 percent. When we compare this figure to the star network (Figure 12.1) with a centralization of 100 percent and the circle (Figure 12.2) with 0 percent, it can be concluded that the network is relatively decentralized. This confirms the second hypothesis.

Centrality scores for individual actors vary widely. There were 25 MPs who sent out ties but received none. There are also some highly central actors. The most central person receives 43 in-degrees, followed by two people with 33 incoming ties each. In all, ten people have a centrality degree greater than 15. Among these are key parliamentary officials, such as the minority and majority leaders and the minority and majority chief whips. This finding is not surprising. These people may have been chosen to hold these offices because they were already influential actors in their respective parties. The function itself further enhances their status and requires them to maintain frequent contact with other MPs. One question that arises is whether the nomination of people in parliamentary leadership positions is just an instance of name dropping. A name dropper is a person 'who knows exactly which contacts are the 'right' names to give, thus placing himself right in the centre of the network'.[87] The survey is indeed vulnerable in this regard, but there are two facts that speak against widespread name dropping. Although 43 in-degrees might seem like a high number, it also means that the most central person was named by only 17 percent of the MPs. Moreover, there are office holders with low in-degree scores, as well as individuals who do not hold an official function but have high in-degrees. These findings suggest that central positions in the network result from a combination of formal and informal power.

As has been shown, the network is densely connected, but to what extent is the formation of ties influenced by shared attributes such as ethnic origin and party affiliation? With regard to party affiliation, there is no indication of a strong tendency towards homophily. Under a model of independence—meaning that the attribute 'party membership' has no influence on the existence of a relationship between two actors—the expected E-I Index for the full network is −0.006. The observed E-I Index is −0.023. Thus, connections among MPs who belong to the same party are slightly more frequent than expected under the model of independence, but the deviation is very low. The results for the individual parties are displayed in Table 12.3. These values are

Table 12.3. Party E-I Index

Party	E-I Index
NDC	−0.114
NPP	0.090

---

[87] Higley *et al.*, 'Elite integration in stable democracies', p. 50.

so close to zero that neither a strong homophilous nor a strong heterophilous tendency can be observed. Only nine MPs out of 271 (3.3 percent) have contacts exclusively within their own party.

Before presenting the results for ethnic homophily, a discussion of the measurement of ethnicity is required. Ethnicity is a contested concept, and many scholars in African Studies emphasize the situational and instrumental aspects of ethnicity. This fluidity makes categorization and measurement extremely difficult. At the same time, however, ethnicity continues to be discussed as a central feature of African politics. In the survey, MPs were asked to indicate to which ethnic group they belonged. What is actually being measured here is the MPs' self-perception. The sensitivity of the question is fully confirmed by the fact that there are a huge number of missing values here. The matter is further complicated by the fact that some people named broad groups like Akan, while others referred to subgroups included in the broader Akan group. Table 12.4 shows the ethnic distribution of MPs according to the categories used in the Population and Housing Census of the Statistical Service of Ghana.

Evidently, the legislature is fairly representative, but the N for many groups is very small. The article therefore refers to the concept of 'politically relevant groups'[88] and codes ethnic groups along the lines of the Ethnic Power Relations Dataset.[89] Thus, the Akan,[90] Ewe, and Ga were included in the analysis

Table 12.4. Representation of ethnic groups

Group	% in the 2010 Census	% in the survey	NDC	NPP
Akan	47.5	57.6	38.5	81.0
Ga-Dangme	7.4	9.4	12.3	6.0
Ewe	13.9	10.7	17.2	3.0
Guan	3.7	4.0	6.6	1.0
Gurma	5.7	4.0	4.1	4.0
Mole-Dangbani	16.6	11.2	16.4	4.0
Grusi	2.5	2.2	3.3	0
Other	2.5	0.9	1.6	0.9
N (missing)	–	224 (18.5)	122	100

[88] Julian Wucherpfennig, Nils B. Weidmann, Luc Girardin, Lars-Erik Cederman, and Andreas Wimmer, 'Politically relevant ethnic groups across space and time: Introducing the GeoEPR Dataset', *Conflict Management and Peace Science* 28 (2011), pp. 423–37.

[89] Lars-Erik Cederman, Brian Min, and Andreas Wimmer, 'Why do ethnic groups rebel? New data and analysis', *World Politics* 62 (2010), pp. 87–119.

[90] The dataset draws a further distinction between 'Asante' and 'other Akans'. Whether or not Akan-speaking people can be treated as a political entity is a controversial issue. For example, the NPP is sometimes portrayed as an Akan party. However, there are political conflicts within the group that involve not only the Asante but also other sub-groups including the Akyem and the Fanti. For this article, the decision to merge all Akan MPs into one group was mainly taken because the information on the subgroups was incomplete (because a large number of MPs indeed identified themselves as Akan).

as individual groups, whereas the Gurma, Grusi, and Mole-Dagbani were merged into the category 'Northerners'. The Guan group and the 'others' were more ambiguous and were therefore excluded. For the four ethnic groups, the expected E-I Index under the model of independence would be 0.169; the observed value is −0.124. The E-I Index is statistically significant. The deviation from the expected value is small, such that we still cannot speak of widespread homophily. There are, however, interesting differences between the groups (see Table 12.5). The Akan group reveals a somewhat homophilous tendency, whereas the other groups seem to form more heterophilous ties. Forty out of 216 MPs (18.51 percent) had contacts only within their own ethnic group.

Table 12.6 displays some network measures for the ethnic sub-networks in comparison to the full network. Among the sub-networks, the Akan group is the most cohesive: the network has fewer components than the other three sub-networks and shows a lower value of fragmentation. The component ratio, which describes the relationship between the components, indicates that the Ga, Ewe, and Northerner networks are composed of a greater number of smaller components or isolated nodes. Compared to the full network, however, all of the sub-networks are significantly less cohesive. This fits very well with the findings on the low presence of ethnic homophily in the overall network. Figure 12.4 visualizes the sub-networks. Party affiliation is shown as different node shades to demonstrate interaction effects between party membership and ethnicity. From the figure, it is evident that NPP and NDC MPs of Akan origin are closely related to one another; in contrast, the Ga and Ewe networks are not only dominated by the NDC but also show a quasi-exclusion of NPP MPs from the interaction structure. For the Northerners, the picture is mixed. These findings confirm the third hypothesis.

Table 12.5. Ethnic groups E-I Index

Group	E-I Index
Akan	−0.451
Ga	0.543
Ewe	0.371
Northerners	0.258

Table 12.6. Ethnic groups' sub-networks

	Akan	Ga	Ewe	North	Full network
Components	4	6	9	9	1
Component ratio	0.02	0.25	0.35	0.21	0
Density	0.04	0.08	0.08	0.05	0.03
Fragmentation	0.046	0.565	0.638	0.429	0
Nodes	129	21	24	41	273

Table 12.7. Inter-party trust

Party	Inter-party trust (mean)
NDC	3.12
NPP	2.79

Finally, it is important to ask whether the various parties trust one another? Overall, most MPs trusted the opposing party only to a certain extent. The mean value for NDC MPs on a five-point scale was 3.12; for NPP MPs, 2.79 (see Table 12.7). Thus, most values are clustered around the answer 'I trust the other parties somewhat'. This relatively moderate level of trust stands in contradiction to the frequent inter-party contacts of individual MPs. It must be noted, however, that the question treats parties as an entity. It is possible for a person to mistrust other parties as political institutions but still entertain friendships with individual members of these parties. Viewed in this way, the finding fits rather well into the overall picture of outwardly displayed party hostilities. Again, it is interesting to compare this to other studies. Based on a survey of German MPs, Best[91] reports that 65 percent of the respondents feel a degree of togetherness with MPs of other parties, while 35 percent state that they have nothing in common with them. Eighty percent of the latter group nevertheless had contacts with MPs from other parties. Obviously, such contradictory patterns are by no means limited to Ghana and deserve further research in future studies. Thus, the fourth hypothesis can be confirmed, albeit with some qualifications.

Conclusion

This article has used new empirical material to corroborate the findings of scholars like Lindsay Whitfield, Alexander Frempong, and Johanna Svanikier, who have argued that Ghana's democratic success is deeply connected to a change in elite behaviour.[92] The observed parliamentary network comes close to what Higley and Burton describe as a *consensually united elite*. The network is densely connected, there are frequent contacts between all MPs, and information can flow easily. Once created, consensually united elites tend to be

---

[91] Heinrich Best, 'Associated rivals: Antagonism and cooperation in the German political elite', in Heinrich Best and John Higley (eds), *Democratic elitism: New theoretical and comparative perspectives* (Brill, Leiden and Boston, MA, 2010), pp. 97–116.

[92] Whitfield, '"Change for a Better Ghana"'; Frempong, 'Political conflict and elite consensus'; Svanikier, 'Political elite circulation'.

remarkably persistent.[93] While this is good news for the future of democracy in Ghana, it is equally important to highlight the conditions under which this elite consensus came into being. Two aspects are particularly important: the role of the two-party system in the process of elite settlement, and the interaction between ethnicity and party loyalties.

The Ghanaian experience fits well into the pattern described by the literature on elite settlements. Tensions between government and opposition were high, especially in the 1992 elections, and when the situation began to seriously threaten the stability of the country, the first steps toward an elite consensus were taken.[94] The process was completed by the opposition victory in 2000 and another peaceful transfer of power in 2008, but such an initial consensus is no guarantee of a consolidated democracy. The deepening of elite unity depends on the creation of institutions that allow the successful management of conflicts.[95] Many authors have stressed the salience of the two main political traditions in the country: the Busia-Danquah tradition and the Nkrumah tradition.[96] These political poles were the source of bitter elite struggles between the 1960s and 1990s, but also laid the foundation for today's two-party system by structuring the political space into easily recognizable camps.

Political parties in every new republic tended to form along the traditional cleavage, and with the weakening of the Nkrumahists in the 1990s, the NDC effectively took over the political space on the left of the NPP. The emerging two-party system had important consequences for elite politics. First, the small number of actors reduces collective action problems and makes cooperation more feasible.[97] Second, the existence of strong parties with high numbers of core voters lends legitimacy to the process of elite settlement. This confirms Levine's view that the successful implementation of elite agreements hinges on strong political parties.[98] The two-party system provides a regular and routine channel for political contestation. Both parties have huge followings, and therefore the costs associated with breaking up the consensus are high. Neither of the parties would be guaranteed to gain anything, but would instead face opposition from a large segment of Ghanaian society. Electoral competition is no longer perceived as a zero-sum-game—today, losers are not threatened with political demise but can hope to be more successful in the next election. In this way, trust and mutual security have been gradually established: 'What

---

[93] Higley and Burton, *Elite foundations of liberal democracy*, p. 12.

[94] Frempong, 'Political conflict and elite consensus', p. 137.

[95] Levine, 'Venezuela since 1958', p. 83.

[96] Jonah, 'Political parties and the transition'; Nugent, 'Living in the past'.

[97] Mancur Olson, *The logic of collective action* (Harvard University Press, Cambridge, MA, 2009 [1965]).

[98] Levine, 'Venezuela since 1958: The consolidation of democratic politics', p. 102.

were once innovations in intergroup relations become, through continuous and routine use, conventional expectations of common treatment.'[99]

This elite consensus is further stabilized by an interaction effect between party loyalties and ethnic affiliation. The role of ethnicity in elections has been debated energetically among scholars of politics in Ghana. Kevin Fridy argues that many voters tend to see the NDC as an Ewe party and the NPP as an Akan party.[100] Nevertheless, none of the parties can win elections by appealing only to its core voters, and this provides a clear incentive for reaching out to all ethnic groups. At the elite level, the dynamics between party loyalties and ethnic identities are equally complex. The data presented in this article add important findings to the discussion. As Figure 12.4 shows, Akan elites tend to network more with each other, but this homophilous tendency is moderated by party membership. In other words, an ethnically based feeling of solidarity bridges political cleavages and, as a result, reduces the potential for violent conflicts between the parties. For some of the smaller groups, however, it is the other way round. Ga and Ewe tend to interact only with those fellow ethnics who are in the same party—in their case, party loyalties override ethnic solidarity. The crisscrossing of party affiliation and ethnic identity at the elite level serves as a major stabilizing factor for Ghana's democracy. The fact that group solidarities of different kinds moderate each other strengthens elite unity and reduces the likelihood of ethnic mobilization strategies.

Elite consensus does not mean the absence of political conflicts. What it does mean, however, is that elites build enough mutual trust to be able to handle these conflicts in a non-violent way. In Ghana, this change in elite behaviour is most obvious in the dispute over the election results in 2012. Although the outward display of political animosities remains a part of the political ritual between the opposition and the ruling party, both parties chose to handle the issue by constitutional means instead of taking it to the streets. This does not automatically imply that more extreme political orientations within the parties are completely repressed. For Parliament (as an important and influential segment of the national elite), however, it can be safely argued that a consensus on the rules of the game has been achieved.

This article has shown that elite structures are central to the democratic process. The evidence suggests that actor-centric approaches, and especially the Higley/Burton thesis, contribute significantly to our understanding of democratization in Africa. Furthermore, the article has introduced social network analysis (SNA) as a useful methodological tool. Although the Higley/Burton theory holds true in the case of Ghana, the findings should be

---

[99] *Ibid.*, p. 103.   [100] Fridy, 'The elephant, umbrella, and quarrelling cocks'.

treated with some caution until comparative studies are conducted. As the relationship between elites and regimes can only be assessed fully when Ghana's elite structure is compared to those of other African countries, there is a pressing need for similar studies in the future.

Acknowledgment

Published in *African Affairs*, 114, 457 (2015), p. 529–554. Funding for this research was provided by the Excellence Initiative of the German Research Foundation (DFG). I wish to thank the Centre for Democratic Development (CDD) in Accra for generous assistance; special thanks go to Professor Emmanuel Gyimah-Boadi, Franklin Oduro, Mohammed Awal, and Regina Oforiwaa-Amanfo. I also thank the editorial team of *African Affairs* and two anonymous reviewers for their helpful comments on an earlier version of the article.

13

Neo-Patrimonial Politics in the ANC

Tom Lodge

WHAT EXPLAINS THE ANC's apparent transformation from a rule-regulated, mass-based party into an organization in which internal dynamics are mostly shaped by personal interests? Increasingly within the ANC, leadership behaviour appears to be characterized by neo-patrimonial pre-dispositions and, while formal distinctions between private and public concerns are widely recognized, officials nevertheless use their public powers for private purposes.[1] Other symptoms of neo-patrimonial political behaviour have also appeared. There is factionalism, that is, the emergence of internal rival groups constituted by personal loyalty rather than shared ideological beliefs. Another manifestation is the affirmation by the ANC leadership of 'traditionalist' representations of indigenous culture, whereby moral legitimation is sought more and more from appeals to 'Africanist' racial solidarity and nostalgic recollections of patriarchal social order rather than on the basis of the quality of government performance.[2]

Neo-patrimonial indicators include the acquisition of business interests by leading politicians and their families, most notably the proliferation of the presidential family's business concerns since Jacob Zuma's accession to the presidency.[3] Despoliation by local office holders through municipal and

---

[1] Following Christopher Clapham's definition of neo-patrimonialism in *Third World Politics* (Helm, London, 1985), p. 48.

[2] For Jacob Zuma's statements on childbearing as 'good training to a woman', see *The Guardian*, 'Jacob Zuma says it is not right for women to remain unmarried', 22 August 2012, <http://www.theguardian.com/world/2012/aug/22/jacob-zuma-women-unmarried> (1 November 2013); on the taking away of 'our dignity…because our traditional system and leadership was undermined', see *City Press*, 'Zuma scolds "clever" blacks', 4 November 2012, <http://www.citypress.co.za/news/zuma-scolds-clever-blacks-20121103/> (1 November 2013).

[3] By March 2010 members of the Zuma family held 134 company directorships. Of the companies in Zuma's official declaration of interests, 83 were registered after Zuma became ANC president. *Mail and Guardian*, 'Keeping it in the family', 19 March 2010.

provincial tendering procedures began earlier.[4] This was a consequence of the 'capture' of municipalities by informal networks that in the ANC's weaker regions could especially easily impose their influence over local branches.[5] This kind of behaviour has been accompanied by sharpening competition for posts in government and within the party organization, which in turn has eroded the decorum that used to characterize the ANC's internal procedures. The ANC's leadership increasingly reinforces its authority and demonstrates its power through displays of ostentation and through elaborate security procedures.[6]

Meanwhile, the ANC's mobilization of public support relies increasingly on patron–client relations.[7] Reminding us that patrimonial power must involve reciprocal exchanges, and, indeed, in contrast to the socially aloof predisposition of his predecessor, President Zuma cultivates a reputation as an accessible man of the people, always ready to entertain petitions.[8] These developments are dynamic and they have yet to become all-encompassing— they do not constitute the entirety of the ANC's internal life, nor do they affect other South African political parties in the same way.[9] Both within the ANC and in the wider political system patrimonial behaviour interacts with norms

---

[4] In a survey undertaken in the Eastern Cape in 2005, 27 percent of local government officials had witnessed the award of jobs or contracts to political allies. Doreen Atkinson, 'Taking to the streets: has developmental local government failed in South Africa' in Sakhela Buhlungu, John Daniel, and Jessica Lutchman (eds), *State of the Nation: South Africa, 2007* (HSRC Press, Cape Town, 2007), pp. 53–77, p. 67.

[5] According to Atkinson, this was a particular feature of political life in the Free State, a region where for most of its history the ANC lacked a strong organized base. Atkinson, 'Taking to the streets', pp. 67–8.

[6] Both grandiose ostentation and extreme security precautions are combined in the features of President Zuma's new residential estate at Nkandla in KwaZulu Natal where R250 million in public funds have been spent on protective arrangements. Disapproval of such measures is by no means universal. On learning that the leader of the parliamentary opposition, Helen Zille, intended to visit Nkandla to inspect the project, the local *inkosi* (chief) expressed outrage. 'She was supposed to first consult traditional leaders before going to the President's home ... we have arrived at a point where we say enough of this disrespectful white girl.' *Sunday Times*, 'Zille told: we will defend Zuma's home', 4 November 2012, <http://www.timeslive.co.za/sundaytimes/2012/11/04/zille-told-we-will-defend-zuma-s-home> (1 November 2013).

[7] A letter in *City Press* may express more widely shared views among the ANC's more partisan supporters: 'Zimbabwe has a life President and Angola is doing well, so this is the best route for us if we are to indigenize and deal with the land question. South Africa needs a big strong man to force things to happen.' Themba D. Ntshangase, 'Former MK Cadre', *City Press*, 4 November 2012.

[8] 'There are often long queues at Mahlamba Ndlopfu, the presidential residence in Pretoria, of people seeking to see him. The situation is no different in Nkandla, his KwaZulu Natal rural home, where Zuma is said to hold one-on-one meetings until the early hours. ... It is people from all walks of life who come to see him: business people, politicians and even ordinary locals who come to complain about pensions and unsafe roads.' *Sunday Times*, 'Who's who in the Zuma web', 5 August 2011.

[9] For example, the Democratic Alliance, traditionally a white middle-class party, is probably more immune to neo-patrimonial compulsions because of its fairly impersonal approaches to the electorate. DA planners favour 'relying on public relations as the primary driver of the party's popularity with voters' and assign a low priority to the task 'of establishing membership structures on the ground', even in black townships. *Business Day*, 'DA not creating homegrown

that reflect bureaucratic legal rationality as well as democratic procedures: that after all is the hallmark of a *neo*-patrimonial polity.[10] Indeed, studies that have explored the ANC's base-level organization have documented key features of a mass-based party with a membership animated by political principles and horizontal ties of solidarity.[11]

This suggests that with respect to the typologies that are used to classify party organizations, the ANC still belongs to the broad family of mass-based parties, and this does make it unusual in the broader African context.[12] But the ANC's patrimonial characteristics are becoming more pronounced, and as a result the argument that South African politics represents an exception to the general trends that shape political life elsewhere in sub-Saharan Africa is becoming less compelling. The behaviour of ANC leaders and their followers is beginning to correspond to conventions associated with clientelistic organizations, in which specific public services and resources are offered to particular groups in exchange for political support.[13] At the rate that this behaviour is proliferating it threatens to overwhelm what used to be a relatively disciplined and well-structured political organization unified by beliefs about programmatic purpose and securing public support through ideological appeals to widely shared collective interests. The consequences of this for the party, its original mission, and South African democracy would be profound.

Explaining neo-patrimonialism

Before considering explanations for this change we need conceptual clarity: what is neo-patrimonialism, and what does it mean to propose that the ANC is becoming a more neo-patrimonial organization? For Gero Erdmann and Ulf Engel, neo-patrimonial systems feature 'a mixture of two coexisting, partly

members', 5 November 2012, <http://www.bdlive.co.za/national/politics/2012/11/05/da-not-creating-home-grown-members> (1 November 2013).

[10] Gero Erdmann and Ulf Engel, 'Neo-patrimonialism reconsidered: critical review and elaboration of an elusive concept', *Commonwealth and Comparative Politics* 45, 1 (2007), pp. 95–119, p. 105.

[11] See Tom Lodge, 'The ANC and the development of party politics in South Africa', *Journal of Modern African Studies* 42, 2 (2004), pp. 189–219; Vincent Darracq, 'The ANC's organization at the grassroots', *African Affairs* 107, 429 (2008), pp. 589–609; Alexander Beresford, 'Comrades back on track: the durability of the Tripartite Alliance', *African Affairs* 108, 432 (2009), pp. 391–412.

[12] Matthijs Bogaards, 'Counting parties and identifying dominant party systems in Africa', *European Journal of Politcal Research* 43 (2004) pp. 173–97, p. 178.

[13] For distinctions between clientelistic, class, and mass parties see Richard Gunther and Larry Diamond, 'Species of political parties: a new typology', *Party Politics* 9, 2 (2004), pp. 167–99.

interwoven, types of domination: namely patrimonial and legal bureaucratic domination'. Personal rule exists alongside bureaucratic order, sometimes 'twist(ing) its logic, functions and output'.[14] In Africa, neo-patrimonial politics is often a residue of authoritarian politics, both colonial and post-colonial, with the result that many of today's ostensible democracies are in fact transitional hybrids, 'neo-patrimonial multi-party systems'.[15] However, the legal-rational element of neo-patrimonialism is not a façade—it can determine key decisions and itself can shape patrimonial behaviour.

The notion of neo-patrimonial rule as a hybrid system in which two kinds of politics co-exist is also central to the way the concept is addressed by Anne Pitcher, Mary Moran, and Michael Johnston. They remind us that in its representation by Weber, patrimonialism meant a specific form of legitimation that included reciprocal exchanges between rulers and groups. In their analysis of neo-patrimonial politics, modern democratic procedures as well as rational legality are built 'on a foundation of traditional and highly personalised reciprocities and loyalties'.[16] Their main point is that neo-patrimonialism is not an anachronistic survival that blocks modernization but rather a form of authority that can function in a range of regimes, authoritarian and democratic.

In this article, I explore three different ways of understanding the rise of neo-patrimonialism and assess their applicability to the South African context. First, I address the possibility that what is happening within the ruling party is the effect of entrenched political habits inherited from colonial rule. In this argument patrimonial leadership has a long history within the ANC, but was curtailed after the movement's embrace of militant activism during the 1950s and during its exile, and has only resurfaced in the era of democratic politics. In other words, over the hundred years of its existence, the ANC has 'moved through a radical arc' only to return to its roots in the present.[17]

Next, I consider explanations centred on institutional uncertainties and the state's legitimation deficits. These affected the ANC in two ways. First, personalized networks constituted through reciprocal exchanges were fostered by the ANC's entanglement with criminal networks during its armed revolutionary phase. The apartheid state's reliance on repression created a moral climate that facilitated such connections between political activists and criminals. Second, there are the effects of the more recent developments following South Africa's democratization. From this perspective, proliferation of rent seeking is partly the consequence of the circumstances that surrounded the

---

[14] Erdmann and Engel, 'Neo-patrimonialism', p. 105.   [15] Ibid., p. 113.
[16] Anne Pitcher, Mary H. Moran, and Michael Johnston, 'Rethinking patrimonialism and neopatrimonialism in Africa', African Studies Review 52, 1 (2009), pp. 125–56, p. 145.
[17] Martin Plaut and Paul Holden, Who Rules South Africa? (Jonathan Ball, Johannesburg, 2012), p. 348.

ANC's abrupt transition from a liberation movement to an electorally oriented political party and the stresses that this has introduced. It is also related to the effect of the ANC's incumbency in office in a setting in which political procedures and allocative entitlements are still novel and untested. Following this view, neo-patrimonialism has been fostered by a series of political insecurities.

The third sort of explanation relates to broader issues arising from the way in which South African economic life is organized, irrespective of the features of particular politicians or parties. The state's use of tenders and licences to empower black businessmen has created fresh opportunities for the exercise of patrimonial capitalism.

The ANC's neo-patrimonialism as a colonial residue

Let us consider our first possible explanation: that the exercise of patrimonial leadership in the modern ANC resonates with historically entrenched habits, norms, and expectations derived from colonial experience. This argument draws upon common explanations of African neo-patrimonialism that attribute its prevalence to the prolonged after-effects of colonialism. Here the state is an alien importation at odds or 'incongruent' with preexisting norms and institutions.[18] Colonial rule confined the legal rational sphere to a small privileged group residing in the administrative centre and most subjects lived under the rule of chiefs whose pre-colonial patrimonial powers were often amplified by colonial authority. In weak post-colonial states bureaucracy expanded very rapidly and 'was challenged and invaded from below by informal relationships'.[19] In the striking phraseology of Peter Ekeh, a new 'public realm' was created, 'in which primordial groupings, ties, and sentiments influence and determine the individual's public behaviour'.[20] Ekeh's notion of a second public realm characterized by neopatrimonial polities reminds us that personalized networks often function in a setting in which there is broad public approval of their operation.

Networks constituted through family, kinship, and childhood friendship certainly played an important role in the formation of the ANC's founding elite. More arguably, such personalized networks continued thereafter to

---

[18] Pierre Englebert, 'Pre-colonial institutions, post-colonial states and economic development in tropical Africa', *Political Research Quarterly* 53, 1 (2000), pp. 7–36, p. 10.

[19] Erdmann and Engel, 'Neo-patrimonialism', p. 106.

[20] Peter P. Ekeh, 'Colonialism and the two publics in Africa: a theoretical statement', *Comparative Studies in Society and History* 17, 1 (1975), pp. 91–2, p. 92.

exercise profound influence. The life of John Langalibalele Dube, the ANC's first president, illustrates this point well. Born at the American Zulu Mission at Inanda, Dube was the son of the Mission's first African pastor and the grandson of the Chief of the Qadi. His upbringing was within the Christian-ized *amakholwa*, a land-owning middle-class elite that supplied political leadership to Africans both within Natal and nationally through the twentieth century. The Champion family were also important members of the Inanda community, and John Dube and A. W. G. Champion, later political rivals in Natal's provincial politics, were classmates. Pixley Isaac Seme, another early ANC president, was a cousin. Dube's school, the Ohlange Institute, itself became an important agency in the socialization of generations of ANC leadership: among Dube's own pupils were members of the Msimang family and Albert Luthuli. Dube was related through marriage to the Cele family, another important family within the provincial ANC leadership.

The linkages that bound this elite were particularly important in a setting in which personal and public concerns were entwined. Members of the *ama-kholwa* shared the aim of 'managing' the introduction of modernity through leadership that would instil progress through 'Christian improvement and industrial education'.[21] In this vision, their own social mobility at the helm of meritocratic hierarchy was the key to broader racial emancipation. In a colonial order in which their own private ambitions were under increasing threat it was easy to conflate personal interests with public concerns. From 1906, Dube began to invest in farmland, and subsequently his standing as a landowner would upgrade his status as a notable. Dube was elected as the ANC's first president in recognition of his achievements as an educationalist and landowner, and his interests in such ventures would always shape his political actions. More widely, Natal's African nationalist politics in its first decades was decisively influenced by two factions, both headed by networks assembled through kinship and schooling: one based around the American mission stations along the coastline; the other formed through the agency of British Methodists in the Natal Midlands. Despite its modernist aspirations, this leadership was often concerned to defend 'a strictly hierarchical social order in which aristocracy and meritocracy combined'.[22]

The way private social connections helped to reinforce and reproduce political leadership was not peculiar to Natal. Similar networks, constituted through clan membership, schooling, friendship, and marriage operated with-in the Barolong elite in the western Transvaal. Here, as with the Qadi settlement around the Inanda mission, a German Lutheran-sponsored Chris-tian elite of rural teachers and professionals allied with the Montshiwa

[21] Heather Hughes, *First President: A life of John L. Dube, founding president of the ANC* (Jacana, Auckland Park, 2011), p. 42.
[22] *Ibid.*, p. xix.

chieftaincy to provide the social base of a tightly interconnected ANC leadership group whose members would include Sol Plaatje, various members of the Molema family, and later Z. K. Matthews and his descendants.[23]

Turning to the ANC's later history, the ascendancy of an Eastern Cape elite, drawn primarily from Methodist converts and 'progressive' peasants[24] and socialized through education at Healdtown and Fort Hare, has been very evident. Within this group, a shared sense of origin and familiarities derived from attending the same schools was bolstered through more intimate ties. As we know from Mandela's early life in Johannesburg, a 'home boy' network facilitated his early induction into the ANC as well as his placement in a legal firm, with his fellow clansman Walter Sisulu supplying the critical brokerage function. Nelson Mandela would cement his friendship with Sisulu through his first marriage, to Sisulu's cousin Evelyn Mase. The success this elite enjoyed in reproducing its influence across generations is particularly obvious in the subsequent political progression of a talented cohort of younger Sisulus.

Another entrenched source of patrimonial politics can be traced to the reflexes developed during the ANC's participation in official institutions that became hubs of clientelistic undertakings during apartheid. During the 1950s, despite resolutions to boycott township advisory board elections, plenty of ANC elders joined the boards and belonged to them. Mia Brandel-Syrier's ethnographic study of the 'upper classes' in a new 'Bantu subsidized housing estate' near Johannesburg includes a portrait of 'Mr S', an ANC member who joined the Advisory Board in 1951 and who became the dominant township 'boss', presiding over a dissolute politics in which 'votes were secured by money payments together with various forms of illegal pressure and extortion'.[25] Though formally consultative bodies, Advisory Boards could influence allocations of public goods: they were centres of clientelist politics and such kinds of political activity retained substantial public legitimacy through the 1960s.

Mia Brandel-Syrier's example of a local ANC leader engaged in 'boss' politics in Germiston was not exceptional: fieldwork at the time encountered ANC personalities at the forefront of advisory boards in Durban—here the Combined Board was chaired by A. W. G. Champion, provincial ANC president until 1951. Certainly, by the 1950s, Champion embodied the more conservative predispositions within the ANC's leadership. However, as Leo Kuper noted, in Durban at the end of the decade there were a number of

---

[23] Andrew Manson and Bernard Mbenga, 'The African National Congress in the Western Transvaal/Northern Cape Platteland, c. 1910–1964', *South African Historical Journal* **64**, 3 (2012), pp. 472–93.
[24] Colin Bundy, 'Introduction' in Govan Mbeki, *Learning from Robben Island* (James Currey, Oxford, 1991), pp. ix–xx.
[25] Mia Brandel-Syrier, *Reeftown Elite* (Routledge and Kegan Paul, London, 1971), p. 11.

'active members of Congress...to be found on the statutory bodies' that included the Boards.[26] In East London, various factions of the ANC won Advisory Board elections between 1947 and 1957.[27] In general, though it is true that by the 1950s more radical ANC leaders and members were openly contemptuous of the Boards and favoured their boycott, this was not a universal position and in practice ANC leaders tolerated participation within them.

To recapitulate: modern patrimonial reflexes within the ANC's leadership were partly the product of two features of the ANC's historical development. First, there were the networks of notables articulated by affective ties that established the organization. Schools, churches, and dynastic marriages helped to reproduce these networks and consolidate their power up to and through the 1950s, and still do so, though to a lesser extent. The second historic tributary are the clientelistic expectations nurtured through the ANC's engagement in Advisory Board politics in the 1940s and 1950s. Though the ANC moved from being a party of notables to a party based on mass membership more than sixty years ago, the continuity in its leadership lineage until quite recently is striking. This is not unusual. Comparative analysis reminds us that 'parties founded when local notables were politically powerful may remain under the domination of elite factions well past the time when a majority of voters ceased to be deferential to notable elites'.[28] As Angelo Panebianco notes, original political choices and ways in which political organizations are formed leave 'indelible marks' on their later development.[29]

Neo-patrimonialism, state legitimation and institutional uncertainty

The next set of explanations for the ANC's neo-patrimonial operations focus on the insecurities resulting from change. A common explanation for the persistence of patrimonial behaviour in ostensibly modern states— neopatrimonialism—views it as the consequence of imposed modernization. As Samuel Huntington has suggested, rapid institutional change generates disorder.[30] What distinguishes this explanation from the first approach is its

[26] Leo Kuper, *An African Bourgeoisie* (Yale University Press, New Haven, CT, 1965), page 329.
[27] Philip and Iona Meyer, *Townsmen and Tribesmen* (Oxford University Press, Cape Town, 1974).
[28] Gunther and Diamond, 'Species of political parties', p. 174.
[29] Angelo Panebianco, *Political Parties: Organization and power* (Cambridge University Press, Cambridge, 1988), p. xiii.
[30] Samuel P. Huntington, *Political Order in Changing Societies* (Yale University Press, New Haven, CT, 1968), pp. 59–64.

emphases on organizational disarray and social insecurity. When institutions change there are no stable public realms in which people can find assurance and comfort. Under such conditions, corruption is an example of the way in which political actors use 'disorder as a political instrument'.[31]

Here too there is an historic dimension to the argument. ANC leaders moving to embrace militant activism during the 1950s defied the law at a time when apartheid criminalized many actions that black South Africans would not have recognized as immoral. This created an environment that drew together political and criminal networks. During the 1950s, certain ANC leaders made a point of trying to rehabilitate *tsotsi* gangsters, motivated partly by a compassionate perception of criminals as victims of social injustice as well as recognition that *tsotsis* 'could be trusted' to promote social disorder and hence might help to reinforce militant activism.[32] In Sophiatown in Johannesburg, ANC activists found themselves on the same side as the gangsters in resisting removals and the local Youth League recruited among the gangs. One explanation for ANC leaders' modern cupidity is to view it as the outcome of routines nurtured through the incorporation of criminal networks, beginning with these efforts to secure *tsotsi* support in the 1950s. The career of one-time Alexandra gangster Joe Modise is illustrative.[33] In 1994 Modise was Minister of Defence in President Mandela's cabinet, an appointment that helped him to become a major beneficiary of the bribery that accompanied the 1997 arms contract. Modise's record of criminal undertakings, including car theft and smuggling, stretched back to his youth in the 1950s. He continued such activities in exile as profitable sidelines to leading Umkhonto we Sizwe. From 1994, foreign arms contractors' access to Modise was facilitated by Fana Hlongwane, ex-Umkhonto commander and—from 1994, as Modise's ministerial 'political adviser'—already in receipt of payments from British Aerospace and SAAB.[34] British Aerospace's relationship with Modise began in 1995 with a R5 million donation to the Umkhonto veterans association, a body that Modise chaired.[35]

Stephen Ellis's research suggests that Modise hardly represented an isolated case. In 1980, ANC leaders expressed alarm over the prevalence of car smuggling by their members and government sources corroborated this concern, alleging also ANC engagement in mandrax smuggling. Later the ANC's

---

[31] Patrick Chabal and Jean-Pascal Daloz, *Africa Works: Disorder as a political instrument* (James Currey, Oxford, 1999), pp. 85–91.

[32] Clive Glaser, *Bo-Tsotsi: The youth gangs of Soweto, 1935–1976* (James Currey, Oxford, 2000), p. 82.

[33] R. W. Johnson, *South Africa's Brave New World: The beloved country since the end of apartheid* (Allen Lane, London, 2009).

[34] Plaut and Holden, *Who Rules South Africa?*, p. 109.

[35] Andrew Feinstein, *After the Party: A personal and political journey inside the ANC* (Jonathan Ball, Johannesburg, 2007), p. 155.

intelligence department under Jacob Zuma's direction enlisted the help of Johannesburg-based criminal syndicates to supply weapons for Operation Vula, the operation to establish a military operational command inside South Africa. In 1987, the Civil Cooperation Bureau, a clandestine counter-insurgency agency, employed Ferdi Barnard, a convicted criminal. His task was to recruit agents within those criminal syndicates engaged in ANC supply operations.[36] Both the SADF and the ANC used the same smuggling routes and criminal agencies in efforts to penetrate each other's organizations and in the process they would increasingly develop mutually beneficial operations.[37]

There is considerable evidence that the legacy of these relationships continues to shape ANC politics. At least two of the major corruption scandals in South Africa's post-democratic political history had their origins in symbiotic relationships that evolved between key ANC officials and businessmen, some of the latter being individuals implicated in organized crime. Well before the 1997/8 arms deal, for example, businessman Shabir Shaik was making gifts to Jacob Zuma, his old comrade in ANC intelligence, and Zuma would later reciprocate in facilitating contracts for Shaik and his clients after his appointment to KwaZulu's regional government in 1994.[38] A rather more sinister relationship would develop, again through initial offers of help in resettling in South Africa, between Jackie Selebi, then head of the ANC's Youth Section, and Glenn Agliotti, a commodity broker with a history of illicit dealing. Agliotti's friendship with Selebi began with his paying an urgent medical bill for the treatment of Selebi's infant daughter. Agliotti would later control a criminalized security firm that would undertake errands for Selebi after the latter's appointment as police commissioner. Meanwhile, Agliotti himself would extract commissions from businessmen wishing to meet Selebi.[39] ANC insiders insist that Selebi's dealings with Agliotti were naïve rather than intentionally criminal: in the words of ex-ANC intelligence operative Barry Gilder, 'Selebi thought he was running Agliotti as a source.'[40] Gilder's views about the incidence of ostensibly corrupt behaviour are probably widely shared among his comrades. As he observes, the obligations arising from tightly knitted camaraderie that had sustained ANC cadres in exile often conflicted with new rules and norms:

---

[36] Peter Stiff, *Warfare by Other Means: South Africa in the 1980s and 1990s* (Galago, Alberton, 2001).

[37] Stephen Ellis, 'Politics and crime: reviewing the ANC's exile history', *South African Historical Journal* **64**, 3 (2012), pp. 622–36.

[38] Feinstein, *After the Party.*

[39] Mandy Weiner, *Killing Kebble: An underworld exposed*, second edition (Macmillan, Johannesburg, 2012), pp. 76–7.

[40] Barry Gilder, *Songs and Secrets: South Africa from liberation to governance* (Jacana, Auckland Park, 2012), p. 430.

The question has to be asked, however controversial it may be: to what extent do the notions of nepotism and cronyism adequately take into account the South African cultural realities of reciprocity and obligation to extended families and communities and, of course, to the solidarity amongst those who gave so much of themselves in the struggle for democracy.... [I]n moment-by-moment individual judgement calls, the cultural instinct to come to the aid of comrade, friend, family and community is strong and, in the eyes of the one who provides, morally correct.[41]

Criminal networks incorporated into the organization during its insurgent phase would certainly strengthen any patrimonial predispositions within the ANC's leadership. Their influence today might be accentuated by the ascent within the ANC hierarchy of a tightly knit group, composed of Jacob Zuma's former comrades within the ANC's intelligence section—that part of the organization most concerned with deploying criminal networks during the anti-apartheid struggle.

The ANC's organizational requirements during the political transition between 1990 and 1994 also help to explain the growing influence of person-alized networks within it. For top leaders it was imperative to build organized political followings in areas where the ANC had little previous support. Indeed, the need to expand the organization's base into new territory may have had an even more profound effect on the ANC's prevalent norms and values than the opportunistic friendships that developed between certain of its officials and dishonest businessmen. To illustrate the point it is helpful to recall the manner of the ANC's organizational entrenchment into what was then the eastern Transvaal.

In the eastern Transvaal—today's Mpumalanga—the provincial organiza-tion chose as its chairman a recently returned exile, Matthews Phosa. He had departed from South Africa in the early 1980s, leaving behind his partnership in a firm of Nelspruit attorneys. Phosa's law practice had continued to function during his absence, the only black attorneys' office in the Lowveld. It provided vital services to traders in their efforts to negotiate licences with the relevant homeland officials, and supplied Phosa on his return with valu-able networks of potential allies within the homeland-based business and bureaucratic elites. Even so, the real power within the Eastern Transvaal ANC lay in the hands of those who helped to 'convene' the organization.

The 'conveners' had emerged from the Youth Congress network. Before the regional executive elections, there were allegations that ANC 'branches' were set up after bulk sales of membership cards to traders.[42] In many districts the ANC's organization rested on a substructure of youth cohorts mobilized

---

[41] *Ibid.*, p. 399.
[42] Edwin Ritchken, *Leadership and Conflict in Bushbuckridge* (Unpublished PhD thesis, Department of Political Studies, University of the Witwatersrand, 1995).

around local 'big men', effectively reproducing customary patterns of patronage. Sitting on the new regional executive were a number of old Bantustan notables, including an MP who underwent a very sudden political conversion after losing his seat and a former chief deposed by his community. After 1994, as new provincial ministers, several former homeland politicians would be engaged in corrupt practices. David Mkhwanazi, for example, MEC for environmental affairs, a former member of the KaNgwane administration, was eventually dismissed in 1998 after accusations that he had appointed family members to positions in his department. The generalized sense of entitlement that helped to prompt such behaviour is evident in the explanation given by another prominent provincial ANC leader, Jackson Mthembu, MEC for Transport in Mpumalanga, when he was asked about his department's purchase of ten BMW 528s for transporting his colleagues on the provincial executive: 'I am a leader in my community and therefore have a certain status—you can't therefore be saying that I should drive a 1600 vehicle.'[43]

After 1994, the need to fund the party's organization also amplified the contribution of patronage and venality to its internal politics. Between 1990 and 1994, the ANC signalled its willingness to accept support from almost any source, no matter how morally compromised donors might have been by previous engagements with the earlier regime. Nelson Mandela's embrace of Sol Kerzner was a case in point. In this case, the ANC's lack of concern about venal associations was underlined by Mandela's retention within his cabinet of Stella Sigcau, the Transkeian minister implicated in a corruption case against Kerzner a decade earlier. Kerzner contributed R500,000 to the ANC's electoral campaign in 1994. Mandela's actions supplied the template for future electoral fundraising. As Andrew Feinstein observes, 'speculation has refused to go away that the ANC received millions of rands from the successful bidders (in the 1998 arms contracting), money that was probably used in our 1999 election campaign'.[44]

Since then, though, the ANC has become increasingly reliant on local funding sources. Accordingly, the ANC nurtures its relationship with the corporate world through initiatives that include the Progressive Business Forum, a body that sells access to key government ministers. Access to such resources enables the ruling party to maintain a very well-paid echelon of senior officials—raising the stakes in the competition for such offices—but it has also helped to instil a culture of 'gatekeeping', in which convivial meetings between businessmen and politicians are expected to be mutually rewarding. Moreover, through the ANC's efforts to extend its influence in the business world by deploying its own cadres in key corporate positions, there has

[43] *Sunday Times*, 'Big wheels', p. 4, 14 December 1997.
[44] Feinstein, *After the Party*, p. 155.

developed a sizeable group of businessmen who continue to view themselves as politicians.

One consequence of the development of an ANC oligarchy is the increasing role that private sources of wealth play *within* the ANC's internal politics. In 2012, Tokyo Sexwale, for example, was reported to be selling his stakeholding in the ABSA group to finance his 'war chest' for contesting the leadership elections at the ANC's national conference.[45] In 2010, Richard Mdluli, then head of the police's Crime Intelligence unit and a key ally of Jacob Zuma, reported that politicians were using proceeds from tendering to build up reserves to fund their leadership campaigns.[46] When candidates for internal offices need to mobilize support through such investments, clearly they are functioning in a milieu in which candidates are expected to reward their followers, in effect operating as patrons looking after their clients. In the 2007 conference at Polokwane, Deputy President Kgalema Motlanthe confirmed as much, admitting that buying the votes of branch delegates had become 'rampant and pronounced'.[47]

Such abuses are much likelier when an organization experiences spurts of very rapid expansion that strain its capacity for regulation. Expansion may also generate challenges to the values that underpin the organization's administrative arrangements. In particular, the recent growth of the Youth League's following has called into question the ANC leadership's authority, which tends to rely on customary deference to age and seniority. The Youth League's rise also threatens to supplant the Communist Party's ascendancy within the ANC's leadership. In contrast to the labour movement that provides the South African Communist Party with its leverage, Youth League power accumulates through its mobilization of a very different constituency, the unemployed school-leavers in rural settlements, people who have gained much less than organized workers from ANC governments. This is a constituency that has very different expectations of leadership from the 'comradely' accountability expected if not always practised by organized workers, taking their cues from the ethics of shop-floor democracy.[48] Indeed Jackson Mthembu might have been quite correct in assuming that in rural Mpumalanga, his own former Youth Congress comrades would have felt affronted if he arrived at meetings in an economical Nissan rather than a prestigious BMW.

[45] *City Press*, 'Tokyo Sexwale to cash in on ABSA shares', 5 August 2012, <http://africajournalismtheworld.com/tag/tokyo-sexwale-share-gains/> (1 November 2013).

[46] *Mail and Guardian*, 'Sexwale's prints all over R10bn tender', 23 March 2012, <http://mg.co.za/article/2012-03-23-sexwales-prints-all-over-r10bn-tender> (1 November 2013).

[47] Susan Booysen, *The African National Congress and the Regeneration of Political Power* (Witwatersrand University Press, Johannesburg, 2011), p. 63.

[48] Beresford, 'Comrades back on track'.

The Youth League, established in 1944, ceased functioning at the time of the prohibition in 1960—but, in any case, had not really played an assertive role of its own during the 1950s.[49] Today's Youth League, re-established in late 1990, is a force in its own right. Following its reformation, the League built its membership structure along the networks supplied by the Youth Congresses, the main rural bases of the United Democratic Front in the 1980s. Through the 1990s, under the charismatic presidency of Peter Mokaba, the League began to play a major role within the ANC's internal politics, in particular in supporting Thabo Mbeki's ascendancy and in enabling Mbeki to offset the influence of the Communist and trade-unionist left. The next stage in the League's trajectory was a swift multiplication of its membership, between 1990 and 1994, up to half a million, much of it in semi-rural settings, especially in KwaZulu-Natal and in Limpopo among unemployed school leavers.

Under the presidencies of Fikile Mbalula from 2004 and Julius Malema from 2008 the League began to confront the authority of older and more senior ANC leaders. Together with the Communist Party and the trade unions, it mobilized the vote against Mbeki at the 2007 Polokwane conference after two years of mutinous support for Jacob Zuma's reinstatement as Deputy President. In mid-2010, however, Julius Malema and other Youth League leaders turned on Zuma, criticizing him for failing to keep his promises to the ANC's poorest supporters and calling for nationalization of the mines and land redistribution. By mid-2011 Malema was proposing Zuma's replacement.

There are several reasons why this incarnation of youth politics is so much more unmanageable than earlier generational challenges to the authority of ANC elders. First, the League itself embodies a major share of the ANC's active support with its own claimed membership rivalling that of the parent body. During the recent branch meetings held to nominate candidates for the ANC's National Congress in December 2012, so often those 'who turned up...were young, unemployed and predominantly male'.[50] In the mainly rural provinces, now the areas of the ANC's firmest voting support, the League's role as an electoral mobilizer is probably more significant than the trade unions' contribution to ANC activism, especially at a time when industrial trade union membership has been declining.[51]

Second, Youth League leaders today have backgrounds that contrast sharply with the social settings that traditionally incubated ANC leadership. They often lack advanced education and they have no real work experience. Julius Malema's upbringing in the poorest of households in Seshego, a settlement

---

[49] Clive Glaser, The ANC Youth League (Jacana, Auckland Park, 2012), p. 46.

[50] City Press, 'Cape branch meeting a damp squib', 3 November 2012, <http://www.citypress. co.za/news/cape-branch-meeting-a-damp-squib-20121103/> (4 November 2012).

[51] Sakhela Buhlungu, A Paradox of Victory: COSATU and the democratic transformation in South Africa (Scottsville, University of KwaZulu Natal Press, 2010), p. 106.

outside Polokwane, and his political ascendancy through COSAS class-room activism at his Senior Primary School, is typical. Notwithstanding their own social mobility, they often retain a polarized worldview shaped by the wretched conditions of their upbringing.

Third, the Youth League leadership's power bases have become consolidated around the most dysfunctional segments of South Africa's public administration—rural, local, and provincial government. In local settings where government itself supplies the main economic impetus and where political venality is already deeply entrenched—classically neo-patrimonial settings—accession to public office or even less formal positions of political influence is a main route for private accumulation. Julius Malema's career again offers illustration. His fortune began with winning a tender to supply school uniforms while he was a COSAS leader. By 2000, through his command of activist support, he had become a decisive figure in determining candidatures in Limpopo's municipal elections. It was his support within the municipalities that enabled him to take on more established figures within Limpopo's ANC hierarchy in competing for tenders. By 2009, Malema controlled the unit that 'outsourced' capital expenditure by the provincial Department of Roads and Transport.[52]

Fourth, quite aside from the personal wealth of certain of its leaders, the League itself has been able to win its own financial support, separately from its parent organization, most notoriously in the sponsorship it received from the mining entrepreneur, Brett Kebble, who helped to set up the League's company, Lembede Investments.

Additionally, and most importantly, it is the League's political volatility that makes it such a difficult constituent for the wider movement. The unruly politics of the Youth League draws upon an inherited repertoire of bellicose and even violent activism. Factionalized divisions are encouraged by an internal organizational politics in which personal accumulation supplies a key dynamic. Such rapid expansion would have tested the procedures of even a well-established organization; unsurprisingly, the Youth League's ballooning membership has been accompanied by organizational disarray within the parent organization, in which Youth Leaguers play an increasingly assertive role. Meanwhile the rags-to-riches progression of individual leaders through their acquisition of political kingdoms has supplied meaning and moral valorization for an ideology of racialized redistribution through the exercise of state power.

A final feature of the environmental insecurity that reinforces neopatrimonial predispositions is apparent in the public expectations engendered when the ANC exercises its incumbent power as a government. Here exchanges

---

[52] Forde, *An Inconvenient Youth*, p. 168.

between the party and its supporters project the idea of support bringing rewards. In such transactions, citizenship is reduced to the passive role of beneficiary. This predisposition is nicely captured in vignettes from the ANC's campaigning during the 2004 election. In Jane Furse in Limpopo, a praise singer opened proceedings before Mbeki's address: 'I may be hungry, I may be poor, but things are good because the ANC takes care of everything.'[53] In northern KwaZulu-Natal, possibly in response to the challenge of contesting for support within Inkatha's home base, ANC electioneering included what were clearly understood as transactional exchanges between regional leaders and the local *amakhosi*. For example the former MEC for transport was invited to hold a special meeting with the *amakhosi* 'to develop a programme of action to deliver the goods in their respective areas'.[54]

To be fair, on the whole ANC campaigning is still largely driven by national programmatic undertakings rather than clientelist promises of special favours to particular groups, a predisposition that is reinforced by the national-list system of proportional representation used in national and regional elections.[55] This might still make South African politics distinctive on the continent, though analysts disagree about the prevalence of clientelism elsewhere.[56] The ANC also tends to eschew narratives about particular personalities, though in the 2009 election a fresh precedent was established when the portraits of regional politicians began to appear on placards. But in rural regions in which the numbers of beneficiaries of welfare have expanded very quickly as a consequence of deliberate efforts to ensure that people entitled to grants actually receive them, it is still quite easy for voters to perceive pensions and other benefits as the reward for their political support.

Let us summarize the argument in this section. From the 1950s the ANC was drawn into extra-legal and armed opposition, processes which led its leadership to incorporate criminal groups into its networks. This helped to strengthen patrimonial political predispositions. Then, after 1990, the ANC needed to transform itself very swiftly into an organization equipped to win elections and maintain its support once ensconced in power. The first requirement was simply to expand its organized following outside the towns, which had been its historic centres of strength, into the countryside where it had been largely absent organizationally, and in parts of which it expected to find electoral opposition. The quickest way to accomplish such expansion was through the incorporation of the elites and networks consolidated around

---

[53] Lodge, 'The African National Congress', p. 119.   [54] *Ibid.*, p. 120.

[55] For comparative insights see Herbert Kitschelt, 'Linkages between citizens and politicians in democratic polities', *Comparative Political Studies* 33, 6–7 (2000), pp. 845–79, p. 859.

[56] See Daniel Young, 'Is clientelism at work in African elections?' (Afro Barometer Working Paper No. 106, IDASA, Pretoria, April 2009) and Staffan Lindberg, 'It is our time to chop: do elections in Africa feed neo-patrimonialism rather than counteract it?', *Democratization* 10, 2 (2003), pp. 121–40.

homeland polities. The corollary to this was that in certain predominantly rural provinces the ANC's local leadership would re-enact the social relationships of established patterns of clientelistic politics.

The second need was financial: the ANC believed it needed massive funding to win its first election and this set expectations for future contests in which it began to rely on resources generated by party-controlled enterprises or by politically motivated contracting. With the appointment of its own cadres onto company boards, internal factional contests for party positions and public office began to be financed by private fortunes. The third dynamic associated with the ANC's movement away from liberation politics was the expansion of its Youth League and the consequential displacement of organized labour as its main power base. Given the backgrounds and aspirations of the League's constituents, the ANC's mass following became increasingly amenable to a politics in which authority is manifest in the exercise of personal power, conspicuous consumption, and individual generosity. After all, clientelist politics tends to thrive in settings in which livelihoods are precarious and quite modest 'selective incentives' offered through face-to-face encounters have especially telling effects. This is more likely among an electorate living in isolated rural locations, in which young unemployed people predominate, than among industrially organized urban residents.[57] The fourth and latest development arising from the ANC's transformation into an electoral machine is the increasing incidence of promises of particular rewards to specific groups of voters in exchange for their electoral support. Each of these developments reinforces patrimonial predispositions within the ANC's leadership and each of them reflects the wider environment in which institutional life is rendered inchoate as it becomes subject to sudden change and consequent disorder.

In other words, in the ANC's case patrimonial predispositions are not simply the consequence of functional imperatives for building and retaining electoral support in this particular environment. They are also a residual effect of liberation movement politics, of the incompleteness of the ANC's organizational change from movement to party. In this setting, politically biased contracting is morally excusable as a strategy to reverse historic racist inequities. The exercise of partisan patronage through 'deployments' of party personnel to positions of influence in business and public institutions is similarly justifiable. The ANC itself resists classification as an electoral party and prefers to view its role as much broader: disciplined members are expected to achieve party goals in a range of arenas, not just electoral and parliamentary politics— in Gunther and Diamond's terminology, the ANC's orientation is still protohegemonic rather than pluralistic.[58] Ironically, though, these aspirations

---

[57] Kitschelt, 'Linkages between citizens', pp. 851–2.
[58] Gunther and Diamond, 'Species of political parties', p. 171.

extend the possibilities for the operation of personal networks. As its own officials admit, such networks ultimately undermine the party's own institutionalized procedures and in the long run might weaken its organizational capacity and ideological authority.

The ANC and the political economy of South Africa

A third kind of explanation for the socio-political orientation of ANC's leadership is to view it as the reflection of deeply instilled characteristics of South Africa's political economy. Here neo-patrimonial politics reflects a particular level of economic development. From this perspective, neopatrimonial political systems consolidate in environments in which the acquisition of political office represents the best avenue for personal accumulation, in settings where the emergence of local capitalist groups has been thwarted by the state. As Pitcher, Moran, and Johnston propose in the case of Botswana, the relative resilience of the legal-rational domain is the consequence of its rulers having emerged as rural capitalists *before* their ascent to national public office. Conversely, recent writing about the political economy of the Arab world has suggested that in weakly institutionalized settings a system of 'patrimonial capitalism' exists in which 'property rights and contract security can best be secured and guaranteed through personal socio-political ties with the "right" individuals'.[59]

An application of this model to post-Soviet experience offers especially close parallels to modern South African developments. Neil Robinson suggests that post-Soviet politics embodies 'patrimonial capitalism'. Here power over the economy is heavily personalized and exchanges require 'a high degree of relational capital'.[60] Relational capital is accumulated through successive personal one-to-one encounters: the resulting affective ties facilitate wealth creation. In such cases, the key issue is that the accumulation requirement for relational capital makes it difficult for other groups to gather the resources needed to challenge the elite. Moreover its operation blunts the impact of external forces. Global economic actors have to work through local holders of relational capital and this limits the transformative potential of global firms. Political power derives from systems of economic control in which local

---

[59] Oliver Schlumberger, 'Structural reform, economic order and development: patrimonial capitalism', *Review of International Political Economy* 15, 4 (2008), pp. 622–49, p. 634.

[60] Neil Robinson, 'Russian patrimonial capitalism and the international financial crisis', *Journal of Communist Studies and Transition Politics* 27, 3–4 (2011), pp. 435–55, pp. 436–7.

ownership is highly concentrated—a situation that in Russia is the consequence of the economy's dependence on energy sales.

Robinson's conception of the Russian political economy is complicated and differs in several important respects from South Africa, but there are striking resemblances. Like Russia, South Africa is dependent upon mineral exports in fields where the state can in effect award monopolistic prospecting rights. In South Africa, legislation in 2004 institutionalized preference to 'historically disadvantaged persons' in the award of such rights. As in Russia, dependence on external investment has prompted programmes of market reform which themselves have helped to create openings for oligarchical accumulation through the privatization of state assets or the 'outsourcing' of public services.[61] In both Russia and South Africa, state and business transactions involving 'relational capital' have become increasingly important, because of the role that political patronage is playing in tendering. In South Africa the role of relational capital is accentuated by policies that have made the black business elite 'a pivot in relations between business and state',[62] despite the relatively small share of the economy it controls directly. Black businessmen's influence certainly exceeds the scale of their actual holdings. In 2004, for example, at a time, when 'empowered' businessmen owned about 10 percent of the shares of the largest companies on the Johannesburg Stock Exchange, nine of them were listed by the *Financial Mail* as among South Africa's twenty top businesspeople, including three heavyweight ANC notables: Cyril Ramaphosa, Tokyo Sexwale, and Saki Macozoma.[63] As government purchasing is regulated by 'preferential procurement' legislation, there are incentives for companies to recruit politically well-connected personalities onto their boards: the rising fortunes of Jacob Zuma's kinsfolk are illustrative of this predisposition.

Of course, Russia represents a much more complete and advanced model of patrimonial capitalism, and in South Africa ownership and economic activity remain more diversified. There also remain in South Africa tougher democratic constraints on the exercise of authoritarian leadership than in Russia. But the correspondence between the broad circumstances of the two political settings is striking: in both neo-patrimonial leadership is consolidated in an environment in which market reform of what was

---

[61] See for example *Mail and Guardian*, 'Sexwale's prints all over R10 billion tender', 23 March 2012, <http://mg.co.za/article/2012-03-23-sexwales-prints-all-over-r10bn-tender> (1 November 2013).

[62] Don Lindsay, 'BEE reform: The case for an institutional perspective' in John Daniel, Prishani Naidoo, Devan Pillay, and Roger Southall (eds), *New South African Review 2: New paths, old dependencies* (Witwatersrand University Press, Johannesburg, 2011), p. 249.

[63] Roger Southall, 'Black empowerment and present limits to a more democratic capitalism in South Africa' in Sakhela Buhlungu, John Daniel, Roger Southall, and Jessica Lutchman (eds), *State of the Nation: South Africa, 2005–2006* (HSRC Press, Cape Town, 2006), pp. 191–3.

previously a heavily *dirigiste* economy has facilitated and continues to reinforce the transformation of a political elite into a tightly networked class of accumulators.

Conclusion: the ANC and the roots of neo-patrimonialism

This article has surveyed three different explanations for the expansion of neo-patrimonial forms of leadership behaviour in South Africa's ruling party. Taken together they supply a comprehensive account of neopatrimonialism within the ANC and indicate its most important drivers. With respect to the roots of ANC patrimonialism, the evidence is compelling. In the organization's early history, family and friendship bound leadership together in strong affective ties. In a social environment where the state restricted black property owning and occupational mobility so tightly, it was understandable that individual success was valorized politically. Meanwhile, in its local settings the ANC was drawn into the township boss-style politics that developed around advisory boards. Today's ANC has certainly incorporated into its municipal representation the legacy of such politics, whether this was part of its local political history or not.

The second proposition regards the expansion of patrimonial behaviour as a corollary of the ANC's interaction with criminal syndicates during its insurgent phases and, more recently, the expediencies the ANC embraced in its efforts to assemble an electoral machine. For this latter purpose, the ANC was willing to accept help from self-interested donors after its legalization. Its territorial expansion was facilitated by the embrace of homeland politicians. As internal competition for office has sharpened, a new generation of politicians-turned-businessmen have financed new kinds of factional rivalry. Meanwhile the ANC's activist base has shifted away from organized labour and towards unemployed youth, for whom a political ideology constructed around patriarchal notions of masculinity has a special appeal.[64] At the same time and increasingly, the ANC has solicited electoral support by promising specific rewards to particular groups, appealing to voters as passive clients rather than assertive citizens.

Finally, it is also clear that powerful environmental compulsions help foster a contemporary politics in which leaders function as patrons. Patrimonial habits are stimulated by an economic setting in which 'relational' capital is an important asset. The role of relational capital is accentuated by the state's

---

[64] Shireen Hassim, 'Democracy's shadows: sexual rights and gender politics in the rape trial of Jacob Zuma', *African Studies* **68**, 1 (2009), pp. 57–77, p. 65.

efforts to nurture a politically loyal oligarchy constituted by black business-men, themselves often former politicians. The structural conditions that favour the operation of patrimonial capitalism include a large share of the national economy being based upon resource extraction in which the state plays a pivotal role as a regulator and licensor. Foreign capital helps to strengthen its hold through the recruitment of local oligarchs as political intermediaries and brokers. These are all features of South Africa's political economy that have become increasingly conspicuous over the last decade and help to explain the changing character of South Africa's ruling party.

The focus in this article has been on the behaviour of leaders and leadership—but South Africa's generalized public sentiment often supplies a receptive setting for neo-patrimonial modes of political incorporation. Amongst former exiles, as Barry Gilder has noted, there are 'cultural instincts to come to the aid of a comrade, friend, family and community'.[65] Such instincts may become more prevalent over time. Peter Ekeh observed two public realms that people inhabit in post-colonial settings, an imposed civic public domain 'from which they gain materially but to which they give only grudgingly', and a 'primordial public' from which they derive little material benefit but to which they give generously and from which they extract moral sustenance.[66] It is within that primordial domain that people confine their proper behaviour, for in the civic or modern realm a person will try only to gain. They will then be admired if they channel at least part of what they appropriate from the civic public into the primordial realm.

Ekeh was writing about West Africa a decade or so after independence—a region arguably much less transformed by the intrusion of colonial political economy than Southern Africa. Writing more recently about about the abrupt repudiation of socialism by former liberation movement leaders in Namibia, Angola, Mozambique, Zimbabwe, and South Africa, John Saul has suggested that the explanation could be that 'social contradictions just do not cut deeply enough in Southern Africa' and that communal kinds of solidarity will 'trump class consciousness every time'.[67]

Ekeh's conceptual distinctions between two normative spheres can explain Jackson Mthembu's defence of ministerial ostentation. Leaders are expected to project glamour. Their own success in extracting resources from the civic public can serve as a beacon of hope for their supporters, who might them-selves become beneficiaries of any redistribution of their patron's store of public goods.[68] Moreover, in a society in which such sharp social inequalities

---

[65] Gilder, *Songs and Secrets*, p. 399.
[66] Ekeh, 'Colonialism and the two publics in Africa', p. 108.
[67] John S. Saul, 'The strange death of liberated South Africa', *Transformation* **64** (2007), pp. 1–26, p. 20.
[68] For evidence from Limpopo, see Isak A. Niehaus, 'Doing politics in Bushbuckridge: work, welfare and the South African Elections of 2004', *Africa* 76, 4 (2006), pp. 526–48, p. 542.

are still so obviously correlated with race, Julius Malema's illicit acquisition of riches becomes a saga of popular empowerment, a story in which a native son has challenged and triumphed over remote and alien citadels. As Jonny Steinberg has noted, in impoverished villages, Malema's name evokes respect. Villagers 'have received as a revelation the story he tells about their country. He says that when black people won South Africa at the ballot box, whites began to hide power in invisible places. . . . He says his mission is to go and find power where it hides and retrieve it.'[69]

Significantly, when power makes itself visible, as may occur during election seasons, its representatives are expected to render tribute to that realm of personal probity. This is Ekeh's 'primordial' arena, the place in which the hungry and the poor can expect their leaders 'to take care of everything'.

Can this South African experience yield insights that are more generalizable? The continuing importance of lineage and other affective ties in the ANC's internal politics is partly an effect of relationships consolidated over generations of political leadership: dynastic succession within the political elite is discernible in other African countries that have parties that embody particular political traditions—Angola's rulers are a case in point.[70] The ANC's history reminds us how enduring the affective ties initially generated through the construction of networks around very personal loyalties can be in political parties, even after successive changes in their form and purpose. They also persist long after the modernization of the settings that nurtured local elites such as the *amakholwa*.

Within an African setting, the ANC belongs to a family of political organizations with their roots in liberation politics that attempted to mobilize a popular following on the basis of mass organization drawing on broad social solidarities among oppressed groups. After their legal incorporation into a newly institutionalized arena of procedural democracy, and pulled by the logic of electoral competition, they extended their organizational base in ways that opened up space for the narrower and more personalized channels of clientelist politics. With adaptations, much the same narrative could be drawn from the modern-day operations of Mozambique's ruling party, as well as the former liberation movements in other ex-Portuguese colonies.[71]

---

[69] Jonny Steinberg, 'Julius Malema: the man who scarred South Africa', *The Guardian*, 10 February 2012, <http://www.theguardian.com/world/2012/feb/10/julius-malema-south-africa.anc> (1 November 2013).

[70] Which, as David Birmingham observed in 1988, constitutes a government 'controlled by a network of a dozen families of the old creole military caste that had dominated the black elite in the nineteenth century'. David Birmingham, 'Angola revisited', *Journal of Southern African Studies* 15, 1 (1988), pp. 1–14, p. 9.

[71] As noted by members of a 'Strategic Conflict Assessment' commissioned by the United Kingdom's DfID, 'the socialist ideology of FRELIMO has long been replaced by pragmatism. . . . Relations based on extended families (and in some cases ethnic affiliations) determine access to

Finally, keeping in mind the third set of arguments about the effect of today's political economy on the ANC's organizational culture, the South African experience can be read as a case study of the implications for party politics of a more general change whereby organized labour has lost political leverage in previously heavily industrialized economies. Mass parties are generally in decline, in part because of the rise of new electoral technologies that render them redundant and in part because of the breakdown of the traditional working class. The degenerative changes that are observable within the ANC thus appear to reflect a global trend in which mass parties are being replaced by electoral machines that depend less and less upon militant activism.[72]

Acknowledgment

Published in *African Affairs*, 113, 450 (2014), p. 1–23.

state resources and political power.' Tony Vaux, Amanda Mavela, Joao Pereira, and Jennifer Stuttle, *Mozambique* (DfID, London, April 2006), p. 19.

[72] See Otto Kirchheimer, 'The transformation of Western European party systems' in Joseph LaPalombara and Myron Weiner (eds), *Political Parties and Political Development* (Princeton University Press, Princeton, NJ, 1966).

Part IV

Africa and the World

14

An Introduction to Africa and the World

Carl Death

AFRICA'S INTERNATIONAL RELATIONS comprises conflict and cooperation, authority and resistance, realist self-interest and the quest for justice and progress—just like international politics in other regions of the world. Yet, while disciplinary generalists within International Relations (IR) have often regarded Africa as marginal or peripheral to the main business of the major powers, African politics has always been constituted through and productive of global power relations: including slavery; colonialism; institutions like the United Nations (UN), the Non-Aligned Movement, and the G77; globalized political economies of trade, aid, and natural resource extraction produced by capitalism; climate change; and the migration of people, goods, and ideas.

The study of Africa's international relations—in *African Affairs* and elsewhere—has therefore been characterized by a number of tensions between the empirical subject-matter and the discipline ("IR"). IR theorists have sometimes regarded Africa as peripheral either because its states were seen as weak and it lacked genuine "Great Powers" able unilaterally to shape world politics, or because it was assumed to be behind the rest of the world (and particularly America and Europe) on a progressive trend towards civilization, democracy, and modernity. For IR theorists, Africa was sometimes seen primarily as a site of fieldwork or data-mining, somewhere to test theories developed elsewhere in the world rather than a place to develop and advance IR theory itself. Viewed from the other perspective, Africanists have sometimes regarded IR as a discipline with scepticism or even disdain: does a set of assumptions about similar sovereign states competing within international anarchy really explain much about African politics? Even liberal studies of evolving international norms and regimes on human rights or environmental protection can sometimes seem very far removed from the realities of life in Abuja, Nairobi, or Pretoria.

Yet, as the work introduced here shows, there has been a great deal of research at the interface of African studies and IR which has used traditional

theories like realism or constructivism to explain African international politics, or which has sought to challenge and develop IR theory through empirically informed accounts of African politics. It has always been recognized that
global events and structures like colonialism and independence, the Cold War
and the new world order after the fall of the Berlin Wall, the economic and
cultural globalization of contemporary capitalism, and the War on Terror,
have profoundly shaped African politics and international relations.

Research in this area has not just reflected global trends and theoretical
debates, but has also shaped and advanced them. The 1990s was animated by
debates over whether ethical foreign policies were possible, given the end of
the Cold War and an apparent shift from a realist world of violence and
competition to a liberal world order of human rights and democracy. Nelson
Mandela's seminal essay in *Foreign Affairs* was a key expression of this
aspiration,[1] and studies of South African foreign policy and international
relations in particular have continued to reflect upon the possibility of a
more idealist outlook on world politics.[2]

Perhaps even more strikingly, however, African studies specialists have
played a major role in challenging and revising some of the supposed 'timeless
truths' of IR: the centrality of states, international anarchy, and universal
values like democracy and the rule of law. African international politics has
informed and helped to develop insights in critical theory and postcolonial
theory which have contributed to broader shifts in the discipline of IR. Thanks
in part to African theorists and Africanist scholars, the study of world politics
now contains much more prominent research on issues of race, gender,
identity, resistance, non-state agency and violence, transboundary migration
and solidarity, and the relationship between society and the natural world.[3]

---

[1] Nelson Mandela, 'South Africa's Future Foreign Policy', *Foreign Affairs* 72, 5 (1993),
pp. 86–97.

[2] Ken Booth and Peter Vale, 'Security in South Africa: After Apartheid, Beyond Realism',
International Affairs 71, 2 (1995), pp. 285–304; Laurie Nathan, 'Interests, Ideas and Ideology:
South Africa's Policy on Darfur', *African Affairs* 110, 438 (2011), pp. 55–74; Peter Vale and Sipho
Maseko, 'South Africa and the African Renaissance', *International Affairs* 74, 2 (1998),
pp. 271–87.

[3] Some of the best general accounts of Africa and IR theory include: Adekeye Adebajo, *The
Curse of Berlin: Africa After the Cold War* (Hurst, London, 2010); William Brown, 'Africa and
International Relations: A Comment on IR Theory, Anarchy and Statehood', *Review of International Studies* 32, 1 (2006), pp. 119–43; William Brown, 'Sovereignty Matters: Africa, Donors,
and the Aid Relationship', *African Affairs*, 112, 447 (2013), pp. 262–82; Christopher Clapham,
Africa and the International System: The Politics of State Survival (Cambridge University Press,
Cambridge, 1996); Christopher Clapham, 'Degrees of Statehood', *Review of International Studies*
24 (1998), pp. 143–57; Scarlett Cornelissen, Fantu Cheru, and Timothy M. Shaw (eds), *Africa
and International Relations in the 21st Century* (Palgrave Macmillan, Basingstoke, 2012); Kevin
C. Dunn and Timothy M. Shaw (eds), *Africa's Challenge to International Relations Theory*
(Palgrave, Basingstoke, 2001); Ali A. Mazrui, *Africa's International Relations: The Diplomacy
of Dependency and Change* (Westview, Boulder, CO, 1977); Tandeka C. Nkiwane, 'Africa and
International Relations: Regional Lessons for a Global Discourse', *International Political Science*

With respect to two crucial global processes—colonialism and capitalism—research on African politics shows how the boundaries between domestic affairs and international relations are never clear-cut. While some IR theorists may seek to "black box" the state in the interests of theoretical parsimony, international and transnational power relations have always shaped African domestic politics, and domestic interests and ideas structure world politics. The articles in Part IV were selected precisely because each provides a different way of thinking about how international and domestic structures and actors interact and relate to each other.

CONFLICT, COOPERATION, AND COLONIALISM IN AFRICAN IR

Traditional or mainstream IR theory has often been characterized in terms set out by E. H. Carr in his classic study of the 1930s: the balance between the realist pursuit of self-interest and security, and the idealist search for progress and justice.[4] The coexistence of conflict and cooperation within international anarchy is thus the starting point for most mainstream IR theorists. But research on African international politics usually begins with a third 'c': colonialism. African engagements with world politics did not begin with colonial encounters, and trade, conflict, and the exchange of people and ideas go back well beyond the formal structures of colonialism.[5] However, it was the so-called "Scramble for Africa" in the nineteenth century as European powers divided the continent into what they thought resembled "modern" territories and boundaries, and carved up colonial possessions to fuel global imperial projects, that created some of the most profound and long-lasting structures of African international politics. The Berlin Conference of 1884–5 encapsulates the interplay of conflict and cooperation in international politics. Bismarck orchestrated European diplomacy to avoid outright war, but in so doing inaugurated decades of colonial and postcolonial conflict in Africa.[6] Whereas the architects of empire saw Africa as the setting for the spread of "Christianity, Civilization, and Commerce", a more appropriate "three Cs" might be conflict, cooperation, and colonialism.

Review 22, 3 (2001), pp. 279–90; Ian Taylor and Paul Williams (eds), *Africa in International Politics: External Involvement on the Continent* (Routledge, London, 2004); Carolyn M. Warner, 'The rise of the state system in Africa', *Review of International Studies* 27, 5 (2001), pp. 65–89.

[4] E. H. Carr, *The Twenty Years' Crisis 1919–1939: An Introduction to the Study of International Relations* (Palgrave Macmillan, Basingstoke, 1939/2001).

[5] Emmanuel Akyeampong, 'Africans in the Diaspora: The Diaspora and Africa', *African Affairs* 99, 395 (2000), pp. 183–215.

[6] Adebajo, *The Curse of Berlin*.

Colonialism was integral to the early identity of *African Affairs*. As the journal of the Royal African Society it provided space for statesmen (and they were predominantly men) to reflect upon the course of world politics. During the 1930s and 1940s the journal was filled with the lectures and reflections of colonial officials and politicians like William Ormsby-Gore (Colonial Secretary and High Commissioner to South Africa) and Lord Hailey (director of the African Survey). As academia changed and professionalized after World War II, and the journal itself took on a new form, the articles became more research-driven rather than policy-focused. This line between practitioners and observers of international relations remains sometimes blurred, however, and the journal continues to publish research by those closely involved with the business of world politics, such as by Omar Touray in 2005, the ambassador from the Gambia to the African Union.[7]

During the Cold War, Africa was often regarded as the battleground of the rival great powers, the theatre of proxy wars in Angola and Mozambique and elsewhere, with newly independent African states often propped up or ravaged by external forces. This is illustrated in an article by Oye Ogunbadejo, 'Soviet policies in Africa', which argues that realist self-interest increasingly trumped ideals of global revolution for the Kremlin's Africanists during the 1970s. Ultimately, he suggests, 'what is important to the Soviet Union is not a doctrinal stance of ideological orthodoxy, but to use Africa to further its own economic development.'[8] This position reflects the assessment of many theorists of neo-colonialism and dependency who argued, following Kwame Nkrumah, that even nominally independent sovereign states found their economic system and political policy 'directed from outside'.[9] Yet even in the teeth of economic dependency, Africanists have drawn attention to the agency that less powerful states can exercise. Some point to transnational pan-Africanist projects, others to the Machiavellian skill of adroit politicians.[10] Ethiopia, for example, was able to play off West and East during the Cold War, although this did not bring safety, stability, or security for either Ethiopia's rulers or its people.[11]

In the 1990s the dominant concerns of IR in Africa turned to the spread of global norms and regimes like human rights and democracy, and the responsibilities of international society in cases where order broke down.[12] The

---

[7] Omar A. Touray, 'The Common African Defence and Security Policy', *African Affairs* 104, 417 (2005), pp. 635–56.

[8] Oye Ogunbadejo, 'Soviet Policies in Africa', *African Affairs* 79, 316 (1980), p. 322.

[9] Kwame Nkrumah, *Neo-colonialism: The Last Stage of Imperialism* (Thomas Nelson and Sons, London, 1965), p. 1.

[10] Ali A. Mazrui, 'Africa: In Search of Self-Pacification', *African Affairs* 93, 370 (1994), pp. 39–42.

[11] See Clapham, *Africa and the International System*, chapter 6.

[12] Rita Abrahamsen, *Disciplining Democracy: Development Discourse and Good Governance in Africa* (Zed Books, London, 2000); Gorm Rye Olsen, 'Europe and the Promotion of

catastrophes of civil war in Somalia and genocide in Rwanda seemed to confirm that Africa was in dire need of 'saving' by the West. Yet in South Africa, the end of apartheid and the transition to democracy under Mandela and the African National Congress (ANC) gave hope to those who believed progress was possible in international politics. International sanctions (even if belated) and support for the ANC in exile (even if sporadic) were seen as contributing to the downfall of a racist, violent, and undemocratic regime, and the ANC confidently espoused a vision of helping to build a more peaceful, just, and secure world order.[13]

By the 2000s, this vision in South Africa had begun to pale, as its foremost architect, President Thabo Mbeki, was increasingly castigated for the failures of "quiet diplomacy" in Zimbabwe and Sudan, as well as on HIV/AIDS, land reform, privatization, and the neoliberal turn.[14] At the same time, liberal faith in a new world order of democracy and security was challenged by the 9/11 attacks on the US and the subsequent wars in Afghanistan and Iraq. Decades of development assistance, structural adjustment, neoliberal trade and financial reforms, and democracy promotion had neither succeeded in modernizing African economies nor made much headway in tackling poverty and social inequality.[15] Critical theorists argued about whether Africa was exploited because of the depth of its penetration by, and integration into, the capitalist global economy—or left vulnerable because of its exclusion and marginalization.[16] A relaunched African Union (AU) was widely regarded as an improvement on the moribund Organisation of African Unity but its limits were revealed by new or continuing conflicts in Somalia, Darfur, the Democratic Republic of the Congo and the Great Lakes region, Côte D'Ivoire, and elsewhere.[17]

Democracy in Post Cold War Africa: How Serious is Europe and for What Reason?', *African Affairs* 97 (1998), pp. 343–67.

[13] Stephen Ellis, 'The ANC in exile', *African Affairs* 90 (1991), pp. 439–47; Audie Klotz, *Norms in International Relations: The Struggle Against Apartheid* (Cornell, Ithaca, NY, 1995).

[14] Richard Ballard, Adam Habib, Imraan Valodia, and Elke Zuern, 'Globalization, Marginalization, and Contemporary Social Movements in South Africa', *African Affairs* 104, 417 (2005), pp. 615–34; Carl Death, 'Troubles at the Top: South African Protests and the 2002 Johannesburg Summit', *African Affairs* 109, 437 (2010), pp. 555–74; Laurie Nathan, 'Consistencies and Inconsistencies in South Africa's Foreign Policy', *International Affairs* 81, 2 (2005), pp. 361–72.

[15] Claude Aké, *Democracy and Development in Africa* (Brookings Institute, Washington, DC, 1996); Graham Harrison, *The World Bank and Africa: The Construction of Governance States* (Routledge, Abingdon, 2004).

[16] Graham Harrison, *Neoliberal Africa: The Impact of Global Social Engineering* (Zed Books, London, 2010).

[17] David M. Anderson and Jacob McKnight, 'Kenya at War: Al-Shabaab and its Enemies in Eastern Africa', *African Affairs* 114, 454 (2014), pp. 1–27; Danny Hoffman, 'The Civilian Target in Sierra Leone and Liberia: Political Power, Military Strategy, and Humanitarian Intervention', *African Affairs* 103, 411 (2004), pp. 211–26; Nathan, 'Interests, Ideas and Ideology'; Touray, 'The Common African Defence and Security Policy'; Paul D. Williams and Arthur Boutellis,

A seminal article by Paul Williams on regional security in Africa explicitly interrogates the value of theoretical frameworks derived from realism, neo-realism, and constructivism in understanding and explaining African international relations.[18] Despite undertaking peace operations in Burundi, the Central African Republic, the Comoros, Mali, Somalia, and Sudan, the basic tension between two norms—the principle of African unity and solidarity, and respect for democracy and human rights—was starkly revealed as African international society split over Libya in 2011. While the AU supported engagement with Gaddafi as a long-time (if unreliable) pan-Africanist, the UN Security Council (including three African states who all voted for intervention) approved the first international intervention under the 'Responsibility to Protect' (R2P) doctrine. Gaddafi fell, Libya descended into protracted conflict, and the AU was left apparently impotent on the sidelines.

The early twenty-first century was also defined by a changing world order in another way, as "rising powers" like Brazil, India, and China challenged the assumptions that the US was the sole superpower in a unipolar world, or that European aid donors could direct policy on development and governance in Africa.[19] Increasing levels of Chinese involvement in African politics have been a particularly important strand of research on African international relations during this period.[20]

As the structures of world politics have shifted, and new emerging or great powers have interacted with Africa in different ways, a recurring concern within the discipline has been the agency of African states.[21] How do smaller states like Uganda, Cameroon, Malawi, and Mozambique exercise agency in world politics? How can we understand their role in international relations as proactive, rather than passive or as perennial victims? Some have done this

'Partnership Peacekeeping: Challenges and Opportunities in the United Nations-African Union Relationship', *African Affairs* 113, 451 (2014), pp. 254–78.

[18] Paul D. Williams, 'From Non-Intervention to Non-Indifference: The Origins and Development of the African Union's Security Culture', *African Affairs* 106, 423 (2007), pp. 253–79.

[19] Brown, 'Sovereignty Matters'; Pádraig Carmody, *The New Scramble for Africa* (Cambridge: Polity, 2011); Fantu Cheru and Cyril Obi, *The Rise of India and China in Africa: Challenges, Opportunities and Critical Interventions* (Zed Books, London, 2010); Scarlett Cornelissen, 'Awkward Embraces: Emerging and Established Powers and the Shifting Fortunes of Africa's International Relations in the Twenty-First Century', *Politikon* 36, 1 (2009), pp. 5–26; Michael Klare and Daniel Volman, 'America, China and the Scramble for Africa's Oil', *Review of African Political Economy* 33, 106 (2006), pp. 297–309; Ian Taylor, *Africa Rising: BRICS Diversifying Dependency* (James Currey, London, 2014).

[20] Deborah Bräutigam, *The Dragon's Gift: The Real Story of China in Africa* (Oxford University Press, Oxford, 2009); Julia Gallagher, 'Ruthless Player or Development Partner? Britain's Ambiguous Reaction to China in Africa', *Review of International Studies* 37, 5 (2011), pp. 2293–310; Daniel Large, 'Beyond "Dragon in the Bush": The Study of China–Africa Relations', *African Affairs* 107, 426 (2008), pp. 45–61.

[21] William Brown and Sophie Harman (eds), *African Agency in International Politics* (Routledge, Abingdon, 2013); Jonathan Fisher, 'Managing Donor Perceptions: Contextualising Uganda's 2007 Intervention in Somalia', *African Affairs* 111, 444 (2012), pp. 404–23.

through IR theory, such as Will Brown who shows that 'sovereignty remains a central organizing device in contemporary aid relations'.[22] Others have sought to go beyond traditional IR theory and explore alternative forms of African agency.

HYBRIDITY AND RESISTANCE IN AFRICA AND THE WORLD

A state-centric perspective, informed by long-standing assumptions from Western political theory about order and authority, progress and civilization, can only ever capture part of the picture of African politics, and it also works to continue to shape and produce the world which it claims to represent objectively. As such, African international politics has also provided inspiration for many to engage with more critical perspectives on world politics, and to explore ways of theorizing and studying African international relations without reproducing many of the biases and omissions of so-called "Eurocentric" theory.[23]

One of the most influential critical essays on Africa's international relations—to be published anywhere, let alone just in *African Affairs*—is Jean-François Bayart's article 'Africa in the world: a history of extraversion', which has been cited over 600 times since its publication in 2000. Bayart brings together Foucauldian and neo-Gramscian theory to write a history of African agency which is essentially global. His argument is that African agency is often 'extraverted', in which elites mobilize 'resources derived from their (possibly unequal) relationship with the external environment',[24] while rejecting the passive renditions of African politics produced by dependency theory approaches. Through strategies of exporting images of either democratic progress or horrific war—both of which have been used to inspire assistance and aid from external actors—African elites have gained economically and politically. As a sociologist rather than an IR theorist, Bayart rejects the state-centrism of classic IR theory and draws attention to the prominence of aid agencies, warlords, private military companies, NGOs, drug traffickers and people smugglers, and so on, in what he famously terms the *politique du*

---

[22] Brown, 'Sovereignty Matters', p. 282.

[23] Pinar Bilgin, 'Thinking Past "Western" IR?', *Third World Quarterly* 29, 1 (2007), pp. 5–23; Robbie Shilliam (ed.), *International Relations and Non-Western Thought: Imperialism, Colonialism and Investigations of Global Modernity* (Routledge, Abingdon, 2011); Amina Mama, 'Is it Ethical to Study Africa? Preliminary Thoughts on Scholarship and Freedom', *African Studies Review* 50, 1 (2007), pp. 1–26.

[24] Jean-François Bayart, 'Africa in the World: A History of Extraversion', *African Affairs* 99, 395 (2000), p. 218.

ventre.[25] This does not supplant or replace the sovereign African state, but reshapes and reconfigures it in a relation of unequal dependence and extraversion with the rest of the world.

Bayart's attention to how colonialism and its disciplinary mechanisms produced certain forms of subjects—both among colonized Africans and "enlightened" colonialists—is taken up by Rita Abrahamsen in another influential article which both reflected and inspired a resurgence of postcolonial theory in African IR. This article effectively dispelled some of the misunderstandings of postcolonial theory (that it necessarily entailed political conservatism, ahistorical generalizations, or baffling theoretical abstractions) and set out one of the clearest and most compelling elaborations of what a postcolonial perspective on power, discourse, and resistance mean for African politics, both domestic and international. The central claim of postcolonial theory, for Abrahamsen, is that the historical experience of colonialism (which is varied and never homogenous) has profoundly shaped and indeed produced the contemporary globalized world of both Africa and Europe.[26] This can be illustrated through the example of Zimbabwe: contemporary political discourses and identities in Zimbabwe remain profoundly shaped by the legacies of colonialism and anti-colonial struggle, as Mugabe's speeches make clear. But modern British identities and discourses are also a product of the experience of empire, whether through the wealth of the British state, a belief in the civilizing, liberalizing mission, or the anti-colonial stance of Clare Short who informed Mugabe in 1997 that the new Labour government was 'without links to former colonial interests'.[27] Abrahamsen's clear exposition of how postcolonial theorists such as Homi Bhabha, Gayatri Spivak, Edward Said, and Achille Mbembe can be used to produce a much richer, more critical, more historically informed picture of African international politics than the neorealist and neoliberal traditions of mainstream IR theory has produced a much more diverse field of African IR in the twenty-first century than was available in the twentieth.[28]

[25] Jean-François Bayart, *The State in Africa: The Politics of the Belly*, 2nd edition (Polity, Cambridge, 2009). See also Rita Abrahamsen and Michael C. Williams, *Security Beyond the State: Private Security in International Politics* (Cambridge University Press, Cambridge, 2011); Clapham, *Africa and the International System*, chapter 10.

[26] Rita Abrahamsen, 'African Studies and the Postcolonial Challenge', *African Affairs* 102, 407 (2003), p. 196.

[27] Julia Gallagher, *Zimbabwe's International Relations: Fantasy, Reality, and the Making of the State* (Cambridge University Press, Cambridge, 2016).

[28] Pal Ahluwalia, *Politics and Post-Colonial Theory: African Inflections* (Routledge, London, 2001); Jean Comaroff and John L. Comaroff, *Theory from the South; Or, How Euro-America is Evolving Toward Africa* (Paradigm, Boulder, CO, 2012); Carl Death, 'Governmentality at the Limits of the International: African Politics and Foucauldian Theory', *Review of International Studies* 39, 3 (2013), pp. 763–87; Clive Gabay and Carl Death (eds), *Critical Perspectives on African Politics: Liberal Interventions, State-Building and Civil Society* (Routledge, Abingdon, 2014); Julia Gallagher (ed.), *Images of Africa: Creation, Negotiation, and Subversion* (Manchester

AFRICAN AGENCY AND THE TRANSFORMATION
OF WORLD POLITICS

This diversity is illustrated by the four articles which follow. They encompass both traditional and more critical approaches to African IR, and include contributions by historians and geographers as well as political scientists and IR scholars. Each of them, in different ways, demonstrates one of the broader features of African IR: an insistence on showing African agency and how African political actors have shaped the world we live in, as well as being shaped by it.

The first article, 'What is the concept of globalization good for?', by historian Frederick Cooper, is an excellent place to start trying to understand Africa in the world. This is both because of what it has to say about Africa and global politics, as well as because it is a seminal article which has profoundly shaped subsequent writing on global studies and Africa. Cooper is a historian of colonialism and labour movements, writing from a critical perspective but (at times) equally scathing of postcolonial theory as well as the universalizing pretensions of theorists who claim that all societies are on the same journey to liberal democracy and free markets. In this article the concept of globalization—as deployed by neoliberals, social democrats, and postmodernists in the 1990s—is his target, and he concludes that it obscures more than it clarifies.

Cooper tells a global history, in which Africa was linked to the Caribbean and Asia by the "globalized" European empires of the seventeenth, eighteenth, and nineteenth centuries. In terms of labour and agricultural produce—slaves, sugar, and manufacturing—Africa was intimately bound up with the development of capitalism in Europe, and thus we must ask what has changed in the current epoch of neoliberal capitalism, and why. Cooper sees a "lumpy" world, in which transnational capitalist networks penetrate some areas quite densely and tail off elsewhere. As such, prescriptions by international financial institutions to open markets need to recognize both that African economies have always been globally connected, benefitting some people while costing others, as well as that some features of African economies can act as obstructions to the transnational flow of goods and labour.

The second article is a good example of the sort of nuanced research Cooper calls for, combining an awareness of changing global structures with an acute

University Press, Manchester, 2015); Siba Grovogui, *Beyond Eurocentrism and Anarchy: Memories of International Order and Institutions* (Palgrave Macmillan, New York, 2006); Achille Mbembe, *On the Postcolony* (University of California Press, Berkeley, CA, 2001); Paul Tiyambe Zeleza, 'Rewriting the African Diaspora: Beyond the Black Atlantic', *African Affairs* 104, 414 (2005), pp. 35–68.

eye for (and empirical research on) local agency and activism. Peace Medie presents the results of interviews with women's rights advocates, police officers, bureaucrats, staff of international organizations, and victims of violence in two Liberian counties, in order to show how non-state actors can influence policy at the implementation stage. She argues that weak state capacity can allow space for local and transnational women's movements to make progress in implementing norms against gender-based violence, which in the case of post-conflict Liberia have contributed to a lower rate of withdrawal of rape cases. This article is an important piece of empirical scholarship on everyday violence in post-conflict contexts, as well as the agency of non-state actors, but it also makes a broader theoretical point about the interaction of global networks with local political opportunity structures in producing progressive change in African politics. This more fine-grained analysis shows that agency exists and progress can happen, even in the context of global structures like capitalism, patriarchy, and racism.

The third article, by Giles Mohan and Ben Lampert, pays attention to a different sort of non-state African agency, in relation to Chinese economic power in Africa. As well as providing a useful overview of the state-of-the-art on China in Africa—a field which has exploded in the last decade—they make a critical argument that African actors have shaped Chinese flows of investment and migration. However, this agency is highly uneven and works to reinforce unequal economic and political relations, providing a salutary reminder that not all non-state activism produces progressive outcomes.

The final piece in Part IV is Tim Murithi's assessment of the AU's attempts to become a norm entrepreneur in the areas of peace and security, democracy, and human rights. Ending with the AU is fitting in several ways. First, the AU represents, at its best, the aspirations for a more unified and positive role for African leaders and states in global politics; not just "African solutions for African problems", but also a regional vehicle for promoting pan-African visions of global progress and security. Second, even for those sceptical of the degree to which the AU is able to articulate either coherent expressions of political agency or more idealist visions of political progress, understanding the new forms of power and authority which are increasingly taking regional rather than national or ethnic forms is an important element of contemporary African politics. Finally, the AU "project" encapsulates all the issues which the collection of essays in this book covers: overcoming the colonial legacy, development, globalization, transnational flows of goods and people (licit and illicit), conflict and security, democracy and good governance, and engaging with old and new external powers.

In this briefing Murithi concludes, quite reasonably, that although the AU has made some progress, 'the dream of African unity remains unfulfilled'. While the AU may seek to promote norms of peace, security, democracy, and development, it is limited by the self-interest of member states.[29] In this respect we might conclude that politics in Africa is quite typical of politics elsewhere in the world. At the time of writing this chapter both Europe and the US are embroiled in fundamental political disputes over who and what they represent in the world, and whether this is defined in terms of narrow self-interest or a more positive contribution to a global humanity. Some might suggest this is inherent to politics itself: realism and idealism, or the art of the possible as well as making the impossible imaginable.[30]

This is what makes the study of world politics—in domestic and international settings, and in settings which blur these artificial boundaries—so exciting and rewarding. Understanding and explaining African politics has been the central aim of *African Affairs* as a scholarly journal, but the journal has also insisted that scholarship is always political, and is always an intervention in the world. This sense of the political agency, and hence responsibility, of the researcher comes through in many of the articles in this volume, and it is also reflected in the work of the Royal African Society. In that sense it is perhaps not too idealistic to invoke Madiba's words, and hope that the study of African international politics can make a 'positive contribution to peace, prosperity and goodwill in the world'.[31]

---

[29] See also Touray, 'The Common African Defence and Security Policy'; Williams and Boutellis, 'Partnership Peacekeeping'.

[30] Contrast the Two Very Different Accounts of World Politics in Nathan, 'Interests, Ideas and Ideology' and Olsen, 'Europe and the Promotion of Democracy in Post Cold War Africa'.

[31] Mandela, 'South Africa's Future Foreign Policy', p. 97.

15

What Is the Concept of Globalization Good For?

An African Historian's Perspective

Frederick Cooper

THERE ARE TWO PROBLEMS WITH THE CONCEPT OF GLOBALIZATION, first the 'global', and second the '-ization'. The implication of the first is that a single system of connection—notably through capital and commodities markets, information flows, and imagined landscapes—has penetrated the entire globe; and the implication of the second is that it is doing so now, that this is the global age. There are certainly those, not least of them the advocates of unrestricted capital markets, who claim that the world should be open to them, but this does not mean that they have got their way. Nevertheless, many critics of market tyranny, social democrats who lament the alleged decline of the nation-state, and people who see the eruption of particularism as a counter-reaction to market homogenization, give the boasts of the globalizers too much credibility. Crucial questions do not get asked: about the limits of interconnection, about the areas where capital cannot go, and about the specificity of the structures necessary to make connections work.

Behind the globalization fad is an important quest for understanding the interconnectedness of different parts of the world, for explaining new mechanisms shaping the movement of capital, people, and culture, and for exploring institutions capable of regulating such transnational movement. What is missing in discussions of globalization today is the historical depth of interconnections and a focus on just what the structures and limits of the connecting mechanisms are. It is salutary to get away from whatever tendencies there may have been to analyze social, economic, political, and cultural processes as if they took place in national or continental containers; but to adopt a language that implies that there is no container at all, except the planetary one, risks defining problems in misleading ways. The world has long been—and still is—

a space where economic and political relations are very uneven; it is filled with lumps, places where power coalesces surrounded by those where it does not, where social relations become dense amidst others that are diffuse. Structures and networks penetrate certain places and do certain things with great intensity, but their effects tail off elsewhere.

The present article is written by a historian whose research has focused on the study of colonial empires, particularly in Africa. Specialists on Africa, among others, have been drawn into the globalization paradigm, positing 'globalization' as a challenge which Africa must meet, or else as a construct through which to understand Africa's place in a world whose boundaries are apparently becoming more problematic.[1] My concern here is with seeking alternative perspectives to a concept that emphasizes change over time but remains ahistorical, and which seems to be about space, but which ends up glossing over the mechanisms and limitations of spatial relationships. Africanists, I shall argue, should be particularly sensitive to the time-depth of cross-territorial processes, for the very notion of 'Africa' has itself been shaped for centuries by linkages within the continent and across oceans and deserts—by the Atlantic slave trade, by the movement of pilgrims, religious networks, and ideas associated with Islam, by cultural and economic connections across the Indian Ocean. The concept cannot, I will also argue, be salvaged by pushing it backwards in time, for the histories of the slave trade, colonizing, and decolonization, as well as the travails of the era of structural adjustment fit poorly any narrative of globalization—unless one so dilutes the term that it becomes meaningless. To study Africa is to appreciate the long-term importance of the exercise of power across space, but also the limitations of such power.[2] The relevance of this history today does not lie in assimilation of old (colonial) and new (global) forms of linkages but in the lessons it provides about both the importance and the boundedness of long-distance connections. Historical analysis does not present a contrast of a past of territorial boundedness with a present of interconnection and fragmentation,

---

[1] Both dimensions were evident in a conference on 'Social Sciences and the Challenges of Globalization in Africa', held in Johannesburg in September 1998 by the influential African research consortium, CODESRIA. The 2001 Congress of the Association of African Historians to be held in Bamako will devote itself to the theme 'African Historians and Globalization'. The conference announcement (from a posting on H-Africa) begins, 'Globalization is an omnipresent and inescapable fact'. For quite different examples of globalization in Africanist literature, see Caroline Thomas and Peter Wilkin, *Globalization, Human Security, and the African Experience* (Lynne Rienner, Boulder, CO, 1999) and Peter Geschiere and Birgit Meyer (eds), *Globalization and Identity: Dialectics of flow and closure* (Blackwell, Oxford, 1999).

[2] Colonial studies now offer not only an argument about the ways in which European societies, and other empires as well, were constituted across space, but also an argument about the limitations and incoherences of colonial systems. See Ann Stoler and Frederick Cooper, 'Between metropole and colony: rethinking a research agenda,' in F. Cooper and A. Stoler (eds), *Tensions of Empire: Colonial cultures in a bourgeois world* (University of California Press, Berkeley, CA, 1997), pp. 1–56.

but a more back-and-forth, varied combination of territorializing and deterritorializing tendencies.

Today, friends and foes of globalization debate 'its' effects. Both assume the reality of such a process, which can either be praised or lamented, encouraged or combated.[3] Are we asking the best questions about issues of contemporary importance when we debate globalization? Instead of assuming the centrality of a powerful juggernaut, might we do better to define more precisely what it is we are debating, to assess the resources which institutions in different locations within patterns of interaction possess, to look towards traditions of transcontinental mobilization with considerable time-depth?

Globalization is clearly a significant 'native's category' for anyone studying contemporary politics. Anyone wishing to know why particular ideological and discursive patterns appear in today's conjuncture needs to examine how it is used. But is it also a useful analytical category? My argument here is that it is not. Scholars who use it analytically risk being trapped in the very discursive structures they wish to analyze. Most important in the term's current popularity in academic circles is how much it reveals about the poverty of contemporary social science faced with processes that are large-scale, but not universal, and with the fact of crucial linkages that cut across state borders and lines of cultural difference but which nonetheless are based on specific mechanisms within certain boundaries. That global should be contrasted with local, even if the point is to analyze their mutual constitution, only underscores the inadequacy of current analytical tools to analyze anything in between.

Can we do better? I would answer with a qualified yes, but mainly if we seek concepts that are less sweeping, more precise, which emphasize both the nature of spatial linkages and their limits, which seek to analyze change with historical specificity rather than in terms of a vaguely defined and unattainable end-point.

---

[3] Early on, globalization was a particularly American fad, but it has become more 'global'. In France, for example, *'mondialisation'* is much debated in politics and increasingly in academic circles. If the 'pros' dominate the American debate, the 'antis' are prominent in France, and they even have their public hero, José Bové, arrested for wrecking a McDonalds. The Socialist Government argues that globalization can and should be regulated and controlled, but it does not question 'its' reality. See 'Procès Bové: la fête de l'antimondialisation', *Le Monde*, 30 June 2000; 'Gouverner les forces qui sont à l'oeuvre dans la mondialisation', *Le Monde*, 27 June 2000. For different uses of the globalization concept by French academics, see GEMDEV (Groupement Economie Mondiale, Tiers-Monde, Développement), *Mondialisation: Les mots et les choses* (Karthala, Paris, 1999); Serge Cordellier (ed.), *La mondialisation au delà des mythes* (La Découverte, Paris, 2000, orig. 1997); Jean-Pierre Faugère, Guy Caire, et Bertrand Bellon (eds), *Convergence et diversité à l'heure de la mondialisation* (Economica, Paris, 1997); Philippe Chantpie *et al.*, *La nouvelle politique économique: l'état face à la mondialisation* (PUF, Paris, 1997).

Views of globalization

The first way in which globalization is frequently talked about can be termed the Banker's Boast. With the collapse of the Soviet Union and the market orientation of Communist China, investments supposedly can go anywhere. Pressure from the United States, the IMF, and transnational corporations brings down national barriers to the movement of capital. This is in part an argument for a new regulatory regime, one which lowers barriers to capital as well as trade flow, and which operates on a global level. It is also an argument about discipline: the world market, conceived of as a web of transactions, now forces governments to conform to its dictates. 'Globalization' is invoked time and time again to tell rich countries to roll back the welfare state and poor ones to reduce social expenditures—all in the name of the necessities of competition in a globalized economy.[4]

Next comes the Social Democrat's Lament. This accepts the reality of globalization as the bankers see it, but instead of claiming that it is beneficial for humankind, it argues the reverse. The social democratic left has devoted much of its energy to using citizenship to blunt the brutality of capitalism. Social movements thus aim for the nation-state, the institutional basis for enforcing social and civic rights. Whereas the enhanced role of the nation-state reflected organized labour's growing place within the polity, 'globalization' has allegedly undermined the social project by marginalizing the political one. In some renderings, globalization must therefore be fought, while, in others, it has already triumphed and there is little to do except lament the passing of the nation-state, of national trade union movements, of empowered citizenries.[5]

---

[4] This is the version of globalization one sees in the newspapers every day, and it can be found in vivid form in the book by *New York Times'* correspondent Thomas Friedman, *The Lexus and the Olive Tree* (Ferrar, Straus & Giroux, New York, 1999). However, the pro-business *The Economist* has long held a more sceptical view, for it thinks the economy is not globalized enough. Among academic economists, advocates of globalization include Paul Krugman, *Pop Internationalism* (MIT Press, Cambridge, MA, 1996) and Kenichi Ohmae, *The Borderless World: Power and strategy in the interlinked world economy* (Harper, New York, 1990). See also Organization for Economic Co-operation and Development, *Toward a New Global Age: Challenges and opportunities (Policy Report)* (OECD, Paris, 1997).

[5] Susan Strange exaggerates the decline of the state but provides a valuable analysis of 'non-state authorities'. She finds the word 'globalization' hopelessly vague. Saskia Sassen embraces 'globalization' and treats it as a causative agent ('Globalization has transformed the meaning of....'). But much of her work consists of useful and insightful discussion of the intersection in cities of transnational migration and financial movements, as well as of the problems of regulation of interstate economic activities. She too emphasizes the declining relevance of states. See Susan Strange, *The Retreat of the State* (Cambridge University Press, Cambridge, 1996); Saskia Sassen, *Globalization and Its Discontents* (New Press, New York, 1998). For other versions of the decline of states see David Held, *Democracy and the Global Order* (Polity Press, Cambridge, 1995); Scott Lash and John Urry, *Economies of Signs and Space* (Sage, London, 1994); Bertrand Badie, *Un monde sans souveraineté: Les états entre ruse et responsabilité* (Fayard, Paris,

Finally comes the Dance of the Flows and the Fragments. This argument accepts much of the other two—the reality of globalization in the present and its destabilizing effect on national societies—but makes another move. Rather than homogenize the world, globalization reconfigures the local. But not in a spatially confined way. People's exposures to media—to dress, to music, to fantasies of the good life—are highly fragmented; bits of imagery are detached from their context, all the more attractive because of the distant associations they evoke. Hollywood imagery influences people in the African bush; tropical exoticism sells on rue du Faubourg St Honoré. This detachment of cultural symbolism from spatial locatedness paradoxically makes people realize the value of their cultural particularity. Hence a sentimental attachment to 'home' by migrants who do not live there but who contribute money and energy to identity politics. As flows of capital, people, ideas, and symbols move separately from one another, the dance of fragments takes place within a globalized, unbounded space.[6]

There is something in each of these conceptions. What is wrong with them is their totalizing pretensions and their presentist periodization. The relationship of territory and connectivity has been reconfigured many times; each deserves particular attention.[7] Changes in capital markets, transnational corporations, and communications in recent decades deserve careful attention, but one should not forget the vast scale on which investment and production decisions were made by the Dutch East Indies Company—linking the Netherlands, Indonesia, and South Africa and connecting to ongoing trading networks throughout south-east Asia—in the sixteenth century. Some scholars argue that the 'really big leap to more globally integrated commodity and factor markets' was in the second half of the nineteenth century, that 'world capital markets were almost certainly as well integrated in the 1890s as they were in the 1990s'. Such arguments work better for OECD countries than elsewhere and do not adequately express qualitative change, but economic historians still stress that the great period of expansion of international trade and investment—and their importance to shaping economic interdependence— was the decades before 1913, followed by a dramatic loss of economic

---

1999). For one of many examples of the denunciatory mode of globalization literature, see Richard Falk, *Predatory Globalization: A critique* (Polity Press, Cambridge, 1999).

[6] Arjun Appadurai, *Modernity at Large: Cultural dimensions of globalization* (University of Minnesota Press, Minneapolis, MN, 1996). What is striking to an historian about this book is Appadurai's assertion of newness without the slightest effort to examine the past and his preference for inventing a new vocabulary (ethnoscapes, etc.) to characterize phenomena at a global level rather than making a sustained effort to describe the mechanisms by which connections occur. A related approach is used by two Africanists in Geschiere and Meyer, *Globalization and Identity.*

[7] Some observers describe the present age as one of the 'annihilation of space by time'. That, of course, is a nineteenth-century idea—from Marx—and space-time compression has had many moments. See David Harvey, *The Condition of Postmodernity* (Blackwell, Oxford, 1989).

integration after that date. For all the growth in international trade in recent decades, as a percentage of world GDP it has only barely regained levels found before the First World War. Paul Bairoch emphasizes 'fast internationalization alternating with drawback' rather than evidence of 'globalization as an irreversible movement'. The extensive work now being done on specific patterns of production, trade, and consumption, on national and international institutions, and on existing and possible forms of regulation is salutary; fitting it all into an '-ization' framework puts the emphasis where it does not belong.[8]

The movement of people, as well as capital, reveals the lumpiness of cross-border connections, not a pattern of steadily increasing integration. The highpoint of intercontinental labour migration was the century after 1815. Now, far from seeing a world of falling barriers, labour migrants have to take seriously what states can do. France, for example, raised its barriers very high in 1974, whereas in the supposedly less globalized 1950s Africans from French colonies, as citizens, could enter France and were much in demand in the labour market. Aside from family reconstitution, labour migrations to France have become 'residual'.[9] Clandestine migration is rampant, but the clandestine migrant cannot afford the illusion that states and institutions matter less than 'flows'. Illegal (and legal) migration depends on networks that take people to some places but not others. Other sorts of movements of people follow equally specific paths. Movements of diasporic Chinese, within and beyond south-east Asia, are based on social and cultural strategies that enable mobile business-men and migrating workers to adjust to different sovereignties while maintaining linkages among themselves. As Aihwa Ong argues, such movements do not reflect the diminishing power of the states whose frontiers they cross, or undermine those states; rather, such states have found new ways of exercising power over people and commodities.[10] We need to understand these institutional mechanisms, and the metaphor of 'global' is a bad way to start.

The deaths of the nation-state and the welfare state are greatly exaggerated. The resources controlled by governments have never been higher. In OECD countries in 1965, governments collected and spent a little over 25 percent of GDP; this has increased steadily, reaching close to 37 percent in the supposed-ly global mid-1990s.[11] Welfare expenditures remain at all-time highs in France

---

[8] Kevin H. O'Rourke and Jeffrey G. Williamson, *Globalization and History: The evolution of a nineteenth-century Atlantic economy* (MIT Press, Cambridge, MA, 1999), pp. 2, 4; Paul Bairoch, 'Globalization myths and realities: one century of external trade and foreign investment', in Robert Boyer and Daniel Drache (eds), *States against Markets: The limits of globalization* (Routledge, London, 1996), p. 190. See also Paul Hirst and Grahame Thompson, *Globalization in Question* (Polity Press, Cambridge, 1996) and Kevin R. Cox, *Spaces of Globalization: Reasserting the power of the local* (Guilford Press, New York, 1997).

[9] *Le Monde*, 20 June 2000.

[10] Aihwa Ong, *Flexible Citizenship: The cultural logics of transnationality* (Duke University Press, Durham, NC, 1999).

[11] 'A survey of globalisation and tax', *The Economist*, 29 January 2000, p. 6.

and Germany, where even marginal reductions are hotly contested by labour unions and social democratic parties and where even conservatives treat the basic edifice as a given. The reason for this is contrary to both the Banker's Boast and the Social Democrat's Lament: politics. This point has been emphasized in regard to Latin America: both France and Brazil face tough international competition, but in France the welfare state can be defended within the political system, whereas in Brazil 'globalization' becomes the rationale for dismantling state services and refraining from the obvious alternative—taxing the wealthy. In the more developed Latin American countries, taxes as a percentage of GNP are less than half the levels of western Europe.[12] There are alternatives to acting in the name of globalization, which the Brazilian state has chosen not to pursue.

But one should not make the opposite mistake and assume that in the past the nation-state enjoyed a period of unchallenged salience and unquestioned reference for political mobilization. Going back to the anti-slavery movements of the eighteenth and early nineteenth centuries, political movements have been transnational, sometimes focused on the 'empire' as a unit, sometimes on 'civilization', sometimes on a universalized humanity. Diasporic imaginations go well back too; the importance of deterritorialized conceptions of 'Africa' to African Americans from the 1830s is a case in point.

What stands against globalization arguments should not be an attempt to stuff history back into national or continental containers. It will not fit. The question is whether the changing meaning over time of spatial linkages can be understood in a better way than globalization.

Globalization is itself a term whose meaning is not clear and over which substantial disagreements exist among those who use it. It can be used so broadly that it embraces everything and therefore means nothing. But for most writers, it carries a powerful set of images, if not a precise definition. Globalization talk takes its inspiration from the fall of the Berlin Wall, which offered the possibility or maybe the illusion that barriers to cross-national economic relations were falling. For friend and foe alike, the ideological framework of globalization is liberalism—arguments for free trade and free movement of capital. The imagery of globalization derives from the World Wide Web, the idea that the web-like connectivity of every site to every other site represents a model for all forms of global communication. Political actors and scholars differ on 'its' effects: diffusion of the benefits of growth versus increasing concentration of wealth, homogenization of culture versus diversification. But if the word means anything, it means expanding integration, and integration on a planetary scale. Even differentiation, the globalizers argue, must be

---

[12] Atilio Boron, 'Globalization: A Latin American perspective'. Unpublished paper for CODESRIA conference, Johannesburg, South Africa, 1998.

seen in a new light, for the new emphasis on cultural specificity and ethnic identification differs from the old in that its basis now is juxtaposition, not isolation.

For all its emphasis on the newness of the last quarter-century, the current interest in the concept of globalization recalls a similar infatuation in the 1950s and 1960s: modernization.[13] Both are '-ization' words, emphasizing a process, not necessarily fully realized yet but ongoing and probably inevitable. Both name the process by its supposed endpoint. Both were inspired by a clearly valid and compelling observation—that change is rapid and pervasive—and both depend for their evocative power on a sense that change is not a series of disparate elements but the movement of them in a common direction. Modernization theory failed to do the job that theory is supposed to do, and its failure should be an illuminating one for scholars working in the globalization framework. Modernization theory's central argument was that key elements of society varied together and this clustering produced the movement from traditional to modern societies: from subsistence to industrial economies, from predominantly rural to predominantly urban societies, from extended to nuclear families, from ascriptive to achieved status, from sacred to secular ideologies, from the politics of the subject to the politics of the participant, from diffuse and multifaceted to contractual relationships.

The flaws of modernization theory parallel those of globalization. The key variables of transition did not vary together, as much research has shown. Most important, modernization, like globalization, appears in this theory as a process that just happens, something self-propelled. Modernization talk masked crucial questions of the day: were its criteria Eurocentric, or even more so, based on an idealized vision of what American society was supposed to be like? Was change along such lines just happening or was it being driven—by American military might or the economic power of capitalist corporations?

The contents of the two approaches are obviously different and I do not wish to push the parallel beyond the observation that modernization and globalization represent similar stances in relation to broad processes. Both define themselves by naming a future as an apparent projection of a present, which is sharply distinguished from the past. For the social scientist, the issue is whether such theories encourage the posing of better, more precise questions or slide over the most interesting and problematic issues about our time.

---

[13] Dean Tipps, 'Modernization theory and the comparative study of societies: a critical perspective', *Comparative Studies in Society and History* 15 (1973), pp. 199–226.

Capitalism in an Atlantic spatial system—and beyond

So let me start somewhere else, with C. L. R. James and Eric Williams.[14] Their books are both solidly researched analyses and political texts. I intend to talk about them in both senses, to emphasize how reading them allows us to juxtapose space and time in a creative way. James was born in the British colony of Trinidad in 1901. He was a Pan-Africanist and a Trotskyite, an activist in anti-imperialist movements in the 1930s that linked Africa, Europe, and the Caribbean. *Black Jacobins* (1938) was a history of the Haitian revolution, from 1791 to 1804, and it showed that in the eighteenth century as much as the twentieth economic processes and political mobilization both crossed oceans.

To James, slavery in the Caribbean was not an archaic system. The organizational forms that became characteristic of modern industrial capitalism—massed labourers working under supervision, time-discipline in cultivation and processing, year-round planning of tasks, control over residential as well as productive space—were pioneered on Caribbean sugar estates as much as in English factories. The slaves were African; the capital came from France; the land was in the Caribbean. Eric Williams, historian and later prime minister of Trinidad, elaborated the process by which the trans-Atlantic connections were forged, arguing that the slave trade helped bring about capitalist development in England, and eventually the industrial revolution.

Slavery was not new in Africa or in Europe. What was new was the interrelationship of Africa, Europe, and the Americas which changed the way actors in all places acted, forced a change in scale, and gave a relentless logic to the expansion of the system into the nineteenth century.

When the declaration of the rights of man and of the citizen was being discussed in Paris, it did not occur to most participants that the categories might embrace people in the colonies. But colonials thought they did, first planters who saw themselves as property-owning Frenchmen, entitled to voice the interests of their colony vis-à-vis the French state, then the *gens de couleurs*, property-owning people of mixed origin, who saw themselves as citizens too, irrespective of race. Then slaves became aware both of universalistic discourse about rights and citizenship coming from Paris and of the weakening of the state as republicans, royalists, and different planters fought with each other. James stresses the 'Jacobin' side of the rebellion: the serious debate in Paris over whether the field of application of the universal

---

[14] C. L. R. James, *The Black Jacobins: Toussaint L'Ouverture and the San Domingo revolution* (Vintage, New York, 1963, orig. 1938); Eric Williams, *Capitalism and Slavery* (University of North Carolina Press, Chapel Hill, NC, 1944). See also Robin Blackburn, *The Making of New World Slavery: From the baroque to the modern* (Verso, London, 1997).

declaration was bounded or not, the seizure by slaves of this discourse of rights, the mixture of ideals and strategy which led a French governor to abolish slavery in 1793 and try to rally slaves to the cause of Republican France, and the multi-sided and shifting struggle of slave-led armies, full of alliances and betrayals, which ended in the independence of Haiti. He mentioned that two-thirds of the slaves at the time of the revolution were born in Africa, but he was not particularly interested in that fact or its implications.

The year of *Black Jacobins'* publication, 1938, was the centenary of Britain's decision to end the intermediary status, 'apprenticeship', through which slaves passed as they were emancipated. The British Government, which had for years emphasized its emancipatory history, now banned all celebrations of the centenary. A series of strikes and riots had taken place in the West Indies and central Africa between 1935 and 1938; celebrating emancipation might have called attention to the meagreness of its fruits. James brings this out in his text. His intervention tied a history of liberation accomplished in 1804 to the liberation he hoped to see—in the British as well as the French empires—in his own time.

His text had another significance. Haiti did not go down in history as the vanguard of emancipation and decolonization; for colonial elites it was the symbol of backwardness and for nineteenth-century abolitionists an embarrassment. James wanted to change that record, to make the Haitian revolution a modern uprising against a modern form of exploitation, the vanguard of a universal process. Michel-Rolph Trouillot has called attention to what James left out in order to do this, what he calls the 'war within the war', another layer of rebellion by slaves of African origin who rejected the compromises the leadership was making—for it was seeking to preserve plantation production, to preserve some kind of state structure, and maybe to preserve some kind of relationship with the French—something these slaves rejected. Trouillot notes that the upper class of Haiti likes to claim direct descent from the nationalists of 1791; to do so takes a deliberate act of silencing.[15]

Much as James left out for his 1938 purposes, he disrupts present-day notions of historical time and space in a fruitful way. The revolution took place too early. It began only two years after the storming of the Bastille. The nation-state was being transcended as it was being born; the universe to which the rights of man applied was extended even as those rights were being specified; slaves were claiming a place in the polity before political philosophers had decided whether they belonged; and transoceanic movements of ideas were having an effect while territorially defined social movements were still coming into their own. Many of the questions being debated in James's

---

[15] Michel-Rolph Trouillot, *The Silences of the Past: The power and the production of history* (Beacon, Boston, MA, 1995); Carolyn E. Fick, *The Making of Haiti:The Saint Domingue revolution from below* (University of Tennessee Press, Knoxville, TN, 1990).

time were already posed, with great forcefulness, between 1791 and 1804. So too some of the questions James did not want to pose, as Trouillot has reminded us.

Looking at 1791 and 1938 together allows us to see politics in cross-continental spatial perspective, not as a binary opposition of local authenticity against global domination, and to emphasize struggle over the meaning of ideas as much as their transmission across space. The French Revolution installed liberty and citizenship in the lexicon of politics, but it did not fix their meanings, the spatial limits of the concepts, or the cultural criteria necessary for their application. If some political currents—in 1791 or 2001—sought a narrow, territorially or culturally bounded definition of the rights-bearing citizen, others—in 1791 or 2001—developed deterritorialized political discourses. This dialectic of territorialization and deterritorialization has undergone many shifts ever since.

James's argument is an 'Atlantic' one, Williams's as well. Both emphasize a specific set of connections, with world-wide implications, to be sure, but the historical actuality of which is more precisely rooted. The development of capitalism is at the core of their argument: capital formation via the African-European-American slave trade, the interconnectedness of labour supply, production, and consumption, and the invention of forms of work discipline in both field and factory. The struggle *against* this transoceanic capitalism was equally transoceanic.

Atlantic perspectives have been considerably extended via Sidney Mintz's analysis of the effects of Caribbean sugar on European culture, class relations, and economy, and Richard Price's studies of the cultural connections of the Caribbean world. Such studies do not point to the mere transmission of culture across space (as in other scholars' search for 'African elements' in Caribbean cultures), but look instead at an intercontinental zone in which cultural inventiveness, synthesis, and adaptation take place, both reflecting and altering power relations.[16]

The Atlantic perpective does not necessarily have this ocean at its core. There were many shorelines and islands that were all but bypassed by the colonizing/enslaving/trading/producing/consuming system, even at its eighteenth-century peak. And there were places in other oceans (such as Indian Ocean sugar-producing islands) that were 'Atlantic' in structure, even if they were in another ocean. Powerful as the forces James and Williams

---

[16] Sidney Mintz, *Sweetness and Power* (Penguin, New York, 1985); Richard Price, *First-time: The historical vision of an Afro-American people* (Johns Hopkins University Press, Baltimore, MD, 1983). For a more recent perspective, see Michael A. Gomez, *Exchanging Our Country Marks: The transformation of African identities in the colonial and antebellum south* (University of North Carolina Press, Chapel Hill, NC, 1998).

wrote about, they had their histories, their limitations, their weaknesses. One can, as these authors show, write about large-scale, long-term processes without overlooking specificity, contingency, and contestation.

Oceans, continents, and intertwined histories

But the history of long-distance connections goes back further than the history of capitalism centred in northwestern Europe and the Atlantic Ocean. Take the following sentence from a historian's article: 'There have been few times in history when the world has been so closely interconnected—not only economically, but also in culture and tradition'.[17] Is she writing about the 'globalization' era of the late twentieth century? Actually, it is about the Mongol empires of the fourteenth century: an imperial system stretching from China to central Europe, laced with trade routes and featuring linked belief systems—a marriage of kinship and warrior ideology from East Asia and Islamic learning and law from western Asia—a balance of nomadic, agricultural, and urban economies, and a communications system based on relays of horsemen that kept the imperial centre informed.

Analyzing regional connections and culture, in large empires or networks of trade and religious linkages, means coming to grips with the lumpiness of power and economic relations and the way such asymmetries have shifted over time.[18] Attempts to posit a transition from multiple worlds to a single world system with a core and a periphery have been mechanistic and inadequate to understand the unevenness and the dynamics of such a spatial system. Rather than argue for a sixteenth- or seventeenth-century world system—and then assign causal weight to the logic of the system itself—one can argue that structures of power and exchange were not so global and not so systematic and that what was new was in the domain of political imagination.[19] With the widespread Portuguese and Dutch voyages and conquests, it became possible to think of the world as the ultimate unit of ambition and

---

[17] B. A. F. Manz, 'Temur and the problem of a conqueror's legacy', *Journal of the Royal Asiatic Society* 8, pt.1 (1998), p. 22.

[18] For an illuminating study of unevenness within a sea-borne regional system in southeast Asia—of the differential impact of political power and the multiple forms of connection and pilgrimage as much as trade—see Sanjay Subrahmanyam, 'Notes on circulation and asymmetry in two "Mediterraneans", 1400–1800', in Claude Guillot, Denys Lombard, and Roderich Ptak (eds), *From the Mediterranean to the China Sea* (Harrassowitz, Wiesbaden, Germany, 1999), pp. 21–43.

[19] Critiques of world-system theory in some ways parallel those of modernization and globalization. See, for example, Frederick Cooper, Allen Isaacman, Florencia Mallon, Steve Stern and William Roseberry, *Confronting Historical Paradigms: Peasants, labor, and the capitalist world system in Africa and Latin America* (University of Wisconsin Press, Madison, WI, 1993).

political and economic strategy. But it still required considerable scientific progress, in cartography for example, to give content to such imaginings, let alone to act on such a basis. The relationship among different regional trading systems, religious networks, projections of power, and geographical under-standings presents a complex and highly uneven historical pattern.

Empires are a particular kind of spatial system, boundary-crossing and also bounded. There is now abundant scholarship on their ambiguity: their structure emphasizes difference and hierarchy, yet they also constitute a single political unit, and hence a potential unit of moral discourse. Jurists in Spain from the sixteenth to the eighteenth century debated the moral authority of an imperial ruler to subordinate certain subjects but not others, to take the land of some but not others. Imperial forces often recognized and profited from pre-existing circuits of commerce, but they could also be threatened by networks which they did not control and by the unpredictable effects of interaction between agents of empire and indigenous commercial and political actors. Empires generated creole societies which might distance themselves from the metropole even as they claimed 'civilizational' authority by association with it.[20]

A seminal intervention into these issues—in some ways breathing new life into the James-Williams argument—comes from a historian of China, Kenneth Pomeranz. He notes that the economies of Europe and China before 1800 operated in quite different ways, but that it makes little sense to say that one was better, more powerful, or more capable of investment and innovation than the other. Instead of a single centre of a world economy, he finds several centres with their own peripheries. The central regions in China and those in north-western Europe were not notably unequal in their access to the resources needed for industrialization. But after 1800, they diverged. He argues that different kinds of relations with regional peripheries shape this divergence. China's trading and political connections with south-east Asia brought it into relation-ship with a periphery that was in many ways too similar: rice-growing, trade-oriented communities. European expansion, however, both built and built upon differentiation, in terms of ecology and of labour. The slave plantation in European colonies developed resource complementarities with key regions in Europe that the Chinese empire could not emulate. China could not overcome resource blockages in food and fuel that the industrializing regions of western Europe were able to surmount. The different forms of imperial projection—the specific blockages overcome or not overcome—shaped the divergence.[21]

[20] Anthony Pagden, *Spanish Imperialism and the Political Imagination* (Yale University Press, New Haven, CT, 1990); Benedict Anderson, *Imagined Communities: Reflections on the origin and spread of nationalism* (Verso, London, 1983).
[21] Kenneth Pomeranz, *The Great Divergence: Europe, China, and the making of the modern world economy* (Princeton University Press, Princeton, NJ, 2000).

Africa's place within such a picture is crucial: the possibility of moving, by force, labour from Africa to parts of the Americas (where indigenous populations had been marginalized or killed off) allowed European empires to develop labour complementarities and to turn land complementarities into something useable. African slaves grew sugar on Caribbean islands that supplied English workers with calories and stimulants. But how could such a frightful complementarity come about? Only with powerful commercial and navigational systems to connect parts of this Atlantic system. Only with an institutional apparatus—the colonial state—capable of backing up the coercive capability of individual Caribbean slaveowners, of defining an increasingly racialized system of law that marked enslaved Africans and their descendants in a particular way, and of enforcing property rights across different parts of an imperial system, but whose power was vulnerable in ways which James pointed out. Only by developing connections with African states, mostly unconquered, and African trading systems, and then by influencing those relationships in a powerful—and horrendous—manner.[22]

But to understand the contrast, and the interrelation, of coastal West Africa and the heartlands of capitalist agriculture and early industrialization in England, one must look at the ways in which production was organized, not just the way it fitted into a wide spatial system. Marx stressed the importance in the seventeenth and eighteenth centuries of 'primitive accumulation', the separation of producers from the means of production. It was this process which forced the possessors of land and the possessors of labour power to face each day the necessity to combine their assets with some degree of efficiency. Feudal landlords, slaveowners, and peasants all could respond, or not respond, to market incentives, but capitalists and workers were trapped.

One can argue that in most of Africa one is at the other extreme, and therefore Africa should play a crucial role in the study of capitalism, however paradoxical this might appear in 2001. For a combination of social and geographic reasons, what Albert Hirschman calls the 'exit option' was particularly open in Africa.[23] There were a few places with the resources for prosperity, but many places with adequate resources for survival, and corporate kinship structures made mobility into a collective process. Africa's islands of exploitation were linked by trading diasporas and other sociocultural linkages, so that movement and the juggling of alternative political and economic possibilities remained key strategies. This does not mean that Africa was a continent of tranquil villages, for efforts were being made to overcome

---

[22] The argument is spelled out in Cooper's essay in *Confronting Historical Paradigms*. For a related argument emphasizing the historical depth of contemporary patterns, see Jean-François Bayart, 'Africa in the world: a history of extraversion', *African Affairs* **99** (2000), pp. 216–67.

[23] Albert O. Hirschman, *Exit, Voice, and Loyalty* (Harvard University Press, Cambridge, MA, 1970).

precisely the challenges of kinship groups and physical dispersal. The would-be king tried to get a hold on detached people—those who fell foul of kinship group elders or whose own groups had fallen apart—to build a patrimonial following. But anyone who built up land resources had to face the problem that labourers would flee or use their corporate strength to resist subordination. Expanding production often meant bringing in outsiders, often through enslavement. Power depended on controlling the external.

And here we have an intertwining of histories that cannot simply be compared. By the seventeenth and eighteenth centuries the British economy was prepared to use its overseas connections in a more dynamic way than the Iberian imperialists of an earlier epoch. African kings were vulnerable at home and found strength in their external connections. The slave trade meant different things to different partners: for the African king it meant gaining resources (guns, metals, cloth and other goods with redistributive potential) by seizing someone else's human assets, not by facing the difficulties of subordinating one's own population. Raiding slaves from another polity and selling them to an outside buyer externalized the supervision problem as well as the recruitment problem. Over time, the external market had increasing effects on the politics and economics of parts of west and central Africa, unpredictable to the rulers who first became enmeshed in this transatlantic system. It fostered militarized states and more efficient slave trading mechanisms. This was, from the point of view of African participants in the process, the unintended consequence of the fatal intertwining: outlets for war captives created a new and insidious logic that began to drive the entire system of slave catching and slave marketing.

So while one set of structures was enhanced in Africa by the slave trade, another set—the 'modern' instititutions of production, commercialization, and capital movement described by James and Williams—developed between the Caribbean and Europe. The Atlantic system depended on the connection of vastly different systems of production and power and had different consequences at each point in the system.

When Europeans finally decided in the early nineteenth century that the slave trade was immoral, the odium of it was attached to Africans who continued to engage in such practices, and Africans moved from being the Enslaveable Other to the Enslaving Other, an object for humanitarian denunciation and intervention.[24] What was most 'global' in the nineteenth century was not the actual structure of economic and political interaction, but the language in which slavery was discussed by its opponents: a language of shared humanity and the rights of man, evoked by a transatlantic social movement,

---

[24] Frederick Cooper, Thomas Holt, and Rebecca Scott, *Beyond Slavery: Explorations of race, labour, and citizenship in post-emancipation societies* (University of North Carolina Press, Chapel Hill, NC, 2000).

Euro-American and Afro-American. This language was used first to expunge an evil from European empires and the Atlantic system and, from the 1870s onwards, to save Africans from their alleged tyranny towards each other. The actual impetus and mechanisms of European conquests were of course more particular than that. Colonial invasions entailed the concentration of military power in small spaces, the movement of colonial armies onward, and a strikingly unimpressive colonial capacity to exercise power systematically and routinely over the territories under European rule. A 'globalizing' language stood alongside a structure of domination and exploitation that was lumpy in the extreme.

This is little more than a sketch of a complex history. From the sixteenth-century slave trade through the nineteenth-century period of imperialism in the name of emancipation, the interrelation of different parts of the world was essential to the histories of each part of it. But the mechanisms of interrelation were contingent and limited in their transformative capacity—as they still are. In this sense, the Atlantic system was not entirely systematic, nor was it an eighteenth-century 'globalization'.

Doing history backwards: colonization and the 'antecedents' of globalization

Scholars working within globalization paradigms differ over whether the present should be considered the latest of a series of globalizations, each more inclusive than the last, or a global age distinct from a past in which economic and social relations were contained within nation-states or empires and in which interaction took place among such internally coherent units. Both conceptions share the same problem: writing history backwards, taking an idealized version of the 'globalized present' and working backwards to show either how everything led up to it ('proto-globalization') or how everything, up to the arrival of the global age itself, deviated from it. In neither version does one watch history unfold over time, producing dead ends as well as pathways leading somewhere, creating conditions and contingencies in which actors made decisions, mobilized other people, and took actions which both opened up and constrained future possibilities.[25]

---

[25] An example of ascending globalizations can be found in the GEMDEV volume (*Mondialisation*), where Michel Beaud writes of 'several globalizations', and about 'archeo-globalizations' and 'proto-globalizations' (p. 11). In the same book, Gérard Kébabdjian makes the opposite argument, distinguishing between today's 'globalized' structure and colonial economies, which entailed exchange within bounded regimes (pp. 54–5). A variant between the two, in the same book, comes from Jean-Louis Margolin, who looks for 'preceding phases of globalization' and then writes of 'the distortion into colonial imperialism of the strong globalizing wave coming

Let us take an example from where I left off in the last section: the colonizations by European powers in Africa in the late nineteenth century. At first glance, this fits a metahistory of integration—however ugly some of its forms may have been—of apparently isolated regions into what was becoming a singular, European-dominated 'globality'. Colonial ideologists themselves claimed that they were 'opening up' the African continent. But colonization does not fit the interactive imagery associated with globalization. Colonial conquests imposed territorial borders on long-distance trading networks within Africa and monopolies on what was then a growing external trade, damaging or destroying more articulated trading systems crossing the Indian Ocean and the Sahara desert and along the West African coast. Africans were forced into imperial economic systems focused on a single European metropole. More profoundly, colonial territories were highly disarticulated politically, socially, and economically: colonizers made their money by focusing investment and infrastructure on extremely narrow, largely extractive, forms of production and exchange.[26] They taught some indigenous peoples some of what they needed to interact with Europeans, and then tried to isolate them from others whose division into allegedly distinct cultural and political units ('tribes') was emphasized and institutionalized. There might be a better case for calling colonization 'deglobalization' than globalization, except that the prior systems were constituted out of specific networks, with their own mechanisms and limits, and that colonial economies were in reality cross-cut by numerous networks of exchange and socio-cultural interaction (also dependent on specific mechanisms and bounded in particular ways). To study colonization *is* to study the reorganization of space, the forging and unforging of linkages; to call it globalization, distorted globalization, or deglobalization is to measure colonization against an abstract standard with little relation to historical processes.

Was decolonization a step towards globalization? It was literally a step toward *internationalization*, that is, a new relationship of nation-states, which is what globalizers, with reason, try to distinguish from globalization. Newly independent states were at pains to emphasize their national quality, and economic policy often relied on import-substitution industrialization and other distinctly national strategies to shape such an economic unit.

---

from the industrial and political revolutions' (p. 127), of 'the aborted globalization surrounding Europe, 1850–1914' (p. 130), then of the 'quasi-retreat of the global economy by a third of Humanity' (under Communism, pp. 127, 130, 131). He ends up with a dazzling non-sequitur: 'All this prepared the globalization, "properly speaking", of today' (p. 132). All three variants reduce history to teleology with little understanding of how human beings act in their own times and their own contexts.

[26] On agriculture in colonial and postcolonial Africa—notably the importance of 'exploitation without dispossession'—see Sara Berry, *No Condition is Permanent: The social dynamics of agrarian change in sub-Saharan Africa* (University of Wisconsin Press, Madison, WI, 1993).

Does the era of Structural Adjustment Plans, imposed on now hapless African states by international financial institutions such as the IMF, at last represent the triumph of globalization on a resistant continent? That certainly was the goal: IMF policy is consistent with the Banker's Boast, an imposed lowering of barriers to capital flows, reduction of tariff barriers, and aligning of currency on world markets.

But was that the effect? It takes a big leap to go from the Banker's Boast to a picture of actual integration. In fact, Africa's contribution to world trade and its intake of investment funds were *larger* in the days of national economic policy than in the days of economic openness.[27] Shall we call this the age of globalizing deglobalization in Africa, or of distorted globalization? Is Africa the exception that proves the rule, the unglobalized continent, and is it paying a heavy price for its obstinacy in the face of the all-powerful world trend? The problem with making integration the standard—and measuring everything else as lack, failure, or distortion—is that one fails to ask what is actually happening in Africa.

The downsizing of governments and the loosening of investment and trade regulations are important trends, but they reflect the force of proglobalization *arguments* within institutions like the IMF rather than an ongoing *process*. Rule-making is not production, exchange, or consumption. All of those depend on specific structures, and these need to be analyzed in all their complexity and particularity. Africa is filled with areas where international investors do not go, even where there are minerals that would repay investors' efforts. To get to such places requires not deregulation, but institutions and networks capable of getting there.

One could make related arguments about China, where the state's economic role and importance in mediating relations with the outside world are far too strong for the globalization paradigm, or Russia, where oligarchies and mafias imply a model focused on networks more than integrative world markets. Africa now appears to be part of the half of the globe that is not globalized. Better, however, to emphasize not a 'globalizing' (or 'deglobalizing') Africa (or China, or Russia), but rather the changing *relationships* of externally based firms and financial organizations, of indigenous regional networks, or trans-continental networks, of states, and of international organizations.[28] Some

---

[27] Africa's share of world trade fell from over 3 percent in the 1950s to less than 2 percent in the 1990s, and to 1.2 percent if one excludes South Africa. Africans have the use of one telephone line per 100 people (1 per 200 outside of South Africa), compared with 50 in the world as a whole. Electricity is unavailable in many rural areas and does not always work in urban ones; mail services have deteriorated, and radio is often unusable because batteries are too expensive; millions of people get their information in an older way—by word of mouth. World Bank, *Can Africa Claim the 21st Century?* (World Bank, Washington, DC, 2000).

[28] Béatrice Hibou, 'De la privatisation des économies à la privatisation des états', in B. Hibou (ed.), *La privatisation des états* (Karthala, Paris, 1999).

linkages, such as the relationships of transnational oil companies to the state in Nigeria or Angola, are narrowly extractive in one direction and provide rewards to gatekeeping elites in the other. There is nothing web-like about this.

At another extreme are the illicit networks that send out diamonds from the rebel-controlled areas of Sierra Leone and Angola and bring in arms and luxury goods for warlords and their followers. Such networks are built out of young people detached (or kidnapped) from their villages of origin, and flourish in contexts where young men have few routes to a future other than joining the forces assembled by a regional warlord. These systems are linked to diamond buyers and arms sellers in Europe (sometimes via South African, Russian, or Serbian pilots), but they depend on quite specific mechanisms of connections. Rather than integrating the regions in which they operate, they reinforce fragmentation and reduce the range of activities in which most people in a violence-torn region can engage.[29] The diamonds-arms nexus recalls the slave trade of the eighteenth and early nineteenth centuries, for there too, as James and Williams understood very well, were historical processes unfolding in Africa that made no sense except by their relationship to the Atlantic system. The modern version provides a product to be enjoyed by people in distant lands, who do not necessarily ask where the diamonds come from any more than the consumers of sugar in nineteenth-century England wanted to know about the blood in which their sugar was soaked. And now there are 'international issue networks' developing to tell the diamond users in Europe and North America about this blood, using a similar universalistic language to that of the anti-slavery movement of the early nineteenth century.

More than local and less than global: networks, social fields, diasporas

How does one think about African history in ways that emphasize spatial connection but do not assume the 'global'? The vision of the colonial official or the 1930s anthropologist of Africa divided neatly into culturally distinct, self-conscious units did not work, despite the tendency of official myths to create their own reality. By the 1950s and 1960s, anthropologists were using other concepts: the 'social situation', the 'social field', and the 'network'. The first two

---

[29] Rather than constitute alternatives to the state, such mechanisms more likely interact with state institutions and agents. See Janet Roitman, 'The garrison-entrepôt', *Cahiers d'Études Africaines* **150–152** (1998), pp. 297–329; Karine Bennafla, 'La fin des territoires nationaux?', *Politique Africaine* **73** (1999), pp. 24–49; Jean-François Bayart, Stephen Ellis, and Béatrice Hibou, *La criminalisation de l'état en Afrique* (Ed. Complexe, Paris, 1997).

emphasized that in different circumstances Africans constructed distinct patterns of affinity and moral sanction and moved back and forth between them; class affiliation might be operative in a mining town, deference to elders in a village. Conquest itself created a 'colonial situation', as Georges Balandier described it in a pathbreaking article in 1951, defined by external coercion and racialized ideology within a space marked by conquest boundaries; Africans, far from living within their bounded tribes, had to manoeuvre within—or try to transform—the colonial situation. The network concept stressed the webs of connection which people developed as they crossed space, countering the somewhat artificial notion of 'situations' as being spatially distinct.[30]

These terms did not provide a template for analyzing a structure, but they directed the researcher towards empirical analysis of how connections were formed, towards defining units of analysis by observation of the boundaries of interaction. They encouraged studying the channels through which power was exercised. These concepts thus had their limits, and they did not address the kinds of macroprocesses in the historical analyses of James or Williams. Nevertheless, one can use such a framework to study the merchant diasporas of West Africa—in which Islamic brotherhoods as well as kinship and ethnic ties maintained trust and information flows across long distances and during transactions with culturally distinct populations—or the long-distance migrant labour networks of southern Africa.[31] The network concept puts as much emphasis on nodes and blockages as on movement, and thus calls attention to institutions, including police controls over migration, licensing, and welfare systems. It thus avoids the amorphous quality of an anthropology of flows and fragments.

These concepts open the door to examination of the wide variety of units of affinity and mobilization, the kinds of subjective attachments people form and the collectivities that are capable of action. One is not limited by supposedly primordial identifications, to the 'tribe' or 'race' for instance, or to a specific space. One can start with identification with 'Africa' itself and study the diasporic imagination, for 'Africa' as a space to which people attached meaning was defined less by processes within the continental boundaries than by its diaspora. If slave traders defined Africa as a place where they could legitimately enslave people, their victims discovered in their ordeal a commonality which defined them as people with a past, with a place, with a collective imagination.

---

[30] Georges Balandier, 'La situation coloniale: approche théorique', *Cahiers Internationaux de Sociologie* 11 (1951), pp. 44–79; Max Gluckman, 'Anthropological problems arising from the African industrial revolution', in Aidan Southall (ed.), *Social Change in Modern Africa* (Oxford University Press, London, 1961), pp. 67–82; J. Clyde Mitchell, *Social Networks in Urban Situations: Analysis of personal relationships in Central African towns* (Manchester University Press, Manchester, 1969).

[31] Abner Cohen, *Custom and Politics in Urban Africa: A study of migrants in Yoruba towns* (University of California Press, Berkeley, CA, 1969).

When African-American activists in the early nineteenth century began to evoke images of 'Africa' or 'Ethiopia', they were making a point within a Christian conception of universal history rather than a reference to particular cultural affinities. The meanings of Africa-consciousness have been varied, and their relationship to the particulars of Africa even more so. J. Lorand Matory argues that certain African 'ethnic groups' defined themselves in the course of an African-American dialogue under the influence of former slaves who returned to the region of their fathers and advocated forms of collective identification that transcended regional divisions and which were based as much on an imagined future as a claimed past.[32]

The spatial imagination of intellectuals, missionaries, and political activists, from the early nineteenth to the mid-twentieth century, was thus varied. It was neither global nor local, but was built out of specific lines of connection and posited regional, continental and transcontinental affinities. These spatial affinities could narrow, expand, and narrow again. Pan-Africanism was more salient in the 1930s and early 1940s than in the 1950s, when territorial units became more accessible foci of claims and when political imagination became (for a time at least) more national. French officials in the post-war decade tried to get Africans to imagine themselves in a different way, as citizens of a Union Française, and African politicians tried to use this imperial version of citizenship to make claims on the metropole. But imperial citizenship was ridden by too many contradictions and hypocrisies to constitute a plausible case to most Africans for supranational identification. French officials, realizing the cost of making imperial citizenship meaningful, backed away from it, using the word 'territorialization' in the mid-1950s to emphasize that in conceding power to Africans the government was devolving on them the responsibility of meeting the demands of citizens with the resources of individual territories.[33] Among the various possibilities—pan-African visions, large-scale federations, and imperial citizenship—the territorially bounded citizenship that Africans received was the product of a specific history of claims and counterclaims.

One needs to look at other circuits: religious pilgrimages to Mecca and networks of training which Muslim clerics followed all over the Sahara desert, from the eighth century and intensely from the eighteenth; regional systems of shrines in central Africa; religious connections between Africans and African-American missionaries. The linkage between intra-African and extra-African networks is an old one: the Brazil-Angola-Portugal slave-trading nexus;

---

[32] James T. Campbell, *Songs of Zion: The African Methodist Episcopal Church in the United States and South Africa* (Oxford University Press, New York, 1995); J. Lorand Matory, 'The English professors of Brazil: on the diasporic roots of the Yoruba nation', *Comparative Studies in Society and History* **41** (1999), pp. 72–103.

[33] Frederick Cooper, *Decolonization and African Society: The labour question in French and British Africa* (Cambridge University Press, Cambridge, 1996).

trans-Saharan commercial, religious, and scholarly networks connecting with Hausa and Mandingo systems within West Africa; a trading system extending from Mozambique Island through the Red Sea, southern Arabia, and the Persian Gulf to Gujarat; a Dutch-pioneered system that connected Indonesia, South Africa, and Europe, with tentacles reaching into the interior of southern Africa; the network of merchants and professionals across coastal West Africa, with links to Brazil, Europe, the Caribbean, and the West African interior, shaping racially and culturally mixed coastal communities; and, more recently, the horrifically effective networks of diamond and arms smugglers connecting Sierra Leone and Angola to Europe. One cannot argue that networks are soft and cosy and structures are hard and domineering.[34]

And one can look at border-crossing 'issue networks', of which the anti-slavery movement of the early nineteenth century was the great pioneer.[35] Anti-colonial movements from the 1930s onwards were able to make the once ordinary category of 'colony' into something unacceptable in international discourse largely because they linked activists in African towns and cities with principled groups in metropoles who in turn tied those issues to the self-conception of democracies. In South Africa in the early twentieth century, scholars have found in a single rural district linkages to church groups emphasizing Christian brotherhood, to liberal constitutionalist reforms in cities, to African-American movements, and to regional organizations of labour tenants.[36] The shifting articulations of local, regional, and international movements shaped a political repertoire which kept a variety of possibilities alive and suggested ways of finding help in the African diaspora and in Euro-American issue networks. In the end, South African whites, who prided themselves on their own connections to the 'Christian' and 'civilized' West, lost the battle of linkages.

Perhaps social democrats have better things to do than lament. The current efforts of trade unions and NGOs to challenge 'global' capitalism via 'global' social movements—such as those against sweat shops and child labour in the international clothing and shoe industries or the movement to ban 'conflict diamonds'—have precedents going back to the late eighteenth century, and they have won a few victories along the way. Arguments based on the 'rights

---

[34] The variety and time-depth of diasporic phenomena, as well as the specificity of the mechanisms by which they were organized, are emphasized in Emmanuel Akyeampong, 'Africans in the diaspora; the diaspora in Africa', *African Affairs* **99** (2000), pp. 183–215. For a detailed study of transcontinental interconnection, see Joseph Miller, *Way of Death: Merchant capitalism and the Angolan slave trade 1730–1820* (University of Wisconsin Press, Madison, WI, 1988).

[35] David Brion Davis, *The Problem of Slavery in the Age of Revolution 1770–1823* (Cornell University Press, Ithaca, NY, 1975); Margaret E. Keck and Kathryn Sikkink, *Activists Beyond Borders: Advocacy networks in international politics* (Cornell University Press, Ithaca, NY, 1988).

[36] William Beinart and Colin Bundy, *Hidden Struggles in Rural South Africa* (University of California Press, Berkeley, CA, 1987).

of man' have as good a claim to 'global' relevance as arguments based on the market. And in both cases, discourse has been far more global than practice.

Rethinking the present

The point of these short narratives is not to say that nothing changes under the sun. Obviously, the commodity exchange system, forms of production, the modalities of state interventions into societies, capital exchange systems, let alone technologies of communication, have changed enormously. The slave-sugar-manufactured goods commodity circuits of the eighteenth century had a vastly different significance for capitalist development in that era from that of the diamond-arms circuit today. My argument is for precision in specifying how such commodity circuits are constituted, how connections across space are extended and bounded, and how large-scale, long-term processes, such as capitalist development, can be analyzed with due attention to their power, their limitations, and the mechanisms which shape them. One can, of course, call all of this globalization, but that is to say little more than that history happens within the boundaries of the planet and therefore all history is global history. However, if one wants to use globalization as the progressive integration of different parts of the world into a singular whole, then the argument falls victim to linearity and teleology. The globalizers are right to tell us to look at long-distance connections. The difficulty is to come up with concepts that are discerning enough to say something significant about them. Like modernization theory, globalization draws its power from uniting diverse phenomena into a singular conceptual framework and a singular notion of change. And that is where both approaches occlude rather than clarify historical processes.

But what about reversing the argument? Or admitting that there is little point in refining globalization by adding a historical dimension, and turning instead to the other position which some globalizers take: that the global age is now and it is clearly distinguished from the past. Here, my argument has been not against the specificity of the present, but whether characterizing it as global distinguishes it from the past. Communications revolutions, capital movements, and regulatory apparatuses all need to be studied and their relationships, mutually reinforcing or contradictory, explored. But we need a more refined theoretical apparatus and a less misleading rhetoric than globalization—Banker's Boast, Social Democrat's Lament, or the Dance of the Flows and Fragments—provides. I have argued this by looking both at the variety and specificity of cross-territorial connecting mechanisms in past and present and at the misleading connotations of the 'global' and the '-ization'.

The point goes beyond the academic's quest for refinement: a lot is at stake in the kinds of questions which a conceptual apparatus brings to the fore. International financial institutions that tell African leaders that development will follow if they open up their economies will not get to the bottom of the continent's problems unless they address how specific structures within African societies, within or across borders, provide opportunities and constraints for production and exchange, and how specific mechanisms in external commodity markets provide opportunities and blockages for African products. State institutions, oligarchies, warlords, regional mafias, commercial diasporas, oligopolistic foreign corporations, and varied networks shape the nature of capitalism and its highly uneven effects. Capitalism remains lumpy.[37]

It is no surprise that journalists and academics alike react with a sense of wonder to the multiplicity of forms of communication that have opened up (but are available only to some) and to the border-crossing strategies of many firms (but not others). The globalization fad is an understandable response to this sense of connectivity and opportunity, just as modernization theory was to the collapsing rigidities of European societies in the 1950s and the escape from the constraints of colonial empires. Globalization can be invoked to make a variety of claims, but it can also constrict the political imagination, occlude the power and importance of the long history of transnational mobilizations, and discourage focus on institutions and networks that can offer opportunities as well as constraints.

Of course, all the changing forms of trans-continental connections, all the forms of integration and differentiation, of flows and blockages, of the past and present can be seen as aspects of a singular but complex process which we can label globalization. But that is to defend the concept by emphasizing how little it signifies. Words matter. The incessant talk about globalization—the word, the images associated with it, and arguments for and against 'it'—both reflects and reinforces fascination in boundless connectivity. Yet scholars do not need to choose between a rhetoric of containers and a rhetoric of flows. They do not need to decide whether Africa is part of a necessary and universal trend or a peculiar and frustrating exception, but they can instead analyze how it and other regions are linked and bounded and how those links and boundaries shift over time. Activists are not faced with a singular force to oppose or promote, but they, like their predecessors in anti-slavery and anti-colonial

---

[37] As Hibou ('De la privatisation') shows, the privatization of nationalized companies in Africa produced something quite different from a 'private sector' of competing firms connected to world markets: officials may privatize state-owned firms to themselves, leading to private accumulation through government, and narrow channels of interaction. Similarly, the Commonwealth of Independent States remains vastly different from post-1989 fantasies of market integration. Markku Lonkila, 'Post-Soviet Russia? A society of networks?' in Markku Kangaspuro (ed.), *Russia: More different than most?* (Kikimora, Helsinki, 1999), pp. 98–112.

movements, need to understand with precision the patterns of interconnection, the choices and constraints which they imply, and the consequences of different sorts of actions along different sorts of interfaces. Not least of the questions which we should be asking concern the present: what is actually new? What are the mechanisms of ongoing change? And above all, can we develop a differentiated vocabulary that encourages thinking about connections and their limits?

Acknowledgment

Published in *African Affairs* 100, 399 (2001), p. 189–213. I would like to thank the Centre d'Études et de Recherches Internationales in Paris for hosting a seminar in June 2000 at which an earlier version of this article received helpful discussion. A French version is being published concurrently in *Critique Internationale*, and I am grateful to Jean-François Bayart and the editors of *African Affairs* for agreeing to this bilingual publication, as well as for their comments on earlier versions.

16

Fighting Gender-Based Violence

The Women's Movement and the Enforcement of Rape Law in Liberia

Peace Medie

GENDER-BASED VIOLENCE HAS RECEIVED increasing attention in recent years, and many African states, often under pressure from local women's movements, have passed laws to criminalize various forms of gender-based violence (GBV), including rape.[1] However, the passage of such laws has not always translated into implementation; victims of GBV often face many obstacles within society and in the criminal justice system that render it difficult, and sometimes impossible, for them to benefit from new laws.[2] This problem is particularly acute in post-war states that have weak implementing agencies, which often prevent victims from receiving justice.[3]

In post-war Liberia, where GBV is prevalent, a large proportion of reported cases never advance to the courts.[4] Instead, police officers withdraw these

---

[1] Aili Mari Tripp, Isabel Casimiro, Joy Kwesiga, and Alice Mungwa, *African Women's Movements: Transforming political landscapes* (Cambridge University Press, New York, NY, 2009).

[2] Amnesty International, '"I can't afford justice": violence against women in Uganda continues unchecked and unpunished' (Amnesty International, London, 2010); Neil Andersson, Sharmila Mhatre, Nzwakie Mootsi, and Marina Penderis, 'How to police sexual violence', *Crime and Conflict* 15 (1999), pp. 18–22; Bruce Baker and Helen Liebling-Kalifani, 'Justice and health provision for survivors of sexual violence in Kitgum, northern Uganda' (Coventry University, Coventry, 2010); Megan Bastick, Karin Grimm, and Rahel Kunz, 'Sexual violence in armed conflict: global overview and implications for the security sector' (Geneva Center for the Democratic Control of Armed Forces, Geneva, 2007); Convention on the Elimination of all Forms of Discrimination against Women, 'NGO report on violence against women in Burundi' (New York, NY, 2008); United Nations Population Fund, 'Gender-based violence in Sierra Leone: a case study' (United Nations Population Fund, New York, NY, 2005).

[3] *Ibid.*

[4] For data on the prevalence of GBV, see Liberia Institute of Statistics and Geo-Information Services [LISGIS], 'Liberia demographic and health survey 2007' (Ministry of Health and Social Welfare, Monrovia, Liberia, 2008); Women and Children Protection Section, Liberia National Police Force, Case Disposal Statistics, (2006–10), in author's possession.

cases from the police station, sometimes upon the request of complainants.[5] The withdrawal of cases, especially when forced upon complainants, undermines the purpose of GBV legislation and raises serious concerns about the translation of formal policies into substantive changes in the lives of women.[6] Yet, despite this problem, scholars of women's movements and women's rights have largely failed to study policy implementation.[7]

This article addresses this gap in the literatures by interrogating how the women's movement in Liberia has influenced police officers' enforcement of the rape law. The rate of withdrawal of rape cases is significantly lower than other forms of GBV, and is lower now than it was in the pre-war period. To assess whether this is the result of the activism of the women's movement, I conducted one-hundred and fifty interviews in 2010 and 2011 with women's rights advocates, police officers, bureaucrats, staff of international organizations (IOs), and victims of violence in two Liberian counties. Based on this evidence, I document the ways in which, since the end of Liberia's civil war in 2003, women's groups have worked—sometimes independently, but mostly in collaboration with the state and IOs—to amend the rape law, create institutions to address rape, and provide education on rape to police officers and the public. Most significantly, I argue that these measures have contributed to a lower rate of withdrawal of rape cases. The article also demonstrates how the state's openness to the participation of NGOs in the crafting of the national response to rape, combined with the material and political support of IOs, has bolstered NGOs' anti-rape efforts and facilitated their ability to influence police enforcement of the rape law. This goes against the grain of much recent literature that has emphasized the limitations of civil society, especially in areas such as women's rights where limited progress in policy implementation has been made over the past forty years.

The article first discusses the literature on social movements and policy implementation, before turning to African women's movements. After outlining the methodology, the article introduces the problem of GBV in Liberia and analyses the strategies that women's groups have adopted since the end of the civil war, as well as the effects of these strategies on police enforcement of

---

[5] Women and Children Protection Section, 'Case Disposal Statistics'.

[6] I am not arguing that police referral of cases to court is sufficient for the prosecution of the offender and for the complainant to receive justice. However, referring a case to court is a necessary condition for the prosecution of offenders.

[7] Some exceptions are Gemma Lucy Burgess, 'When the personal becomes political: using legal reform to combat violence against women in Ethiopia', *Gender, Place and Culture: A Journal of Feminist Geography* 19, 2 (2012), pp. 153–74; Shereen Usdin, Nicola Christofides, Lebo Malepe, and Aadielah Maker, 'The value of advocacy in promoting social change: implementing the new domestic violence act in South Africa', *Reproductive Health Matters* 8, 16 (2000), pp. 55–65.

the rape law. I conclude with a discussion of how future studies can further advance knowledge of the implementation of women's rights policies.

Social movements and policy implementation

An extensive body of literature in the fields of public administration, public policy, and other disciplines investigates policy implementation, and although numerous research questions and policy areas are examined the focus is generally on explaining three broad outcomes: why policies are implemented, why policies are not implemented, and how policies are implemented.[8] Studies probe how the presence, absence, and characteristics of certain actors, structures, resources, norms, and policy instruments affect one or more of these themes. While earlier studies produced long lists of variables to explain implementation, without specifying the importance and effects of each variable, comparative case studies and large-n quantitative studies conducted over the last two decades have aimed for parsimony in explaining the implementation process, its outputs, and outcomes.[9]

Scholars have identified four categories of factors that explain the behaviours of policy implementers such as police officers: political control, organizational control, individual-level characteristics, and external pressures.[10] Political control is exerted by political officials, while organizational control emanates from actors and conditions within the implementing agency. The individual level refers to the norms and beliefs of individual implementers, while external pressures are produced by actors and conditions that are outside the state and its bureaucracies. IOs and interest groups, such as social movements, are sources of external pressure. While some scholars have argued that individual-level characteristics best explain implementation behaviour, others have found that social movements are important to implementation

---

[8] For a review of major methodological and theoretical themes and debates in the implementation literature, see B. Guy Peters and Jon Pierre (eds), *Handbook of Public Administration* (Sage, London, 2007), pp. 131–63.

[9] For a discussion of the problem of over-determination and how it has hindered theory development in implementation studies see, Michael Goggin, 'The "too few cases/too many variables" problem in implementation research', *Political Research Quarterly* 39, 2 (1986), pp. 328–47. The author also notes the failure of most studies to specify the causal patterns that correspond to the outcomes under observation, p. 329.

[10] Peter J. May and Soren C. Winter, 'Politicians, managers, and street-level bureaucrats: influences on policy implementation', *Journal of Public Administration Research and Theory* 19, 3 (2009), pp. 453–76; Marcia K. Meyers and Susan Vorsanger, 'Street-level bureaucrats and the implementation of public policy' in Peter and Pierre (eds), *Handbook of Public Administration*, pp. 153–63.

and that they also shape the individual-level characteristics of implementers.[11] The weak implementing capacity within many African states suggests a more prominent role for social movements in policy implementation.

Social movements' influence on implementation is first determined by the political context; the openness of the political environment conditions movements' involvement in the implementation process. A democracy, therefore, offers more opportunities for movements to influence policy implementation than an authoritarian regime.[12] Furthermore, the political opportunity structure affects the strategies adopted by movements. In a study of anti-nuclear movements in Europe and America, Herbert Kitschelt found that movements operating in 'open' political systems adopted assimilative strategies such as lobbying while those in 'closed' systems opted for more confrontational strategies such as public demonstrations.[13] Movements also find that the conditions and strategies that make it possible for them to influence agenda setting and policy adoption do not necessarily support their involvement in policy implementation.[14]

Once movements gain access to the political system, they typically try to influence implementation from the policy design stage.[15] By directly participating in policy design or lobbying lawmakers, movements attempt to imbue policies with their ideas of how a problem should be addressed, which agency should be responsible for addressing this problem, and which instruments should be employed. In doing so, they shape the directives that implementers eventually receive and contribute to setting the organizational rules and procedures that guide implementation. They also attempt to shape the organizational structure and capacity of implementing agencies, thus moulding the systems and processes through which policies are delivered.[16] Opportunities to participate in the development or restructuring of implementing agencies, therefore, present opportunities to influence the implementation process.

[11] John Brehm and Scott Gates, *Working, Shirking, and Sabotage: Bureaucratic response to a democratic public* (University of Michigan Press, Ann Arbor, MI, 1997); Steven Williams Maynard-Moody and Michael Craig Musheno, *Cops, Teachers, Counselors: Stories from the front lines of public service* (University of Michigan Press, Ann Arbor, MI, 2003).

[12] May, 'Policy design and implementation'; Burgess, 'When the personal becomes political'.

[13] Herbert P. Kitschelt, 'Political opportunity structures and political protest: anti nuclear movements in four democracies', *British Journal of Political Science* 16, 1 (1986), pp. 57–85.

[14] Edwin Amenta, Neal Caren, Elizabeth Chiarello, and Yang Su, 'The political consequences of social movements', *American Review of Sociology* 36 (2010), pp. 287–307.

[15] Evelyn Z. Brodkin, 'Implementation as policy politics' in Dennis James Palumbo and Donald J. Calista (eds), *Implementation and the Policy Process: Opening up the black box* (Greenwood Press, Westport, CT, 1990), pp. 107–18; Eugene Bardach, *The Implementation Game: What happens after a bill becomes law* (MIT Press, Cambridge, MA, 1977).

[16] Susan Franceschet, 'Explaining domestic violence policy outcomes in Chile and Argentina', *Latin American Politics and Society* 52, 3 (2010), pp. 1–29.

Social movements also seek to affect policy implementation from the bottom up, exerting influence on both policy implementers and beneficiaries. They employ strategies such as lawsuits and negotiations to compel implementers to change how they implement policies,[17] and they educate policy beneficiaries on their rights and help them in formulating the demands that they make of implementers.[18]

Scholars, focusing mostly on the US and Europe, have found that the effects of these mobilization strategies vary across policy issue areas, because influence on implementation is not determined solely by the strategies adopted but is contingent upon other factors.[19] In a study of how the creation of agency-level hate crime policies affects police officers' official recording of such crimes in California, Ryken Grattet and Valerie Jenness found that the effect of policies depends on characteristics of the police force (such as police integration in the community) and the presence of human relations commissions (organizations that serve as community watchdogs).[20] Thus, 'Communities with a human relations commission and neighbourhood-based police stations experience the largest payoff for creating a policy.'[21] In a study of the civil rights movement's influence on the implementation of poverty policies in Mississippi, Kenneth Andrews found that communities with strong movement infrastructures (leadership, organizational capacity, and resources) generated greater funding for programme implementation and succeeded in shaping programme content.[22] In South Africa, the Soul City Institute for Health and Development Communication in partnership with the National Network on Violence against Women used strategies such as lobbying and media advocacy successfully to pressure the government to implement the 1998 Domestic Violence Act.[23] After this intervention, a 'growing sense of urgency was discernible from within government ranks to move the process forward'.[24] However, advocates were excluded from many aspects of how the act was implemented, including the development of the national instructions and the training of police officers, and had less impact in this regard.

---

[17] Diane Mitsch Bush, 'Women's movements and state policy reform aimed at domestic violence against women: a comparison of the consequences of women's mobilization in US and India', *Gender and Society* 6, 4 (1992), pp. 587–608.

[18] Jelke Boesten, 'Pushing back the boundaries: social policy, domestic violence and women's organizations in Peru', *Journal of Latin American Studies* 38, 2 (2006), pp. 355–78.

[19] Amenta et al., 'The political consequences of social movements'.

[20] Ryken Grattet and Valerie Jenness, 'Transforming symbolic law into organizational action: hate crime policy and law enforcement practice', *Social Forces* 87, 1 (2008), pp. 501–27.

[21] *Ibid.*, p. 516.

[22] Kenneth T. Andrews, 'Social movements and policy implementation: the Mississippi civil rights movement and the war on poverty, 1965–1971', *American Sociological Review* 66, 1 (2001), pp. 71–95.

[23] Usdin et al., 'The value of advocacy in promoting social change'.

[24] *Ibid.*, p. 60.

These findings show that movements' influence is conditioned by their organizational characteristics, the mobilization strategies adopted, the policy issue area, the structure of implementing agencies, and the political environment, factors which vary temporally within and across states. However, 'there are no specific organizational forms, strategies, or political contexts that will always help challengers'.[25] The political, social, and economic conditions in Liberia, and many other African countries, differ significantly from those of the developed countries addressed in the literature, providing an opportunity to examine these issues in a new context.

African women's movements and policy implementation

I adopt Myra Max Ferree's definition of a women's movement as one that 'organizes women as women to make social change'.[26] Such movements are characterized by women's mobilization around a shared gender identity and a focus on the concerns of women in specific issue areas. In Africa, women's groups have a long history; Filomena Steady, for example, describes how 10,000 Sierra Leonean women under British rule in 1951 staged a demonstration against a proposed increase in market dues and the steep rise in food prices caused by the monopolization of wholesale food distribution by Lebanese traders.[27] The women subsequently won the rights to purchase directly from the government and coalesced to form the Sierra Leone Women's Movement (SLWM). Despite some weaknesses and constraints, women's movements have continued to protest political and socio-economic injustices in the post-colonial period and in transitions to democracy.[28] However, with the end of colonial rule, many women's movements were co-opted into ruling parties and several one-party states established women's wings. Similar forms of co-option and incorporation occurred in the immediate aftermath of transitions to democracy,[29] and this absorption of women's movements by

[25] Amenta et al., 'The political consequences of social movements', p. 296.

[26] Myra Marx Ferree, 'Globalization and feminism: opportunities and obstacles for activism in the global era' in Myra Marx Ferree and Aili Mari Tripp (eds), *Global Feminism: Transnational women's activism, organizing, and human rights* (New York University Press, New York, NY, 2006). pp. 3–23.

[27] Filomena Chioma Steady, *Women and Collective Action in Africa: Development, democratization and empowerment* (Palgrave Macmillan, Gordonsville, VA, 2005).

[28] Malehoko Tshoaedi, '(En)gendering the transition in South Africa: the role of COSATU women activists', *Transformation* 78, (2012), pp. 1–26, p. 7.

[29] Aili Mari Tripp, 'Women's movements and challenges to neopatrimonial rule: preliminary observations from Africa', *Development and Change* 32, 1 (2001), pp. 33–54; Sylvia Tamale, '"Point of order Mr Speaker": African women claiming their place in parliament', *Gender and Development* 8, 3 (2000), pp. 8–15.

ruling parties weakened these groups' ability to hold the state accountable as they began to function as extensions of governments.[30]

The growth of civil society over the last two decades has expanded the political space outside of state control, and challenged governments' ability to control women's movements.[31] Consequently, some movements have managed to effect important changes despite the barriers that they continue to face. One important aspect of this activism has been women's efforts to promote the adoption of laws and institutions to overturn existing structures and practices that discriminate against women. For example, a collection of gender and women's rights advocates successfully lobbied for the passage of Ghana's 2007 Domestic Violence Bill.[32] However, it is clear that policy adoption is not sufficient for policy implementation.[33] Many governments have been quick to pass women's rights legislation, but lack the political will and/or the resources to effectively deliver and implement. This is evident in the implementation of GBV policies; despite laws that criminalize rape and other forms of GBV, police officers encourage and sometimes compel victims to accept reconciliation instead of pursuing the prosecution of the offenders.[34] Describing police response to GBV in Ethiopia, Gemma Lucy Burgess states that:

> Police often do not follow correct procedure when a rape is reported. One activist said that police think it is better if the woman marries her rapist than pursues a criminal case. Rape cases are often dismissed when the victim is not a virgin.[35]

This gap in law enforcement demonstrates that getting GBV legislation on the statute book is only half the struggle; where progressive policies have been introduced the question becomes how state agents can translate and deliver GBV policies in ways that will protect and empower women, and how women's movements can help them to achieve that goal. The movement literature demonstrates that the influence of social movements does not end

---

[30] Studies have demonstrated, however, that the presence of a strong and autonomous women's movement is not a necessary condition for policy change. See this argument articulated in, Mala Htun, *Sex and the State: Abortion, divorce, and the family under Latin American dictatorships and democracies* (Cambridge University Press, New York, NY, 2003).

[31] Tripp, 'Women's movements and challenges to neopatrimonial rule'.

[32] Akosua Adomako Ampofo, 'Collective activism: the domestic violence bill becoming law in Ghana', *African and Asian Studies* 7, 4 (2008), pp. 395–421, p. 413.

[33] Amnesty International, 'I can't afford justice'; Andersson *et al.*, 'How to police sexual violence'; Baker and Liebling-Kalifani, 'Justice and health provision'; Convention on the Elimination of all Forms of Discrimination against Women, 'NGO Report on Violence against Women in Burundi'; Burgess, 'When the personal becomes political'; United Nations Population Fund, 'Gender-based violence in Sierra Leone'.

[34] *Ibid.*   [35] Burgess, 'When the personal becomes political', p. 162.

at the point of policy adoption, but extends to the implementation phase and is contingent on the mobilization strategies, the political environment, the characteristics and structures of implementing agencies and of social movements, and the issue area. It is, therefore, necessary to examine the influence of women's movements on the implementation of GBV and other women's rights policies.

In post-conflict Liberia, the rate of withdrawal of rape cases has declined and in order to assess whether the activism of the Liberian women's movement contributed to this decline, I employed the method of structured, focused comparison in two locations: Monrovia and Gbarnga.[36] In this method the questions, reflecting the research objectives, are standardized and focused across cases. Monrovia and Gbarnga were selected to allow for variations in the levels of a key factor, the presence of women's NGOs. There is a greater NGO presence in Monrovia than in Gbarnga and most organizations are headquartered in the capital, but the women's movement has nevertheless been able to organize and use its advocacy strategies to influence implementation in both locations.

Data were collected through semi-structured interviews, participant observation, and reviews of official documents and grey literature. I observed police officers as they interacted with complainants and collected documents produced by government agencies, media houses, IOs, and NGOs. Interviewees were identified through purposive and snowball sampling techniques, and included staff of the ministries of Gender and Development (MoGD), Justice (MoJ), and Labor (MoL); staff of IOs; and GBV survivors. They also included 28 women's rights advocates from 12 women's NGOs and 50 police officers. Information on the role of the women's movement was gathered directly from the advocates as well as from the other interviewees, enabling the production of a holistic picture of the movement's structures and activities and its impact on police responses and on the behaviour of survivors of violence. I also observed the staff of women's NGOs at work and attended meetings of the national GBV task-force. The deliberations of the taskforce shed light on the movement's involvement in the anti-rape efforts in Liberia, its weaknesses and constraints, and its influence on how the state and its agents have responded to rape. I found this influence to be both direct and indirect, defining direct influence as the outcome of NGOs' interaction with police officers and indirect influence as a product of the movement's efforts at changing law enforcement procedures and institutions as well as target group behaviour.

---

[36] See Alexander L. George and Andrew Bennett, *Case Studies and Theory Development in the Social Sciences* (MIT Press, Cambridge, MA, 2005, p. 67).

Gender-based violence in Liberia

All warring factions in Liberia's civil war targeted violence at women.[37] Although the level of violence has fallen since the war's end, physical and sexual violence remain major problems and the victims in most reported cases of rape are minors. Some women's rights advocates argue that the incidence of GBV in post-war Liberia is higher than before the war, while others contend that it is not the incidence, but the reporting of GBV that has increased.[38] The absence of pre-war data makes it difficult to establish the validity of either claim, but reports show that rape was the most reported crime in 2007 and currently, rape and domestic violence are two of the crimes most reported to the Women and Children Protection Section (WACPS) of the Liberia National Police (LNP).[39] Nonetheless, the majority of crimes are not reported to the police. Instead, victims turn to family palavers and customary courts for adjudication.

Informal means of adjudication are preferred for several reasons. Some view the court system as divisive as it focuses on establishing guilt and punishment instead of reconciling disputing parties.[40] People also view the criminal justice system as corrupt.[41] The unofficial fees levied on complainants by the police and the courts dissuade people from reporting GBV. The length of trials and the time that it takes away from work is also a burden on survivors. The fear of retaliation, stigmatization, and being accused of lying (in the case of rape) also discourages reporting.[42] Some survivors and/or their families also accept payment from rapists in exchange for keeping cases out of the police stations and courts. Liberia's crippling poverty has made this a common practice.[43] These factors also contribute to the withdrawal of cases after they have been reported to the police.

Public attitudes toward GBV, though improving, are largely negative. A high percentage of men (30) and women (59) believe that domestic violence is justifiable.[44] In the case of rape, people tend to blame the victim. In a 2008

---

[37] Human Rights Watch, 'How to fight, how to kill: child soldiers in Liberia', *Human Rights Watch* **16**, 2 (2004), pp. 1–43.

[38] Interview, Sallimatu Kamara, Women Aid Incorporated, Monrovia, 28 June 2010.

[39] Women and Children Protection Section, 'Case Disposal Statistics'.

[40] Deborah H. Isser, Stephen C. Lubkemann and Saah N'Tow 'Looking for justice: Liberian experiences with and perceptions of local justice options' (Peaceworks, 63, United States Institute of Peace, Washington, DC, 2009).

[41] *Ibid.*

[42] United Nations Mission in Liberia [UNMIL], 'Research on prevalence and attitudes to rape in Liberia' (UNMIL, Legal and Judicial Support Division, Monrovia, Liberia, 2008).

[43] Interview, female member of staff, Women Aid Incorporated, Monrovia, 13 September 2010. Kofi Annan Institute for Conflict Transformation, 'FAQs on rape and the revised rape law' (Kofi Annan Institute for Conflict Transformation, Monrovia, Liberia, 2011).

[44] LISGIS, 'Demographic and health survey', pp. 214–15.

survey of 1,000 households in all 15 counties, 69 percent of respondents agreed that 'women contribute to rape by flirting with men' and 61.9 percent agreed that 'women contribute to rape by being alone with a man in a room'.[45] Victims are also stigmatized and viewed as 'damaged goods' and 'leftovers'.[46] Nonetheless, 96.3 percent of respondents agreed that 'rape is a serious crime' and 90.5 percent agreed that 'men who commit rape should be given harsh sentences'.[47] Liberians, however, do not rank all types of rape equally. Rape against children is viewed as serious whereas the rape of women, especially where they are perceived to have caused it, is seen as less serious. Some people think that the law should allow for 'restorative remedies' for these 'less egregious' forms of rape.[48] These negative attitudes toward rape and other forms of GBV have made it harder to promote women's rights, but have contributed to the mobilization of the women's movement.

Women organizing against rape

The women's movement in post-war Liberia, though facing internal challenges, has organized to prevent rape and to seek justice for survivors.[49] Historically, Liberian women have mobilized to challenge policies and institutions that negatively affected them.[50] There were instances where women mobilized against forms of GBV prior to the 14-year civil war, but these were typically not sustained and inclusive national campaigns. Instead, their activism was usually in reaction to a series of public and particularly violent attacks against women and involved a few communities protesting for a short period.[51] The outbreak of the war in 1989 led women's groups to mount national campaigns against GBV and other injustices. Starting in early 1990, female politicians and women's organizations began to appeal to the warring factions to come to a peace agreement, and, as the conflict progressed, the

---

[45] UNMIL, 'Research on prevalence', p. 41.   [46] *Ibid.*   [47] *Ibid.*, pp. 41–2.
[48] Isser *et al.*, 'Looking for justice', p. 6.
[49] For a discussion of the causes and consequences of women's movements' focus on sexual violence see Peace A. Medie, *Police Behavior in Post-Conflict States: Explaining variation in responses to domestic violence, internal human trafficking, and rape* (University of Pittsburgh, unpublished PhD dissertation, 2012), pp. 193–200; Benjamin de Carvalho and Niels Nagelhus Schia, 'Sexual and gender-based violence in Liberia and the case for a comprehensive approach to the rule of law', *Journal of International Relations and Development* 14, 1 (2011), pp. 134–41.
[50] Mary Moran, *Liberia: The violence of democracy* (University of Pennsylvania Press, Philadelphia, PA, 2006).
[51] For example, in March 1988 female residents of the Matadi Estates in Monrovia criticized the police for poor handling of the investigation into the rape and murder of one of the estate's female residents. They appealed to several government agencies that were involved in the case to make it a priority. See *Daily Observer* [Monrovia], 'Estate women', 1 March 1989, pp. 1 and 6.

various groups coalesced into a women's movement, pressuring both national and international actors to end the war.[52]

During the war, some groups within the movement were active for short periods of time and on a small scale, while others functioned at the national level for several years.[53] Since the end of the war, some groups have continued within the movement, although its main focus has shifted from conflict resolution to the promotion of women's rights. The post-war movement consists of small, medium, and large NGOs led and mainly staffed by women, and national networks such as the Women's NGO Secretariat, which maintain links between the various groups. While organizations such as the Women in Peacebuilding Network (WIPNET) have branches across the country, most are only present in Monrovia or a few of the larger towns. Similarly, organizations such as the Association of Female Lawyers of Liberia (AFELL) and Touching Humanity in Need of Kindness (THINK) are more active and influential than others, drawing on their greater expertise and capacity to provide services.[54] Given this diversity, rape has emerged as one of the principal issues around which the movement has organized in a more coherent fashion.

The political opportunity structure has favoured women's organizing and provided openings for NGOs to have a voice in policy design and implementation.[55] Many lawmakers in the transitional government, cognizant of the prevalence and brutality of rape during the civil war, supported the adoption of the rape law.[56] This reflects a commitment and willingness to combat rape that did not exist prior to the war.[57] President Ellen Johnson Sirleaf encouraged the efforts of women's NGOs and voiced her commitment to combating GBV.[58] Although this has not translated into steady and adequate funding for anti-rape initiatives or the commitment of all bureaucrats and implementers, it has created a political and bureaucratic environment that is mostly open to and sometimes welcoming of NGO involvement. On the other hand, some

---

[52] Abigial E. Disney and Gina Reticker, *Pray the Devil Back to Hell* [film] (Fork Films, USA, 2008); African Women and Peace Support Group, *Liberian Women Fighting for the Right to Be Seen, Heard and Counted* (Africa World Press, Trenton, NJ, 2004); *Daily Observer* [Monrovia], 'It is time for peace', 8 June 1990, pp. 1 and 6; S. Togba Slewion, 'Christian women want an end to Nimba crisis', *Daily Observer* [Monrovia], 16 May 1990, p. 6.; *Daily Observer* [Monrovia], 'Women call for ceasefire', 30 May 1990, pp. 1 and 6.

[53] African Women and Peace Support Group, 'Liberian women fighting for the right to be seen'.

[54] All organizations are underfunded and face resource constraints.

[55] The political opportunity structure is defined as the allies and structures within state institutions that determine movement involvement in the policy process.

[56] Interview, Ruth Caesar, former Chairperson of the Committee on Gender Equity, Women, and Child Development in the National Transitional Legislative Assembly, Monrovia, 5 June 2011.

[57] Medie, *Police Behavior in Post-Conflict States*.

[58] United Nations Population Fund, 'Liberia's Gender Based Violence National Action Plan' (United Nations Population Fund, 2006).

interviewees complained that the MoGD has attempted to dominate the GBV conversation and the activities of all organizations, showing favouritism towards some NGOs and marginalizing others who express dissenting views.[59] This has created resentment amongst some advocates and hindered the extent to which they have shared ideas and information with other organizations.

Nonetheless, NGOs have worked with allies in government to achieve policy and institutional changes, but have also pressured these entities when their efforts have been resisted. They have also worked closely with IOs (the UN—the organization with the largest presence in the country—as well as other multilateral agencies, bilateral agencies, and international NGOs) who have prioritized the issue of rape, relying on them for financial and technical support to lobby the state and to fund programmes. The movement, often in collaboration with the state and IOs, has focused its anti-rape efforts on three areas: legal and policy changes, institutional and programmatic changes, and education and awareness-raising.

Laws and policies

Women's NGOs initiated action against rape through their participation in the creation of several women's rights policy documents including the 2006 GBV National Action Plan. The movement has also engendered legal change, lobbying for the amendment of the rape law in 2004 in response to frequent reports of rape, including gang rape and statutory rapes. AFELL identified the absence of a comprehensive rape law as an impediment to providing justice to victims and to deterring the crime, and began to work with other NGOs, IOs, and the state towards strengthening the existing law.[60] The amended law significantly enhanced the pre-existing statute on rape in the penal code, broadening the categories of acts that are included in the legal definition of rape, categorizing some forms of rapes as first-degree felonies, and mandating harsher punishment for those found guilty.

However, the amendment of the law highlighted the weaknesses of the judicial system. Rape cases sent to court were often left pending on the docket. Liberia lacked sufficient lawyers, judges, and courtrooms to adequately handle the wave of cases. This led to the prioritization of offences such as murder and treason over cases of rape and other forms of GBV.[61] Men accused of rape were sometimes held in custody for extended periods of time without trial and

---

[59] Interview, female member of staff of Liberian NGO, Monrovia, 29 June 2010; interview, female member of staff of Liberian NGO, Monrovia, 15 July 2010.

[60] Interview, Zeor Bernard, Interim President, AFELL, Monrovia, 7 September 2010.

[61] Interview, Deweh Gray, Commissioner, Law Reform Commission, Monrovia, 19 August 2010.

eventually released on humanitarian grounds.[62] Advocates also complained that rapists were bribing their way out of police custody.[63] This state of affairs underscored the need for the creation of new anti-rape institutions and programmes.

Creating new institutions and programmes

The women's movement has also advocated for the creation of new state agencies to address rape, while its members have developed and implemented programmes to prevent rape and support survivors. Within the government, the GBV Secretariat of the MoGD oversees all anti-GBV activity in the country and also chairs the National GBV Taskforce. Established in 2006 by a coalition of women's NGOs, IOs, and the government, the taskforce meets monthly in every county to strategize on plans of action, develop policies, evaluate existing programmes, and report on the successes and challenges that members experience in their day-to-day operations. NGOs in Monrovia and Gbarnga use the taskforce as a forum to discuss problems related to the police force and to bring their concerns to the attention of representatives of the WACPS, who sometimes attend taskforce meetings.[64] The taskforce provides a reasonably united front of activists advocating for change. It is relatively easy for a corrupt police officer to ignore the demands of a small NGO but significantly more difficult to disregard the taskforce.

The women's movement has also contributed to changes in the judicial system. In 2009, AFELL, with the support of several IOs, advocated for the passage of an act to create Criminal Court E, a court that is mandated exclusively to prosecute all cases of sexual violence, in Montserrado County. As of January 2011, there was one courtroom dedicated to hearing cases of sexual violence and trials were conducted *in camera* to protect the victim's confidentiality. Once this had been achieved, women's NGOs publicized the court and its function to the public. However, the prosecution of cases has proceeded at a glacial pace because there is only one courtroom dedicated to rape cases. Furthermore, as of August 2011, funding constraints had restricted the court to Montserrado County, meaning that survivors in the other 13 counties continue to face major barriers to justice.

AFELL, in collaboration with the MoJ and donors, was also a central figure in the creation of the ministry's Sexual and Gender Based Violence (SGBV) Crimes Unit in 2009 to complement Criminal Court E and the WACPS. The

---

[62] The problem persists.

[63] Interview, female member of staff of Liberian NGO, Monrovia, 15 July 2010.

[64] Interview, Anita Rennie, Bong County Gender Coordinator, Gbarnga, 5 May 2011; observation of GBV Taskforce meetings, Monrovia, 27 August 2010 and 30 September 2010.

unit is mandated to assist in the investigation and prosecution of sexual offences but is 'concerned about the whole being of the victim'.[65] It provides counsellors to work with victims during trial. The unit also supports the WACPS and complements its effort. WACPS officers liaise with and receive legal advice and guidance from staff of the unit when they investigate sexual violence cases. As of August 2011, however, the unit remained a pilot project that was operational only in Montserrado County.

Women's NGOs have not limited their efforts to the state. Organizations such as Women Aid Incorporated and THINK run safe homes, which, although severely under-resourced, shelter women and protect them from their abusers and the public. They sometimes resettle survivors in new communities and, when they are willing, NGOs guide them through the criminal justice system to reduce their fear of cooperating with the police and going to court. Staffs of some women's NGOs visit police stations to pressure the police to prioritize reported cases and to follow up on those that are pending. NGOs also serve as liaisons between complainants and the police, and their efforts facilitate the investigations. They sometimes provide transportation and phone airtime to enable investigating officers to follow up on cases. Although they are heavily underfunded and the services they provide are limited, they fill a crucial gap, as the state largely fails to provide these services.

Education and awareness-raising

Women's NGOs have also participated in the development of several awareness-raising programmes, including the 2007 Anti-Rape Campaign. NGOs also have myriad community education programmes. Development Education Network–Liberia organizes community workshops and dramas to raise awareness of rape in Gbarnga, while the Bassa Women Development Organization airs radio programmes that educate on a range of women's rights issues, including rape. With support from donors, NGOs have also trained journalists on rape reporting, and newspapers now regularly report on rape crimes although the majority of these stories focus on the rape of minors.[66] Their reports not only frame rape as a serious problem but also aim to encourage those affected to seek justice through the state. Police officers are exposed to these messages and they also receive training from NGOs such as AFELL and THINK. During these training sessions, they are taught the importance of and procedures for ensuring prosecution. Moreover, NGOs reach police officers through their participation in the crafting of police

---

[65] Interview, Felicia Coleman, Chief Prosecutor, SGBV Crime Unit, Monrovia, 14 July 2010.
[66] *Daily Observer* [Monrovia], 'Two get ten year jail each', 10 March 2011, p. 20; *Front Page* [Monrovia], 'Two men held for rape', 30 July 2010, p. 8b.

training documents. For example, AFELL contributed to the development of the MoJ's 2009 Sexual Assault and Abuse Police Handbook, which has been used to train police officers on how to respond to sexual violence cases.

Overall, it is clear that women's NGOs have launched anti-rape initiatives in a wide range of areas that influence policy implementation.[67] Their design of policies and institutions has affected the political and bureaucratic structures. They have trained and monitored implementers and implementing agencies, and they have educated and encouraged victims of violence to seek prosecution. They have, therefore, reached police officers through multiple pathways. Opportunities in the state's political and bureaucratic structures to participate in policy and programme design and support from IOs have facilitated NGOs' ability to engage the wide range of factors categorized in the literature as having an effect on policy implementation.[68]

The women's movement is, however, beset by challenges. Most NGOs face severe financial constraints and are heavily dependent on donor funding. This has enabled donors to set the agenda of some organizations. Donors have been overwhelmingly focused on sexual violence, leading one staff of an international NGO to comment that donors' attention to sexual violence has created a situation in which women's NGOs are 'blinded' by rape and mostly ignore other prevalent forms of GBV such as domestic violence.[69] Indeed I noticed that staff of some NGOs used the terms 'rape' and 'GBV' interchangeably. Other researchers have noted this problem.[70] This raises questions about the relationship between IOs and women's NGOs and the latter's ability to address non-sexual forms of GBV.

The GBV taskforce is also beset by dissent. Staff of some women's NGOs accused the MoGD, which chairs the taskforce, of punishing them for expressing opposing views. As mentioned above, they claimed that they have been sidelined from planning discussions and have been excluded from representing the taskforce at national and international anti-GBV meetings. This has led some member NGOs to respond negatively by failing to attend meetings, refusing to contribute to policy discussions, and failing to report on the progress of their respective programmes. This problem stems from the fierce competition for resources and recognition that exists among some activists and institutions. It hinders collaboration and limits the degree to which the movement can address rape. Nonetheless, the steps taken so far have affected how police officers enforce the rape law.

---

[67] Meyers and Vorsanger, 'Street-level bureaucrats and the implementation of public policy'.
[68] *Ibid.*
[69] Interview, female international NGO staff member, Monrovia, 1 September 2010.
[70] Carvalho and Schia, 'Sexual and gender-based violence in Liberia'.

The influence of the women's movement on police officers

By amending the rape law and introducing new rape policies, creating programmes and institutions, and educating the police and the public about rape, the women's movement has contributed to increased police referral of rape cases to court. The influence of women's NGOs on police officers has been facilitated by the political and material support provided by IOs and the state's openness to NGOs' participation in policy development. My suggestion is not that the withdrawal of rape cases is no longer a concern in Liberia, but that the rate of withdrawal of rape cases has fallen—relative both to the past and to other forms of GBV. Between January and December 2009, police referred 40 percent of rape cases to court, withdrew 4 percent, transferred 3 percent to other agencies, and left 53 percent pending. Over that same period, police referred 36.5 percent of domestic violence cases to court (prosecuted as aggravated assault), withdrew 29.6 percent, transferred 1 percent, and left 33.3 percent pending. Furthermore, the proportion of rape cases referred to court is significantly higher than prior to the civil war. None of the 49 rapes reported to the Montserrado County police from July 1967 to August 1968 were referred to court in this period.[71] In 1972 there were only two rape cases on record in the courts and four in 1977: these figures do not reflect a low incidence of rape but, rather, low reporting and referral to court.[72]

The interviews revealed that there are two factors that lead the police to respond differently to rape than other forms of GBV, and explain the lower rate of withdrawal. One is the perception that rape is a crime whose adjudication is above the jurisdiction of the police. The other is the existence of a non-withdrawal policy for rape in the WACPS. While this perception and policy existed before the war, both have recently been more purposely crafted and promoted by NGOs, IOs, and the state. I found that in addition to cultural beliefs, officers' perception of rape has been shaped by training, the WACPS' policies, and the framing of the rape law. The WACPS' non-withdrawal policy has been structured primarily by IOs but also by women's activism for a tougher response to rape. Women's NGOs have, therefore, directly and indirectly influenced police behaviour.

---

[71] Ministry of Justice, 'Annual Report of the Attorney General of the Republic of Liberia—October 1, 1967 to September 30, 1968' (Ministry of Justice, Monrovia).

[72] Ministry of Justice Annual Reports covering the periods: 1 October 1971–30 September 1972; 1 October 1972–31 December 1972; 1 January 1977–31 December 1977. Many of the reports were destroyed during the war.

Direct influence

The training sessions organized by women's NGOs, IOs, and the state have taught that prosecution is the only acceptable response to rape and have provided step-by-step guidance that aims to prevent the withdrawal of cases. AFELL's participation in the development of the 2009 Sexual Assault and Abuse Police Handbook, which reinforces this message, has further increased the organization's input into police training. This training aims to dispel any negative attitudes towards rape and to (re)form how officers think about the crime. The contrast in police officers' and the public's attitudes toward rape victims illustrates the effectiveness of this training. As discussed above, the public views some rapes as less serious and blames adult victims. The police officers interviewed did not express these views. Officers' references to their training when explaining their decision to refer cases to court underscores its importance. Officer No. 41 stated that, 'we have been told time and time in all trainings that rape is not compromisable'.[73]

Even where training is not explicitly given as a reason for referring cases to court, it underlies officers' decisions, as other explanations such as the role of the state as prosecutor and the magnitude of the offence are conveyed to officers in training.[74] This effect of training is expressed by Officer No. 36:

> We have been receiving cases where the [victim's] parents just do not want to prosecute the person but then for the police, we look at the crime committed, it's a state crime. So we tell them that since you do not want to prosecute this person, but for us you will be serving as a state witness, even though you serve as a complainant in our document. Once we have evidence linking this man to the crime, whether you do not want to prosecute, we will still send this man to court and the state will prosecute him.[75]

In another example, Officer No. 32 stated that 'with rape cases, everyone is aware…we don't take it lightly. It's not a minor offence. All major offences have to go to court. We don't compromise rape cases.'[76] These statements illustrate the effect of training on officers' perception of rape and, ultimately, their response to the crime.

Women's NGOs also directly influence police officers when they aid survivors in navigating the criminal justice system and when they lobby the WACPS to regulate officers' actions. Their presence places pressure on and provides resources for the police to conduct investigations, to do so in a timely

---

[73] Interview, male police officer, Monrovia, 10 June 2010.
[74] Ministry of Justice, 'Sexual assault and abuse handbook: for the women and children protection section of the Liberian National Police Force' (Ministry of Justice, Liberia, 2009).
[75] Interview, male police officer, Monrovia, 15 September 2010.
[76] Interview, male police officer, Monrovia, 14 September 2010.

manner, and to eschew actions—including the demand of bribes—that lead complainants to withdraw cases. The pressure exerted on the police through the GBV Taskforce and other organizational platforms is also important in this regard. A staff member of WIPNET explained that when the local police fail to investigate adequately the reports of women who come to her organization for help, or refuse to make arrests, her organization makes a report to the central police headquarters and, if that fails, to the MoJ.[77] She explained that women in the organization's sub-branches in the counties do not stop pressuring the police until the case proceeds to court. By taking these steps, women's NGOs lobby the WACPS to enforce its non-withdrawal policy, and hold it accountable. This accountability is important to ensure that policies on paper are effectively put into practice.

Indirect influence

AFELL spearheaded the campaign to strengthen the rape law and to eliminate all gaps that would lead to police withdrawal of cases. This amended law has signalled the gravity of the crime to police officers and conveyed the message that rapes should be prosecuted. It also provides clarity and direction and does not leave space for officers to use their discretion to determine if a case is 'serious' (and thus should be forwarded to court) or 'not serious' (and therefore should be withdrawn). In explaining their decisions to refer cases to court, some officers cited the provisions of the law. A female officer stationed in Monrovia stated that:

> Rape cases, they [complainants] come in talking about withdrawal but there is nothing like withdrawal in rape cases...Because, it's a first degree felony in Liberia, it is viewed just as murder cases are viewed.[78]

A male officer stationed in Monrovia explained why he employs his discretion when responding to domestic violence (aggravated assault) but not to rape:

> Rape cases are first degree felonies and aggravated assault is a second degree felony. For rape aspect we can't make our own decisions, we have to consult our superiors or the courts.[79]

Another officer, a male stationed in Monrovia, summarized the importance of the law in saying that he does not withdraw cases only because he fears disciplinary action from the WACPS but because 'the laws says that anyone

---

[77] Interview, member of staff, WIPNET, Monrovia, 30 June 2010.
[78] Interview, Officer No. 19, Monrovia, 29 September 2010.
[79] Interview, Officer No. 50, Monrovia, 10 July 2010.

who rapes needs to be prosecuted'.[80] These statements convey how the framing of the law has shaped officers' views and response to the crime.

In Monrovia, the creation of Criminal Court E and the SGBV Crime Unit has also led officers to refer cases to court. These institutions convey to officers the seriousness of the crime, institute measures that make it difficult for officers to use their discretion to withdraw rape cases, and support officers to refer cases to court. Officer No. 26 summarized the importance of the unit:

> If anybody comes to say I don't want to go to court, that is my relative, I don't want to go to court, we will tell you when you go to the SGBV [unit] you can tell them that but for now we have already turned the case over to SGBV.[81]

An officer discussing the role of the unit explained that,

> We have constructive partners that we work with that help us a lot in the SGBV Unit. They provide the legal technical know-how about the process of handling cases and how to avoid the contamination of evidence.[82]

Another officer explained that 'anytime cases of rape are reported, we contact the SGBV Unit and they advise us on what to do'.[83]

The support and supervision that the unit provides to investigating officers enhance investigations and contribute to their decision to refer rape cases to court. In the absence of an SGBV Unit in Gbarnga, officers relied on other less-resourced units within the MoJ. Officer No. 28 explained that 'when a woman chooses not to prosecute, we contact the County Attorney to seek advice. If the office is closed, we get to the magisterial court.'[84]

Women's NGOs also provide support to rape survivors. Their presence gives confidence to women, many of whom are intimidated by the criminal justice system and who lack the financial resources to usher a case through the system. Their involvement not only empowers some women to report their rapes to the police, but also to persist until justice is served by the courts.[85] Furthermore, the information that women's NGOs provide through radio programmes and other media encourages survivors to seek help from these NGOs and to cooperate with the police. In the absence of these programmes, many women would be ignorant of their rights under the law and, therefore, would continue to perceive customary courts and family meetings as the sole means of adjudication.

The decision of WACPS officers to refer cases to court has been shaped by their perception of the crime and by WACPS' policies. Officers' perception of

---

[80] Interview, Officer No. 16, Monrovia, 10 October 2010.
[81] Interview, female police officer, Monrovia, 16 September 2010.
[82] Interview, Officer No. 2, male, Monrovia, 12 July 2010.
[83] Interview, Officer No. 4, male, Monrovia, 20 September 2010.
[84] Interview, male police officer, Gbarnga, 24 May 2011.
[85] Interview, Zoe Bernard, Interim President, AFELL, Monrovia, 7 September 2010.

the crime has been influenced by NGOs. AFELL's spearheading of the amendment of the rape law enabled them to play a central role in laying the foundation for Liberia's response to rape, as this law guides the behaviour of police officers. NGOs' participation in police training has also enabled them to influence police officers directly. Policing the police and holding them accountable is another avenue through which women's NGOs have shaped police response to rape.

Opportunities within the state for women's NGOs to participate in the design of policies and institutions have enabled them to influence implementation. IOs' focus on sexual violence and the political and financial support that they have provided to NGOs and the state have also bolstered the efforts of the women's movement. Furthermore, the strategies used and members' efforts at organizing across Monrovia and Gbarnga have allowed the women's movement to reach politicians, bureaucrats, implementers, and the public—all of whom matter to the implementation process.[86] Building on the social movement literature, these findings show the conditions under which a social movement in a post-war African state has succeeded in influencing policy implementation.

Conclusion

Referring a rape case to court is no guarantee that it will be prosecuted, but it is a necessary step for victims to get justice. However, getting cases to court is an uphill battle for survivors of rape in Liberia and elsewhere. The case of Liberia demonstrates that police perception of the crime, and the organizational rules relating to it, shape the decision to refer cases to court. This article argues that women's NGOs in Liberia have contributed to shaping both police perceptions and the organizational rules, and in doing so have made police more likely to forward rape cases to court. Although some of their initiatives remain concentrated in Monrovia and resource constraints prevent them from reaching a significant proportion of women in other areas, they have set an important precedent and ensured that more women have their cases proceed to trial. Although police response to rape in Liberia remains deeply problematic, it is important to recognize the improvements that have been made, consider how these improvements have occurred, and use these lessons to think about how the implementation of rape and other GBV policies can be furthered across the continent.

---

[86] Meyers and Vorsanger, 'Street-level bureaucrats and the implementation of public policy'.

This article has demonstrated that women's movements matter beyond policy adoption. Two conditions, a relatively open political environment and political and material support from IOs, have enabled women's NGOs to access and impact the implementation process. Future studies can build upon these findings to further advance our understanding of the influence of women's movements on policy implementation. There is a need to investigate implementation across policy issue areas and socio-economic and political contexts. The case of Liberia demonstrates the central role played by the women's movement in a state that is mostly open to the involvement of non-state actors in the policy process, in part because it is characterized by weak institutions. It will be important for theory building to probe the extent to which the presence of the movement matters in other contexts where the state actually has the resources to perform the services that are being provided by women's NGOs in Liberia, and so is less dependent on non-state actors. The relationship between the women's movement and IOs also needs to be probed. In Liberia, IOs have provided material and political support to women's NGOs but there is a gap in understanding the degree to which they set the movement's agenda and the tension that this causes on the ground. It is, therefore, important to examine how IOs, which have a strong presence in post-war states, are affecting women's movements.

The outputs and outcomes of the policy implementation process are determined by a complex interaction of factors. The women's movement is only one actor in this process and it faces many internal and external challenges. Nonetheless, this article demonstrates that despite significant constraints, the Liberian women's movement has succeeded in changing how police officers respond to victims of rape. This finding offers many opportunities to better understand and improve the delivery of rape policies in Africa and beyond.

Acknowledgment

Published in *African Affairs*, 112, 448 (2013), p. 377–397. I am grateful to the research participants. Thanks to Taylor B. Seybolt, Lisa D. Brush, Muge Kokten Finkel, and Harvey White for insightful comments and suggestions. I also thank the editors of *African Affairs* and two anonymous reviewers for helpful comments and suggestions. An earlier version of this article was presented at the International Studies Association's Annual Convention, Montreal, 2011. A dissertation fellowship from the African and African Diaspora Studies Program at Boston College supported the writing of this project. All opinions and conclusions presented are my own.

17

Negotiating China

Reinserting African Agency into China–Africa Relations

Giles Mohan and Ben Lampert

CHINA'S RESURGENT ROLE IN AFRICA IS OFTEN presented as a relationship in which Chinese actors dominate the agenda and act in coordinated ways.[1] The flipside is that African actors are treated as passive and lacking agency. Yet recent moves by the Sata government in Zambia to double mining royalties highlight how African states are acting to leverage benefits from Chinese investment.[2] This article explores the role of African agency in shaping the dynamics and outcomes of China's renewed engagement with the continent. While not crudely reversing the analytical lens, we suggest that African actors also exercise agency outside the confines of the state, even as these actions are shaped by and in turn shape processes of state formation and function.

The first section of this article reviews existing political analyses of China–Africa relations and shows how these treat China as the dominant force and acknowledge little African agency beyond that located in the state. The following section reinserts African agency and advances a conceptual framework for understanding agency both within and beyond the state. We then investigate African agency by focusing on Chinese state investments in Angola, and on Chinese migrants in Ghana and Nigeria. It is argued that, at a variety of levels, African actors have negotiated and even shaped Chinese engagements in important ways—and in so doing have carved out more opportunities than is

---

[1] See Ted Fishman, *China, Inc.: How the rise of the next superpower challenges America and the world* (Simon and Schuster, London, 2005); Joshua Ramo, *The Beijing Consensus: Notes on the new physics of Chinese power* (The Foreign Policy Centre, London, 2004).
[2] Andrew England, 'Zambia to double mine royalties', *The Financial Times*, 11 November 2011, <http://www.ft.com/cms/s/0/5a64a96c-0c8c-11e1-88c6-00144feabdc0.html> (4 October 2012).

often recognized for their own benefit and advancement. However, the ability of African actors to exercise such agency is highly uneven and can have as much to do with African politics as it does with the politics of China–Africa relations.

Existing explanations of China—Africa politics: bilateral relations and state elites

Recent studies of the politics of China–Africa relations tend to focus on a particular set of actors and political relationships, which has the effect of attributing much of the power to China at the expense of Africa.[3] These studies are generally international and so focus on Chinese state actors qua African state actors.[4] Moreover the African actors that appear in this literature are overwhelmingly state elites and even then many of the instances of agency in action are occluded by a lack of data. Under-pinning this focus on state actors and inter-state relationships is the evident reality that these actors have been driving the growing engagement between China and Africa, which is reflected in the few studies which theorize across cases. Christopher Alden, Denis Tull, and Ian Taylor have all called for a focus on the African state when analysing China's impacts on Africa.[5]

From this inter-state focus a number of studies usefully highlight relational political dynamics. For example, Dan Haglund's work on Zambia focuses on 'the interface between Chinese investors and local regulatory institutions', or what he terms 'political embeddedness'.[6] Likewise Daniel Large's series of studies on Sudan is based on the premise that 'China's involvement has developed within, influenced and itself been affected by Sudanese politics

---

[3] Chris Alden and Daniel Large, 'China's exceptionalism and the challenges of delivering difference in Africa', *Journal of Contemporary China* 20, 68 (2011), pp. 21–38; Daniel Large, 'China's Sudan engagement: changing northern and southern political trajectories in peace and war', *The China Quarterly* 199 (September 2009), pp. 610–26.

[4] For example, Pádraig Carmody, Godfrey Hampwaye, and Enock Sakala, 'Globalisation and the rise of the state? Chinese geogovernance in Zambia', *New Political Economy* 17, 2 (2012), pp. 209–29; Sanusha Naidu, 'Balancing a strategic partnership? South Africa–China Relations' in Kweku Ampiah and Sanusha Naidu (eds), *Crouching Tiger, Hidden Dragon? Africa and China* (University of KwaZulu-Natal Press, Scottsville, 2008), pp. 167–219.

[5] Chris Alden, *China in Africa* (Zed Books, London, 2007); Denis Tull, 'China's engagement in Africa: scope, significance and consequences', *Journal of Modern African Studies* 44, 3 (2006), pp. 459–79; Ian Taylor, *The International Relations of Sub-Saharan Africa* (Continuum, London, 2010).

[6] Dan Haglund, 'Regulating FDI in weak African states: a case study of Chinese copper mining in Zambia', *Journal of Modern African Studies* 46, 4 (2008), pp. 547–75; see also Oliver Hensengerth, *Interaction of Chinese Institutions with Host Governments in Dam Construction: The Bui Dam in Ghana* (German Development Institute, Bonn, 2011).

since 1989'.[7] Beyond individual cases, Pádraig Carmody and Ian Taylor use the term 'flexigemony' to capture the more dynamic interactions between China and a differentiated landscape of African politics. For them flexigemony denotes how 'Chinese actors adapt their strategies to suit the particular histories and geographies of the African states with which they engage'.[8] While useful in examining the elite nature of these processes, the 'flexi-' prefix is about China's hegemonic intent rather than the agency of African actors, even if this is implicit in the notion of 'particular histories and geographies'.

This tendency to acknowledge African agency but then focus largely on the flexibility of the Chinese also appears in studies that rightly stress the 'pragmatism' of the Chinese. Jonathan Holslag sees China operating in a 'diffuse mercantilist' fashion where the Chinese state directs its economic actors. However, his useful analysis of China's responses to African coups, by its nature, examines the role of Chinese actors rather than African agency, beyond the reduction of Africa to an 'unstable' place.[9]

Even in those studies that attempt to drill down into these bilateral relationships the analysis invariably focuses on state elites. Pádraig Carmody, Godfrey Hampwaye, and Enock Sakala conclude their study of China–Zambia 'geogovernance' by arguing that the relationship is 'based on an (il)liberal bargain between domestic and Chinese political elites', and as we shall see a similar pattern pervades China's relations with Angola. But even when African agency is invoked in political analysis of China–Africa relations it is rarely conceptualized or demonstrated empirically, especially in the wider social arena beyond the state. As a result, there is a pressing need for research that goes beyond Chinese actors and the role of high-level state officials to address the 'informal operation of power and influence which may be at play' and conducts 'on-the-ground' analysis as opposed to theorizing from supposition.[10]

Reinserting (African) agency

Contemporary analyses of China in Africa have much in common with earlier debates about dependency, where African developments were seen as

---

[7] Large, 'China's Sudan engagement', p. 613.

[8] Pádraig Carmody and Ian Taylor, 'Flexigemony and force in China's geoeconomic strategy in Africa: Sudan and Zambia compared', *Geopolitics* 15, 3 (2010), pp. 496–515, p. 497.

[9] Jonathan Holslag, 'China and the coups: coping with political instability in Africa', *African Affairs* 110, 440 (2011), pp. 367–86. This is echoed in Alden and Large's discussion of China's 'adaptive impulse', in 'China's exceptionalism', p. 36.

[10] Carmody, Hampwaye, and Sakala, 'Chinese geogovernance in Zambia', p. 213. See also Joshua Eisenman, 'China's political outreach to Africa' in Robert Rotberg (ed.), *China into Africa: Trade, aid and influence* (Brookings Institution Press, Washington, DC, 2008).

determined by external capitalism.[11] Analysis of Africa's contemporary engagements with China often repeats this, but China's resurgence in spheres of influence that have traditionally been the purview of the Western powers has been one of the forces that has impelled a rethinking of African agency. Will Brown argues that the greater prominence of African states over the past decade is due to changes at the international level including growing demand for strategic minerals and energy resources, the global ramifications of the post-9/11 securitization process, and the rise of various 'Southern' actors.[12] According to some accounts, these developments give African states more space to manoeuvre.

As Colin Wight notes, there is a dearth of work in international relations (IR) on state agency.[13] In response Wight developed a three-layered theorization.[14] The first meaning he ascribes to agency relates to the more commonsense view in which agents have accountability, intentionality, and subjectivity. This notion of 'embodied intentionality' Wight terms 'agency$_1$'.[15] However, as we are all reflexive and embedded actors there is no pure 'I' unencumbered by social forces. Here Wight identifies 'agency$_2$', in which agents are 'an agent of something'. This emphasizes social context, particularly 'the socio-cultural system into which persons are born and develop'.[16] There is a recursive aspect to this since individuals can reproduce or transform these collective identities, although Wight acknowledges 'not all agents are equally placed or positioned'.[17] The third dimension of this framework is the roles that agents inhabit, although Wight prefers the term 'positioned practices' to reflect the non-normative aspect of this. However, these positioned practices—or agency$_3$—are structural in so far as they refer to properties that 'persist irrespective of the agents that occupy them', as illustrated for example by the diplomat. For Wight any invocation of agency requires all three dimensions; that is, they are 'co-constituted' and can only be analysed empirically.

Two implications arise from a critical engagement with Wight's framework. First, while Wight focuses on actors in social context, he underplays the conditioning effects of economic relations and fails to recognize that state agents have to be situated in the context of wider capitalist relations. Capital is fragmented in such a way that state activity and politics cannot be homogenized

---

[11] Colin Leys, *The Rise and Fall of Development Theory* (James Currey, London, 2006).

[12] Will Brown, 'African agency in international politics' (unpublished paper, ESRC African Agency in International Politics Seminar, University of Stellenbosch, 2–3 November 2011), <http://www.open.ac.uk/socialsciences/bisa-africa/african-agency> (4 October 2012).

[13] Colin Wight, 'State agency: social action without human activity', *Review of International Studies* 30, 2 (2004), pp. 269–80.

[14] Colin Wight, 'They shoot dead horses don't they? Locating agency in the agent-structure problematique', *European Journal of International Relations* 5, 1 (1999), pp. 109–42.

[15] *Ibid.*, p. 132.   [16] *Ibid.*, p. 133.   [17] *Ibid.*, p. 133.

by reducing them to the needs of a 'unitary' capital.[18] In terms of China's heightened role in Africa, one of the important differentiating factors is the scale and type of Chinese enterprise.[19] Much of the debate has focused on the bundling of Chinese aid, trade, and investment but this relates primarily to the ties between key Chinese ministries, development banks, and large state-owned enterprises.[20] These projects are often spatially enclaved with relatively few multipliers in the local economy or deep linkages to local society. By contrast we see private Chinese TNCs entering to compete for sales and contracts in the local open market, where they often lack the protection afforded by the tying of loans to investment. Finally there are independent Chinese entrepreneurs who have established a diverse array of small and medium-scale enterprises, some dating back to the colonial period.

A second analytical implication of Wight's tripartite approach to agency, especially the social context and roles, is to diversify what we might mean by political action. Here Tobias Hagmann and Didier Péclard have sought to 'understand how local, national and transnational actors forge and remake the state through processes of negotiation, contestation and bricolage'.[21] Their 'analytic of statehood' is about the dynamic and always undetermined process of state (de)construction, which is a multi-level phenomenon, although Martin Doornbos rightly cautions that social demands in Africa are often 'negated' rather than negotiated.[22] Hagmann and Péclard's framework comprises diverse actors, many of whom lie outside formal political structures, thereby extending beyond Wight's focus on official state roles. This move into the realm of 'social agency' acknowledges that 'all forms of external intervention necessarily enter the existing life-worlds of the individuals and social groups affected, and in this way are mediated and transformed by these same actors and structures'.[23] What also becomes apparent is that there is a strong class- and interest-based dimension to political and social agency. In the context of the opportunities and threats raised by China's entry into Africa, civil society action is often—but not exclusively—about protecting the class privileges of

---

[18] Jim Glassman, 'State power beyond the "territorial trap": the internationalization of the state', *Political Geography* 18, 6 (1999), pp. 669–96.

[19] Jing Gu, 'China's private enterprises in Africa and the implications for African development', *European Journal of Development Research* 24, 1 (2009), pp. 570–87.

[20] Paul Hubbard, 'Chinese concessional loans', in Rotberg (ed.), *China into Africa*, pp. 217–29.

[21] Tobias Hagmann and Didier Péclard, 'Negotiating statehood: dynamics of power and domination in Africa', *Development and Change* 41, 4 (2010), pp. 539–62, p. 544.

[22] Martin Doornbos, 'Researching African statehood dynamics: negotiability and its limits', *Development and Change* 41, 4 (2010), pp. 747–69.

[23] Norman Long, 'From paradigm lost to paradigm regained?' in Norman Long and Ann Long (eds), *Battlefields of Knowledge: The interlocking of theory and practice in social research and development* (Routledge: London, 1994), p. 20.

the African petit-bourgeoisie, while the sections of the state that benefit from (and so fight for) Chinese investment are often part of a highly select elite.

The power of Angola's state elites

The Angola case has been one of the most studied in the context of China's renewed engagement with Africa and is used here to demonstrate how the agency of African state elites is operating through the bespoke institutions set up to manage the China–Angola relationship.[24] Following Chris Alden, Angola can be seen as an 'illiberal regime with weak democracy', with an economy heavily based on oil extraction and export.[25] In this sense Angola shares many structural similarities with the Sudan case, in which a determined and insulated leadership used its political agency to shape the Chinese engagement to their own national and regional aspirations.[26]

Angola's post-war economy required huge amounts of social and infra-structural investment and so external financing was actively sought.[27] It was in this context that China, in need of energy resources, offered Angola a series of oil-backed credit lines with little conditionality.[28] China's Construction Bank provided the first funding for infrastructure development in 2002 and a 'framework agreement' was formally signed in 2003. In March 2004 the first ExIm Bank US$2 billion financing package for public investment projects was approved.

[24] Indira Campos and Alex Vines, 'Angola and China: a pragmatic partnership?' (Working Paper, CSIS Conference, 'Prospects for Improving US-China-Africa Cooperation', 5 December 2007), <http://www.csis.org/media/csis/pubs/080306_angolachina.pdf> (4 October 2012); Lucy Corkin, 'Uneasy allies: China's evolving relations with Angola', *Journal of Contemporary African Studies* 29, 2 (2011), pp. 169–80; Lucy Corkin, 'Chinese construction companies in Angola: a local linkages perspective' (Discussion Paper No. 2, MCCP, Open University, 2011); Alex Vines, Lillian Wong, Markus Weimer, and Indira Campos, *Thirst for African Oil: Asian national oil companies in Nigeria and Angola* (Chatham House, London, 2009); Lee Levkowitz, Marta McLellan Ross, and J. R. Warner, *The 88 Queensway Group: A case study in Chinese investors' operations in Angola and beyond* (US-China Economic and Security Review Commission, Washington, DC, 2009), <http://www.uscc.gov/The_88_Queensway_Group.pdf> (4 October 2012); Manuel Ferreira, 'China in Angola: just a passion for oil?' in Chris Alden, Daniel Large, and Ricardo Soares de Oliveira (eds), *China Returns to Africa: A rising power and a continent embrace* (Hurst, London, 2008), pp. 295–317.

[25] Alden, *China in Africa*.

[26] Ali Askouri, 'China's investment in Sudan: displacing villages and destroying communities', in Firoze Manji and Stephen Marks (eds), *African Perspectives on China in Africa* (Pambazuka Books, London, 2007), pp. 71–86; Daniel Large, 'From non-interference to constructive engagement? China's evolving relations with Sudan' in Alden, Large, and Soares de Oliveira (eds), *China Returns to Africa*, pp. 275–94.

[27] Tony Hodges, *Angola from Afro-Stalinism to Petro-Diamond Capitalism* (James Currey, Oxford, 2011).

[28] Corkin, 'Uneasy allies'.

Two additional ExIm loans of US$500 million and US$2 billion were made in 2007 with the repayment terms increased to 15 years and the interest rate revised downward.[29] A further US$1 billion loan from the China Development Bank was granted in March 2009 (rising to US$1.5 billion in 2010) with a view to supporting the development of Angolan agriculture. In the first official estimate of Chinese credit to Angola, the Chinese ambassador said in 2011 that US$14.5 billion in credit had been provided since the end of the war from China's three state banks.[30] Project proposals identified as priorities by the various Angolan ministries are put forward to the Grupo de Trabalho Conjunto (GTC, Joint Work Programme), a committee comprising Angola's Ministry of Finance and China's Ministry of Commerce (MOFCOM). Implementation then passes over to a multi-sectoral technical group, the GAT (Gabinete de apoio tecnico de gestão da linha de crédito da China, Technical Support Office for the Management of the Chinese Credit Line). For each project put to tender, the Chinese government proposes three to four Chinese companies, while sectoral ministries manage these public works and ensuring that sufficient staff are trained. Through these institutional arrangements, the Angolan government has been able to use Chinese credit to undertake over 100 projects that correspond to its strategy of prioritizing the (re)construction of key infrastructure.

Additionally, oil-backed loans amounting to as much as US$10 billion have been provided by a private equity firm based in Hong Kong called the China International Fund (CIF). Lee Levkowitz, Marta McLellan Ross, and J. R. Warner have shown that many of the Chinese companies currently operating in Angola have the same address in Hong Kong.[31] The ownership and management structures of these firms are diffuse and opaque with the same individuals holding varying stakes in a number of joint ventures. Crucially, the CIF credit facility has been managed by Angola's Reconstruction Office, the Gabinete de Reconstrução Nacional (GRN), which has been exclusively accountable to the Angolan presidency.[32] The various *gabinetes* founded by President Dos Santos have always been highly personalized vehicles for economic management as part of what Ricardo Soares de Oliveira terms a 'successful failed state'.[33] In the major government reshuffle of March 2010, the GRN was replaced by a company called Sonangol Imobiliária (Sonangal Real Estate) that took over responsibility for implementing various

[29] Campos and Vines, *Angola and China*.
[30] Marcus Power, Giles Mohan, and May Tan-Mullins, *China's Resource Diplomacy in Africa: Powering development?* (Palgrave Macmillan, London, 2012).
[31] Levkowitz, McLellan Ross, and Warner, *The 88 Queensway Group*.
[32] Campos and Vines, *Angola and China*.
[33] Ricardo Soares de Oliveira, 'Business success, Angola-style: postcolonial politics and the rise of Sonangol', *Journal of Modern African Studies* 45, 4 (2007), pp. 595–619.

infrastructure projects. However, there was a wider perception that transferring control to a branch of the state oil company would be unlikely to enhance transparency compared to 'strengthening the relevant state institutions'.[34]

These institutional fixes suggest a particular form of African political agency. In the relationship between the CIF and the GRN/Sonangol Imobiliaria the agency of a small number of Chinese and Angolan actors has produced a node that sits within the state but is only connected to clandestine elements within it—what Lucy Corkin terms 'closed door negotiations'.[35] This is reminiscent of the unaccountable enclaves within states during the structural adjustment era when 'parallel governments' were established in finance ministries by appointed technocrats.[36] The model of 'parallel government' in Angola today is in keeping with the patterns of accumulation prior to the entry of the Chinese, in which a coterie around Dos Santos used the state oil company, Sonangol, to buttress their power.[37] As Corkin notes, the China–Angola model of engagement arose out of an 'opportune moment of equal need' when Dos Santos needed the economic and social infrastructure to build his regime's legitimacy and support base in the run-up to elections.[38] For their part the Chinese needed access to oil in an environment where other supplier states were already dominated by Western oil companies; they were also seeking new markets for Chinese manufacturers.[39] For the Chinese, structures like the GRN and GTC are, as Corkin argues, a way of minimizing risk since their close surveillance allows Chinese actors to monitor expenditure and delivery in a way that less ring-fenced forms of financing could not.[40]

Such agency therefore profoundly questions a unitary understanding of the state and also highlights state building as an ongoing process involving actors within and outside the state. Moreover, Chinese relations with many African countries are maturing and moving beyond state-to-state deals, implicating many more actors. So, the need to move beyond statist, elite dialogues is not simply a theoretical exercise, but one made more pressing by this growing 'embeddedness' of mutual political and economic ties.

---

[34] Sylvia Croese, '1 million houses? Angola's national reconstruction and Chinese and Brazilian engagement' in Fahamu (ed.), *Strengthening the Civil Society Perspective Series II: China and other emerging powers in Africa* (Fahamu, Oxford, 2011), p. 8, <http://www.fahamu.org/images/empowers_report_0311.pdf> (4 October 2012).

[35] Lucy Corkin, 'All's fair in loans and war: the development of China–Angola relations' in Ampiah and Naidu (eds), *Crouching Tiger, Hidden Dragon?*, pp. 108–23.

[36] Eboe Hutchful, 'From "revolution" to monetarism: the economics and politics of the adjustment programme in Ghana', in Bonnie Campbell and John Loxley (eds), *Structural Adjustment in Africa* (Macmillan, London, 1989).

[37] Soares de Oliveira, 'Business success'.   [38] Corkin, 'Uneasy allies', p. 178.

[39] Campos and Vines, *Angola and China.*

[40] Corkin, 'Uneasy allies'; Ferreira, 'China in Angola'.

African social agency in action: encouraging and facilitating the Chinese presence

Just as many African governments have consciously turned to China as a potential partner in national development and regime legitimacy, African citizens have increasingly reached out to China as a source of useful resources for personal and business progression. For example, Gregor Dobler's work on Namibia mentions town twinning as a semi-formal means of encouraging inward Chinese investment and trade.[41] Another manifestation of this is significant numbers of African traders who, since the mid-1990s, have travelled to China, especially Guangzhou, to buy Chinese consumer goods for export to Africa.[42] Significantly, local manufacturers that we interviewed in Ghana and Nigeria often argued that it is these African traders in China, rather than Chinese traders in Africa, who have been primarily responsible for the massive influx of cheap Chinese goods in recent years.[43] Indeed, Chinese traders in these countries regularly reported that their greatest competition came not from their co-nationals but rather from African traders who source goods from China, the latter seen as having a better understanding of the local market.[44] In the sense of Wight's agency$_2$, these African traders are agents embedded in particular cultural contexts that give them a distinct commercial advantage.

The forging of connections to China by African traders also appears to be one of the factors that has encouraged Chinese entrepreneurs and companies to come to the continent. Respondents from Chinese manufacturing companies that have established outlets and/or factories in Ghana and Nigeria often remarked that they had first been alerted to the West African market by the quantity of orders they received from traders from the region. For example, a Chinese entrepreneur who came to Nigeria in 2001 to sell textiles and subsequently established a furniture factory in Lagos in 2006 recalls, 'I had a

---

[41] Gregor Dobler, 'Solidarity, xenophobia and the regulation of Chinese businesses in Namibia', in Alden, Large, and Soares de Oliveira (eds), *China Returns to Africa*, pp. 237–55.

[42] See, for example, Adams Bodomo, 'The African trading community in Guangzhou: an emerging bridge for Africa–China relations', *The China Quarterly* 203 (September 2010), pp. 693–707; Sylvie Bredeloup, 'African trading post in Guangzhou: emergent or recurrent commercial form?', *African Diaspora* 5, 1 (2012), pp. 27–50; Michal Lyons, Alison Brown, and Li Zhigang, 'In the dragon's den: African traders in Guangzhou', *Journal of Ethnic and Migration Studies* 38, 5 (2012), pp. 869–88.

[43] See also Laurence Marfaing and Alena Thiel, 'Chinese commodity imports in Ghana and Senegal: demystifying Chinese business strength in urban West Africa' (Working Paper 180, German Institute of Global and Area Studies, Hamburg, 2011).

[44] See also Heidi Østbø Haugen, 'Chinese exports to Africa: competition, complementarity and cooperation between micro-level actors', *Forum for Development Studies* 38, 2 (2011), pp. 157–76.

small-scale factory in [China] and we knew that Nigeria was a large market because Nigerians were importing from my factory.... So that was why I knew that there's a market in Nigeria. So I came to Nigeria.'[45]

Furthermore, we found that Ghanaian and Nigerian entrepreneurs are playing a much more direct role in encouraging the Chinese presence by sourcing not only consumer goods but also partners, workers, and capital goods from China—something that Deborah Brautigam noted in the case of autoparts manufacturers in south-east Nigeria.[46] Among manufacturers in the two countries, purchasing relatively cheap machinery from China has become an increasingly important way of maintaining production in the face of almost prohibitively high costs linked largely to unreliable and expensive power supplies and limited transport infrastructure.[47] Central to this strategy of taking advantage of more affordable Chinese technology is recruiting Chinese technicians to oversee installation and train their local counterparts in operating, maintaining, and repairing the machinery. For example, a Nigerian engineering component manufacturer reported that when he replaced his ageing Europe-sourced production lines for half the cost by turning to a supplier in China, he also negotiated for nine technicians to be seconded to his Lagos factory for six months.[48] To assist the Chinese technicians he employed the services of a Chinese-speaking Nigerian man who had recently returned to Nigeria with his Chinese wife to establish a translation company after studying and working in China for 6 years.

In an important twist to the dominant narrative around Chinese firms importing their own labour we found evidence that African companies across a range of sectors increasingly view China as a source of skilled and/or hardworking labour and are actively bringing over Chinese workers in an attempt to increase productivity and provide higher quality goods and services.[49] This evolution in African business connections with China is exemplified by Mr Daniel, a Nigerian entrepreneur based in Lagos who has employed Chinese staff in a number of his businesses.[50] Mr Daniel's furniture business had been based on importing finished furniture from Europe and, more recently, China. When the Nigerian government banned the importation of furniture in 2004 he realized his only option was to manufacture locally, but was concerned that

---

[45] Interview, Chinese factory owner, Lagos, 20 December 2010. This is our interpreter's translation from the Chinese.

[46] Deborah Brautigam, 'Close encounters: Chinese business networks as industrial catalysts in sub-Saharan Africa', *African Affairs* **102**, 408 (2003), pp. 447–67.

[47] See also Dulue Mbachu, 'Nigerian resources: changing the playing field', *South African Journal of International Affairs* **13** (2006), pp. 77–82.

[48] Interview, Nigerian manufacturer, Lagos, 9 October 2010.

[49] See also Mario Esteban, 'A silent invasion? African views on the growing Chinese presence in Africa: the case of Equatorial Guinea', *African and Asian Studies* **9**, 3 (2010), pp. 232–51.

[50] Interview, Mr Daniel, Nigerian businessman, Lagos, 12 October 2010. The names of individuals and companies have been changed to protect the identity of respondents.

local labour would not be sufficiently skilled or reliable, while expatriate labour from Europe would be far too expensive. Having been impressed by the quality of the Chinese furniture he had previously imported, he learned from the extensive network of contacts he had established in southern China that Chinese labour was 'cheap' and able to bear basic living conditions. He therefore recruited a team of four furniture makers from one of his former suppliers in Guangdong Province.

On the basis of this positive experience Mr Daniel made recruiting labour from China an explicit strategy in the expansion of his business empire. Most recently, he hired 14 workers from China for a construction company he has established with a Chinese partner. One of their first projects is to convert a large building owned by Mr Daniel into a hotel, for which he is in the process of recruiting from China a manager, chef and two masseurs. Indeed, hospitality is one of the sectors in which Nigerian and Ghanaian entrepreneurs have been most active in recruiting Chinese staff for the skills and professionalism they are seen to offer. This is particularly evident among the growing number of African entrepreneurs in Accra and Lagos who have established up-market Chinese restaurants in order to capture the growing middle-class and elite demand for 'authentic' cuisine. A key strategy for achieving this is to recruit experienced Chinese chefs and restaurant managers, either directly from China or, to quote a Ghanaian restaurateur, by 'poaching' them from local Chinese-owned competitors.[51]

Significantly, Chinese partners and workers brought to Ghana and Nigeria by African entrepreneurs have gone on to facilitate further Chinese immigration, initiating an African-induced process of chain migration and investment.[52] In one of the most notable cases, the founder of the 'China Town' shopping complex in Lagos, which has served as an important gateway for Chinese migrants to Nigeria, was first brought into the country from China by Chief Oladipo, a prominent Nigerian businessman and politician. Chief Oladipo, having established strong business links with China in the 1980s, wanted to set up a business to extract salt from the lagoons of Lagos; he was able to recruit a Chinese partner, Mr Wu, with the necessary experience.

Mr Wu arrived in Nigeria in 1990 but, just as the venture was taking off, it collapsed when Chief Oladipo was forced into political exile.[53] Observing that there were openings for affordable consumer goods in Nigeria, Mr Wu remained in Lagos and began trading in products imported from China. Chief Oladipo returned to Nigeria in 1998 and, when he was elected to an

---

[51] Interview, Ghanaian businessman, Accra, 30 June 2011.

[52] See Dobler, 'Solidarity, xenophobia' for how local officials help facilitate Chinese chain migration to Namibia.

[53] Interview, Mr Wu, Chinese entrepreneur, Lagos, 9 September 2010.

important political position the following year, helped Mr Wu to establish Nigeria's first 'China Town' shopping complex in the up-market Lagos district of Ikoyi. A political ally of Chief Oladipo argues that his intention in supporting the 'China Town' project was to attract Chinese entrepreneurs who would go on to establish factories in Lagos, thereby generating local employment and supporting economic development.[54] However, another respondent involved with the complex points out that it became a useful outlet for close relatives of Chief Oladipo involved in the textile business, particularly for retailing the substantial volumes of affordable material they imported from China.[55] This could be indicative of a discourse of 'local development' being used to justify mutually beneficial interpersonal ties to Chinese entrepreneurs, as Dobler found in the case of Namibia.[56]

Whatever Chief Oladipo's intentions, 'China Town' soon became a thriving centre for the distribution of Chinese consumer goods. By 2002 the complex was full and Chief Oladipo facilitated its relocation to a larger site in Ojota, where a new structure was commissioned in 2005. By then, several hundred Chinese were trading there with many using the complex as an initial base before moving on to pursue other commercial opportunities within and beyond Lagos. Mr Wu became a major Chinese migration and investment broker, not only bringing in traders to 'China Town' but also working to advise and assist Chinese entrepreneurs and companies wishing to establish operations in Nigeria. Furthermore, with 'China Town' having aroused some significant resistance from important economic and political forces in Nigeria, it is suggested by associates of Mr Wu that he has been able to continue to function in this way thanks to the continuing support and protection of Chief Oladipo, who remains a highly influential figure both in Lagos and Nigeria as whole. As Mr Wu himself observes, '[Y]ou must become friends with the Nigerian person. That's the only way you will be able to move forward in Nigeria.'[57]

The case of Chief Oladipo illustrates not only how African entrepreneurs can initiate inward flows of Chinese migrants and investment but also how Chinese enterprises in Ghana and Nigeria often depend on local patrons in order to survive and prosper. Clearly, through the positions they inhabit in the local social context, African patrons are able to enact agency in ways that can have an important influence over the fortunes of Chinese ventures.

---

[54] Interview, Nigerian associate of Chief Oladipo, Lagos, 16 September 2010.
[55] Interview, Nigerian associate of 'China Town' complex, Lagos, 8 September 2010.
[56] Dobler, 'Solidarity, xenophobia'.
[57] Interview, 9 September 2010. For more on the elite connections of prominent Chinese entrepreneurs in Nigeria see Serge Michel, Michel Beuret, and Paolo Woods, *China Safari: On the trail of Beijing's expansion in Africa* (Nation Books, New York, NY, 2009).

African workers: agency and advancement in Chinese enterprises

Contrary to the dominant assertion that Chinese companies operating in Africa tend to rely on labour imported from China, in most of the 85 Chinese enterprises we studied in Ghana and Nigeria, a substantial proportion, and often the majority, of the workforce was African. This was seen at a range of scales, from the independent Chinese traders in markets in Lagos and Accra who generally employ at least a couple of local assistants all the way through to the largest Hong Kong Chinese-owned industrial groups that employ thousands of African workers.[58] Even where these Chinese enterprises have not been encouraged or facilitated by an African patron, it was clear that their success depended on African actors in the form of their local workers. Chinese entrepreneurs often emphasized that employing African labour was central to their business strategy and sustainability; it was not only seen to be considerably cheaper than bringing in workers from China, but was also deemed essential to understanding the local market.

For instance, the two Chinese managers of the Nigeria office of a Chinese quarry machinery manufacturing company argue that beyond the highly competitive price of their product range, it is their two Nigerian sales directors that have been key to the rapid success of the outlet.[59] The Chinese managers report that while they had a limited ability to communicate in English, and particularly Nigerian English, the Nigerian sales directors were able to initiate a strategy of visiting local quarries to talk directly to the owners—and that it was through the personal relationships they initiated that the first orders came in. Furthermore, the Nigerian sales directors built on this by contracting some of the initial cohort of satisfied customers to act as sales agents for the company, thereby establishing a wide-reaching marketing network.

While management positions tend to be dominated by Chinese staff, having at least some locals in these roles is often considered useful, particularly in negotiating the demands of government agencies and officials and in recruiting, managing, and motivating local workers, agents, and subcontractors.[60] In some cases, African staff constitute a significant proportion of management

---

[58] See also Françoise Bourdarias, 'Chinese migrants and society in Mali: local constructions of globalization', *African and Asian Studies* **9**, 3 (2010), pp. 269–85; Karsten Giese and Alena Thiel, 'The vulnerable other—distorted equity in Chinese–Ghanaian employment relations', *Ethnic and Racial Studies* (forthcoming); Antoine Kernen, 'Small and medium-sized Chinese businesses in Mali and Senegal', *African and Asian Studies* **9**, 3 (2010), pp. 252–68; Ching Kwan Lee, 'Raw encounters: Chinese managers, African workers and the politics of casualization in Africa's Chinese enclaves', *The China Quarterly* **199** (September 2009), pp. 647–66; Yan Hairong and Barry Sautman, 'Chinese farms in Zambia: from socialist to "agro-imperialist" engagement?' *African and Asian Studies* **9**, 3 (2010), pp. 307–33.

[59] Interview, Chinese managers, Lagos, 13 December 2010.

[60] See also Bourdarias, 'Chinese migrants'; Lee, 'Raw encounters'; Hairong and Sautman 'Chinese farms'.

and/or have become their Chinese bosses' closest and most trusted managers. In one of the Chinese-owned manufacturing companies we visited in Tema, for example, the factory manager is a Ghanaian who has worked there since the company was founded some 30 years ago.[61] Reporting directly to the Chinese owner, he is the most senior manager at the company and helps oversee not only the 58 local staff but also the three Chinese technicians.

As this example suggests, African workers have carved out significant opportunities for their own advancement. This is especially apparent in Golden Telecoms, one of the three major Chinese telecommunication companies that have entered the Nigerian market since the late 1990s. Golden Telecoms has explicitly pursued a strategy of recruiting a high proportion of local staff. Former and current local Golden Telecoms staff report that as a result of this strategy the company has developed the reputation as a good place to launch a career in Nigeria's rapidly growing telecoms industry and wider corporate sector.[62] While Golden Telecoms is known to pay less than its American and European competitors, it is seen to promote locals more rapidly and in greater numbers than its rivals and, significantly, to invest much more in their training and development. Indeed, with the intensive, often hands-on training programmes that it offers its local staff, Golden Telecoms is regarded as something of a commercial finishing school, particularly for those interested in gaining specialized telecoms knowledge or more general expertise in marketing and project management. As a Chinese Golden Telecoms executive acknowledged, local staff often spend a few years at the company and then move on to attain more lucrative jobs with its rivals and other major 'blue-chip' firms operating in Nigeria.[63]

Furthermore, some Nigerian Golden Telecoms staff have used the skills and experience they have acquired at the company to establish or significantly augment dynamic new Nigerian companies both in and beyond the telecoms sector. For example, a former Golden Telecoms senior staff member argues that the knowledge and experience he gained at the company enabled him to establish a fast-growing telecoms engineering services firm in 2007. 'We started by saying that we will sell knowledge', he recalls, 'and all this came from my last place of work.... The Chinese trained me.'[64] His company now enjoys significant contracts not only with Golden Telecoms but also most of the other big telecoms companies and employs over a hundred staff, many of whom he has trained directly by drawing on his Golden Telecoms expertise. Such cases support Brautigam's assertion that contact with Chinese businesses

---

[61] Interviews, Chinese factory owner and Ghanaian factory manager, Tema, 23 August 2011.
[62] Interviews, five current and three former Nigerian Golden Telecoms staff, Lagos, 29 September–19 October 2010.
[63] Interview, Chinese Golden Telecoms executive, Lagos, 13 September 2010.
[64] Interview, Nigerian former Golden Telecoms staff member, Lagos, 5 October 2010.

can enable African entrepreneurs to develop new skills and capabilities and establish spin-off ventures of their own.[65]

African resistance: challenging the Chinese presence

While some African actors have actively assisted, and carved out opportunities from, the Chinese presence in Ghana and Nigeria, others have felt that it damages their interests and have sought to contest it. As elsewhere in Africa, the growing Chinese presence has excited considerable public debate and even protest.[66] Some Ghanaian and Nigerian actors have taken direct action to regulate the activities of the Chinese and on occasion have attracted some degree of support from elements of the state. Such action has in some cases produced tangible effects, disrupting and/or constraining Chinese enterprise and forcing Chinese actors to adapt their strategies and activities.[67] All of this is especially evident in the response to Chinese traders and their importation of 'cheap' Chinese consumer goods, which has been one of the most contentious issues related to the Chinese presence in both Ghana and Nigeria.[68]

In Nigeria, much of the agitation has focused on the 'China Town' in Lagos discussed earlier.[69] By the time the complex relocated to Ojota in 2002,

---

[65] Deborah Brautigam, '"Flying geese" or "hidden dragon"? Chinese business and African industrial development' in Alden, Large, and Soares de Oliveira (eds), *China Returns to Africa*, pp. 51–68.

[66] Dobler, 'Solidarity, xenophobia'; Dirk Kohnert, *Are the Chinese in Africa More Innovative than the Africans? Comparing Chinese and Nigerian entrepreneurial cultures of innovation* (GIGA, Hamburg, 2010); Margaret Lee, 'Uganda and China: unleashing the power of the dragon' in Henning Melber (ed.), *China in Africa* (Nordiska Afrikainstitutet, Uppsala, 2007); Lee, 'Raw encounters'; Terence McNamee, *Africa in Their Words: A study of Chinese traders in South Africa, Lesotho, Botswana, Zambia and Angola* (Brenthurst Foundation, Johannesburg, 2012); Cyril Obi, 'Enter the dragon? Chinese oil companies and resistance in the Niger Delta', *Review of African Political Economy* 35, 117 (2008), pp. 417–34; Barry Sautman and Yan Hairong, 'African perspectives on China–Africa links', *The China Quarterly* 199 (September 2009), pp. 728–59.

[67] For other cases see Dobler, 'Solidarity, xenophobia'; Lee, 'Raw encounters'; Human Rights Watch, *"You'll Be Fired If You Refuse": Labor abuses in Zambia's Chinese state-owned copper mines* (Human Rights Watch, New York, NY, 2011), <http://www.hrw.org/sites/default/files/reports/zambia1111ForWebUpload.pdf> (4 October 2012).

[68] Isaac Idun-Arkhurst, *Ghana's Relations with China* (South African Institute of International Affairs, Johannesburg, 2008); Kohnert, *Are the Chinese in Africa More Innovative*; Jing Lui, 'Contact and identity: the experience of China goods in a Ghanaian marketplace', *Journal of Community and Applied Social Psychology* 20, 3 (2010), pp. 184–201; Ndubisi Obiorah, Darrean Kew, and Yusuf Tanko, 'Peaceful rise and human rights: China's expanding relations with Nigeria' in Rotberg (ed.), *China into Africa*, pp. 272–95; Alaba Ogunsanwo, 'A tale of two giants: Nigeria and China' in Ampiah and Naidu (eds), *Crouching Tiger, Hidden Dragon?*, pp. 192–207.

[69] See also Sola Akinrinade and Olukoya Ogen, 'Globalization and de-industrialization: South–South neo-liberalism and the collapse of the Nigerian textile industry', *The Global South* 2, 2 (2008), pp. 159–70; Mbachu, 'Nigerian resources'; Olukoya Ogen, 'Contemporary China–Nigeria economic relations: Chinese imperialism or South–South mutual partnership?',

prominent Nigerian manufacturers and the Manufacturers Association of Nigeria had begun to mobilize against it. They argued that the importation of cheap and often sub-standard Chinese goods was fatally undermining local producers. Indeed, this agitation only increased as the new complex became more popular with Chinese traders and African consumers alike. 'They challenged it with all their powers', recalls a Nigerian closely involved with 'China Town' since its early days. 'They did not want the influx of these people because they know they will take over all their markets. So it was bad . . . What they do is they go to the authorities, right from the presidency to every arms of the government, to say look at these people . . . their product is not good, their business is not right, cross check very well.'[70] As a result of such calls by the manufacturing lobby, the federal government added a number of goods, such as textiles and furniture, to its import prohibition list between 2003 and 2004. In late 2005, just nine months after the new 'China Town' was officially commissioned by President Obasanjo's wife, officers of the Nigeria Customs Service descended upon the complex, seized banned imported goods and closed it for three months.

The impact of this action was considerable. The vast majority of the Chinese traders lost most or all of their stock. Some simply went out of business and returned to China. Many others moved to another country or attempted to relocate within Nigeria. A good number fled to Kano but here the local traders' association promptly banned 'foreigners' from the city's famous textiles market and sought to restrict the Chinese to wholesaling at the perimeter.[71] For those who remained in the Lagos 'China Town', business never recovered. Some traders stopped importing the banned goods while others continued to bring them in, particularly textiles, but faced the increasingly high costs of 'settling' officials. With a reduced quantity and range of goods on offer, the remaining Chinese traders complain that the complex has won back few of its old customers. Such political agency enacted by lower-tier officials can clearly modify Chinese behaviours and is arguably a material gain for these 'street level bureaucrats'.[72] However, Haglund's work on the regulatory weaknesses of the Zambian state shows that weak local political capacity is a toxic cocktail in which Chinese firms are relatively free to abuse labour and environmental laws.[73]

While Nigeria's manufacturers have enjoyed some success in encouraging the state to disrupt the activities of Chinese traders operating in the country,

---

China aktuell 3 (2008), pp. 78–102; Pat Utomi, *China and Nigeria* (Center for Strategic and International Studies, Washington, DC, 2008).

[70] Interview, Nigerian associate of 'China Town' complex, Lagos, 16 September 2010.

[71] Interviews, Nigerian traders' association official and Chinese textile outlet manager, Kano, 18 December 2010.

[72] See also Dobler, 'Solidarity, xenophobia'.   [73] Haglund, 'In it for the long term'.

less elite groups have gained little state support in their attempts to contest the Chinese presence. In late 2010, the second in what was planned to be a nation-wide series of protests was held to challenge the growing tendency of major international and Nigerian firms to employ large numbers of foreign workers, particularly from India and China. Organized by a group of trade unions and civil society organizations, one of the campaign's main targets was the Nigerian-owned Dangote Group, which stood accused of employing 3,000 Chinese work-ers in the construction of its new cement factory, many apparently doing low- and semi-skilled jobs for which Nigerians could have been found easily.[74] The Dangote Group attracted criticism not only because it proudly claims to be Nigeria's foremost indigenous conglomerate but also because its owner, Alhaji Aliko Dangote, was, rather ironically, the chairman of the federal government's National Committee on Job Creation. Despite their well-publicized public pro-tests appealing to the President and ministers, the campaigners failed to elicit any government response.

It appears that the Dangote Group has continued unhindered in its utiliza-tion of Chinese labour: Chinese workers were conspicuous at the recent opening of one of its new cement factories.[75] In Doornbos's terms, it would seem that the social demands advanced in this case have been negated rather than negotiated by state elites, reminding us of Wight's assertion that 'not all agents are equally placed or positioned'.[76] This can also be seen in the mixed results African trade unions have had in improving the pay and conditions of local workers in Chinese enterprises, where the quality of leadership and degree of government support have been key factors in the effectiveness of organized labour.[77]

Conclusion

Africa cannot be seen as simply a passive space increasingly subject to intervention by China. While we must be wary of reversing the analytical lens too far, reinserting African agency into the dominant discourse of China-in-Africa reveals Sino-African relationships that are more locally driven and mediated than is generally recognized. Just as Kobena Mercer noted that identity only becomes an issue when it is threatened, agency becomes

---

[74] Interviews, two male Nigerian leaders of the campaign, Lagos, 30 September and 4 October 2010.

[75] BBC News, 'Aliko Dangote opens Nigeria's biggest cement plant', 11 June 2012, <http://www.bbc.co.uk/news/world-africa-18400028> (11 June 2012).

[76] Doornbos, 'Researching African statehood'; Wight, 'They shoot dead horses', p. 133.

[77] Lee, 'Raw encounters'; Anthony Baah and Herbert Jauch, *Chinese Investments in Africa: A labour perspective* (African Labour Research Network, Namibia, 2009); Power, Mohan, and Tan-Mullins, *China's Resource Development*.

important where it is denied.[78] It is here that academics as interlocutors have to avoid overly structural accounts that deny African agency and simply produce political nihilism that forecloses a future in which African agency can be realized in more transformative ways.

African actors have been able to shape these relationships in ways that advance their own interests and aspirations and/or produce forms of wider social benefit. This agency is found at the individual level, but also within more organized civil society activity and within parts of the African state. While cases of John Lonsdale's African 'agency in tight corners' clearly exist, contexts also emerge in which multiple forms of African agency work to bring some benefits to African development.[79] However, the ability of African actors to express this agency is highly contingent: the space for African agency varies significantly, and it is thus neither possible nor wise to homogenize or reify this agency outside of particular contexts.[80]

Indeed, the African actors that appear to benefit most are often political and business elites and this might reinforce unaccountable modes of political and economic governance as well as highly uneven distributions of wealth and power. In terms of scale, Chinese and African elites enter relationships at the local level where discourses of 'local development' are used to legitimate what are largely private agendas. Likewise at the central state level small elite 'nodes' provide protection, albeit quite fragile, for Chinese firms to accumulate and deploy the rhetoric of 'South–South cooperation' to legitimize these essentially narrow interests.[81] But as the cases of resistance demonstrate, there are emerging sites in which these inequalities are being contested within African societies, and not in straightforwardly 'anti-Chinese' ways.

Acknowledgment

Published in *African Affairs*, 112, 446 (2012), p. 92–110. The research for this article was conducted within two ESRC-funded projects (RES-062-23-0487 and RES 062-23-1893). The authors are grateful to the editors and three anonymous referees for helpful comments on previous drafts.

---

[78] Kobena Mercer, 'Welcome to the jungle: identity and diversity in postmodern politics' in Jonathan Rutherford (ed.), *Identity: Community, culture, difference* (Lawrence and Wishart, London, 1990).

[79] John Lonsdale, 'Agency in tight corners: narrative and initiative in African history', *Journal of African Cultural Studies* 13, 1 (2000), pp. 5–16.

[80] Mirjam de Bruijn, Rijk van Dijk, and Jan-Bart Gewald, 'Social and historical trajectories of agency in Africa' in Patrick Chabal, Ulf Engel, and Leo de Haan (eds), *African Alternatives* (Brill, Leiden, 2007), pp. 9–20.

[81] See also Christopher Clapham, 'Fitting China in', in Alden, Large, and Soares de Oliveira (eds), *China Returns to Africa*, pp. 361–9.

18

Briefing

The African Union at Ten: An Appraisal

Tim Murithi

As THE AFRICAN UNION MARKED ITS TENTH ANNIVERSARY on 9 July 2012, it was still recovering from one of its most public disagreements. At the heart of this disagreement was the AU's interpretation of and commitment to good governance and humanitarian intervention. Sparked by the uprisings in Tunisia, Egypt, and Libya, and the contested November 2010 elections in Côte d'Ivoire, these issues came under intense debate. The NATO-led intervention in Libya—the AU's backyard—caught the organization unaware and divided its members on whether the military incursion, under the rubric of the UN doctrine of the 'responsibility to protect' (R2P), was warranted. Similarly, the earlier crisis in Côte d'Ivoire and the involvement of the UN and France led to criticisms of the AU's failure to respond in a unified and coherent manner.

The key issue of debate was whether the AU should act as a bulwark against external intervention and become the primary agent of humanitarian intervention and democratic consolidation on the continent, or whether this role should continue to be usurped by foreign actors who are often perceived to pursue their own strategic self-interests. South Africa, which was involved in the AU efforts to mediate the crisis in both Libya and Côte d'Ivoire, adopted a strategic position premised on moulding the leadership institutions of the African Union, with a view to making it a more effective and professional regional organization. Arguing that the AU Commission, and by extension its membership, was slow and indecisive in addressing the two crises, South Africa attempted to take over the leadership of the Commission towards the end of 2011. It did so by proposing its former Minister for International Relations and Cooperation, Nkosazana Dlamini-Zuma, as the Southern African Development Community (SADC) candidate for the position of Chairperson of the AU Commission. This was an unprecedented move, and a direct critique of the existing chairperson, Jean Ping of Gabon. The subsequent vote to elect the Chairperson was conducted through a secret ballot so the exact break down of the voting pattern is difficult to discern, but initially the incumbent Ping received sufficient votes to prevent an outright majority for Dlamini-Zuma. However, in July 2012, Dlamini-Zuma secured the support she required to be crowned as Chair at the Summit of Heads of State and Governement. The very public disagreement over who should lead the AU revealed two competing notions of the nature and character of the organization. At the heart of this debate lies the question of whether the AU should make a robust transition towards becoming an effective norm entrepreneur as far as the ideals of peace, security, democracy, and development are concerned.

This Briefing provides an assessment of the AU's achievements to date. It focuses on the Union's attempts to become a norm entrepreneur, particularly in the areas of peace and security, democracy, and human rights. It also assesses the organization's achievements in terms of establishing itself as 'a voice of Africa' and concludes that the project of Pan-Africanism has made some progress under the AU, but that the dream of African unity remains unfulfilled.

The AU as a norm enterpreneur: from Pan-Africanism to regional integration

An endeavour to re-animate Pan-Africanism was the directing force behind the establishment of the African Union.[1] Pan-Africanism is an invented notion, but with the purpose of addressing Africa's insecurity and underdevelopment.[2] The ideal of African solidarity was first institutionalized in the form of the Organization of African Unity (OAU) in 1963, and subsequently re-articulated in the establishment of the AU in 2002. It continues to act as the animating drive behind the AU and its commitment to regional integration. However, the first ten years of the AU reveal that the Pan-Africanist project remains predominantly a top-down affair with elites from across Africa crafting and moulding the institutions to govern the continent, often without sufficiently consulting their publics. That said, there are social movements developing across African borders, which are also fuelling Pan-Africanism from below.

In the ten years of its existence, the AU has attempted to play a continental role as a norm entrepreneur, understood here as a normative leader who encourages others to uphold a range of norms for the improvement of the

---

[1] Hakim Adi and Marika Sherwood, *Pan-African History: Political figures from Africa and the Disapora since 1787* (Routledge, London, 2003), p. vii.

[2] Timothy Murithi, *The African Union: Pan-Africanism, peacebuilding and development* (Ashgate, Aldershot, 2005).

livelihood of people within their jurisdiction or authority. The AU has sought to advance norms related to peace and stability and to function as a collective security regime. The AU Constitutive Act ascribes to the Union the right to intervene and a responsibility to protect in situations of war crimes, crimes against humanity, and genocide. In terms of norms and policy this means that African countries have to agreed to pool their sovereignty to enable the AU to act as the continental guarantor and protector of the security, rights, and well-being of the African people. The African Union Peace and Security Council (PSC) was established as a legal institution of the Union through the 'Protocol Relating to the Establishment of the Peace and Security Council of the African Union' in 2002, and in this sense the AU has undoubtedly led in promoting the norms of peace and security on the continent. Currently the AU is seeking to operationalize these norms through its peace operations in Somalia, the African Union Mission in Somalia (AMISOM, launched in 2007), its Electoral and Security Assistance Mission to the Comoros (AU-MAES, launched in 2008), and its contribution to the Joint AU-UN Hybrid Mission in Darfur (UNAMID, launched in 2007). In addition, Union personnel contributed towards stabilizing the situation in Burundi, through the AU Mission in Burundi (AMIB) from 2003 to 2004.

Promoting governance and development norms

Similarly, on issues relating to governance the AU has sought to establish norms to guide the behaviour of its member states. In particular, the African Union Charter on Democracy, Elections and Governance is a seminal document, which has been ratified by the required fifteen member states and is accordingly a living document that outlines a range of provisions on how countries can improve their governance. The challenge is to ensure that these norms are actually adopted and implemented.

African countries have consistently expressed their desire to regain control of their economic development policies, in order to improve their citizens' access to education and health care. The Structural Adjustment Programmes (SAPs) and so-called Poverty Reduction Strategy Papers (PRSPs) promoted and enforced by the International Monetary Fund (IMF) and World Bank have had a negative impact on development. Both the IMF and the Bank have admitted that these programmes did not achieve the desired results, while the United Nations Conference on Trade and Development (UNCTAD) estimates that IMF/World Bank policies led to a 10 percent decline in economic growth in Africa.[3]

---

[3] United Nations Conference on Trade and Development (UNCTAD), 'Trade performance and commodity dependence' (UNCTAD, Geneva, 26 February 2004).

The AU's New Partnership for Africa's Development (NEPAD) should be understood in this context. NEPAD was conceived as the means to enable Africa to accelerate its active participation on equal terms in the international economic sphere, and was endorsed by the Group of Eight (G8) in June 2002.[4] The key objectives of NEPAD include developing a viable Pan-African market economy, through infrastructure development and the promotion of intra-African trade, as well as improved access to education, training, and healthcare.[5] NEPAD has now been fully integrated into the AU with a Coordinating Agency based at the Union's headquarters in Addis Ababa.

At the African Union's Assembly in 2002, held in Durban, the Declaration on the Implementation of NEPAD was adopted. It included a more specific 'Declaration on Democracy, Political Economic and Corporate Governance', which also established the African Peer Review Mechanism (APRM). The objectives of the APRM are to enhance African ownership of its development and governance agenda, to identify, evaluate, and disseminate best practices, and to monitor progress towards agreed goals. Member states are invited to join the APRM to participate in a self-monitoring programme with a clear timeframe for achieving certain standards of inclusive governance, premised on a commitment to accountability through peer pressure. However, as with many good intentions both NEPAD and the APRM have fallen short when it comes to implementation.[6] The G8 (now the G20) have not lived up to the development promises that they made in 2002 in terms of approaching Africa as a partner rather than a patron, while critics of NEPAD argue that the programme cannot succeed because it tries to integrate Africa into a global framework of neo-liberal laissez-faire economics, which is part of the reason why the continent found itself in such a difficult economic position in the first place.[7] In addition, African governments have only paid lip service to the APRM, due to its intrusive approach to domestic governance issues.

---

[4] Godwin Dogbey, 'Towards a strategic vision for a continent in distress' in Olubenga Adesida and Arunma Oteh (eds.), *African Voices, African Visions* (Nordic Africa Institute, Stockholm, 2001).

[5] New Partnership for Africa's Development, 'The African Peer Review Mechanism' (Base Document, Sixth Summit of the NEPAD Heads of State and Government Implementation Committee, NEPAD/HSGIC/03-2003/APRM/MOU/Annex II, 9 March 2003, Abuja, Nigeria).

[6] Ayesha Kajee, 'NEPAD's APRM: a progress report, practical limitations and challenges' in *South African Yearbook of International Affairs* (South African Institute of International Affairs, Johannesburg, 2004).

[7] George Monbiot, 'At the seat of empire: Africa is forced to take the blame for the devastation inflicted on it by the rich world', *The Guardian*, 25 June 2002 <http://www.guardian.co.uk/politics/2002/jun/25/foreignpolicy.greenpolitics?INTCMP=SRCH> (1 July 2012).

The AU as an international actor: the voice of Africa

The continental body has a dual role of forging unity among its member states and advocating their interests internationally. During its first ten years of existence the AU's role as an international actor has been complicated by the difficulty of promoting consensus among African states and then maintaining that consensus in the face of often divergent national interests. The Africa Group at the UN General Assembly works to forge consensus on key issues of Pan-African interest, such as development, trade, debt cancellation, infectious diseases, small arms and light weapons, nuclear, chemical and biological weapons, climate negotiations, trans-national crime prevention, and the election of Africans to various UN activities and bodies.[8]

In March 2005, the AU issued a declaration known as 'The Common African Position on the Proposed Reform of the United Nations: the Ezulwini Consensus', which highlighted issues pertaining to HIV/AIDS and security, poverty, debt, environmental degradation, trade negotiations, the responsibility to protect, peacekeeping, and peacebuilding.[9] In addition, the AU issued a position on UN reform and in particular on the reform of the Security Council by noting that 'in 1945, when the UN was formed, most of Africa was not represented and that in 1963, when the first reform took place, Africa was represented but was not in a particularly strong position'.[10] It continues that 'Africa's goal is to be fully represented in all the decision-making organs of the UN, particularly in the Security Council'.[11] The Common Position enumerates what 'full representation' of Africa in the Security Council means by demanding 'not less than two permanent seats with all the prerogatives and privileges of permanent membership including the right to veto' and 'five non-permanent seats'.[12]

On paper, the AU was attempting to establish and maintain a common position, but in practice some countries, including South Africa, broke ranks with the Ezulwini Consensus and sought ways to ascend individually to become permanent members of the Security Council. This in effect undermined efforts to demonstrate African 'unity of purpose'. It was not the first time this had happened: time and again African countries have shown that

---

[8] See the statement of the Africa Group at the 11th UN Congress on Crime Prevention and Criminal Justice, 18–25 April 2005; the statement of the Coordinator of the Africa Group to the Chemical Weapons Convention, April 2003; and the Africa Group position statement to the UN Climate Negotiations, August 1997. Controversially, in May 2004, the Africa Group submitted and successfully achieved the election of Sudan to the UN Commission on Human Rights, see Economic and Social Council, press release ECOSOC/6110.

[9] African Union, 'The Common African Position on the Proposed Reform of the United Nations: the Ezulwini Consensus' (EXT/EX.CL/2 (VII), African Union, Addis Ababa, 7–8 March 2005).

[10] *Ibid.*, p. 9.   [11] *Ibid.*   [12] *Ibid.*

they are unlikely to vote as a collective on matters before, or pertaining to, the Security Council—a clear indication that member states are not respecting the AU as a norm entrepreneur. Governments generally tend to adopt positions that best serve their interests, or positions that enable them to receive certain benefits from more powerful countries that 'pick and choose' which countries they want to work with. Malawi's move to deny President Omar Al Bashir of Sudan access to the AU Summit, due to be hosted in Lilongwe in July 2012, is a case in point. Explaining Malawi's reasons for taking this stance, President Joyce Banda stated that her country's commitment to its donors, notably the United Kingdom as the largest bilateral contributor, and its desire to uphold the ICC's Rome Statute, would not allow it to host Bashir, an alleged war criminal. The AU Commission subsequently took the decision to relocate the Summit to Addis Ababa, rather than submit to Banda's injunction. The logic of national self-interest and political realism can thus be seen to have prevailed among African countries, as well as member states at the UN.[13]

The AU's discontents

Those who are discontented with the African Union acknowledge the formal existence of unity, but fault the genuineness of its Pan-African commitment and its achievements. This is evident at several levels. While the political and business elite, as well civil society actors, who work across borders, are often supportive of Pan-African interaction and solidarity, the vast majority of citizens across the continent do not know that the AU exists. For this silent majority, Pan-Africanism is not yet a lived experience. Stringent visa restrictions, for example, remain in place, making a mockery of the notion of unity as citizens from African countries are deported from other African countries. Freedom of movement to and from the headquarters of the African Union in Addis Ababa, in particular, should not be constrained by visa restrictions on African citizens, and the AU leadership should commit in principle to removing visa restrictions on the travel of African citizens across borders.

At its inception the AU waxed lyrically about its commitment to reaching out and engaging civil society. Its founding document, the Constitutive Act, is unambiguous in its commitment 'to build a partnership between governments and all segments of civil society' and to promote the 'participation of the African peoples in the activities of the Union'.[14] However, ten years on, it is

---

[13] Currently there is no systematic analysis of the history of the voting record of the Africa Group.

[14] African Union, *Constitutive Act of the African Union* (African Union, Lome, 2000), preamble.

clear that the AU has mainly paid lip service to empowering African citizens to engage and influence their states.[15] This is particularly evident in the difficulties faced by African civil society organizations that seek to engage the AU in Addis Ababa, as well as its liaison offices around the continent.

The regional economic communities (RECs) are another issue where genuine Pan-Africanism is challenged. The RECs have often positioned themselves as countervailing focal points for collective action and the AU has yet to ensure effective coordination, particularly on issues pertaining to peace, security, governance, the rule of law, citizen participation, and development. The AU and the RECs need to increase their level of interaction and communication in order to ensure effective coordination and collective action.

The AU has also faced criticism for being lethargic and slow in responding to crisis and conflict situations across the continent.[16] This is due to the administrative bottlenecks that constrain the emergence of a culture of professionalism and efficiency, particularly within the AU Commission. These administrative challenges also undermine the morale of AU staff in its various offices around the continent and ultimately affects the AU's ability to engage member states, African citizens, and partners effectively.

In the pursuit of its peace and security interventions the AU has not always seen eye-to-eye with the UN, the International Criminal Court (ICC) or NATO. The UN Security Council's referral of the President of Sudan to the ICC for alleged war crimes, crimes against humanity, and genocide in Darfur in 2009 precipitated a tense stand-off between the AU and the ICC, which is yet to be resolved. In the interest of peace and security, it is essential that the relationship between the AU and these key international organizations is improved.

Conclusion

At its tenth anniversary, the African Union remains, at its core, a disparate collection of nation states that recognizes the value of collective action and solidarity on a range of regional and international issues. The AU, since it holds primary responsibility for establishing and operationalizing the continent's peace and security architecture, has become the leading norm entrepreneur on issues pertaining to peace, security, democracy, and development on the

---

[15] Mammo Muchie, Adam Habib, and V. Panayachee, 'African integration and civil society: the case of the African Union', *Transformation: Critical Perspectives on Southern Africa* **61**, 1 (2006), pp. 3–24.

[16] Sadiki Koko and Martha Bakwesegha-Osula, 'Assessing the African Union's response to the Libyan crisis', *Conflict Trends* 1 (2012), pp. 3–15.

continent. However, this role is tempered by the primary character that continues to define the constituents of the Westphalian system, namely the self-interest of nation states and the persistence of political realism in their day-to-day interactions. A decade after its establishment, the AU is only just beginning to assert its voice in the international system. Even though the AU is not always taken seriously by its interlocutors and powerful countries in the global north, it is laying the foundation to empower its member states to play a more proactive role in international relations. The AU has emerged as a home-grown initiative to take the destiny of the continent into the hands of the African people. However, there is a long way to go before the AU's role as a norm entrepreneur is actualized and its vision and mission realized. The injunction that the great Pan-Africanist Kwame Nkrumah bequeathed to subsequent generations continues to animate the African Union and is still valid: 'Africa must unite, or disintegrate individually.'[17]

Acknowledgment

Published in *African Affairs*, 111, 445 (2012), p. 662–669.

[17] Kwame Nkrumah, *Africa Must Unite* (Heinemann, London, 1963).

Index